# Contemporary Europe

# Macmillan Foundations

*A series of introductory texts across a wide range of subject areas to meet the needs of today's lecturers and students*

*Foundations* texts provide complete yet concise coverage of core topics and skills based on detailed research of course requirements suitable for both independent study and class use – *the firm foundations for future study.*

**Published**

*Biology*
*Chemistry*
*Contemporary Europe*
*Economics*
*A History of English Literature*
*Modern British History since 1900*
*Physics*
*Politics*

**Forthcoming**

*British Politics*
*Economics for Business*
*Mathematics for Science and Engineering*
*Modern European History*
*Nineteenth-Century Britain*
*Sociology*

# Contemporary Europe

**RICHARD SAKWA and ANNE STEVENS**

First published 2000 by
MACMILLAN PRESS LTD
Houndmills, Basingstoke, Hampshire RG21 6XS
and London
Companies and representatives
throughout the world

ISBN 0–333–77270–9

A catalogue record for this book is available
from the British Library.

This book is printed on paper suitable for recycling and
made from fully managed and sustained forest sources.

10   9   8   7   6   5   4   3   2   1
09   08   07   06   05   04   03   02   01   00

Typeset by Footnote Graphics, Warminster, Wilts
Printed in Great Britain by
Antony Rowe Ltd, Chippenham, Wilts

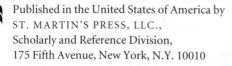

Published in the United States of America by
ST. MARTIN'S PRESS, LLC.,
Scholarly and Reference Division,
175 Fifth Avenue, New York, N.Y. 10010

ISBN 0–312–23615–8 (cloth)
ISBN 0–312–23616–6 (paperback)

# Contents

# List of Illustrations

## Maps

## Figures

## Tables

## Boxes

## Portraits

# Preface

Among the many changes provoked by the fall of the Berlin Wall in 1989 and the end of the revolutionary socialist challenge to capitalism is the renewed attention to territory and space. The politics of identity have come to the fore, asking questions like: Who are we? With whom do we identify? How did we become what we are? The inter-relationship of peoples and space, the definition of 'us-ness' and 'other-ness', and the proper forms of political community are now the issues that confront the European continent, and it is these questions that we shall examine in this book.

The enormity of the change from ideological to identity politics cannot be exaggerated. For over a century the great ideologies of the modern epoch marched over Europe. The ideology of nationalism gave birth to the new states of Italy and Germany and provoked the most destructive of Europe's many 'civil wars', the First World War of 1914–18. The rise of fascism in the interwar years provoked yet another bout in the form of the Second World War in 1939–45. This war, the most destructive that the world has seen, ended only to see Europe divided between the country that had adopted communism as its ideology, the Union of Soviet Socialist Republics (USSR), and an exhausted Western half of the continent and its transatlantic protector, the United States of America (USA). For half a century European politics was overlain by the struggle between these two superpowers, their associated blocs, and the contrasting ideologies that they espoused. Only with the end of the Cold War in 1989–91, accompanied by the disintegration of the USSR into fifteen separate countries, has this overlay ended and Europe taken control of its own destiny once again. The nature and meaning of Europe has become the centre of discussion, while the dynamics of its international and domestic politics has taken on a new prominence.

This book is a contribution to these debates. The aim has been to provide an accessible introduction to some of the main issues in contemporary European development. The expertise of a broad range of scholars has been drawn on to contribute various perspectives to the analysis of contemporary Europe. While it has not always been an easy task to marshal the various authors in the same direction at the same time, it has nevertheless been a rewarding exercise. We have not sought to impose upon the contents of the book, nor upon our contributors, too narrow a vision. The consequence is that some themes and events reappear in a number of places throughout the text, often in a slightly different guise and subject to varying interpretations. We feel that this is appropriate in a work that seeks to illuminate debates and to consider very diverse situations and approaches. We have sought to avoid over-simplification, or reducing complex issues to mere wordbites, but rather to provide throughout an analysis suitable for those coming to the field for the first time. We believe that even an introductory text like this has a responsibility to challenge and to question, to stretch and to inspire students to go and pursue in greater depth some of the issues raised here. We have sought to provide a nuanced yet accessible text for those new to the field, while providing material for thought for those already familiar with the area.

The first chapter focuses on what may be called the 'civilisational' aspect of the identity of Europe. To what degree is Europe today a separate and distinct civilisation with a fundamental unity crossing the old dividing line of ideological confrontation, the iron curtain stretching, as Winston Churchill so memorably put it in 1946, from Trieste in the Adriatic to Stettin on the Baltic? Is there something that transcends the individual histories of particular countries and peoples to suggest a coherence drawn from history and the dynamics of modern development? In short, what is specifically European about Europe? It is this question that is addressed in the first chapter and that is touched on and developed at various points in the book.

The second chapter provides a historical survey of political development in Europe in the twentieth century. Following the Second World War, Europe emerged devastated and unable to control its own destiny. Under the umbrella of the superpower rivalry formalised in the conventions of the Cold War, the Western part of the continent not only rebuilt its economy but entered into an era of unprecedented prosperity, accompanied by the creation of what was to become the European Union (EU). The Eastern part of the continent, however, was wracked by sporadic attempts to reform the Soviet-type systems imposed after 1945. Only after 1989 could the two parts of the continent begin to come together, a process that will stretch well into the twenty-first century.

The third chapter examines the territorial organisation of European space. The late nineteenth century was the high point of nationalist thinking, with intellectual groups everywhere trying to create new states if they did not already have them, above all in the territories of the four European empires – the Russian, German, Austro-Hungarian and Ottoman – together with the British as far as the Irish were concerned. The tensions generated by the great era of nation building after the fall of these empires at the end of the First World War helped provoke the Second War. Today the nation-state appears as the ubiquitous form in which human communities organise themselves, but, as Brian Jenkins shows in his discussion of nations and regions, the traditional notion of the undiluted sovereignty of the nation-state is under challenge from below by the rise of regionalism. It is also challenged from above, as Anne Stevens notes in her discussion of the development of the European Union (Chapter 7). Her chapter examines the history, dynamics and impact of integration. In Chapter 8, Irene Brennan extends the discussion to examine the challenges posed by the enlargement of the European Union, particularly to the East. Chapter 9 allows us to broaden our gaze still further to examine the relationship between global processes and developments in Europe. The fundamental question discussed by Ian Manners can be posed as follows: is the deepening of European integration a rejection of globalisation or itself part of the trend? Are the two processes in fact complementary? Chapter 10, by Mike Bowker, examines in greater depth some of the related questions over security.

William Outhwaite in Chapter 4 focuses on the theme of European identity in relation to social structures and social change, while the chapter by Dieter Rucht takes up some of the issues raised in the previous chapter to examine the way that political participation in society is organised. The politics of protest and the new social movements are deeply rooted in the main social and cultural developments in society, and these are explored in this chapter. In Chapter 6 the focus is more narrowly political. Thomas Saalfeld examines questions of contemporary political organisation, looking at ways in which the people can influence and control governments. The chapter by John Coombes analyses some of the cultural movements of our time, suggesting that the tension between modernism and more traditional forms of artistic production is far from resolved by the emerging postmodern trend.

Finally, the editors consider some of the possible interpretations of Europe, the nature of its identity and some of the implications of this for the future.

These themes are not separated by iron curtains but weave in and out of the various chapters. Together they constitute the tapestry that is contemporary Europe. The debts of gratitude accumulated in the preparation of a work of this sort can only be acknowledged but not repaid. Above all, we must thank the contributors themselves, who have endured the various tribulations of moulding their individual styles to that required to ensure consistency across the book as the whole. The patience and understanding of the editors at our publishers, Frances Arnold and Houri Alavi, have been exemplary and provided the encouragement and incentives to see this work to a conclusion. This book is itself a tapestry of various styles, approaches and themes, and thus reflects in miniature the larger tapestry that is contemporary Europe. We hope that the picture it presents is relatively faithful to the original and, like the great Bayeux tapestry of an earlier age, provides a source of learning and wonderment.

RICHARD SAKWA AND ANNE STEVENS
*Canterbury and Aston, April 2000*

# Acknowledgements

As with all edited volumes, this collection would not have been possible without the cooperation and enthusiasm of all the authors. From the very beginning all have devoted themselves to the project in a way that rendered our job as editors much easier and, although we barely dare say it, enjoyable. With the text now complete in front of us, the commitment of all the contributors appears to have been worthwhile. The contributors took our general indications and requests on board and submitted to editorial direction. Our profound thanks to them all.

We are also grateful to Clive Church at the University of Kent for his steady encouragement and always wise good sense. Ian Manners was particularly helpful in rooting out maps and other materials at short notice. The editors at the publishers no doubt at times felt that this was a project too far, and yet they remained committed and enthusiastic throughout the various tortuous stages in the evolution of the book. Our thanks in particular go to Steven Kennedy, for his initial inspiration and patience. The actual team overseeing the development of the book from concept to fruition have been unfailingly helpful: Frances Arnold, Houri Alavi and Suzannah Tipple. Valery Rose's work in getting the text into shape has been a model of professionalism combined with an extraordinary patience. On the domestic front, Handley Stevens put up with all the preoccupation, long days and missed weekends while the book was being put together with helpful understanding; while Roza Sakwa had to live with a text that at times appeared to want to move in and live with us permanently. Our thanks to them all.

The editors and publishers wish to thank the following for permission to use copyright material:

Chatham House Publishers for **Table 5.4**, based on Russell J. Dalton (1996), *Citizen Politics: Public Opinion and Political Parties in Advanced Industrial Democracies*, 2nd edition, p. 76; and **Figure 6.8**, based on Giovanni Sartori (1987), *The Theory of Democracy Revisited*, Part 1: *The Contemporary Debate*, p. 219.

Macmillan Ltd for **Figures 6.5 and 6.6**, based on data from M. Cotta (1991), 'Conclusions', in J. Blondell and J.-L. Thiébault (eds), *The Profession of Government Minister in Western Europe*, pp. 174–98.

St Martin's Press LLC and Campus Verlag for **Table 6.3**, based on data from M. Wiberg, 'Parliamentary Questioning: Control by Communication?', in H. Döring (ed.), *Parliaments and Majority Rule in Western Europe*, pp. 187–8; © H. Döring.

Pearson Education Ltd for **Tables 5.1–5.3**, based on I. Budge et al. (1997), *The Politics of the New Europe: Atlantic to Urals*, pp. 215, 163, © 1997 Addison Wesley Longman Ltd; and **Figure 7.2**, from Clive H. Church and David Phinnemore (1994), *European Union and European Community*, p. 43, © C. Church and D. Phinnemore 1993.

Taylor & Francis Ltd for **Table 6.1**, from Douglas V. Verney, 'Parliamentary Government and Presidential Government', in A. Lijphart (ed.), *Parliamentary versus Presidential Government* (Routledge, 1992), pp. 31–47.

The University of Minnesota Press for **Table 5.6**, from Hanspeter Kriesi et al. (1995), *New Social Movements in Western Europe: A Comparative Analysis*, p. 20.

World Trade Organization for data in **Table 9.2**, from World Trade Press Release, 16 April 1999, p. 128.

### Photographs and illustrations

AKG, Photo London, pp. 107, 111; BBC Hulton Picture Library, p. 237; *The Economist*, p. 142; Edifice, pp. 239, 241; Farabolafoto/Marco Lanni, p. 134; GAMMA, Paris/Christian Vioujard, p. 115; The Hulton Getty Picture Collection Ltd, pp. 32, 208, 227, 228, 244; Image Select International, pp. 8, 229; Jane Reed, courtesy of Harvard University Office, p. 210; Rex Features, pp. 9, 12, 17, 34, 35, 37, 39, 40, 57, 92, 206; Roger Viollet, p. 230; Ann Ronan at ISI, p. 207; The University of Chicago Office of Public Affairs, p. 209; UPPA, pp. 31, 53; Ian Whadock, p. 74.

Every effort has been made to trace the copyright holders, but if any have been inadvertently overlooked the publishers will be pleased to make the necessary arrangement at the first opportunity.

# List of Abbreviations

| | |
|---|---|
| ABM | Anti-ballistic missile |
| APEC | Asia-Pacific Economic Co-operation |
| ASEAN | Association of South-East Asian Nations |
| CAP | Common Agricultural Policy |
| CDU | Christlich Demokratische Union (Christian Democratic Union) |
| CEE | Central and Eastern Europe/European |
| CEECs | Central and Eastern European countries |
| CET | Common External Tariff |
| CFE | Conventional Forces in Europe |
| CFSP | Common Foreign and Security Policy |
| CIS | Commonwealth of Independent States |
| CJTF | Combined Joint Task Force |
| CMEA/Comecon | Council for Mutual Economic Assistance |
| CPSU | Communist Party of the Soviet Union |
| CSBM | Confidence and Security Building Measures |
| CSCE | Conference on Security and Co-operation in Europe |
| CSU | Christlich-Soziale Union (Christian Social Union) |
| EBRD | European Bank for Reconstruction and Development |
| EC | European Communities |
| ECB | European Central Bank |
| ECSC | European Coal and Steel Community |
| EDC | European Defence Community |
| EEA | European Economic Area |
| EEC | European Economic Community |
| EFTA | European Free Trade Area |
| EMU | European Monetary Union |
| EP | European Parliament |
| ESDI | European Security and Defence Identity |
| EU | European Union |
| Euratom | European Atomic Energy Community |
| FDI | Foreign Direct Investment |
| FRG | Federal Republic of Germany |
| FRY | Federal Republic of Yugoslavia |
| FYROM | Former Yugoslav Republic of Macedonia |
| GATT | General Agreement on Tariffs and Trade |
| GDP | Gross Domestic Product |
| GDR | German Democratic Republic |
| GNP | Gross National Product |
| IGC | Intergovernmental Conference |
| IMF | International Monetary Fund |
| INF | Intermediate Nuclear Forces |
| MEP | Member of the European Parliament |
| MNCs | Multinational companies |

| | |
|---|---|
| NAFTA | North American Free Trade Agreement |
| NATO | North Atlantic Treaty Organisation |
| NHS | National Health Service |
| NICs | Newly industrialising countries |
| NPT | New Political Thinking |
| OPEC | Organisation of Petroleum Exporting Countries |
| OSCE | Organisation for Security and Cooperation in Europe |
| PACE | Parliamentary Assembly of the Council of Europe |
| PDS | Partei des Demokratischen Sozialismus (Party of Democratic Socialism) |
| PPP | Purchasing power parity |
| PR | Proportional representation |
| QMV | Qualified Majority Voting |
| RDA | Regional Development Agency |
| RIAs | Regional integration arrangements |
| RSDLP | Russian Social Democratic Labour Party |
| SDI | Strategic Defence Initiative |
| SEA | Single European Act |
| SED | Sozialistische Einheitspartei Deutschland (Socialist Unity Party) |
| SLBM | Submarine-launched ballistic missile |
| SPD | Social Democratic Party of Germany |
| TEU | Treaty of European Union |
| UN | United Nations |
| USA | United States of America |
| USSR | Union of Soviet Socialist Republics |
| WEU | Western European Union |
| WTO | Warsaw Treaty Organisation |
| WTO | World Trade Organisation |

# Notes on the Contributors

**Mike Bowker** is Lecturer in Politics at the University of East Anglia, Norwich. He has written on Russian foreign policy and the Cold War. His publications include *Superpower Detente: A Reappraisal*, with Phil Williams (1998), *Russian Foreign Policy and the End of the Cold War* (1997), and he has just completed co-editing with Cameron Ross, *Russia after the Cold War* (2000).

**Irene Brennan** is a Jean Monnet Professor of European Integration Studies at the University of Westminster. In the area of European Studies, she has published on integration theory, EU–Russia relations, and *Demos* in the European Union. She has also written on politics, philosophy and Christian–Marxist dialogue. She has higher degrees in both philosophy and international relations.

**John Coombes** is a member of the Department of Literature at the University of Essex, which he joined in 1972 from the University of St Andrews. He has taught and lectured extensively abroad, including Paris, East Berlin, Katowice, Tokyo, Albuquerque and Las Vegas. His principal field of interest is the relationship between literature, politics and society in modern Europe (including England). He is also interested in comparisons of Japanese and European literature. He is the author of *Writing from the Left: Socialism, Liberalism and the Popular Front* (1989) and of numerous articles on English, French and comparative literature since 1600.

**Brian Jenkins** is Professor of French Area Studies at the University of Portsmouth. He is the author of *Nationalism in France: Class and Nation since 1789* (1990) and co-editor of *Nation and Identity in Contemporary Europe* (1996). He is also editor of the *Journal of European Area Studies*.

**Robert Ladrech** is Lecturer in Politics at Keele University. His work focuses on social democratic parties, French politics, and European integration. He is the author of *Social Democracy and the Challenge of European Union* (2000) and co-author of *Europe since 1945: A Concise History* (1996). He has published articles in such journals as *Comparative Politics*, *Journal of Common Market Studies* and the *European Journal of Political Research*.

**Ian Manners** is Lecturer in European Studies in the Department of Politics and International Relations at the University of Kent at Canterbury. He studied for his first degree in international studies in the USA, took an MA in area studies in London, and then joined the News and Current Affairs Department of the BBC. Following the collapse of communism in Eastern Europe he joined the Department of Politics at the University of Bristol to write his PhD on intergovernmental co-operation amongst EC member states in the response to the end of the Cold War. He has published on the Association Agreements with the Visegrad countries and on the Common Foreign and Security Policy of the European Union. He is currently working on two books, *The International Identity of the European Union* and *European Union Foreign Policy*.

**William Outhwaite** is Professor of Sociology in the School of European Studies at the University of Sussex, where he has taught since 1973. He is the author of *Understanding Social Life: The Method Called Verstehen* (1975; 2nd edn, 1986); *Concept Formation in Social Science* (1983), *New Philosophies of Social Science: Realism, Hermeneutics and Critical Theory* (1987), and *Habermas: A Critical Introduction* (1994). He edited *The Habermas Reader* (1996) and (with Tom Bottomore) *The Blackwell Dictionary of Twentieth-Century Social Thought* (1993), and (with Luke Martell) *The Sociology of Politics* (1998). He is currently working on books on post-communism, contemporary Europe and Germany.

**Dieter Rucht** is Professor of Sociology at the University of Kent at Canterbury (England). His research interests include modernisation processes in a comparative perspective, social change, social movements and political protest. Among his recent books are *Acts of Dissent: New Developments in the Study of Protest* (co-edited with Jürgen Gerhards and Friedhelm Neidhardt, 1999) and *Social Movements in a Globalizing World* (co-edited with Donatella della Porta and Hanspeter Kriesi, 1999).

**Thomas Saalfeld** is Senior Lecturer in Politics at the University of Kent at Canterbury. His research focuses on comparative legislatures, coalition government in Western Europe and German government and politics. His recent publications include *Members of Parliament in Western Europe* (co-editor with Wolfgang C. Müller, 1997); *Großbritannien* (in German, 1998) and *Bundestagswahl '98* (co-editor with Stephen Padgett, 1999).

**Richard Sakwa** is Professor of Russian and European Politics in the Department of Politics and International Relations at the University of Kent at Canterbury. His publications include *Soviet Politics* (1989; 2nd edn published in 1998 as *Soviet Politics in Perspective*), *Gorbachev and His Reforms, 1985–1990* (1990), *Russian Politics and Society* (1993; 2nd edn 1996) and *Postcommunism* (1999). He has also written numerous articles on contemporary Russian affairs and given many television and radio interviews. His main research interest at present is the development of democracy and the state in Russia, in particular the evolution of parliamentarianism and political parties.

**Anne Stevens** is Professor of European Studies in the School of Languages and European Studies, Aston University, Birmingham. She is the author of *The Government and Politics of France* (2nd edn 1996) and *Brussels Bureaucrats? The Administration of the European Union* (2000). She has a particular interest in the relations between politics and administration in France, the United Kingdom and the institutions of the European Union.

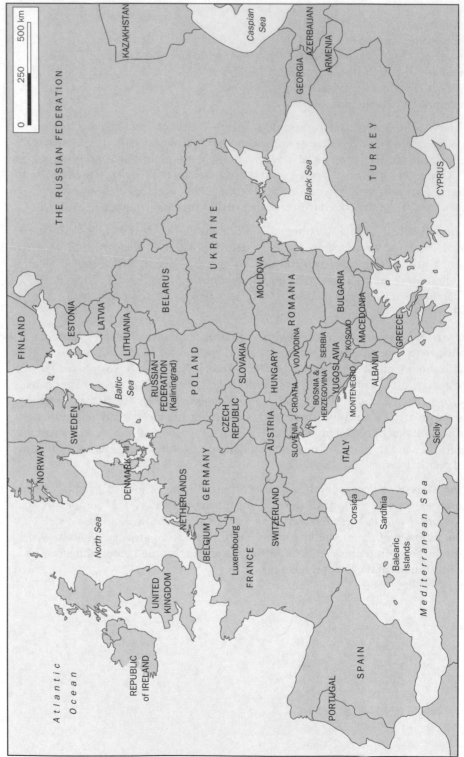

**Contemporary Europe**

# Introduction: The Many Dimensions of Europe

Richard Sakwa

> 'Europe, the homeland of my heart's choice, is lost to me, since it has torn itself apart suicidally a second time in a war of brother against brother.... I have seen the great mass ideologies grow and spread before my eyes – Fascism in Italy, National Socialism in Germany, Bolshevism in Russia and above all else that arch-plague nationalism which has poisoned the flower of our European culture.... It was reserved for us, after centuries, again to see wars without declarations of war, concentration camps, persecution, mass robbery, bombing attacks on helpless cities, all bestialities unknown to the last fifty generations, things which future generations, it is hoped, will not allow to happen. But paradoxically, in the same era when our world fell back morally a thousand years, I have seen that same humankind lift itself, in technical and intellectual matters, to unheard-of deeds, surpassing the achievement of a million years with a single beat of wings.... Not until our time has mankind as a whole behaved so infernally, and never before has it accomplished so much that is godlike.'
>
> STEFAN ZWEIG, *The World of Yesterday* (1943) pp. 7–8

**Polis:** The Greek word for a city state. Used to denote a complete set of political arrangements, usually with the implication that the existence of such arrangements is desirable.

**Humanism:** A system of thought and belief which rejects dependence upon the notion of the existence of God as the source of values and ethics and sees human beings as containing within themselves the highest values.

**Renaissance:** The historical period during the fifteenth and sixteenth centuries which saw the rediscovery of Classical literature and thought, and the development of new forms of art, music, architecture and literature.

As one chapter in Europe's multi-volume history closed in 1989 with the fall of the communist regimes of Eastern Europe, a new era began in which we are now embroiled. What are the main patterns and challenges of this new episode in the European saga? What is it in any case that is distinctively 'European' about Europe? We will examine these questions in this chapter, indicating where the themes will be developed in later chapters.

Students of Europe may be forgiven for thinking that Europe has more political history than perhaps any other continent. The birth of democracy in the Greek **polis** in the fifth century BCE, the articulation of the fundamental concepts of Roman law that remain the cornerstone of modern concepts of law to this day, the anguished debates over individual responsibility, conscience and the relationship between church and state that accompanied the whole trajectory of the development of Christendom, and the rebirth of classical **humanism** and of the very exercise of politics as a sphere of autonomous decision-making in the **Renaissance** of the fifteenth century, have

**Reformation:** The historical period during the sixteenth century which saw the emergence in Western Europe of Christian denominations, most of them described as 'Protestant', which broke away from the leadership of the papacy and rejected what they saw as the excesses, abuses and errors of the Roman Catholic Church.

**Enlightenment:** The name given to a period of intellectual history during the eighteenth century when philosophers and other thinkers stressed the importance of reason, of freedom of thought and of proceeding by observation and deduction.

all shaped the modern world. It was in Europe that the main movements of modernity took shape, like the individualism associated with the Protestant **Reformation**, the questioning spirit of the eighteenth-century **Enlightenment**, and then the triumph of the idea of progress in the nineteenth century accompanied by the emergence of the world's first industrial civilisations and liberal democracies. It was here, too, that Europe's restless energy gave birth to overseas expansion and the creation of the great European empires. It is against this background that we begin an examination of contemporary problems.

The central point here and in later contributions is that these questions can only be understood in the context of the long-term development of Europe; hence we will begin by examining some of the patterns in European history before discussing contemporary European challenges. The central notion will be the concept of *modernity*. Something unique happened in Europe as it left the Middle Ages, something with roots in antiquity and ancient Greece but given new force by intellectual, socio-economic and political developments at this time. The new element was a questing spirit that repudiated the authority of tradition and instead sought to place the individual and his or her conscience and intellect at the heart of the new world. While the traditional authority structures continued, in the form of institutions like the Roman Catholic Church, aristocracies and the family, their authority was challenged by a sense that the past could no longer define the future. Thus the short answer to the question of 'What is Europe?' is that it is a society turned to the future. By the late eighteenth and early nineteenth century this dynamic future-oriented world-view gave the continent a pre-eminent economic and military role in the world, and this gave birth to the strong idea of Europe as a civilisation. In the twentieth century, however, Europe's dominance was challenged by outside powers (above all, the United States), by its own 'civil wars', and by its own alarm at the darker side of its civilisation. The fall of the Eastern European regimes in 1989 put an end effectively to the greatest future-oriented ideology of all, communism, whose dark side had by then become apparent to all. In a paradoxical way, however, Europe is now living without a future, in the sense of a clearly formulated set of aspirations, but is trying to find a compass to determine its own fate and its place in the world.

## ■ What is Europe?

Europe was the crucible of the modern world. It was here that the great movements of our time were forged and, indeed, the very notion of modernity itself was first given form. This theme recurs in Chapter 4. By 'modernity' we mean, to borrow Therborn's succinct definition, 'an epoch turned to the future' (Therborn, 1995, p. 4). From this perspective the present is no more than the preparation for a future that is perceived to be something better than what exists now, while the present itself is considered to be only a leftover from the backwardness of the past. Thus modernity is a future-oriented restless striving for a better future based on notions of progress and development. Modernity is accompanied by notions of modernisation and reform, together with the idea of revolution as a way of leaping into the radiant future. The idea of reform was well represented in European modernity and, among other things, gave rise to the powerful current of social reformism known as social democracy. The idea of progress had by the nineteenth century seized the European imagination, reflecting Europe's striving to move out of the darkness and limitations of the past and to build a better world based on science and human reason. Europe was, indeed, in Therborn's words, 'the pioneer of modernity and the centre of it' (Therborn, 1995, p. 19). There was, however, a darker side to modernity's aspiration to dispense with the past. By focusing on the future, the present becomes no more than the brushwood to be cleared as the foundations of the future are laid. This was the basis for various revolutionary ideologies (including fascism and communism) that took shape in Europe, launching destructive programmes for the establishment of a better future world by destroying aspects of the present one. It is these ambiguities in Europe's civilisational identity that we explore in this chapter.

Europe can be studied through the examination of specific countries or the trajectories of particular movements and ideas. Our focus here, however, is on Europe as a civilisation, that is, as a distinctive arena of social, political and intellectual interaction. The histories of countries, movements and ideas weave together to create an entity that differs from other civilisations. Above all, European civilisation has tended to be dynamic and expansive, whereas comparable civilisations, like that of the Chinese, valued stability and introspection. Europe's dynamism has come from conflict and divisions, in part derived from its geography and ethnography (see Diamond, 1997). Peninsular Europe in particular, jutting out into the Atlantic with its outlying islands of Britain and Ireland, is divided by high mountain ranges, broad rivers, sea channels and a highly indented coastline (see Map 1.1), and has been

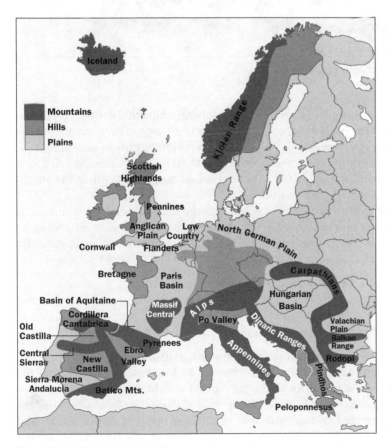

**Map 1.1** Physical geography of Europe

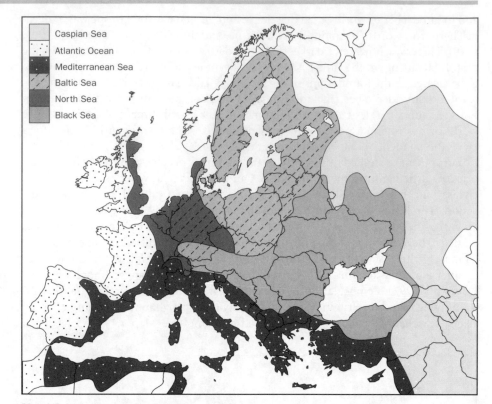

Caspian Sea
Atlantic Ocean
Mediterranean Sea
Baltic Sea
North Sea
Black Sea

**Map 1.2** Watersheds and drainage

peopled by successive waves of invasions and settlement from the East, North and South; it still remains possible to talk of the tribes of Europe. There remain at least 225 autochthonous (indigenous) languages in Europe, joined now by dozens more as new migrant communities become established. In the European Union, out of a total population of 370 million, at least 50 million speak a language other than the official language of the state in which they live.

Unlike the Confucian civilisations of Asia, then, whose underlying principle is *fusion*, the European model, like a nuclear reactor, is based on *fission*, generating an extraordinary creativity. The following tensions and divisions have been particularly important.

### 1    The separation of religious and political authority
Determining the dividing line between church and state has produced a tension that for most of the last millennium in Western Europe was the source of a rich debate over the proper relationship between temporal and secular authority.

### 2    The division between Byzantine and Catholic Christianity
In 1054 the Western half of Christendom, headed by the Pope, separated from the Eastern half under the authority of the patriarch based in Constantinople (today Istanbul) and practising the Orthodox form of Christianity. Relations between the two halves were strained to the degree that in 1204 the Fourth Crusade sacked and looted Constantinople. The crusades, beginning in 1099 and trying to recapture the Holy Land from Islam, transformed Western Christianity into a more militant and

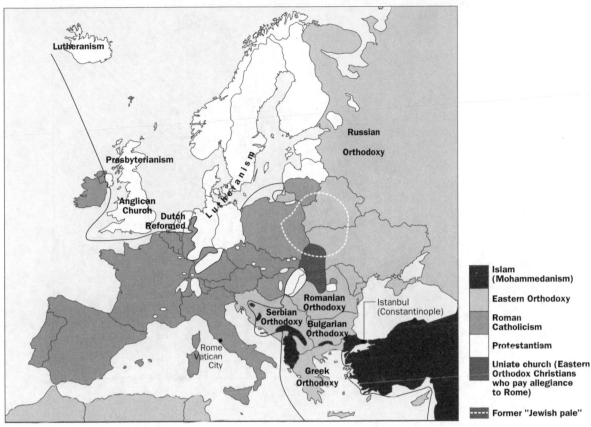

**Map 1.3** Religions of Europe

worldly institution, whereas Orthodoxy tended to be more contemplative, mystical and devotional, although less independent from the secular authorities. The Orthodox churches derived from Byzantium were historically more closely identified with their princes and states, an ideal of fusion and 'symphonia' that deprived these countries of one of the sources of dynamism that characterised the Western part of the continent. This historic cultural division has a powerful resonance to this day, with the Orthodox world of Russia, Ukraine, Belarus, Serbia, Montenegro, Macedonia, Greece and Romania sharing a distinctive religious culture and view of political authority that distinguishes them from the rest of Catholic, Protestant, Jewish and Islamic Europe.

### 3  The separation of knowledge and power

Out of the fundamental divide between church and state came the separation of knowledge and power. In the Islamic world, by contrast, there is a tendency towards a theocratic fusion of the religious and political worlds. In western Catholic Europe already by the twelfth century such a fusion came increasingly under challenge. The growing gulf between secular and temporal power created a space for the development not only of science but also of political philosophy and, ultimately, the critique of authority that lay at the heart of Enlightenment thinking.

### 4  States versus empires

The division of Europe's territory between small states struggling for survival and

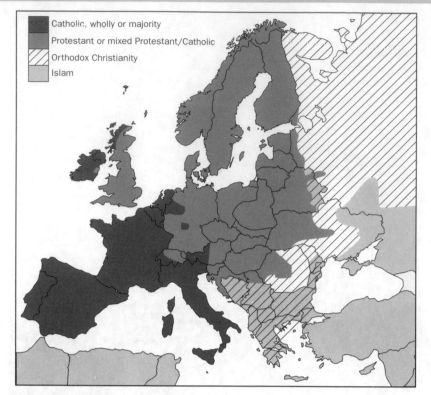

**Map 1.4** The religious situation in 1560

supremacy amongst themselves and against the supra-national ambitions of empires was something that distinguished Europe from, for example, China, where the authority of the emperor (despite numerous invasions, rebellions and secessions) had, since the unification of the most productive parts in 221 BC, extended for thousands of miles without interruption, united by a single written form of a single dominant language. By contrast, Europe in the fourteenth century was fragmented into over a thousand independent principalities, a number reduced by half by 1500 and thereafter steadily falling to reach a low point of 33 in the 1970s, only to start increasing again after the fall of communism as Europe once again fragmented as part of what some have called the 'new medievalism'. The division of Europe into relatively small statelets, something encouraged by its terrain and patterns of settlement, promoted the development not only of the military arts but also of the organisational abilities of states to conduct wars, and above all the development of fiscal systems that could pay for arms and men. Paul Kennedy argued that it was the intense military competition between the relatively small states of Western Europe in early modern times that prompted the creation of highly centralised governments, something that the larger empires of the East (the Russian, Habsburg and Ottoman) did not need to do because their security concerns were less intense and immediate. They were therefore unable to muster the political will for reform (Kennedy, 1987). Concentrated state power in the West prompted technological, administrative and economic changes. Herein lies the origin of the modern banking system in northern Italy, followed by the emergence of the Rothschilds and other great banking families. The development of systems of taxation and the struggle to control revenue collection provoked revolutions in England and France, and of course in America.

The culmination of this long struggle of relatively small states against the power of a supra-national empire was resolved only in the wake of the First World War, when the four great continental empires (German, Russian, Ottoman and Austro-Hungarian) broke up to spawn what were intended to be national states (see Chapter 3). It was at the Paris Peace Conference in 1919 that Woodrow Wilson, who had come to Europe with his 'fourteen points' defending the right of nations to self-determination, was asked: 'Must every little language have a country all its own?' The answer, apparently, was 'Yes', and the Treaty of Versailles ensured that out of the dissolution of the four empires numerous small states were born. The fall of communism was accompanied once again by a wave of state formation. For some seven decades the USSR represented the last attempt to maintain a supra-national 'empire' on fundamentally new principles, namely working-class solidarity and socialist internationalism, but with its disintegration the nation-state became the universal political form in Europe. As we shall see below, the wars of Yugoslav succession can be seen as part of the long struggle to establish relatively homogeneous nation-states. In this headlong rush to establish nation-states the relative advantages of the European multinational 'empires' should not be forgotten. The Austro-Hungarian Empire (see Map 2.1) allowed a multiplicity of peoples to live in communion and relative harmony, while the wars in the Balkans in the 1990s were far from inevitable and in any case failed to resolve the issue of how communities fated to live in proximity with each other can co-exist.

## 5   Civil society versus the state

The tension between state and society in Western Europe took diverse forms, but gradually allowed the emergence of civil society, the realm of civil associations and conscience. This is the source of the pluralism that is characteristic of European civilisation. Civil society is the basis of democratic politics since without the social hinterland of a critical and active public, organised not only in political parties but also in innumerable interest groups, communities of common concern and local self-government, democracy becomes not only formal and lifeless, but also brittle and vulnerable. The issue of participation will be discussed further in Chapter 5, but it might be noted here that Marx took a far more gloomy view of civil society, considering it the source of egotism, selfishness and economic exploitation. He was quite willing to see the baby of civil society thrown out with the bath water of capitalist exploitation, but failed to see how the individual could be defended against the might of the state if all autonomous intermediate institutions had been swept away. It is for this reason that the restoration of civil society became one of the main demands of the anti-communist movements in Eastern Europe from the 1970s onwards. The concept of civil society thus became the focus of *resistance*, but it was also sometimes seen as the site of a possible future *emancipation* from traditional forms of politics (see Keane, 1988). In the event, it soon became clear that a vibrant partnership between the state and civil society is the most effective basis for democracy.

## 6   The guild versus economic society

Perhaps the most crucial of all these divisions was that between the principle of the guild, the closed corporation that strictly regulated the work of its members, access to the market, and prices, and the development of market-oriented capitalism based on entrepreneurial capital. From its birth in northern Italy in the early modern period, market capitalism has now become the universal principle of economic organisation,

### Vladimir Il'ich Lenin (1870–1924)

Born Vladimir Il'ich Ulyanov of a minor gentry family in Samara, he became the major theorist of the practice of revolutionary socialism in the twentieth century. In his seminal work of 1902, *What Is to Be Done?*, Lenin outlined his theory of a tightly knit party of dedicated revolutionaries separate from the working class who would offer leadership. Left to their own devices, in Lenin's view, the working class would develop only a 'trade union' consciousness, devoted only to the amelioration of workers' conditions as opposed to dealing with the root cause of deprivation, capitalist exploitation; and therefore a force had to come from outside – the revolutionary party. Lenin's ideas provoked a split in the Russian Social Democratic Labour Party (RSDLP) in 1903,

with his radical wing becoming the Bolsheviks, and the moderates the Mensheviks. On his return to Russia from Swiss exile on 4 April 1917 Lenin's April Theses suggested an immediate transition from the first stage of revolution (the 'bourgeois democratic') to the second ('revolutionary socialist'), based on his theory of imperialism: the world capitalist system was marked by the concentration of financial and industrial capital, and it would take only a break of the 'weakest link of the imperialist chain' to bring the whole capitalist world crashing down. Under his leadership the Bolsheviks were able to seize power in October 1917 and thereafter established the first revolutionary state in the world.

but it must be stressed that this was by no means a foregone conclusion. In its own way, the state socialism practised in the former Soviet Union represented an attempt to destroy market forces and to regulate economic life in a manner reminiscent of the old guilds, although of course for modern industrial purposes. Today the market is taken for granted not only as the source of wealth but also as the guarantor of freedom, although the debate over the relationship between the two is far from exhausted. A similar debate rages over the intrusion of the values of the market into spheres that are considered by many not to be its proper concern, giving rise to fears that altruism will give way to the universal imposition of the 'cash nexus', undermining traditional cultures and eroding selfless concern for others.

### 7   Class struggles versus liberalism

The hierarchical division of society and inequalities of wealth and privilege have been the universal features of all civilisations. What marks Europe out is not the presence of class divisions, but that these have taken on a systematic and theorised form of class conflict. During the French Revolution new ideas of social equality emerged, advanced above all by the so-called *sans-culottes* during the period of Jacobin dominance between 1791 and 1794. In 1797 Gracchus Babeuf for the first time advanced the cause of the proletariat, and thus signalled the beginning of the class struggles between labour and capital. But the French Revolution signalled above all the consolidation of the power of what in that context was called the 'Third Estate', otherwise known as the bourgeoisie and now more commonly known as the middle class. Through their striving for individual rights in the sphere of politics and the economy, liberalism was forcefully placed on the European agenda, and the nineteenth and twentieth centuries were, above all, the history of the travails and, from the perspective of the early twenty-first century, the apparent triumph of liberalism.

### 8   Revolutionary versus evolutionary socialism

We now come to the period that has just ended, the period that can symbolically be considered to have begun in 1848 with the publication of Karl Marx's and Friedrich

## Joseph Vissarionovich Djugashvili-Stalin (1879–1953)

As Secretary-General of the Communist Party of the Soviet Union from 1922, Stalin came to power following Lenin's death in 1924. He was born in Georgia and had been active in Marxist revolutionary politics, joining the Bolshevik Party in 1903. From the late 1920s onwards Stalin ruled the Soviet Union through a totalitarian dictatorship underpinned by terror. His political approach, which came to be known as Stalinism, involved a cult of his personality, the re-writing of history, the pursuit of a policy of massive industrialisation based on heavy industry and organised by the state through five-year plans, and the collectivisation of agriculture. This caused famine and great loss of life. In the 1930s show trials and purges directed against the Communist Party itself, the army, intellectuals and many others consolidated his personal domination. Anxious to defend the Soviet Union against the rising power of Nazi Germany, Stalin made a pact with Hitler in 1939 and then annexed eastern Poland, Estonia, Latvia, Lithuania, and parts of Romania; he also attacked Finland. However, in June 1941 Hitler invaded the Soviet Union. Stalin organised the Soviet Union's heroic resistance, and joined the Western powers as a valued ally (see Box 2.1). After the war he imposed the Stalinist system on the Soviet Union's satellites in Eastern and Central Europe (except for Yugoslavia, see Portrait 2.3). His totalitarian system based on terror continued until his death in 1953. Stalinism was denounced by Khrushchev (see Portrait 2.4) in 1956.

Engels' *The Communist Manifesto*, proclaiming in its opening sentence that 'A spectre is haunting Europe, the spectre of communism.' Systematised by Marx, revolutionary socialism argued against the ameliorative policies of reformists and insisted that only a socialist revolution could put an end to the exploitation of the working class and, by doing that, put an end to the exploitation of all of suffering humanity. Others, however, argued that socialism could exploit the opportunities offered by liberal rights and institutions to advance the interests of the working class and to improve its living conditions through electoral politics and parliamentary parties. Socialism thus divided into revolutionary and socialist wings, although the starkness of the choice between the two was shot through with ambiguities.

In Russia, where the achievement of liberal rights lagged behind Western Europe, socialism took a radical form. Vladimir Il'ich Lenin organised a revolutionary wing of social democracy in the form of the **Bolshevik Party**, which seized power in October 1917. The course of twentieth-century European history was changed.

Communism had claimed to be able to achieve most of what liberalism aspired to, plus a lot more, above all the emancipation of humanity from the thrall of cold economic laws and from the exploitation of workers by capitalists, but in practice the Soviet republic established by the Bolsheviks under Lenin and his successor, Stalin, became a despotic political system.

The abolition of the capitalist mode of production did not on its own lead to the end of exploitation, but only replaced one form of exploitation by another, this time based on the political dominance of the Communist Party and its bureaucracy. Part of the reason for the evolution of the actually existing communist systems towards authoritarianism is that instead of communism coming *after* capitalism had matured, the revolutionary socialist systems acted as an *alternative* to capitalist development, inheriting relatively backward societies. Development thus took the place of emancipation in Soviet thinking. This is, however, only part of the explanation for the authoritarian turn taken by communist regimes everywhere. Marxist–Leninist ideology simply had no role for civil society and the separation of knowledge and power, let

**Bolshevik Party:** A revolutionary Marxist party which originated from the part of the Russian Social Democratic Labour Party which supported Lenin after 1903. Under Lenin the Bolsheviks seized control of Russia in the October Revolution in 1917. Renamed the Communist Party of the Soviet Union in 1951.

alone the market, and thus represented a repudiation of much of what had made Europe *Europe* in the first place while claiming, paradoxically, to be fulfilling European ideals of modernity.

In Western Europe evolutionary socialism in the form of social democracy brought about a veritable revolution of social reform, producing the modern welfare states of Europe, as Chapter 2 indicates. In the East, however, revolutionary socialism became exhausted, having proved unable to achieve consistent economic growth and improvements in standards of living and welfare that could match those of the West. In 1989 the Communist regimes in Eastern Europe came tumbling down, and in August 1991, following a failed coup by hardliners in the Soviet Union, revolutionary socialism there, too, collapsed. The fall of the revolutionary socialist systems removed any lingering doubts within social democracy over whether it sought to destroy capitalism or to improve it (Sassoon, 1996). One of the first social democratic parties to reject revolutionary socialism was the Social Democratic Party (SPD) in the Federal Republic of Germany (FRG) at its epochal Bad Godesberg conference in 1959, but in Britain the Labour Party remained formally committed to the nationalisation of the 'commanding heights' of the economy until the mid-1990s. By that time collectivist ideologies calling for the direct state management of the economy had everywhere waned. In the early 1980s the failure of President François Mitterrand's (see Portrait 2.6) government's attempt at strongly interventionist management of the French economy discredited all future moves in this direction (see Chapter 2).

### 9    Foreign influences and domestic development

The role of external influences of non-European provenance in Europe's development is relatively slight. While Islamic scholars reintroduced Aristotle to Western intellectual life and provided the bases of algebra, and indeed the very numbers that we use (cf. Lewis, 1982), European development was overwhelmingly endogenous. At least by the sixteenth century the fear of external conquest had declined, although the Eastern marches of Europe remained under threat from the Ottomans until their defeat at the gates of Vienna in 1683. Most of Europe's wars have been genuine civil wars, in the sense that they were between groups that probably had more in common with each other than with those outside. In the modern period wars were fought within the framework of the balance of power, the attempt to achieve a rough parity between the European great powers to avoid the dominance of any single power on the continent. The religious wars of the sixteenth century (various types of Protestants against Catholics) and the ideological wars of the twentieth (communism versus capitalism) were the exception.

However, while non-European cultures had a relatively limited influence on Europe politically, an enduring aspect of Europe's dynamism was the tension between extra- and intra-European developments. The voyage to America in 1492 by the Genoan adventurer Christopher Columbus, in the employ of Ferdinand and Isabella of Spain, marked the beginning of the modern European state system. Competition and wealth derived from the new empires overseas fuelled the competition between states in Europe. Colonial ventures in the Americas, Africa and Asia exported European values and economic organisation to new territories, and 'Europeanisation' by the nineteenth century had become a synonym for modernisation (see Map 2.2). Today the values that had earlier been exported to the rest of the world have come back to Europe in new forms. America in the West has taken European cultures and transformed them to create something new, while from East Asia a different model of capitalism and its social relations challenges Europe to redefine its own developmental path.

Out of these fissures and processes was generated the energy and dynamism that propelled Europe to the forefront of technological and cultural development. Much no doubt was lost in abandoning the fusion model of society, and the Soviet experiment in a way represented an attempt to recreate old harmonious ideals of social life, but out of these various reactions were created the very sinews of modern development. A distinctive civilisation was born with a coherence that transcends the many divisions to which it is prey.

**Cold War:** A state of hostility, animosity and tension between the Communist bloc and the Western World, embodied particularly in the relationship between the USSR and the USA. It lasted from the period soon after the end of the Second World War until the end of the Communist regimes in 1989.

# Endings and beginnings

After the Second World War the global struggle between the superpowers and between ideologies was focused on Europe, but at the same time the struggle diminished Europe's standing and ability to play an independent role. Europe was overlain by the struggle of external powers, each representing facets of ideologies (liberalism and communism) that had, ironically, been born in Europe. The **Cold War** meant the primacy of military power, but once again, in a curious inversion, promoted the demilitarisation of European international politics. No war was fought in Europe between 1945 and 1991 and instead energies were concentrated on economic development, although large military establishments were maintained.

The most profound ending on the European continent in our generation was the fall of the Communist regimes in Eastern Europe between 1989 and 1991. The extension of communism to Eastern Europe from the Soviet Union in 1944–8 in the wake of the defeat of Nazi Germany initially fulfilled certain national and social developmental tasks but by the 1970s it was clear that the Soviet-type systems in Europe were in crisis. Economic growth rates were falling and everywhere the allure of socialism was fading. Various attempts to renovate socialism, above all during the Prague Spring of 1968, when the Czechoslovak Communist Party sought to introduce a more humanistic 'socialism with a human face', were crushed by an invasion of Czechoslovakia by Warsaw Pact forces on 21 August 1968, and thereafter oppositional movements no longer sought to 'renew' socialism but to transcend it. The Soviet Union and its Communist allies, in their eagerness to achieve the formal ratification of post-war borders and other security and economic advantages established in the first two 'baskets' of the Helsinki Final Act of August 1975 (see Box 10.2), signed up to a third 'basket' dealing with a number of issues subsumed under the rubric of human rights (Mastny, 1993, pp. 421–42). This proved one of the more significant catalysts for the fall of the Communist systems, in that it gave the populations a legal document to cite, signed by all the Communist states, promising to defend free speech, freedom of movement and many other aspects. Against the background of declining economic performance and concerns over human rights, by 1989 popular support for the Communist regimes had largely evaporated. Much of Communist officialdom itself realised that the old regimes were exhausted, and prepared for the transition to something new.

With the appointment of Mikhail Sergeevich Gorbachev as leader of the Soviet Union in March 1985 Soviet history entered its endgame. Beginning with a programme of *perestroika* (restructuring), Gorbachev's policies gradually became more

### Mikhail Sergeevich Gorbachev (1931– )

Born in 1931 and pursuing an orthodox career in the Communist Party of the Soviet Union as local Party leader in Stavropol Krai, in March 1985 he was elected General-Secretary of the CPSU. He immediately launched what he called *perestroika*, the restructuring of the Soviet political system and the economy. This was accompanied by *glasnost*, meaning 'openness', allowing a more critical and truthful discussion of the past – above all, the crimes of Stalin. Initial hopes that some fine-tuning of the Soviet system would allow significant improvements in economic performance were dashed, and instead Gorbachev concentrated on political reform. In March 1990 the CPSU was stripped of its 'leading role' in managing society, but conditions continued to deteriorate. The Baltic republics, forcibly incorporated into the USSR by Stalin in 1940, demanded independence, the working class became more militant, and intellectuals were no longer satisfied with 'socialist' democracy, but simply wanted democracy. By 1991 the accumulation of crises overwhelmed Gorbachev's vision of a reformed, humane and democratic socialism. Following the failed coup of August 1991 the Communist Party in Russia was banned, and in December of that year the USSR itself was abolished. Gorbachev resigned on 25 December 1991, and since then has headed the Gorbachev Foundation, a policy think-tank, in Moscow.

radical as he embraced most of the agenda of the Prague Spring, to achieve a type of democratic renewed socialism. His clear signals that the East European countries could go their own way precipitated the various negotiated revolutions (Poland, Hungary), mass movements (Czechoslovakia, Bulgaria) and popular uprisings (Romania) that put an end to the Communist experiment in Eastern Europe in 1989 and in the USSR itself in 1991. The end of revolutionary socialism raised questions about the role of any sort of socialism in the postcommunist world and helped rekindle interest in various 'third way' projects (between revolutionary socialism and neo-liberal capitalism), particularly in Britain under Tony Blair's New Labour after their crushing electoral victory in May 1997. It also seemed to suggest that a distinctive phase in European modernity had come to an end, including the modernist project in art (see Chapter 11). The idea of never-ending progress, of revolutionary leaps into freedom, and of the liberating effects of science, gave way to fears about emancipatory despotism (where the search for absolute emancipation leads to absolute servitude) and the risks attendant on scientific development (Beck, 1992).

The end of communism was accompanied by the end of the last multinational 'empires'. The USSR ceased to exist as a state on 31 December 1991 leaving fifteen successor republics, including Russia and Ukraine (see Map 2.4). Czechoslovakia underwent a 'velvet divorce' on 1 January 1993 when it divided into the Czech Republic and Slovakia. In contrast the disintegration of Yugoslavia between 1990 and 1999 provoked bitter warfare (see Chapter 2 and Map 2.5).

The end of the Cold War allowed an immediate peace dividend, and most countries slashed their defence budgets. It also ended the continent's subordination to the two contesting blocs, although the Western military alliance was forced to rethink its role. The **Truman Doctrine**, announced in 1947, outlining the principles for the 'containment' of the Soviet threat, provided the rationale for the North Atlantic Treaty Organisation (NATO), founded in 1949, based first in Paris and then, from 1966, in Brussels.

The creation of NATO gave Atlanticism concrete form, with Canada and the USA

**Truman Doctrine:** Ideologically expressed commitment made by US president Truman in 1947 to maintain freedom throughout the world by 'containing' the spread of communism. The Doctrine laid the basis for subsequent US involvement in the Greek civil war, the creation of NATO, and long-term US global military presence.

## Box 1.1

## NATO

The North Atlantic Treaty Organisation was established in 1949. The previous year Britain, France, the Netherlands, Belgium and Luxembourg had created the Brussels Treaty Organisation as a mutual defence organisation against the possibility that Germany might once again revive and prove aggressive, and against the menace that the Soviet Union was perceived as constituting. In 1949 these states joined with the United States, Canada, Italy, Portugal, Denmark, Iceland and Norway to sign the North Atlantic Treaty. The intention was to ensure that the United States was firmly committed to the defence of Europe. From this time until the 1990s the Soviet Union was clearly identified as the main threat. Greece and Turkey joined the alliance in 1951. In 1954, following a failed attempt to set up a European Defence Community, the Western

European Union was created, superseding the Brussels Treaty Organisation, and incorporating West Germany alongside the original members. The Western European Union was first and foremost a device to enable West Germany to be admitted to NATO, and in 1955 that took place. Spain joined in 1982. Meanwhile, in 1964, General de Gaulle had symbolised his desire to assert French independence from the USA by withdrawing France from NATO's integrated military command, as well as requesting NATO to move its headquarters out of France.

In 1999 the alliance was expanded by the accession of Poland, Hungary and the Czech Republic. Defensive throughout the Cold War, its first military action took place in the 1990s in the Balkans.

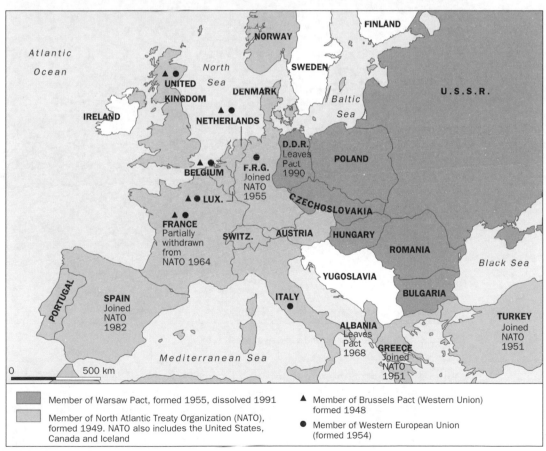

**Map 1.5** The NATO and the Warsaw Pact countries

Box 1.2

## The Warsaw Pact

This military alliance, linking the Soviet Union and its Central and East European satellites, was created in 1955, over and above a series of bilateral treaties between the USSR and its satellites which had allowed for large numbers of Soviet troops to be stationed in those countries. Its creation was primarily, though not solely, a response to the admission of the Federal Republic of Germany to NATO. Its founder members were the Union of Soviet Socialist Republics, Romania, Poland, Hungary, Czechoslovakia, Bulgaria, and Albania, which ceased participation in 1961 and formally left in 1968. East Germany was admitted in 1956. It was nominally an intergovernmental organisation but the military command structure was always under Soviet control. The alliance collapsed with the fall of Communism in 1990–1 and its military structure was formally dissolved on 31 March 1991.

**Map 1.6** European economic and defensive blocs

joining with most non-communist West European nations. The existence of NATO demonstrated that security threats were too big for any one country on its own, even one as powerful as the USA. In the East the counterpart to NATO, the Warsaw Treaty Organisation (WTO), established in 1955, was disbanded in 1991.

For the countries involved there was a 'return of history' as the countries could now pursue their own destinies. The enlargement of NATO to the East proved one of the most contentious issues, with Russia resolutely opposed on the grounds that with the end of the communist threat NATO had outlived its usefulness. For the new and aspirant members of NATO, however, membership gave them a sense of security that they had not enjoyed since the end of the First World War. The Atlantic security partnership remains central to post-Cold War security in Europe and represents an obstacle to the re-emergence of balance-of-power politics, a concept that had spawned so many wars in Europe. As we shall see in Chapter 10, however, the relevance of NATO to a world without communism has been disputed.

One of the superpowers (the USSR) disappeared, while Europe's relationship with the other (the USA) had to be placed on a new footing. Moreover the overlay of the Cold War was withdrawn from Europe just as global market forces were challenging the very basis of independent political existence (see Chapter 9).

Under these conditions economic transitions in Eastern Europe have been taking place, with mixed success. While Poland managed to forge ahead with economic transformation, its economy by the end of the 1990s was still smaller than it had been before the rise of Solidarity in 1980. Slovenia was the only other transition country to restore its 1990 GDP level by the end of the decade, with the Czech Republic, Slovakia and Hungary coming up fast. Elsewhere the picture was far gloomier. The Russian economy shrank by some 60 per cent by the end of the decade, leaving the mass of the population worse off than they had been under communism, and with at least a third below the poverty line. Even in the former German Democratic Republic (GDR) – since 1990 united with the Federal Republic of Germany and thus not obliged to start from scratch as all other postcommunist countries did and enjoying advantages that no other transitional country had: a sound currency in the form of the Deutschmark (exchanged in 1990 at the very advantageous rate of one-to-one for the communist-era Ostmark), massive budget transfers from the West, billions of Deutschmarks in private direct investment, and the whole panoply of democratic institutions and law (property, commercial, bankruptcy, civil and so on) – even here the transition depression was deep, and only in 1999 did the five Eastern *länder* reach their pre-unification levels of GDP. The gulf between per capita GDP in the East and the West remained enormous: in the EU the average income in 1999 was $21,600 per head whereas in Poland, one of the most successful transition economies, it was a mere $4,096, while in Russia it was just over a thousand US dollars. Trends suggested a gradual convergence with the Central European economies and polities moving towards those of the West, whereas in the former Soviet Union the direction was, if anything, in the opposite direction.

Europe had a nightmarish twentieth century, wracked by wars, genocide, mass deportations and ideological hatreds. According to Mazower (1998), some 60 million European deaths before 1950 are attributable to war or to violence by the state. If democracy is now the universal aspiration, this was far from always being so. Fascism and communism rejected the softness and lack of resolution of 'bourgeois' parliamentarianism, particularly in the interwar years, and to this day nationalist myth-making tears societies apart. While the Western part of the continent might see the second half of the century as one of peace and increasing affluence, the Eastern part was effectively subjugated to an at times murderous but always oppressive social system. The West did little to bring about the end of the Cold War, other than existing as an alternative, and for large parts of the East 1989 represented the triumph not so much of democracy as of capitalism. As Mazower (1998) has vividly argued, Europe is far from being the natural home of **liberal democracy**, and liberal democracy is certainly not the natural conclusion to its history.

**Liberal democracy:** A form of democracy which incorporates limited government, accountability of government to the legislature and the people, and a system of regular and competitive elections.

# ■ The struggle for unity and its limits

The post-Cold War era in Europe is marked by three main principles: political democracy, economic liberalism, and integration. Although plagued by divisions and wars, the aspiration to European unity is far from new. There have been attempts to unite Europe in the past, and these continue today, although in radically new forms. In the Roman Empire there was one law, one defence system, a road system radiating from Rome and a single currency for the many peoples sheltering under the *Pax Romana*. This peace lasted until the end of the fourth century when the Goths, Huns and Vandals moved in. The second unificatory project was represented by Christendom, a temporal power that united all of Europe until the fateful split of 1054 between Byzantium and the Roman Catholic Church. In the Western part the popes became the rivals of emperors as the Catholic (or universal) Church emulated the Roman Empire through a system of bishops and monks, with Latin the *lingua franca* once again of a huge territory. In the Middle Ages neither priests nor scholars recognised frontiers or countries but were part of the single cultural entity of Christendom.

The third attempt to unite Europe was launched by the crowning of Charlemagne in 800 as Holy Roman Emperor. The empire survived until 1806, from 1273 to 1806 in the hands of the Habsburgs, the rulers of the Austrian lands. By the end, of course, not much remained of former glories; Voltaire characterised the remnants as 'neither Holy, Roman, nor an empire'. It was Napoleon who in 1806 put the empire out of its misery, but he in turn represented the fourth great unificatory mission. The French Revolution of 1789 brought to the forefront the two great principles of popular sovereignty (democracy) and self-determination (nationalism), although in the meantime Europe had to endure the Napoleonic empire and the long decay of the other empires. Napoleon built a supra-national empire, but he also represented the principles of the Enlightenment. **Democracy** and **nationalism** thereafter were to go together, since for the people to rule there had to be a limit and definition of who exactly were the people. Europe suffered yet one more military attempt to unite the continent, under Hitler's Germany, before Europe, destroyed and overshadowed by the emergent superpowers, embarked on the current, sixth, attempt to contain its diversity in a single political form.

Europe's divisions have been a source of dynamism, but they increasingly became a source of weakness. After 1945 it became clear that Europe, devastated by two world wars within a generation, could not continue in the old way. European politics began to move from fission to fusion. Some visionaries began to hark back to the idea of one law and one defence system to cover a larger area of Europe than the Roman Empire. Victory in the Second World War revived hopes for a continent united and at peace. In Zurich in September 1946 Churchill made a speech calling for a United States of Europe, although he was not advancing the idea that Britain would actually be part of this new 'official' Europe. The new Labour government in Britain under Clement Attlee, absorbed by the creation of the welfare state and by its defence ties with the United States, also saw no reason for British involvement in any movement towards European unity. Calls such as Churchill's, however, fell on more receptive ground in Germany (Konrad Adenauer), in France (Jean Monnet and Robert Schuman) and Italy (Alcide De Gasperi). All were devout Catholics, and it is often suggested that some of their commitment to European unity derived from the universalism of the Roman Catholic Church harking back to the unity of Christendom

**Democracy:** Rule by the people. According to Abraham Lincoln in his address at Gettysburg in 1864, 'government of the people, by the people and for the people'. Democracy is a much contested concept, subject to many varying interpretations.

**Nationalism:** A set of beliefs, which may take varied forms, which asserts the primacy of the nation as the source of sovereignty and the main basis for politics and government.

## Adolf Hitler (1889–1945)

Born in Austria, Hitler began a rather unsuccessful career as an artist. He served in the German army in the First World War, in which he was wounded and gassed. He joined the National Socialist (Nazi) Party in Munich after the war, and rapidly rose to be its leader. During imprisonment for his part in an attempted political take-over (*putsch*) in Munich in 1923 he wrote *Mein Kampf* (*My Struggle*), expressing his racial theories, his sense of German destiny and his virulent anti-Jewish views. Elected into office as Chancellor in 1933, he quickly imposed a totalitarian one-party state with himself as Führer (leader). His aims for German territorial aggrandisement led to the annexation of Austria and of the German-speaking areas of Czechoslovakia in 1938 and the invasion of Poland in 1939 which prompted the outbreak of war. The Nazi pursuit of the 'final solution' and of 'racial purity' led to the holocaust – the mass murder of millions of Jews, along with gypsies, homosexuals, communists and resisters, in the death camps. He committed suicide in Berlin as the Allied forces were about to occupy the city.

of old. Britain's ambivalence about relations with 'Europe', however, is a pronounced form of a tension now experienced more widely, as the challenges of reconciling national politics with the political expression of aspirations to European unity though the European Union become apparent. These themes are further explored in Chapters 7 and 8.

Otto von Bismarck, the 'iron chancellor' who had united Germany through 'blood and iron' in the 1860s, had once dismissed Italy as 'no more than a geographical expression', and while now both Italy and Germany have united, it is Europe that remains a 'geographical expression'. The initial aim of European integration was largely negative, to ensure that never again would war be possible between Germany and France, but a more positive agenda has gradually emerged. This encompasses at the minimum a powerful economic trading bloc that could match the economic power of America and the Far East, but at the maximum there is clearly a dynamic involved that may one day lead to the creation of an integrated state that would supersede the smaller states out of which it is composed.

The process so far is limited to Western Europe, with some tentative advances towards Central Europe. In the East, as we have seen, disintegration rather than integration remains prevalent. Europe remains a geographical expression looking for a political form. But what are the geographical borders of Europe? What are its limits and how can it be physically defined? Europe's borders are poorly delineated, merging into Asia in the East and separated from Asia by the Hellespont in Turkey, making it no more than a sub-continent jutting out into the Atlantic Ocean. In the discussion that follows, it is clear that geography is never absolute but is politically defined: geography, in short, is politics. If we look to the west we see the USA, a country of largely European origins and values and one that by 1913 had a GNP that was already nearly three times that of Britain and four times that of Germany. The eclipse of Europe and the shift of the locus of power over the Atlantic was evident in all fields after 1945. The United Nations, established in San Francisco in April–June 1945, made New York its home, whereas the old and discredited League of Nations was based in Geneva.

In the post-war world the fate of Western Europe and North America appeared to be so closely bound together as to have established a new Atlantic community. This, at least, was the traditional British view, but one that was sharply contested by France

## Box 1.3

### Finlandisation

The condition whereby a country loses its freedom of action in foreign policy, but is free to pursue domestic policies of its choice. The term was historically applied to Finland. After 1945 Finland was forced to take into account the wishes of its giant eastern neighbour, the Soviet Union, in external affairs, but internally the country remained capitalist and democratic. Only in 1989, with the fall of communism, did Finland stop being 'Finlandised'.

in particular. The concept of Atlanticism in Britain was sometimes expressed in the form of the notion of the 'special relationship' between the USA and Britain, an idea that was forged in the early post-war years as Britain's growing economic weakness forced it to pass the baton of world leadership to the USA. The special relationship has always been something accorded greater respect in Britain than in America. The Atlantic ideal, however, has been a weak force outside of security issues and, except in Britain, was soon overshadowed by the idea of European unity. Even the United States took a benign view of European integration, seeing it as a way of strengthening Europe's economic independence, achieving security against communism and guaranteeing no return to the European civil wars of the past.

If we look to the north, the Scandinavian countries during the Cold War espoused the notion of the 'Nordic balance' between the capitalist West and the communist East. Finland found itself in exceptional circumstances, and while internally capitalist, the country accepted some limitations on its freedom of action in foreign policy (a condition known as 'Finlandisation'). Sweden was the main driving force of neutrality and non-alignment in the North, pursuing social democracy at home and refusing NATO membership abroad. With the end of the Cold War, Sweden and Finland joined the EU but not NATO, while Norway remained a member of NATO but not the EU. Denmark was a member of both organisations, and had always been sceptical regarding notions of a Nordic 'Third Way'.

Looking east, the anti-communist revolutions of 1989 represented a long-delayed end to the Second World War, and in a broader sense an end to the division of Europe. However, the end of the Cold War may have brought down the iron curtain but there remains a fundamental division between the prosperity of the West and the travails of transition in the East. The Eastern part of the continent is still engaged in the nation-state building process that is largely completed in the West. With the fall of communism, twenty-two new nation-states were born, fifteen alone out of the former USSR, five (so far) out of Yugoslavia, and two out of Czechoslovakia. In the Balkans this endeavour, trying to carve relatively ethnically homogeneous states out of multinational entities, was accompanied by forced migration on a massive scale. The three Baltic republics (Estonia, Latvia and Lithuania), however, managed to restore their statehood relatively peacefully, although in the first two there were tensions with the large Russian minorities, focusing on issues of citizenship (see Box 8.3). It might be noted that membership of the EU and NATO was out of the question as long as these issues remained unresolved. Everywhere a condition required for accession talks was the resolution of border disputes and the repudiation of territorial claims, something that Latvia did over its claim to territories in Russia.

The Central European countries of Poland, Hungary, the Czech Republic and Slovakia are on the fast track (as we shall see in Chapter 8) for EU membership. Poland, the Czech Republic and Hungary joined the NATO Alliance in April 1999, and the door remained open for a new wave of enlargement to the East. But how far to the East? There is no real eastern geographical border to Europe, with the Ural mountains a symbolic rather than a physical barrier, and with most of Siberia and the Russian Far East as far as the Pacific Ocean brought firmly into the European sphere of civilisation by Russian colonisation. As for the Central Asian states (Kazakhstan, Kyrgyzstan, Tajikistan, Turkmenistan and Uzbekistan) and the South Caucasus (Armenia, Azerbaijan and Georgia), in the period following the end of the Cold War they joined a number of pan-European bodies, but their status on the borderlands of Europe remains contested.

The question of Russia is, as ever, ambivalent. Is it the most western of the Asiatic countries, or the most eastern of the European states? Is it part of European civilisation, or the core of a distinct Eurasian civilisation of its own? While Catherine the Great may have issued a famous *ukaz* (decree) declaring that 'Russia is a European nation', the very fact that such a decree was required suggests at least some uncertainty over the issue. These questions came most sharply to the fore when NATO launched its air war against Serbia on 24 March 1999 in response to Serbian repression in Kosovo. The Balkans, as in 1914, provided the spark that brought out the underlying tensions in the post-Cold War order. Russia's role in helping broker peace in Kosovo, however, confirmed that there could be no enduring peace in Europe *without* Russia, however uncomfortable it may be to live *with* Russia.

The status of Ukraine is perhaps even more ambivalent. The country was not included in either the fast or slow track of eleven future EU members for two main reasons: the slow pace of its domestic reform; and its identification with Russia, especially through joint membership of the Commonwealth of Independent States (CIS). Ukraine had done itself no favours under its first postcommunist president, Leonid Kravchuk, when it had insisted that Russia was not part of 'Europe', and had thus involuntarily placed itself outside as well. Ukraine, however, openly declared that its objective was EU membership; and although it might have unofficially wanted to join NATO, its stated position at first was that of neutrality.

Finally, the south may well ultimately prove Europe's greatest challenge. Turkey first talked about EU membership two decades ago and put in its official bid in 1987, yet political instability, economic weakness, the human-rights record and ethnic conflict (in particular in the Kurdish areas of Eastern Anatolia) meant that its application was shelved. The European South (Portugal, Spain, Italy, Greece) has joined 'official' Europe, although there remain some smaller countries now embarking on membership of the EU (Cyprus, Malta). For centuries under the Greeks and the Romans, and indeed for Napoleon and Hitler, the Mediterranean was the centre of a civilisation that extended into the Levant and North Africa. The capture of Granada and the destruction of the Islamic civilisation of Andalusia in the 1490s secured (in strictly Euronationalistic terms) the southern border of western Europe. Today the Maghreb (stretching from Morocco to Egypt) is firmly on the further shore, and for most European policy-makers the continent ends on the sea's northern strand. The Mediterranean most sharply delineates Europe's zone of prosperity from the South, where various struggles for development, democracy and survival are being waged.

The mention of Europe's Islamic and Southern neighbours draws attention to the contradictory process of European border formation. Just as the external borders are taking on a harder character, migration has brought non-European cultures into the heart of Europe. The retreat from empire gave rise to a reverse flow of former colonial peoples into Europe to work in its factories and to staff its public and social services. In France the movement of Algerians (Algeria was considered part of metropolitan France) had begun before the First World War, but became a mass phenomenon following the conclusion of the Algerian war of independence (1954–61). In Britain the age of mass immigration is considered to have begun with the landing of 547 Jamaicans on the SS *Empire Windrush* in 1948, followed by large numbers from the Indian sub-continent. The migration of large numbers of Turkish *Gastarbeiter* (guest workers) into Germany may be considered a case of intra-European movement if one considers Turkey part of Europe.

While the populations of most West European states have become more heterogeneous since the war, those in the East repudiated centuries of mixed populations during and after the Second World War. The Jewish population was destroyed as a conscious act of policy by Nazi Germany and its local supporters; and from 1945 the German populations were summarily expelled from East Prussia, Silesia, the Sudetenland and elsewhere. At a stroke eight hundred years of German civilisation and settlement came to an end. By 1948 some 10.7 million had been expelled or had fled from Eastern Europe, most of whom went to West Germany; the country by 1950 had become home to 8 million 'out-settlers' (*Aussiedler*), who remain a significant political force there. The legacy of the expulsions continues to haunt relations between Germany and its Eastern neighbours. Poland alone had lost some 3 million Jews and 5 million Germans, and had become one of the most ethnically homogeneous countries in Europe, with 98 per cent of the population claiming to be ethnic Poles before the fall of the Wall. The states of the former Soviet Union remain heterogeneous, with Russia alone hosting at least 126 different peoples. Renewed ethnic cleansing in the Balkans after the end of the Cold War displaced some 2 million from Bosnia, and led to the deaths of about a quarter of a million. It appeared that the future of Europe hinged on its ability to manage and resolve the Balkan crisis. The issue, starkly put, was either the Europeanisation of the Balkans, or the Balkanisation of Europe (Mestrovic, 1994).

As Europe entered the twenty-first century some of the optimism that followed the end of the Cold War in 1989–91 had dissipated. Instead of a new era of peace and prosperity, new divisions came to the fore. The West European zone of prosperity only hesitantly moved to the East, while democracy was far from consolidated in much of the postcommunist world, in particular the area (with the exception of the three Baltic republics) that had once comprised the Soviet Union. The war in Kosovo in 1999 had revealed the underlying tensions between Russia and Europe, while the second Chechen war beginning in September of that year demonstrated once again (as in the Bosnian war of 1991–5) the inability of pan-European institutions to avert or to mediate conflicts. It appeared that a new 'post-ideological' cold war was latent between Russia and the West. Contrary to the view of Francis Fukuyama (see Portrait 10.1), history had certainly not ended in 1989. The features of Europe's twentieth century and in particular the problems facing the continent in the post-Cold War era will be the subject of the following chapters.

## ■ Summary

◆ The meaning of 'Europe' is contested but a peculiar pattern of historical evolution has given the continent a distinctive identity, although this common identity is divided between a Western and an Eastern part. At the base of Europe's civilisational identity is the notion of modernity, whereby a society is turned to the future in the belief that societies progress towards constant improvements.

◆ Europe differs from other civilisations in its dynamism, which is in part derived from its 'fission' (i.e. explosive) pattern of development, based not on stability and continuity but on change and division. A number of key divisions can be identified, but cumulatively they allowed a distinctive relationship between the individual and the community to emerge, generally understood by the term 'liberalism'.

◆ The challenge to liberalism in the form of communism proved unviable in Eastern

Europe. Socialism, however, took two main forms, and while the revolutionary socialism developed by Marx and Lenin ultimately was unable, literally, to deliver the goods, evolutionary socialism (otherwise known as social democracy) left a permanent mark in creating the modern welfare states of Europe. Both evolutionary and revolutionary socialism are themselves now being transcended by 'third way' agendas.

◆ The geography and settlement pattern of Western Europe encouraged territorial fragmentation and the creation of numerous statelets fighting against each other, and this in turn encouraged the creation of the modern administrative state, concentrating fiscal, economic and military resources in its hands. The attempt to maintain multinational empires failed and today the nation-state is the dominant political form in Europe. The disintegration of the USSR, Czechoslovakia and Yugoslavia can be seen as only the latest stage in the development of nation-states.

◆ The emergence of the European Union, however, is a way of re-creating a multinational community on wholly new principles. The European Union is moving away from being simply a trading bloc and is beginning to take on some of the attributes of a state in its own right. The question of enlargement to the East for most of the 1990s was subordinated to the aim of intensifying integration within the organisation itself, a set of priorities that has been questioned by many.

◆ The end of the Cold War in 1989 has not inaugurated an era of peace but, notably in the former Yugoslavia, allowed regional wars to be fought in Europe for the first time since 1945. In response, NATO has rethought its role and is enlarging to the East. This in turn threatens Europe with a new division, between those who are members of the Western European alliance system and those who are not.

◆ New patterns of inclusion and exclusion are emerging, reflecting the ambiguities over Europe's own borders. The question of where Europe, as a geographical and political entity, ends and begins is one of the most important facing the continent today.

## Questions for discussion

▶ What was so distinctive about European modernity?

▶ What were the main divisions that have fuelled European development?

▶ What have been the main consequences of the end of the Cold War?

▶ What are the natural limits to Europe?

## Further reading

Davies, Norman, *Europe: A History* (Oxford: Oxford University Press, 1996). A magisterial survey of the history of Europe from the very beginning until the present.

Dussen, Jan van der and Kevin Wilson (eds), *The History of the Idea of Europe* (London: Routledge, 1995). A very useful introduction to the main intellectual currents underlying European development.

Hayward, Jack and Edward C. Page (eds), *Governing the New Europe* (Cambridge: Polity Press, 1995). An essential collection of essays on politics in contemporary Europe.

Lane, Jan-Erik and Svante O. Ersson, *European Politics: An Introduction* (London: Sage, 1996). An accessible introduction to the main political processes in Europe today.

Urwin, Derek W., *A Political History of Western Europe since 1945*, 5th edn (Harlow: Longman, 1997). A concise history of Europe since the Second World War.

# Historical Background

Robert Ladrech

'The contribution which an organised and living Europe can bring to civilisation is indispensable to the maintenance of peaceful relations.'

ROBERT SCHUMAN, *The Schuman Declaration* (1950)

Europe at the end of the twentieth century is the product of several world-historical dynamics and the unpredictability of human choice. In the fifty-plus years since the end of the Second World War in 1945, the colonial empires of Britain, Belgium, France, Portugal and the Netherlands have disappeared – in many cases as a result of armed independence movements; the establishment of the USA and USSR as superpowers with Europe at the centre of their rivalry turned the continent into the most heavily armed territory on earth; rival ideological systems each produced political–socio-economic systems vastly different from each other – the democratic welfare state in the West, and the communist command economy in the East; and finally, in the last decade of the century, concerted efforts by people, elites as well as ordinary citizens, have undermined institutions and systems of thought and practice held to be nearly immutable – the nation-state in the West, and Soviet rule in the East.

## Europe between the wars

The Europe that entered the twentieth century was a continent characterised by extremes – in the gap between rich and poor; between industrialising and growing consumerist cultures on the one hand, and agrarian, peasant societies on the other; autocratic forms of government as well as parliamentary party government; and modernism and positivism in the arts, philosophy and sciences co-existing with traditional religious social control and patron–client relations. Europe was, in other words, a mix, volatile in some areas, of the promises of material and cultural progress and the ageless traditions and authority of Church and King. By the end of the First World War, these juxtapositions had begun to change, and the certainties that imbued these different dimensions of European society were tested. Europe had entered what E. H. Carr (1939) termed its 'twenty years' crisis'.

By 1919 four European empires ceased to exist – the German, Russian, Austro-Hungarian and Ottoman. Defeat and social and economic collapse brought about by the course of the war were the immediate causes, and ill-adapted forms of governance

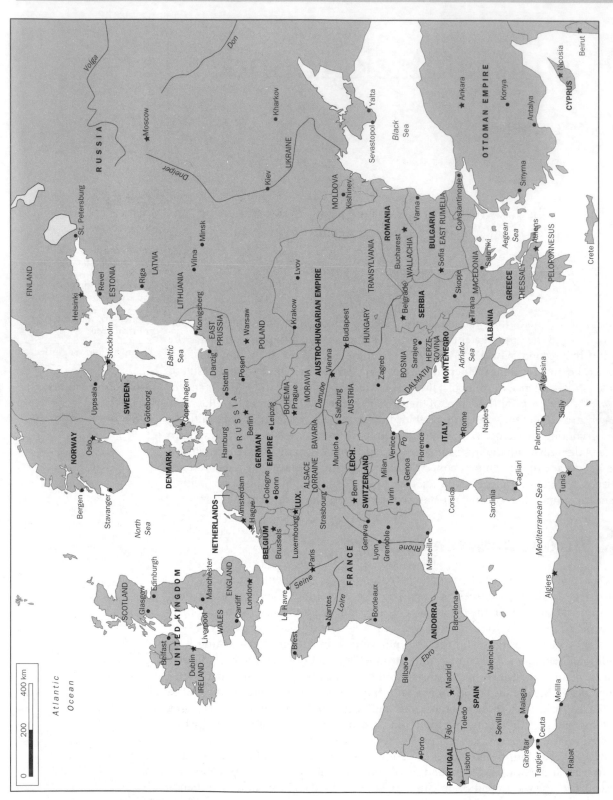

**Map 2.1** Europe prior to the First World War.

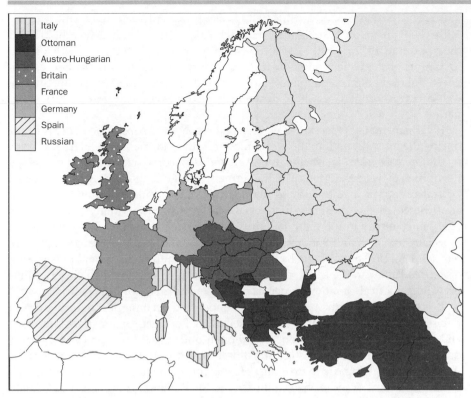

**Map 2.2** Balance of power of the empires, 1871

and administration help to explain why conditions were ripe for the overthrow of these governments. In their wake, successor governments, many of them constituting newly independent countries, especially in the case of the **Austro-Hungarian Empire**, were established in a variety of political forms, ranging from parliamentary to authoritarian. In many cases, initial acceptance of parliamentary and constitutional government was soon supplanted with authoritarian rule, whether in its traditional form as in Poland, Hungary, and Yugoslavia, or in the new one-party state of the Communist-ruled Union of Soviet Socialist Republics (USSR).

In addition to the patchwork of liberal democracies and authoritarian states, the political landscape began to polarise even within the democracies. The success of the Bolsheviks (in 1918 named Communists) in Russia inspired other left-wing groups to organise on a similar basis. Consequently, often as a result of a split within a social democratic or labour party, Communist parties appeared in many European countries, most often in the industrialising states of northern and western Europe. In some, attempts, ultimately unsuccessful, were made to seize power, as in the case of Germany in 1918 and Hungary in 1919. In others, the Communist Party became a small but sometimes decisive factor in parliamentary coalition government, as in the French Third Republic. On the other side of the political spectrum, discontent with parliamentary rule, fuelled by resentment with the terms of the peace treaty ending the war, led to the development of right-wing extremist movements, some constituting themselves as political parties. In the two most famous cases, Italy and Germany, **fascism** took the form of resistance to the liberal democratic state. Together with Communists, the anti-democratic bloc in many countries sometimes nearly

**Austro-Hungarian Empire:** A multinational empire which comprised, among other political units, Austria proper, the Kingdom of Hungary, Bohemia, northern Italian provinces such as Lombardy, etc. The people who inhabited the Empire differed in language, customs, and historical background, and included Germans, Czechs, Slovaks, Poles, Magyars, Croats, Serbs and Slovenes, among others. The Empire fell at the end of the First World War.

**Fascism:** An ideology characterised by a belief in anti-rationalism, struggle, charismatic leadership, elitism and extreme nationalism; associated historically with the Mussolini regime in Italy.

**Depression:** An economic contraction resulting in high unemployment. The Great Depression was triggered by the stock market crash on Wall Street in New York in October 1929 and lasted throughout the 1930s.

approached a majority, as in the 1932 German legislative elections which led to Hitler being named Chancellor. In Italy, the Fascist Party led by Mussolini simply took power in 1922 from the constitutional monarchy and replaced it with a fascist 'corporate' state. Other countries, from Sweden to France to Austria, also experienced political polarisation, manifesting itself both in parliamentary competition as well as in paramilitary clashes. Democracy was indeed sorely tested during this period.

If parliamentary democracy in western and northern Europe came under pressure during the interwar period, the economies of most countries were severely affected by the Great **Depression**, whether they were industrial or agrarian. Added to this was the burden of war reparations paid by Germany, whose economy was part of a wider central European investment and development area. Widespread unemployment contributed to the instability of the political environment. Many of the poorer agrarian countries in the south and the east experienced high levels of emigration, especially to North and South America. Even in countries not experiencing the intensity of political polarisation by fascist and/or communist parties and movements, organised labour in the form of trade unions mounted concerted challenges to the prevailing political-economic order, as in the General Strike of 1926 in Britain.

By 1939, several of the trends sketched above had become clear. Communist or fascist regimes had consolidated themselves in Portugal, Spain, Italy, Germany and Russia. Parliamentary democracy, though under strain from powerful nearby dictatorships and their domestic sympathisers, clung onto the hope of ameliorating the conditions giving rise to extremist movements through the creation of the welfare state in some Scandinavian countries and the Popular Front reforms in France. Economically, a rise in industrial output linked to rearmament in Germany helped to attenuate the worst aspects of the Depression. Forced industrialisation in the USSR, though terrible in the toll on human life, led many to believe a rise in living standards had occurred. Free-market capitalism had therefore given way, in many cases, either to the new Soviet centrally planned economy, or to state-led industrialisation in fascist countries, or to state interventionist policies in the remaining democracies. In many countries of Eastern Europe, stretching from Lithuania in the north to Yugoslavia in the south, economic modernisation had failed to be sustained, and they co-existed with the rest of Europe as generally subsistence-type peasant societies combined with traditional dictatorships.

As we shall see below, life for most Europeans in the period after the Second World War differed markedly from the turmoil of the years between 1914 and 1945. For the generation born in the years soon after the turn of the century, their experience of the dislocations of war, economic deprivation and political extremism translated into strong support for leaders and regimes promising stability and security. Europe after 1945, although divided for the next 45 years owing to the bitter rivalry of two competing ideological systems, represented a peaceful and stable environment compared with that which preceded the Second World War.

## ◼ Post-war Europe: Cold War and bipolar division

At the end of the war in 1945, with the defeat of fascism, one might have expected a return to the European state system which had arisen in the previous two centuries, that is, a system of independent states engaged in various levels of competition and accommodation – militarily by way of alliances and occasional wars outside or else at the periphery of Europe, and economically through trade and investment among themselves and their colonial possessions. Yet this system was already being undermined by the events and trends of the interwar period from 1918 to the outbreak of war in 1939 – the Russian Revolution and rise of the Soviet Union on a course of development isolated from the rest of Europe; the collapse of tentative attempts at liberal democracy in Italy and Germany and in the process the rise of fascist states and movements; the increasing lethalness of armaments and the breaching of the prohibition against targeting civilian populations, i.e. total war; and the growing challenges to Europe's empires by independence movements in the colonies, for example in India.

Instead, the 'new order' that emerged from the ashes of the Second World War was largely determined by the new superpowers, the USA and USSR. Within a few years from the ending of the war in May 1945, the USA and USSR became more intimately involved in the affairs of Europe than at any previous time. During the interwar period, both of these countries had been marginal to the events and dynamics convulsing Europe. This is not to say they were totally absent, as American financial power in the years immediately after the Second World War was influential in the reparations debate concerning Germany. Certainly the establishment of Communist parties in Europe owed some debt to resources sent from the Soviet Union via the Comintern (the Communist International). But in general, the USA and USSR were preoccupied with domestic priorities. In the case of the USA, its isolationist foreign policy and economic problems following the stock market crash of 1929 kept it out of European affairs and the League of Nations (a forerunner of the United Nations) for most of the 1920s and 1930s. The newly established Soviet state took until the early 1920s to consolidate itself, and then crash industrialisation and collectivisation under Stalin rendered the country effectively isolated from the rest of Europe during the 1930s, a situation well expressed by Stalin's phrase regarding 'socialism in one country'. Yet at the war's end, both countries were effectively the dominant country in their respective areas of Europe. How this came about depended to a large degree on the condition of the other formerly 'great' powers.

Within several years of the end of the war, it had become clear that the two former wartime allies were now securing their respective spheres of influence in Europe, and the bipolar division of Europe ensued, not to be overcome for another fifty years. This period of armed confrontation came to be known as the Cold War, and although two mighty military alliances faced each other across the political–ideological divide in Europe – most notably in the divided Germany – actual fighting between the two camps – the American-led North Atlantic Treaty Organisation (NATO – see Box 1.1) and the Soviet-led Warsaw Pact (see Box 1.2) – never occurred. The very possibility of nuclear war taking place in the heart of Europe was in itself a deterrent to using warfare as simply a 'continuation of politics by other means'. This Cold War environment permitted, perhaps paradoxically, a period of stability never before seen in Europe in modern times, which allowed economic development to reach unprecedented heights and spread its affluence throughout societies, both East and West. Before we turn to the details of this 'golden age' and its later trends, let us recall the state of affairs in Europe on the eve of the Second World War. This is important in order to understand just how much the political and military stability and economic development of the period after the Second World War meant to the generation born soon after the turn of the century, and how it came to represent the core of political competition and issues up to our present day.

## Political and economic conditions in 1945–9

The war ended in Europe with the defeat of Nazi Germany in May 1945. Germany was occupied by Allied armies led in the West by the USA and in the East by the Soviet Red Army. Bitter fighting to the end rendered Germany a devastated country, and its formal occupation by the USA, USSR, Britain and France presaged the eventual division of Germany into two states, each allied with one or the other superpower. At the same time, all of the principal combatants save the USA had suffered enormous damage due to bombardment and heavy fighting in the effort to repulse the German armies. The USSR emerged essentially as a military superpower, its industrial base converted to produce arms. Britain, although not occupied by Germany, sustained damage to its industry from German bomb and rocket attacks, and its financial reserves were dangerously depleted by the war effort. France also sustained physical damage, together with deep social and political divisions created by the years of collaboration with the Nazis. Italy and south-eastern Europe also were physically traumatised by the war, an added factor being the unleashing of ethnic and political vendettas by groups in the Balkans against those having allied themselves with the occupying Germans. France and Italy also had large, and as a result of participation in the resistance, well-developed, Communist parties. In all, the political and economic situation at the end of the war represented a vacuum into which the USA and USSR stepped.

Mutual suspicion and miscomprehension of the others' intentions and motivations contributed in large part to the developing hostility between the USA and USSR. The Soviet leader, Joseph Stalin, had what he considered to be good reasons to assume that Soviet occupation of Eastern Europe – accomplished during the drive towards Berlin – would be accepted by the West as *de facto* political control, a buffer zone between

### Box 2.1

### Yalta, Potsdam and the division of Europe

The leaders of the Second World War Allies (the United States, the Soviet Union and the United Kingdom) met inTeheran in November 1943, in Yalta in February 1945 and, after the end of the war, in Potsdam in July and August 1945, to discuss their plans for a post-war world. In October 1944 Stalin, the leader of the Soviet Union, and the British Prime Minister Churchill had come to a 'deal' agreement in which eastern and south-eastern Europe was carved up into respective 'zones of influence' for either side. The USSR would have 90 per cent control over Romania and 75 per cent control over Bulgaria, but there would be 90 per cent control over Greece by the West, and Hungary and Yugoslavia were to be controlled equally. At the conference at Yalta, boundaries were settled between Poland, the Soviet Union and Germany, with the Soviet Union gaining the borders it sought in the East, with the Polish westward frontier on the Oder–Neisse line. These arrangements were said to be temporary. In addition the organisation of the United Nations was agreed upon and the issue of German reparations was raised. At Potsdam they agreed that Germany was to be demilitarised, de-Nazified, decentralised and democratised. The decisions of these conferences resulted in the division of Germany into four zones of occupation – French, British and American in the West, Soviet in the East – and a similar division of Berlin, which lay within the Soviet zone. In the event, the frontiers persisted and the dividing lines came to mark the great division between the West and the Communist bloc until 1989.

the Soviet Union and a possibly resurgent Germany. First, there was the simple fact that the Red Army was in place from Bulgaria through to the eastern half of Germany and all points in between (except Albania and Yugoslavia, where Communist partisans consolidated their positions on their own). Secondly, the fact that the Western Allies chose to invade Germany not from the Balkans but instead from the west, across France, seemed to leave the area to the east open to Soviet strategies. The third factor was an understanding Stalin thought he had from the Western Allies through his 'deal' with British leader Winston Churchill, in which eastern and south-eastern Europe was carved up into respective 'zones of influence' for either side.

The Americans had expected free elections to take place in all of the liberated countries; instead, governments sympathetic to the USSR were set up, many of them dominated outright by Communist parties. The question of what to do with Germany, though, represented the centre of debate. Should Germany be neutralised as much as possible to prevent it ever rising again as a threat to peace in Europe? What sort of reparations would be required? Many of these questions were first addressed in a series of wartime and post-war conferences, including Yalta and Potsdam. For instance, the Yalta Conference produced, in February 1945, a Declaration on Liberated Europe, which called for, among others things, governments responsive to the will of their people throughout Europe, and more specifically, disarmament of Germany by the Allies as they saw fit 'for future peace and security'. In the end, the occupation zones of the Allies in Germany crystallised into two, a fused Western half and an Eastern Soviet-dominated half. Between 1946 and 1949, a number of events and crises took place in which American and Soviet stances hardened towards each other and laid the foundations – politically and militarily – for the next forty years of 'cold war'. These included the articulation of what came to be known as the Truman Doctrine (February 1947), the offer of **Marshall Plan** economic aid to Europe and Stalin's rejection of it (July 1947), the expulsion of Communists in coalition governments in Italy, France and Belgium (May 1947), a coup d'état in Czechoslovakia (February 1948), the Berlin Blockade (June 1948), and in 1949 the establishment of a West and an East German state, and a new military alliance of eleven European countries under American leadership, NATO. In many of these cases, each side interpreted as aggressive what the other considered defensive. The Truman Doctrine, in particular, gave an ideological hue to diplomatic manoeuvrings, and together with the political–military concept of **containment**, the rivalry between the USA and USSR permeated many aspects of European and American society.

## Foundations of divided Europe

By the mid-1950s, the division of Europe seemed set to continue for the foreseeable future. Each superpower, in a *de facto* manner, recognised the other's sphere of influence, and despite American rhetoric of 'rolling back' Soviet military dominance over Eastern Europe, when apparent opportunities arose to give support to domestic moves towards removing such control, as in the Hungarian Uprising of 1956, none was forthcoming. As the Soviet Union sought to extend its type of economic model – the command economy – to its new 'satellite' states, the Western countries began rebuilding their economies with American Marshall Plan aid, and in the process formed part of what became known as Bretton Woods (see Box 2.2), essentially a global, capitalist, US-dominated trade regime. With the formation of a formal Soviet-led military alliance, the Warsaw Pact, in 1955, the bipolar division of Europe seemed fixed, with Soviet-supported Communist governments and command economies in

**Marshall Plan:** Officially named the European Recovery Program, this US initiative involved massive financial aid and loans to European countries (totalling some $14 billion in contemporary prices) in order to hasten their economic recovery following the Second World War, and thereby, hopefully, strengthen their political stability. Although offered to East European countries as well, most recipients were Western European.

**Containment:** The US-inspired doctrine of the Cold War aimed at stopping the spread of Communist influence, through the use of military alliances, subversion, and diplomatic and economic isolation.

## Bretton Woods

Even before the end of the war a meeting in Bretton Woods in New Hampshire in September 1944 established the foundations of the post-war economic system that lasted until the early 1970s and whose institutions remain to this day, establishing a monetary system based in Washington, DC, where the World Bank and the International Monetary Fund (IMF) have their headquarters. At the conference the 44 delegates agreed to create common institutions to avoid a return to the protectionism of the interwar years that had turned an economic slump in 1929 into the Great Depression. In order to achieve this, the International Monetary Fund (IMF) and International Bank for Reconstruction and Development (known as the World Bank) were created, together with a system of fixed exchange rates based on the gold–dollar standard. The IMF had the task of holding the currency or gold deposits of its 29 original members and using them to regulate the international exchange-rate mechanism. The World Bank was to act in parallel with the IMF as a development bank providing long-term loans on a profit-making basis to projects which could not find funding from private sources. The IMF and the World Bank were intended to oversee the creation of a single world market based on fixed exchange rates and the use of the dollar and the pound Sterling as reserve currencies. Many of the principles espoused by John Maynard Keynes, including demand-led management of economies, were accepted. The formal Bretton Woods system of fixed exchange rates collapsed in the early 1970s under the double impact of the oil crisis and stagflation (a combination of stagnation and inflation that was not foreseen in the Keynesian scheme of things), but in the postcommunist era the IMF reshaped itself as the main Western agency policing the economic transitions in Eastern Europe.

the East, and American-supported liberal democracies and market economies in the West.

In Western Europe, economic recovery during the 1950s was complemented by moves towards formal economic integration. Some of the lessons learned from the mistakes of the interwar period, especially economic nationalism, practised in 'beggar thy neighbour' policies, translated into a belief among many elites that co-operation rather than cut-throat competition would hasten economic reconstruction. Promoted by influential individuals such as Jean Monnet, an initial attempt to pool resources and planning in the areas of coal and steel – vital for the rebuilding of industry – was launched in 1950, known as the European Coal and Steel Community (ECSC). Building upon its success, the countries involved – France, Germany, Italy, Belgium, the Netherlands and Luxembourg – created a much more ambitious effort in economic integration, the European Economic Community (EEC), established by the Treaties of Rome in 1957 (which also included co-operation in atomic energy – Euratom). More than simply a **free trade** area – this option was pursued by Britain, Austria, Denmark, Norway, Portugal, Sweden and Switzerland beginning in 1959 as the European Free Trade Association (EFTA) – but less than a federal United States of Europe, the EEC began as a free trade area with a common tariff and supra-national institutions. By the end of the 1960s, common policies in atomic energy and agriculture were in place, and some of the supra-national institutions, especially the European Commission, had become significant institutional players on the political and diplomatic front.

Economic recovery was rapid and unprecedented, so much so that the years of high growth in the 1950s and 1960s are known variously as the economic miracle, the **trente glorieuses** in France, the **Wirtschaftswunder** in Germany, and so on (although Britain actually experienced a relative economic decline during this period). Relations

**Free trade:** The notion that the pursuit of barrier-free trade will benefit all those involved, regardless of relative economic strength.

**Trente glorieuses:** Literally the 'thirty glorious years' of economic expansion in France, this phase of post-Second World War economic growth ended in the mid-1970s, and was characterised by rising personal incomes, affluence and low unemployment.

**Wirtschaftswunder:** Literally the 'economic miracle' of West German post-war economic expansion, characterised by rising incomes and affluence. This unprecedented economic performance helped to legitimise the new West German state in the first few decades after the end of the Second World War. The 'miracle' ended in the mid-1970s.

## Jean Monnet (1888–1979)

French economist, statesman and 'father of Europe'. He found employment during the First World War co-ordinating Franco-British war supplies, and was later appointed Deputy Secretary-General of the League of Nations. During the Second World War he acted as a senior official in the British Supply Council for war purchases in the United States and in 1943 he helped to form the French Committee of National Liberation. In 1946, backed by de Gaulle, Monnet launched a five-year investment and modernisation plan to rebuild the French economy. In 1950,

together with French Foreign Minister Robert Schuman, Monnet produced the Schuman Plan, from which the European Coal and Steel Community (ECSC) and the European Economic Community (EEC) were subsequently developed. Monnet was president of the ECSC High Authority from 1952 to 1955, whereupon he set up the Action Committee for the United States of Europe (ACUSE), intended to bring together leaders of political parties and labour unions in the cause of European unification.

between organised labour and business, never harmonious in the interwar period, became in many countries much less confrontational and in fact more co-operative, especially in Scandinavian countries, the Lowlands, Germany and Austria. In most of these cases, the state, along with business and labour, became part of a system of economic management known as '*neocorporatism*', whereby under the auspices of the state, business and labour elites worked out accommodations among themselves. This relationship was very significant in the development of the welfare state. In southern European countries (apart from Portugal and Spain, which carried over into the post-war period dictatorships that had established themselves in the 1920s and 1930s, respectively) business and labour relations continued to be characterised in confrontational and ideological terms, especially as major industrial labour confederations were allied to Communist parties, most notably in France and Italy.

At the same time, the proceeds of this economic growth and expansion were directed by governments into income-redistribution and social-welfare policies. This macro-economic management was influenced very much by the writings of the British economist John Maynard Keynes, who argued for explicit government manipulation of expenditure and taxation as a means of promoting demand for goods and services, thus helping to keep employment levels high. Thus in complementing rising wages and salaries, the state actively set about to build and strengthen the social infrastructure – in health, education, unemployment insurance, pensions etc. – to create, in other words, the welfare state. The prosperity accruing from economic reconstruction in the late 1950s and 1960s spread to just about all levels of society, a state of affairs never before witnessed in Europe.

The 'stability' of the Cold War, co-operation between labour and business, rising affluence among the working class and an expansion of the salaried middle class, all of this was in stark contrast to the conditions of the interwar period, and this was reflected in politics as well. The political polarisation of the interwar period, between Communist and other left-wing parties on the one hand, and fascist groups and parties on the other, gave way by the late 1950s and early 1960s to a much more stable and accommodating environment. First, parties which had actively supported Nazi and other fascist governments were de-legitimised by this experience in the post-war period. Secondly, although many Communist parties joined the anti-fascist struggle

Box 2.3

### Key points of the Treaty of Rome

- The free movement of goods, persons, services, and capital;

- A customs union and common external tariffs;

- Various Community policies (e.g., the Common Agricultural Policy, transport);

- Supervision by common institutions: the Council of Ministers, Commission, and assembly (the future European Parliament).

## John Maynard Keynes (1883–1946)

A UK economist whose major work, *The General Theory of Employment, Interest and Money*, written in 1936, departed significantly from neoclassical economic theories, and went a long way towards establishing the discipline now known as macroeconomics. In recasting traditional laissez-faire principles, Keynes contended that full employment led to high consumption and increased productivity. He provided the theoretical basis for the policy of demand management, a policy of governmental manipulation of taxation and expenditure, which was widely adopted by Western governments in the early post-Second World War period. Keynesian theories have had a profound effect upon both modern liberalism and social democracy.

after 1941 (Hitler's invasion of the USSR) and emerged from this experience as national heroes, it was primarily only the French and Italian parties which profited in electoral terms. With a taste of government responsibility in the immediate post-war coalitions, these parties moderated their programmatic identities as they strove to be accepted as 'governmental' rather than revolutionary actors. Thirdly, the Social Democratic and Labour parties, many of which lost members to newly formed Communist parties in the 1920s, began to focus their policies and attraction to the electoral centre, and in the process began to emphasise a multi-class appeal rather than being seen as strictly working-class parties. And finally, centre-right parties, both conservative and confessional, came to accept many of the basic foundations of the welfare state, thus reducing the hostility with centre-left parties. By 1960 then, a political scientist observing the political landscape in Western Europe could posit the creation of an ideological consensus between the major parties of the centre-left and centre-right. If we add to this a general anti-communist perspective by these two political blocs, then the main issues around which politics turned during this time were essentially how to manage the economy and further improve the lot of all citizens.

This picture of political stability and economic growth must be supplemented by another consideration, specific to certain countries and having implications up to the present day, and this was the process of **decolonisation**. By 1960, the major colonial powers (minus Portugal), had granted independence to most of their former overseas possessions (the most significant exception was France and its relationship with Algeria). In many cases, independence was won only after bitter and protracted fighting between national liberation forces and the colonial power, for example France and its war in Indochina. In some cases, for instance Britain and Jamaica, the process was relatively smooth. One significant result of decolonisation was large-scale migration of indigenous peoples from the newly independent countries to their European 'mother' country, so much so that the ethnic and racial balances were noticeably altered. This was the case concerning Belgium and the Congo; France and North Africa; Britain and the Caribbean and South Asia; and the Netherlands and Indonesia. In the expanding economies of the day, many found work in the new factories, while others became part of a marginalised underclass, either unemployed or under-employed.

In Eastern Europe, economic reconstruction was from the start undertaken on

**Decolonisation:** The retreat of European powers from their colonies during the twentieth century.

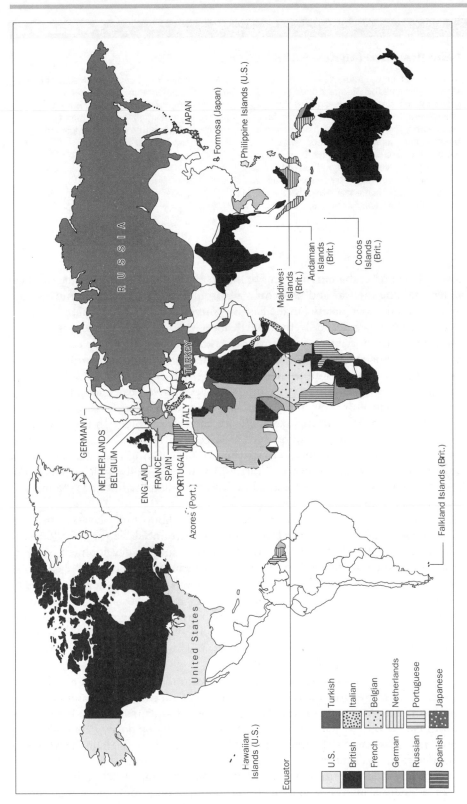

Philippine Islands (U.S.)

JAPAN

Formosa (Japan)

RUSSIA

Andaman
Islands
(Brit.)

Cocos
Islands
(Brit.)

Maldives
Islands
(Brit.)

TURKEY

GERMANY

ITALY

NETHERLANDS
BELGIUM

SPAIN

ENGLAND
FRANCE

PORTUGAL

Azores (Port.)

Falkland Islands (Brit.)

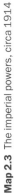

Hawaiian
Islands (U.S.)

United States

Equator

| | |
|---|---|
| U.S. | Turkish |
| British | Italian |
| French | Belgian |
| German | Netherlands |
| Russian | Portuguese |
| Spanish | Japanese |

**Map 2.3** The imperial powers, circa 1914

### Josip Broz Tito (1892–1980)

Yugoslav statesman. As leader of the partisans fighting the Germans during the Second World War, Tito was in place to assume leadership of post-war Yugoslavia. In 1948 he broke with Stalin and pioneered a 'national path' to socialism based on self-managing enterprises. Himself a Croat, he maintained a decentralised and federal territorial organisation of the country, which was made up of six republics and two autonomous provinces. In the early 1950s, along with Nasser of Egypt and Nehru of India, he was instrumental in setting up the movement of non-aligned countries, an attempt to remain independent from the two superpowers (and to exploit this position).

very different bases than in the West. In the first place, as a result of the devastation suffered during the war and its victor status immediately afterwards, much of the remaining industrial matériel in the East was shipped to the Soviet Union for use in its rebuilding efforts. Secondly, the Soviet Union was intent on maintaining political control of its territorial gains, and this translated into structuring the economies of Eastern Europe along a Soviet model. The Soviet-type economy, sometimes referred to as intensive in its developmental orientation, emphasised rapid industrialisation, especially of heavy industry, according to a series of Five-Year Plans. The collectivisation of agriculture was also part of the model, whereby the displacement of peasants from their land supplied labour for the new factories. In the case of the Eastern European countries, some, such as Czechoslovakia and to a certain extent Poland, had already developed industrial economies during the interwar period, while others, for example Bulgaria and Hungary, were basically agrarian. Nevertheless, forced industrialisation promoted rapid economic growth, but at the price of enormous problems.

Another dimension of the Soviet model was its levelling of social classes. In order to accomplish this, massive social upheaval was introduced via the abandonment of private property, the nationalisation of industry, and the development of social measures, rudimentary in the beginning, such as education and health care for all citizens. After Stalin's death in 1953, his successor, Nikita Khrushchev, attempted to moderate several aspects of the Stalinist economic model. He sought to introduce greater specialisation into the Soviet economy by regionalising production, a form of economic decentralisation. In the end, his method of re-directing Soviet production upset too many Communist Party officials, and his reform was ended, as was his position at the head of the Party in 1964.

In many respects, the political situation between the Soviet Union and Eastern European states mirrored the economic reality. If Stalin sought a monolithic Communist order in Europe, resistance to this view was soon apparent. By 1949, Communist parties loyal to Stalin had succeeded in consolidating power (Yugoslavia was the exception, when in 1948 its leader Josip Broz Tito broke with Stalin in favour of a 'national path' to socialism).

As mentioned above, the Soviet economic model was imposed, but the harshness of forced industrialisation and agricultural collectivisation soon generated protests

**Portrait 2.4**

## Nikita Khrushchev (1894–1971)

Born in southern Russia close to the Ukrainian border, Nikita Khrushchev worked as a fitter in the mines. He joined the Communist Party in 1918. He rose in the Party, moving to Moscow in 1929, and after serving as a political officer with the Red Army in the Second World War he became head of the government and Party leader in the Ukraine. He returned to Moscow in 1949 and became first Secretary of the Communist Party after Stalin's death in 1953. In 1958 he became head of both Party and government.

In 1956 his speech to the Twentieth Party Congress denouncing Stalin began the process of 'destalinisation'. He attempted reforms of agriculture, with a marked lack of success, and encouraged technological advance. His deployment of missiles to Cuba led to the confrontation with the United States known as the Cuban missile crisis of 1962. He was forced out of office in 1964 and lived effectively under house arrest until his death in 1971.

outside government – as in Berlin, and the Czechoslovakian demonstrations in 1953 – and within ruling Communist parties, between nationalists and those loyal to Stalinist methods and plans. The assumption of power by Khrushchev, and his denunciation of Stalin in 1956, led to a slightly wider latitude for some Communist governments, particularly in Poland where collectivisation of agriculture was abandoned.

By the mid-1950s, Khrushchev maintained Soviet political control over some Eastern European states by accommodating more nationalist leaders who took full advantage of the relaxed economic trends. However, these leaders had acquired their positions as a result of political crises between their countries and the Soviet Union. Thus Poland and Hungary both emerged by the end of 1956 with Communist Party leaders given a relatively free hand to pursue more nationalist (meaning less orthodox) economic programmes, but only after such calamitous events as the Hungarian Uprising of November 1956, in which pitched battles between Hungarians and Soviet Red Army troops took place in Budapest. In other countries, for instance Bulgaria and Romania, Communist Party bosses playing the 'nationalist hand' came to power in the late 1950s and early 1960s and virtually ruled these countries in an autocratic manner for the next thirty years until their overthrow with the downfall of communism generally.

The overall effect upon East European societies of the changes in Soviet economic planning, the political crises of the early and mid-1950s, and the imposition of a Communist model of society, was that by the 1960s many of these countries began to settle into a pattern of authoritarian political rule and modest economic growth, where a balance was attempted between the requirements of heavy industrialisation and attention to consumer needs. With the end of Khrushchev's economic experimentations came a relatively peaceful and orderly period of growth in the Soviet economy throughout the 1960s, from which East European countries benefited (with the exception of Albania, which pursued an autarchic policy). Although far behind the material gains of West European economies, which were then experiencing their economic 'miracles', most East Europeans and Soviets compared their situation in the 1960s with the pre-war period, much as adults in the West also did. Of all the social changes introduced into Eastern Europe, apart from the elimination of the aristocracy, probably the most dramatic was the expansion of education, especially higher education. Thus a high percentage of professionals, including academics, judges, industrial managers, etc., came from working-class backgrounds, a far higher proportion than in Western European countries such as France, Britain or West Germany.

By the late 1960s, Soviet-style modernisation had transformed many of the countries of Eastern Europe. Although imbalances between countries remained, usually owing to pre-war levels of development, in general the distinction between industrial and agrarian societies disappeared, especially as collectivisation of agriculture destroyed the peasant basis of rural economies. Although Communist Party rule did not allow for opposition parties, and a secret police was used to stifle any attempts at co-ordinating opposition among individuals, the countries also varied in the intensity of Communist rule. One could say that by the late 1960s a Communist European society had been created, but unlike the liberal democracies in the West, official conformity to the Soviet Union in terms of political, economic, and even cultural directions, necessitated the authoritarian nature of these regimes. The apparent stability of both East and West Europe, however, was soon to unravel, as underlying political and economic dynamics came to the fore, beginning in the pivotal year 1968.

# ■ Diversity within blocs and economic slowdown

The year 1968 was a watershed in that the events associated with it represented a puncturing of the mindset that 'business as usual' in political, social and even economic and military affairs could go on undisturbed. Although there were of course antecedents to the events of 1968, the challenge to both Western and Eastern European orthodox views of society laid the foundation for trends in the latter 1970s and 1980s which eventually changed the very complexion of European politics.

## 1968 and the challenge to authority

The two most singular events which occurred in 1968 took place in France and Czechoslovakia. In each of these countries, the political status quo was directly challenged by mass demonstrations involving students, workers, and professionals. In France, student resentment of the de Gaulle government's educational policies sparked a widespread strike at universities that was then joined by trade unions. For a moment in May, it almost seemed as if the very legitimacy of the Fifth French Republic, and its president, was about to fall. In Czechoslovakia, a reformist Communist, Alexander Dubček, became head of the Party, and set about instituting reforms opening up the political process, such as freedom of assembly and organisation, and other measures which were clearly out of step with prevailing Communist orthodoxy in the Soviet Union and surrounding Communist states. The 'Prague Spring' was, in fact, seen as a threat by other Communist leaders, who saw the Czechoslovak changes as possibly spreading into their countries and thereby challenging their grip on power. In late August, a Warsaw Pact force led by the Soviet Union ousted Dubček's government and crushed the experiment in 'socialism with a human face'.

These two episodes shared a common theme, that is, a desire to challenge centralised, bureaucratic, authoritarian structures. Although the 'events of May' in France and the 'Prague Spring' in Czechoslovakia were the most spectacular of the chal-

Portrait 2.5

## Charles de Gaulle (1890–1970)

Pivotal French general and statesman. In the years from the outbreak of the Second World War until his death, de Gaulle was France's most influential and controversial leader. During the war he organised France's resistance to German occupation and briefly headed its first post-war government. Resigning in protest at what he called a return to 'politics as usual', he retired from active politics but capitalised on his authority to argue for a new and modern force in French politics. Thus began the first of many political parties that were dubbed 'Gaullist'. Recalled to power by the French parliament during the Algerian crisis in 1958, de Gaulle put an end to the French Fourth Republic's unstable governance by inaugurating the Fifth Republic, built upon the premise that France needed a strong executive. Elected as the first president of the new Republic, de Gaulle put an end to the Algerian issue by granting independence to it and other African colonies, asserted French sovereignty *vis-à-vis* the United States by emphasising an independent foreign policy along with the development of a nuclear deterrent, and continued with a programme of economic modernisation begun under the Fourth Republic.

lenges to political orthodoxy, other dynamics were also at play in the late 1960s. The bipolar division of Europe had, by the late 1960s, begun to become much more diverse in terms of the relations within each bloc. Ironically, in the West, it was French foreign policy under President de Gaulle that challenged American leadership, particularly over military and political relations between East and West and within NATO. NATO strategy was itself an issue during this period, as the USA sought to substitute its strategic doctrine of the 1950s – massive retaliation – with a 'war-fighting' strategy known as 'flexible response'. Although presented as a better form of deterrence, the very thought of positioning battlefield nuclear weapons on European soil caused much consternation in Allied capitals.

Similarly, in economic matters, de Gaulle threatened to unravel part of the US-dominated global monetary system, Bretton Woods (see Box 2.2), by 'cashing in' dollars for gold held in Fort Knox, USA. The US promise of backing the dollar by gold was one of the foundations of the international trading regime. For a country to actually test this promise was a direct challenge to American top-currency status and its management of the system, especially its use of running deficits. German support for the US position caused some friction between France and Germany, which highlighted the great difference in these two countries' relations with the USA. France emphasised autonomy in foreign policy, and Germany saw its interests as congruent with those of the US regarding East–West relations. In the end, although de Gaulle's action did not alter US behaviour, it was part of a series of events that eventually led to the demise of the Bretton Woods system in 1971.

In the East, although Yugoslavia went its own way in 1948 in escaping Stalin's control, it was under Khrushchev that the seeds of relative diversity in the Communist world were planted. Romania by the 1960s had joined Yugoslavia in managing to pursue a more independent foreign policy, while remaining an ultra-orthodox Communist country. Politically, although Communist regimes were not overtly threatened again by domestic change after the Prague Spring, each country evolved its own system of internal relations, ranging from Poland, where the Catholic Church enjoyed a degree of autonomy not found elsewhere in the Communist world, to Albania, which practised an autarchic policy, maintaining relations generally only with the People's Republic of China and Romania. When it comes to Communist economics, the variation was greater. Poland had turned from collectivisation in the 1950s, Hungary pursued a somewhat market-oriented socialist economy, while others followed the Soviet model in the main. Deviation from the Soviet model was tolerated by Moscow as long as the political and military status quo was unchallenged. The suppression of the Czechoslovakian political reforms was a demonstration of the Soviet Union's resolve in this matter.

By the early 1970s, then, although the bipolar division of Europe was still in place, a loosening of internal bloc relations had taken place. Beginning in 1969, under the newly elected Social Democratic chancellor, Willy Brandt, West Germany pursued a foreign policy which aimed to normalise relations with Eastern European countries, including East Germany. This policy, which had the blessing of a new American administration, was known as *ostpolitik*. In an improved international environment between the USA and USSR, known as **détente**, contacts, especially economic and financial relations, began to multiply between the two sides. By 1975, under the auspices of the Helsinki Accords (see Box 10.2), an agreement on mutual recognition of both sides' boundaries, although with commitments to respect human rights and in fact monitor infractions against them, was signed. Thus stability in political and military matters on the continent appeared at hand in the early to mid-1970s. Such was not to be the case in economic matters.

## Economic downturn in the West, failure of reform in the East

Clouds on the economic horizon had begun to gather in the West in the 1960s, and de Gaulle's challenge to US global economic leadership was in a way a complaint about the 'mismanagement' of the system. In 1971, the US unilaterally declared an end to gold–dollar convertibility, and in 1973 the fixed-exchange-rate system, upon which international trade had grown during the 1950s and 1960s, was ended. In 1973, another dramatic event hit Western industrial economies, and this was the leap in the price charged for oil by the cartel OPEC (Organisation of Petroleum Exporting Countries) – in effect, a price shock. The politics of OPEC's move was also bound up in the vagaries of Middle Eastern politics, in particular the Arab–Israeli conflict. To a certain extent, the manner in which Europe and the USA responded to this event added another division in intra-West foreign-policy cohesion. The West European countries were heavily dependent on oil imports to supply their industries (except countries such as Norway who had off-shore oil supplies), whereas the USA had large domestic reserves, especially with the opening of a pipeline from the Alaskan oilfields in the 1970s. The combination of now floating, or competitive, exchange rates and their impact on trade, together with the oil price shock, precipitated the worst recession in Europe since the Great Depression of the 1930s. As the 1970s wore on, very sluggish growth (or none at all), together with continued high levels of inflation, resulted in a condition called '**stagflation**'. Whereas most economists assumed a trade-off between employment and inflation, persistent high inflation and not enough economic growth to generate employment confounded government economic policy-makers. The Keynesian consensus began to unravel.

How each government went about coping with this predicament led, by the mid-1980s, to a more co-ordinated response, and therefore to a revival of the economic integration process, which had languished during most of the 1970s and early 1980s. Every country's situation varied of course, and some national economies were more

**Détente:** Literally this means loosening, but it is used to describe the relaxation of tension between previously antagonistic states, for example between the USA and USSR following the Cold War.

**Stagflation:** A combination of stagnating output and inflationary pressures which typified the depression of the late 1970s and early 1980s.

**Portrait 2.6**

## François Mitterrand (1916–96)

A French politician and statesman who served for two full seven-year terms as President of the French Republic. As a student in pre-war Paris his closest links were with right-wing political organisations. He was mobilised in 1939, captured, and after escaping, worked as an official of the Vichy government before going into hiding as a resistance activist. He was elected to Parliament in 1946 as a centre-left independent, and occupied ministerial posts throughout most of the Fourth Republic period. He opposed de Gaulle's return to power in 1958. It was not the least of the paradoxes of this complex man that, having opposed the Fifth Republic's constitution, he later presided over a period where the role of that constitution in the working of the presidency and in political life was accentuated. In 1971 he joined the Socialist Party and two days later became its leader. He renewed the structures and alliances of the party and in 1981, at his third attempt, was elected President. The early years of his presidency were marked by economic and social reform, including the nationalisation of key industries. Economic difficulties forced an about-turn in 1983. Between 1986 and 1988 and again from 1993 to 1995 he shared power, in what was known as 'cohabitation', with a right-wing government. He was a partisan of the 'construction of Europe' though doubtful about German reunification. He was a subtle and clever politician, even if astuteness grew, during his second term of office, to look more like deviousness, and cleverness seemed mere machination. He was also a noted author of political books, and the instigator of a number of major architectural projects in Paris including the renewal of the Louvre museum.

at risk from global economic trends than others. The French economy, very much influenced by state intervention in investment and a large public sector, witnessed double-digit unemployment and inflation rates by 1980. The British economy was also in a parlous state, having to approach the IMF (International Monetary Fund) for a loan to meet government expenditures. Although some of the smaller economies, such as Sweden and Austria, weathered this period relatively unscathed, most governments by the end of the 1970s began to impose economic austerity policies, seeking to reduce expenditure rather than generate revenue by raising already high levels of taxation. The election in 1981 of the French Socialist Party, the first time the Left had come to power in the French Fifth Republic, saw probably the last effort to buck the international trend of cutting back on state expenditures, and instead attempted a massive Keynesian-style reflation of the economy. Within two years, the French government under President Mitterrand reversed policy direction, and essentially followed the course of its neighbours.

It was during the 1980s that an alternative economic orientation, dubbed 'neo-liberalism', and associated with the British prime minister elected in 1979, Margaret Thatcher, came to the political fore. Arguing that business was hampered by high taxation and over-regulation, and that this was a primary cause of under-investment by business and thus the absence of growth in the economy, the neo-liberal cause sought to reduce the presence of the state in the economy by privatising public companies such as national airlines, public utilities, etc.; reducing taxes; and limiting the influence of trade unions. Although never adopted elsewhere as rigorously as in Britain, elements of this economic recipe were implemented by many governments in the 1980s. Complementing these national strategies was the resumption of broader, more co-ordinated attempts to revive the West European economy, namely European economic integration.

## Margaret Thatcher (born 1925)

Margaret Thatcher, who was British Prime Minister from 1979 to 1990, took a degree in chemistry and was called to the Bar before her election as Conservative MP for Finchley in 1959. Having served in the Heath government of 1970–4 as Secretary of State for Education and Science she became leader of the Conservative Party in 1975. A politician of conviction and determination, her approach, which came to be known as 'Thatcherism', espoused robust values of monetarism, competition and self-help. She declared herself an advocate of rolling back the frontiers of the state. She attempted to reduce public expenditure, introduced legislation to curb the privileges and powers of the trade unions, undertook substantial bureaucratic reforms in the interests of efficiency and good management, capped the spending of local government, and abolished the Greater London Council. Privatisation was a major theme of her programme after the re-election of the Conservative government in 1983, to which her performance as leader during the Falklands War in 1982 certainly contributed. She supported the deregulation and free-trade elements of European Community policy as embodied in the single market programme, but stoutly opposed closer economic and political union, an opposition which became even more prominent after her resignation, which was caused by her party's increasing distrust of her domineering style, her strident anti-Europeanism, and the unpopularity of her introduction of the system of local taxation known as the 'poll tax'.

## Re-starting the European integration process

By the mid-1980s, West European economies generally had not been able to discover any magic formula allowing a return to the 'golden age' of high growth, expanding employment, and more extensive public services. In fact, compared with the US and Japanese economies, Europe appeared to be 'falling behind'. The failure of the French Socialist government in applying a neo-Keynesian strategy, and the fears of some European companies that advances in computer technology and their broad application by American and Japanese firms would eliminate domestic European rivals, led to a re-examination of the benefits of co-ordinated action at the European level. The European Commission obliged with a White Paper that proposed an accelerated drive to dismantle the barriers to trade within the EC by 1992. Thus the Single Market programme was initiated as a means to revive European economies and, by virtue of the new economies of scale that were to be created, compete globally with the USA and Japan. Essentially neo-liberal in character because it focused on eliminating barriers to trade – negative integration – it also had a few provisions for social concerns and the enhancement of European institutions' decision-making power – positive integration. Adopted by all 12 member states of the EC as the Single European Act in 1986, it created a certain dynamism in the integration process that led, by the early 1990s, to an agreement to create a single European currency (see Chapter 7).

## The failure of reform and modernisation in the East

The 'thaw' in relations between the USA and USSR in the 1970s allowed many East European governments to involve themselves in the wider capitalist system, though usually on very elementary levels. In a drive to satisfy consumer needs, many governments went deeply into debt to import consumer goods from the West. In the Soviet Union itself, under Brezhnev in the 1970s and 1980s, similar small openings to the

West occurred, especially the exchange of certain goods and grain for energy exports, gas in particular. East European governments were permitted to experiment in economic reform, especially after their growth rates of the 1960s had begun to slow in the 1970s. Where reformers tried to introduce some measure of market dynamics into their economies, however, their efforts were frustrated by a coalition of vested interests, ranging from mid-level government bureaucrats, plant managers (especially in the big heavy industry and defence sectors), workers fearing for their job security, and finally, by the limits of what the Soviet leadership would tolerate. Thus in many cases, reform programmes were never fully implemented, and sometimes partial reform policies actually made the situation worse than no reform at all. By the mid-1980s, then, many East European countries found themselves heavily in debt to Western funding agencies, countries and banks, and a lack of capital meant that their industrial plant was woefully outdated. Growth rates for countries as varied as Hungary and Romania declined all through the 1980s, while the rest generally stagnated. The Soviet economy had also entered a stagnant phase from the mid-1970s on, and with political and bureaucratic barriers to innovation, the entire region sank into an economic malaise.

# Challenging the Cold War political order

By the late 1970s, new social movements and political dynamics began to appear in both East and West European states. In the West, many new issues appeared on political and social agendas, and by the end of the decade, some had been transformed into political parties. Issues ignored by or outside the usual policy programmes of major political parties included opposition to nuclear energy, ecological and women's issues, human rights, etc. Extra-parliamentary movements pushed these causes in new and often dramatic ways. In the East, as a result of the 1975 Helsinki Accords, human-rights watch groups were set up to monitor government compliance with human-rights obligations. Under the threat of harassment and even imprisonment, many of these groups criticised the performance of their governments. Recognition from Western governments of these groups and prominent individuals associated with them, and pressure on Eastern governments in the form of withholding economic aid, became part of the wider political environment. By the end of the 1980s, this unofficial opposition in Eastern countries often came from those spearheading the efforts to push Communist governments out. In the West, the issue agenda was changed such that the new issues became part of everyday politics, and new parties associated with them affected the party systems of many countries.

## New social and political movements in Western democracies

A portion of the student activists from the 1968 events across Western Europe continued after their studies to put their ideals into practice. In challenging the political order of the day, many became advocates of more freedom in lifestyles and were opponents of top-down bureaucratic practices and policies. The environmental movement varied according to specific issues in different countries – from opposition to nuclear energy in France to the promotion of sustainable economic development in West Germany. The women's movement sought to change legislation in the areas of divorce and abortion, as well as calling for equality in the workplace in terms of wages, etc. Continuing the critique of bureaucratic structures from the late 1960s, many of these movements resolved to reject hierarchical forms of organisation, and their tactics – including peaceful protests and demonstrations, encouraging boycotts, even theatrical and dramatic events to focus media attention – represented a call for a 'new politics'. In the late 1970s, another issue was taken up by many in these movements, and that was opposition to NATO's decision to deploy Cruise and Pershing II nuclear-armed medium-range missiles in Germany, Italy and elsewhere as a response to the Soviet Union's deployment of a new generation of nuclear-armed missiles (SS-20s) with ranges that included most of Western Europe. The massive protests, particularly in Germany, were a trying period for participating governments, and the anti-American critique of the demonstrators signalled a generational difference with their parents on the credibility of US Cold War strategy.

Although in the end the missiles were deployed, the momentum from the protests was a factor in the decision to transform many of the loosely organised movements into political parties, in order to attempt to change public policy directly 'from within'. In many countries, these parties adopted the name 'Greens', as in Die Grüne in West Germany, or else a label suggesting their placement on the left of the political spectrum, but sufficiently different in order to distance themselves from traditional labour and social democratic parties, for instance the Danish Socialist People's Party. The German Greens, winning their first parliamentary seats in 1983, have gone the furthest of these 'new politics' parties in terms of electoral support, averaging close to 10 per cent in national elections and participating in German state (*Land*) coalition governments, and finally becoming junior coalition partners in an SPD-led government after the September 1998 German elections. In the competition between these parties and the traditional social democratic and labour parties for members and voters, one of the most widespread results was the broadening of the new-issues' appeal into the political mainstream, so that by the 1990s even Conservative and Christian Democratic parties had 'greened' many of their policies.

## The rise of Solidarity, crises of legitimation and the impact of Gorbachev

Emerging from a series of workers' protests in 1976, a self-government movement calling itself Self-organisation of Polish Society represented a sort of anti-government focal point in Poland in the late 1970s. With the election as Pope of a Polish archbishop, Cardinal Karol Wojtyla, in 1978 and his subsequent visit to huge crowds around the country in 1979, coupled with widespread resentment at the decline in economic well being, momentum was generated more forcefully to oppose the discredited government. A workers' organisation emerged from the movement, calling itself Solidarity, led by Lech Wałęsa, and quickly attracted mass support, securing the unprecedented right in a Communist country to strike and organise independent unions in 1980. The following year witnessed more concessions by the government until Solidarity appeared to be a counter-government itself. In December 1981, martial law was declared and Solidarity was banned, its leaders arrested and imprisoned. Although pushed underground, Solidarity survived and, with international support, eventually was recognised by the government, leading to roundtable talks on the opening up of the political system. In August 1989, a Solidarity-led coalition government was installed, the first non-Communist-led government in the Eastern bloc.

The dynamics helping to propel Solidarity into power were apparent in other

Eastern states, namely economic stagnation and the consequent decline of living standards. Apart from the ideology of Marxism–Leninism, the other foundation that Communist parties could suggest to legitimise their rule was an improvement in the standard of living. Between 1960 and 1980 this appeared to be the case, although increasing contacts with the West revealed the comparative backwardness of social and economic achievements. Poland was but the tip of the iceberg when it came to the lack of popular support for ruling Communist parties. Indeed, against this background of declining economic performance and concerns over human rights throughout the Eastern bloc, by 1989 popular support for the Communist regimes had largely evaporated. Much of Communist officialdom itself realised that the old regimes were exhausted, and prepared for the transition to something new.

Mikhail Sergeevich Gorbachev (see Portrait 1.3) was elected as General Secretary of the Communist Party of the Soviet Union in March 1985. Within two years he had begun to encourage reform with the aim of winning popular support (see Chapter 1). Emboldened by the change in Soviet expectations as well as by the experience of Poland, some parties, such as in Hungary, began a concerted effort at political as well as economic reform. Others, for instance in East Germany or Romania, simply kept the 'lid' on even harder, refusing to acknowledge the depth of resentment.

## The end of the Cold War era

Between 1989 and 1991, events of a historic nature unfolded, and all were quite unexpected. On 9 November 1989, the Berlin Wall was breached, and hundreds, then thousands of East Germans poured over into West Berlin. The political dynamics within the East German government quickly slipped out of the control of the ruling Communist Party, and within a year (October 1990) the unification of the two Germanies was officially sealed. The speed with which events transpired – the East German currency disappeared in July 1990 and the West German mark took over, and all-German parliamentary elections took place in December – left not only Germans stunned, but their surrounding neighbours as well. The French president and British prime minister, while not opposed outright to the unification of East and West Germany, urged prudence in the steps towards unification, if not a 'go slow' policy. With the support of the United States, the German chancellor, Helmut Kohl, nevertheless proceeded with a rapid approach to unification and to settling international agreements regarding Germany dating back to the end of the war. However, perhaps as a way of demonstrating that the new Germany was still a 'good European', the German government joined the French in launching a move towards an even greater degree of European integration, monetary unification, of which the outcome was the Maastricht Treaty (see Chapter 7).

Events in the East accelerated from this point onwards. Although Solidarity had managed in mid-1989 to establish itself at the head of a coalition government, within two years Communist parties in other Eastern European countries had either been forced from government – as in Czechoslovakia – or else changed their character such that open and free elections were held which they then lost, for example in Hungary. Most of these changes would no doubt not have happened, or else would have been much more complicated, were it not for the 'critical distance' Gorbachev in the Soviet Union put between himself and those Communist leaders opposed to reform. On the other hand, Gorbachev had given himself a gigantic task, that is, to reform the Soviet Union. Through policies such as openness – **glasnost** – in society,

**Glasnost:** Literally, this means 'openness', but was used to describe the relaxation of censorship and cultural repression during Gorbachev's time in power in the USSR, 1985–91.

**Perestroika:** This literally means 'restructuring' but was used by Gorbachev to describe his attempts to reform the Soviet Union between 1985 and 1991, suggesting plans to liberalise and democratise the Soviet system within a communist framework.

the introduction of some competitiveness in the economy with a view towards its restructuring – **perestroika** – and 'new political thinking' (NPT) in foreign policy, Gorbachev hoped to turn around the dire state of the Soviet economy in order to remain a superpower. Consequently, Gorbachev made it plain that East European Communist governments would have to depend upon the support of their citizens in order to stay in power, not Soviet tanks.

Gorbachev set into motion forces over which he eventually lost control. The limited democratisation he introduced led the Russian Republic, and its elected leader Boris Yeltsin, to form its own power base independent of Union and Party control. After a failed coup in August 1991, events rapidly unfolded and by the end of the year, Gorbachev resigned as the last leader of the USSR. This followed just weeks after the announcement by Yeltsin and the leaders of Ukraine and Belarus of the formal establishment of the Commonwealth of Independent States, or CIS, of eleven of the fifteen successor states from the former Soviet Union, leaving out Georgia (which joined in 1993) and the Baltic states.

It was Ukraine's overwhelming vote for independence on 1 December 1991 that precipitated the break-up of the USSR, since without Ukraine there was not much point to the continuation of the union, or so it appeared at the time. All of the successor states began a search for formulas with which to continue on the road to economic and political reform. Many of these new states suffered violence internally – Russia and the Chechen war, Georgia and breakaway Abkhazia and South Ossetia – or else disputes with neighbours – Armenia and Azerbaijan over Nagorno Karabakh.

**Map 2.4** Member states of the CIS

**Map 2.5** Post-1945 Yugoslavia

By the end of the 1990s, many of the former communist states of Eastern Europe, such as Poland, Hungary and the Czech Republic (on 1 January 1993 Czechoslovakia divided itself into two, the Czech Republic and Slovakia), had sought stability and assistance by turning westward, and had applied to join the European Union (see Chapter 8).

Although the 'velvet divorce' between the Czech Republic and Slovakia was fairly smooth, the disintegration of Yugoslavia in 1990–1 was less peaceful, accompanied by genocidal wars provoked by President Slobodan Milosevic's dream of a 'greater Serbia' to encompass Serbian populations in Croatia and Bosnia. In 1991, four out of Yugoslavia's six republics effectively left to become independent countries (Bosnia, Croatia, Macedonia – sometimes known as the Former Yugoslav Republic of Macedonia, FYROM – and Slovenia), leaving a rump Federal Republic of Yugoslavia (FRY) comprising Montenegro and Serbia. Serbia itself potentially contained two other republics, Vojvodina and Kosovo, which according to the 1974 Yugoslav constitution enjoyed autonomous status that in effect made them equal voting members of the collective presidency. In 1989 Milosevic stripped the two provinces of their autonomy, ultimately provoking a war in Kosovo from 1998 that was potentially yet another war of state formation. Kosovo had only been conquered by Serbia in 1912 but was considered the spiritual homeland of Serbian Orthodoxy and was the site of Serbia's great defeat by the advancing Turks in 1389 at Kosovo Pole. In 1999 nearly the whole Albanian population was driven out in an operation reminiscent of the Second World War. Despite vows of 'never again' in 1945, the evil spirit of a virulent and exclusive nationalism once again stalked Europe. Unlike in the Bosnian war of 1992–5, this time the 'international community' refused to stand by, and forced a settlement on Milosevic, allowing the refugees to return.

## ◼ The post-Cold War order

Over a decade after the fall of the Berlin Wall and the setting into motion of events and pressures which demolished the Cold War order, it would still be prudent to talk of an *emergent* European order, as there is still much that remains in flux. In the West, although the plans for monetary union have proceeded apace, the success of steps towards further convergence of the participating economies is uncertain. Some member states have chosen to stay outside 'Euroland', at least initially. They are Britain, Sweden and Denmark. Greece did not qualify at the time, but is pledged to do so at the earliest moment. The European Union, now with fifteen members, still operates with a system originally set up to accommodate six members. Far-reaching reform is already pressing but discussions were only beginning in 2000. It will thus be bound up with negotiations with the Eastern European applicant states.

In the East, political and economic reform has not been uniform. Some countries, such as Poland, the Czech Republic and Hungary, have progressed far in both spheres, while others, such as Slovakia and Romania, continue to struggle with the legacies of their recent past, in some cases with personnel from the Communist system still wielding power. Elsewhere, tragic events have forestalled political and economic development, for instance the wars in the former Yugoslavia. In the CIS countries, democratisation has similarly been patchy, with parliamentary procedures apparently secure in the Baltic states, but autocratic rule prevalent in Belarus and Central Asia. As for Russia, compared with its Communist past, great progress has been made in opening up both the political and the economic system. Still, the immensity of the country, and the legacy of 70 years of communism, has meant that reform of the economy has proceeded in fits and starts.

Establishing a new European order will mean confronting at least two challenges. First, firmly to ground democratic norms and procedures across all of Europe in order to forestall a new segregation of the postcommunist states. Secondly, to respond creatively to globalisation and European integration, in the sense that these processes can complicate the relationship between state and nation. Meeting both of these challenges may result in new notions of European citizenship.

## ◼ Summary

◆ Europe emerged from the Second World War physically devastated and exhausted.

◆ The remaking of Europe included two new powers, the USA and USSR, each with predominant influence in their half of Europe.

◆ This chapter traces the division of Europe into two, the political and economic events and trends in each half, and then describes the eventual demise of the Cold War and the division of Europe.

## ◼ Questions for discussion

▶ In what ways were the Cold War and political and economic stability related?

▶ In what ways was the year 1968 a turning-point in bipolar politics?

▶ Why was the USA considered the leader of the Western nations?

▶ What were some of the components of Soviet-style modernisation?

▶ What role did Gorbachev play in ending the Cold War?

# Further reading

Wegs, J. R. and R. Ladrech (1996) *Europe since 1945: A Concise History* (New York: St Martin's Press). A good and accessible coverage of political events, and social and economic trends in both eastern and western Europe.

Gaddis, J. L. (1998) *We Now Know: Rethinking Cold War History* (Oxford: Oxford University Press). A stimulating, comprehensive comparative history of the conflict from its origins to its most dangerous moment, the Cuban Missile Crisis.

Dinan, D. (1994) *Ever Closer Union: An Introduction to European Union*, 2nd edn (London: Macmillan). A useful introduction to the history of the European integration process as well as an accessible presentation of the workings of its institutions.

Unwin, T. (1998) *A European Geography* (Harlow, Essex: Longman). A competent introduction to various dimensions of European society, especially in the post-Second World War period, covering cultural issues, politics including European integration, economic issues and social agendas.

Glenny, M. (1996) *The Fall of Yugoslavia: The Third Balkan War* (London: Penguin). A fascinating exploration of the tragedy and wars unleashed by the break-up of Yugoslavia in the first half of the 1990s.

# CHAPTER 3

# The Europe of Nations and Regions

Brian Jenkins

## Contents

*Realpolitik:* A policy emanating
from realist ideas in
international relations. It
argues for a state to pursue its
own national interests rather
than act in an ethical way or for
the common good.

'Nations are not something eternal. They have begun, they will end. They will be replaced, in all probability, by a European confederation.'

ERNEST RENAN, *Qu'est-ce qu'une nation?* (1882)

Of the 190-odd states that demarcate the territory of the globe, 188 (at the last count) are affiliated to an organisation that calls itself the United *Nations*. The idea that the state represents a community called the 'nation' has become so commonplace that the two terms are often used interchangeably. When we describe the behaviour of these actors on the world stage we often say that *France* says this, or *Iraq* does that, rather than referring to the regime or temporary government of the country concerned. We talk about inter*national* relations rather than the relationship between the governing elites of *states*. In other words, the political legitimacy of states world-wide is rooted primarily in the concept of nationhood.

## Nation-state formation and nationalism

Europe was the cradle of this concept. In the sixteenth to eighteenth centuries monarchies began to create centralised institutions (royal bureaucracies, state taxation, professional standing armies) which prefigured the modern state. In some cases (Britain, France and Spain) these structures operated within relatively stable territorial frontiers, and an embryonic form of national consciousness began to emerge, so in retrospect these may be seen as 'prototype' nation-states. However, it was eventually not the absolutist monarchies, but the challenge to them, which launched the political ideology of nationalism and the process of nation-state formation in Europe. The legitimacy of absolutism, for all its *realpolitik*, drew on notions of the divine origins of human authority, of a natural order of things, of a social hierarchy based on birth, which were still rooted in the feudal era. The social and philosophical bases of this Old Order were being undermined by the rise of the new middle classes and the impact of Enlightenment thought. The ground was being laid for new principles of legitimacy involving the organisation of consent from below, representative institutions and constitutional government.

It was the French Revolution, however, which gave this process a radical democratic cutting edge, and linked it to the concept of nationhood. By drawing the masses onto the political stage, it gave substance to the idea of the 'people', but by equating this with the 'nation' it unleashed a concept which would gather a distinctive momentum of its own. In the French context, 'nation' expressed the will to create a self-governing community of citizens *within* the boundaries carved out by dynastic rulers.

It reflected the sentimental unity of the 'Third Estate' (see Box 3.1), the lifeblood of France, ranged against parasitic elites who would soon prove their lack of patriotism by emigrating or conspiring with their reactionary allies abroad. Membership of the nation was defined by residence, and by an act of political will – in the words of the Jacobin revolutionary Jean-Lambert Tallien's words 'the only foreigners in France are the bad citizens' (Brubaker, 1992, p. 7).

However, when this ideal of national self-government was transported in the wake of the Revolutionary and Napoleonic armies into the loosely federated and ethnically diverse territorial empires of continental Europe, it set in motion a very different kind of process. The Hohenzollern, Habsburg, Romanov and Ottoman dynasties had not yet achieved sufficient political and cultural unity within their domains (see Map 2.1) for them to be credible as future 'nation-states'. The state system of the mid-nineteenth century was thus no basis for the translation into practice of liberal and radical–democratic aspirations, which instead attached themselves to movements seeking to build 'nations' along the cultural fault-lines of language and religion. Unlike 'state-nations' such as Britain and France, the nation had to be created as an 'imagined community' (see Anderson, 1983, though here I use his evocative phrase to describe a 'nation' which does not yet exist as a 'state') before it could claim the right to statehood. This process, which necessarily involved the dismantling of the territorial dynastic empires, could take the form of *unification* (as in the cases of Italy and Germany in the 1860s–70s) or *secession* (the final implosion of the Habsburg, Romanov and Ottoman empires in 1917–19).

As the revolutions of 1848 indicate, the new nationalisms were originally very much inspired by the radical–democratic thrust of the French revolutionary legacy. However, the emphasis on cultural affinities and solidarities, especially in Eastern Europe where the movements were led by intellectuals (and in Poland by nobles) with largely peasant support, introduced a romantic *ethnic* (see Box 3.2) dimension which contrasted with the more rationalist civic version of the original French model (this reflecting a more diversified middle class and a more urbanised popular base). Where the latter invoked the assimilationist incorporation of all those who resided on national territory (*ius solis*) and was therefore voluntarist and universalist (exportable as a model), the former invoked a community of blood descent (*ius sanguinis*) and was therefore determinist and particularist (*sui generis*).

At the end of the nineteenth century, this ethnic definition of nationality gained a much wider currency in Western Europe too (and not least in France itself), where it was influenced (and perverted) by *fin de siècle* pessimism and anti-modernism, by elitist theory and by the pseudo-scientific racist theories of Social Darwinism. The fusion of these elements has been seen as laying the ideological foundations of future fascism. At the more popular level, the main manifestations of this rightward 'turn' of nationalism at the end of the century were the rising tide of anti-Semitism, xenophobia against immigrants and chauvinism towards foreign powers.

This, however, is only part of the story of how nationalism migrated from Left to Right in the period between 1870 and 1914. Established nation-states like Britain, France and Germany were soon to recognise the power of nationalism as an ideology,

**Box 3.1**

**The Three Estates**

Under the *Ancien Régime*, French society was divided into three orders – the aristocracy, the clergy and the Third Estate (which represented the remaining 98 per cent of the population). In his famous pamphlet of 1789, *What is the Third Estate?*, the Abbé Sièyes wrote 'Who would dare to say that the Third Estate does not contain within itself all that is required to form a complete nation? What would it be without the privileged orders? Everything, but an everything that would be free and prosperous.'

Box 3.2

## Some European thinkers, 1850–1914, and their impact on nationalism

In terms of the history of ideas, the 'ethnic' version of nationalism is usually traced back to Johann Gottfried von Herder (1744–1803) and therefore often seen as essentially 'German' in origin; but while Herder was fascinated by folk-lore and saw each nation as having a distinctive cultural heritage, he celebrated the diversity of cultures as contributing to a universal 'humanity'. For him, particularism did not lead to exclusivism or doctrines of national superiority, but with German successors like Fichte (1762–1814) this was soon to change. The anti-rationalist mood is reflected in the works of Henri Bergson and Georges Sorel, but also in the study of the unconscious developed by Sigmund Freud and Carl Jung. Elitist theory, and its anti-democratic vision of the manipulable masses, drew on Gustave Le Bon's theories of crowd psychology, and was developed systematically by Vilfredo Pareto and Gaetano Mosca. Darwin's evolutionary theories were embraced by social scientists to underpin notions of racial inequality already developed earlier by the Comte de Gobineau in his *Essay on the Inequality of Human Races* (1855). Popularisers of ethnology and the new science of eugenics, like Houston Stewart Chamberlain who extolled the virtues of the Teutons, laid some of the bases for Nazi racial theories. In France, Charles Maurras and Maurice Barrès wedded an exclusivist definition of nationhood (which discriminated as much against political enemies as against religious and ethnic minorities) to classless social corporatism and various models of the authoritarian state. Zeev Sternhell (1978) controversially claims that turn-of-the-century France was the most important intellectual laboratory for fascist ideas.

no longer of liberation and democratic emancipation, but of social integration and bourgeois stabilisation. Whether they had inherited the more 'civic' or the more 'ethnic' definitions of nationality, whether or not they were evolving into liberal democracies, they were intent on maximising citizen loyalty and strengthening state legitimacy, and the concept of 'nation' was the key vehicle. This was, as Eric Hobsbawm (Hobsbawm and Ranger, 1993) has indicated, the age of the 'invention of (national) tradition', of flags, anthems and other national icons, of the inculcation of patriotic virtues through mass primary education and mass conscription, all of this against a background of rising international tension. And the process was inevitably sharpened by the rise of organised labour and the socialist movement, whose rhetoric of class and indeed of internationalism provided both a target and a spur for a more determined emphasis on the priority of national identities and loyalties.

In this context it is not surprising that this 'state-sponsored patriotism' absorbed some of the features of the new extreme-Right nationalism, whose populist manipu-lation of xenophobic, bellicose and anti-Marxist sentiments provided the conserva-tive establishment with an urban plebeian base. And to the extent that the ruling classes were successful in persuading a majority of inhabitants that like it or not there was no practical alternative to the political framework of the nation-state, that they were 'citizens' and enjoyed benefits which (however meagre) were better than those enjoyed elsewhere, and that in the event of war these were worth defending, the stage was set for the mutual massacre of 1914–18.

The construction of nation-statehood in this period was also facilitated by rapid economic modernisation which, at whatever social costs, did begin to break down local and regional parochialism, to widen markets, to accelerate the concentration of populations in towns and of labour in factory production, to increase social mobility and cultural exchanges, and, especially through the revolutions in the railways and the media, to transform communications and make the 'nation' a more credible physical reality. In established nation-states the efforts of central government to pro-mote national consciousness were greatly assisted by this process, notwithstanding those who remained apprehensive about encouraging the drift of 'governable' peas-

Box 3.3

## Woodrow Wilson, the 'fourteen points' and the Versailles settlement

Woodrow Wilson was an academic social scientist . As the United States joined the First World War President Woodrow Wilson, a Princeton professor before he became President, set out, in an address to the US Congress on 18 January 1918, fourteen points which constituted the chief war aims of the United States, and set out a coherent programme which was the basis on which Germany sued for peace in November 1918. He strongly advocated the principle of national self-determination and he hoped not only to see the war ended, but also the causes of war eliminated. The first five points were general: that there should be open covenants of peace openly arrived at, freedom of navigation on the seas, the removal of economic barriers and the establishment of free trade, guaranteed

reduction in armaments, and an open-minded and impartial adjustment of all 'colonial claims'. There followed eight points related to specific territorial dispositions, including the return to France of Alsace-Lorraine, the independence of Poland, and the settlement of territories in the Balkans 'along historical lines of allegiance and nationality'. The final point stipulated the formation of 'a general association of nations under specific covenants for the purpose of affording mutual guarantees of political independence and territorial integrity to great and small states alike'.

The formation of the League of Nations was the direct outcome of this final point, and its founding covenant formed part of the Treaty of Versailles. But the terms of the peace were much harsher than the

fourteen points had led the Germans to suppose they would be. German representatives were excluded from the negotiations and compelled to accept the Treaty, concluded at Versailles, that was eventually presented to them. They were made to disarm and to shoulder the full blame for the war, and attempts were made to ensure that, through reparations, they bore the full costs. A sense of betrayal fuelled the sentiment that supported Hitler and the Second World War. Moreover, in the multitude of settlements that resulted in the emergence of a new map of Europe from the remnants of the old empires the principle of self-determination, though supported in some cases by plebiscites, was applied rather sporadically and selectively.

ants to the 'unruly' towns. However, in less developed Eastern Europe, where the effects were more localised and where states were far less cohesive and tentacular, 'uneven economic development' (see Immanuel Wallerstein, in Balibar and Waller-stein, 1991; and Tom Nairn, 1977) and the regional disparities it induced fuelled the *disintegrative* tendencies besetting the doomed territorial empires and paved the way for the new national settlement which followed their final collapse in the Great War.

The Versailles settlement's creation of a battery of new nation-states in Central and Eastern Europe sought to endorse and enshrine nationalist aspirations, and to set the seal on the continental process of nation-building. However, the democratic logic of Woodrow Wilson's 'fourteen points' (see Box 3.3) was soon to be under-mined. The attempt to draw national boundaries along 'ethnic' fault-lines (albeit in the hope of forging 'civic' nations) was a vain exercise, especially in the ethnically mixed zones of the former Habsburg territories. It inevitably left linguistic and reli-gious minorities (and, most fatally, German ones) trapped on the wrong side of the new frontiers. Germany's humiliation (and Italy's frustration) at the terms of the Versailles Treaty paved the way for the darkest period in the history of nationalism. Fuelled by the deep social and political divisions engendered first by the Russian Revolution and later by the Great Depression of the 1930s, fascism and Nazism are seen by some as the ghastly apogee of Statist and ethnic nationalism, defeated only by the combined military might of the two future superpowers, one through its vast economic and technological resources, and the other through massive human sacrifices, themselves mobilised as much by nationalism as by communism.

Others, including myself, would see fascism and Nazism as qualitatively distinct-ive phenomena, the products of a specific historical conjuncture, in symbiotic re-lationship with certain forms of nationalism, but certainly not reducible as a logical (or even aberrant) culmination of its long and multi-faceted history. Here is not the place to engage in that complex debate (see Smith, 1979). But it is certainly the case that the legacy of the 1918–45 period cast a long shadow over perceptions of nationalism.

# Nationalism in the post-war era

It is of course true that a very different 'nationalism' reasserted itself in the resistance and liberation struggles in Nazi-occupied Europe, and indeed in beleaguered Britain. A 'people's war' restored the nation-states of Western Europe on the basis of a social and political 'new deal', not only with a strengthened commitment to liberal democracy but also with a major extension of the state's responsibilities in the social and economic spheres. Though the capitalist economy remained intact, what became a 'social-democratic consensus' lasting 30 years sought to extend citizenship, guarantee welfare protection, achieve full employment, promote collective bargaining, redistribute wealth through progressive taxation, and regulate or control public utilities. The techniques differed from country to country, but the overall effect through the years of prosperity was to bind 'state' and 'nation' more closely together than ever before. And in the view of one author, the process of economic and political integration in the 1950s, which led eventually to the establishment of the European Economic Community (EEC) in 1957, should be regarded less as a dilution of state sovereignty than as 'the European rescue of the nation-state' (Milward, 1994; and see Chapter 7). The transfer of certain decisions to the supra-national level has allowed member states to escape responsibility for actions that might otherwise have imperilled their legitimacy.

However, in other respects the post-war settlement created a new world order in which the autonomy of even the strongest European nation-states was increasingly called into question. The economic reconstruction of an exhausted and devastated continent fell largely to the two emerging superpowers, whose military intervention had eventually been decisive. Their dominance of the post-war scene, and their geopolitical and ideological rivalry, now ensured that they would intervene decisively in the affairs of the old continent that had been the cradle of the nation-state. Europe was divided into American and Soviet spheres of influence reflecting the advance lines of military 'liberation' from East and West, and of course cutting defeated Germany in half. Eventually two new states, the Federal Republic of Germany (FRG) and the German Democratic Republic (GDR), would emerge as the 'front line' of this system, but by then the breakdown of the wartime Alliance had degenerated into the 'Cold War' and the notion of an 'Iron Curtain' between East and West. This would be the basis for the emergence of so-called 'bloc politics', which would put pressure on states worldwide to 'align' themselves with one or other of the two superpowers, but whose disciplining effects were most decisively felt in Europe itself where the new 'bloc architecture' made its first impact (see Chapters 2 and 10).

This bloc architecture was embodied in both military and economic institutions (see Box 1.1, NATO; Box 1.2, The Warsaw Pact; Box 2.2, Bretton Woods; Box 9.3, GATT). It must also be recognised, however, that the first attempts to construct supra-national institutions in Western Europe (the Organisation for European Co-operation and Development, the European Coal and Steel Community, the Council of Europe, the ill-fated European Defence Community) were part of this same process (see Chapters 2 and 7). Although European integration was driven by genuine political idealism (peace and democracy) as much as by the demands of economic

**Portr**

## Nicolae Ceauşescu (1918–1989)

Nicolae Ceauşescu of Romania joined the Communist Party as a young factory worker, and was imprisoned for his political activity. He became a minister in the Romanian government in 1948, and in 1965 became General-Secretary of the Party. He encouraged a cult of personality, and buttressed his power through a ruthless use of the *Securitate* secret police. He maintained a measure of independence from the Soviet line, especially in foreign policy, avoiding involvement in the Warsaw Pact invasion of Czechoslovakia in 1968, resisting the policy of the Council for Mutual Economic Assistance, fostering good relations with China and recognising Israel. His social and economic policies, involving, for example, a closed economy that, while eschewing external debt, produced dreadful poverty and deprivation, the forcible clearance of villages, and the encouragement of a high birth-rate, resulted in great suffering and hardship. Romania was the only country where the revolution of 1989 was violent as the *Securitate* fought back, and Ceauşescu and his wife were executed in the course of it.

reconstruction, and although there were those who aspired to a non-aligned (and in some cases democratic-socialist) Europe that might transcend the bloc divide (Cornick, 1996), the fact remains that the EEC took shape in the context of the Cold War and was designed to consolidate the Western Alliance, albeit in the name of defence of the 'free world' rather than overtly in the name of 'capitalism'.

The framework of the Cold War certainly promoted economic and cultural homogenisation in both 'halves' of the continent, and limited the scope for national self-assertiveness. The Soviet military intervention in East Germany (1953), Hungary (1956) and Czechoslovakia (1968), and the less direct pressure it brought to bear on Poland (1981), indicated that in the communist bloc the internal affairs of client states were subject to what in 1968 became known as the **Brezhnev Doctrine** of limited sovereignty. The USA's **hegemony** in Western Europe was generally achieved by more subtle economic and ideological means, though the covert operations of intelligence services against perceived communist subversion told of an equally ruthless determination to maintain the integrity of the American sphere of influence. Of course, there were exceptions to this pattern, notably the success of Gaullist France in negotiating for itself a 'space' between the blocs where it could project at least the image of an 'independent' foreign policy (Cerny, 1980). In the East, Tito's non-aligned Yugoslavia was a special case, but a closer parallel is Ceauşescu's Romania, which was allowed some eccentric foreign policy flourishes.

However, while periods of relative *détente* left some scope for such departures from the norm, in times of greater tension (Cuba 1962, the 'Euromissile' crisis of the early 1980s) the discipline of the bloc system reasserted itself. Whatever the domestic resentment at the constraints imposed on nation-state autonomy, governments accepted the *Realpolitik* of bloc alignment as an unassailable European reality.

The processes which were undermining the freedom of action of the nation-state in the economic sphere were less visible. The increasing internationalisation of advanced capitalist economies, accelerated in Western Europe by the processes of integration, was masked by the survival of the post-war *social-democratic* consensus in the years of prosperity. The liberalisation of capital markets in 1971, and the first oil shock in 1973 – which ushered in a new era of economic uncertainty, and of intensified international competition and periodic recession – exposed the limits of the social-democratic model. Its Keynesian perspectives were deemed no longer operable, its

**Brezhnev Doctrine:** Named after the violent suppression of socialist reforms in communist Czechoslovakia in 1968. According to the doctrine, Moscow arrogated the right to intervene in the internal affairs of Warsaw Pact members to protect the supposed gains of communism.

**Hegemony:** In global terms this refers to the pre-eminence or domination of one power over others.

bureaucratic structures not capable of responding to a more competitive world environment, the massive costs of its multiple social and economic responsibilities no longer supportable.

Ironically it was the New Left politics of the late 1960s and 1970s that had first developed a critique of bureaucratic, over-centralised social-democracy, although in the name of a radical self-managed socialism. But it was the neo-liberal economics of a New Right which was eventually to lead the political offensive and to establish a new orthodoxy in the 1980s, based on 'rolling back the state', restricting public expenditure, privatising nationalised companies, deregulating financial and labour markets, and generally 'liberating' market forces. This soon became the basis of a new 'consensus' as the former social-democratic parties of Western Europe increasingly moved onto this ground, albeit less wholeheartedly and with deeper reservations about the social costs. The last attempt to buck this trend was the French Left's reflationary interventionist programme of 1981, and the policy reversal which swiftly followed may now be seen as symbolic. But the way that this was rationalised is particularly relevant in the context of the 'nation-state' and its future. It was attributed above all to the inoperability of 'Keynesianism in one country' and the government's failure to recognise how deeply France was integrated into the world economy and the new international division of labour. Allegedly it was the tyranny of external constraints, rather than any lack of political will, which forced the government's hand.

The collapse of the social-democratic consensus weakens the political commitment to high levels of job security and full-scale welfare protection on which the legitimacy of the post-war nation-state was constructed. In the case of former 'great powers' like Britain and France this problem of legitimacy is compounded by a forced recognition of their declining autonomy in a range of areas, from foreign and defence, to economic and social policy. While they may kick against this (from Thatcher's Falklands adventure and her anti-European invective to Blair's 'cool Britannia', or Mitterrand and Chirac's unconvincing presidential attempts to maintain the Gaullist discourse of national independence and *grandeur*), rhetoric cannot disguise the fact that the endorsement of economic liberalism and the global market weakens the ties that once bound the community of the 'nation' to the representative agencies of the 'state'.

This process has a cultural dimension as well. Many of the structures and value systems that provided national identities with ideological substance – class, religion, pride in Empire or other symbols of a collective past – have been eroded by the emergence of 'post-industrial' societies, more socially pluralistic and multicultural, more individualistic in tastes and lifestyles, progressively 'Americanised' in their mass consumerism. The rapid post-war increase in migratory flows, both between West European countries and from outside (first from former colonial territories and more recently from Eastern Europe), has in many cases also created genuinely 'multi-ethnic' societies which are even less amenable to the historic myths which once forged national communities.

Weakened from above in its freedom of action, and from below in its cohesion, the West European nation-state is thus in a crucial transitional phase, and adaptation to new realities is inevitably more difficult for those with a difficult legacy of former world influence (Jenkins and Sofos, 1996, pp. 1–5). States can no longer credibly base an entire political programme on nationalism and, despite the occasional rhetorical flourishes, the policies of mainstream political parties acknowledge the fact, notwithstanding the ideological tensions this produces. Centre-right parties may be more willing to endorse the 'market' logic of this process (and the European Union in its liberal economic version), but their moral and social conservatism is reluctant to let go of 'nation' as a vehicle of discipline and cohesion. Centre-left parties, historically more inclined to mobilise 'nation' behind State economic interventionism, and traditionally suspicious of Europe as a 'capitalist club', now tend to see the European Union as potentially a more effective framework than the nation-state for the social regulation of market forces.

At the same time, it is above all the centre-left that has become more sensitive to increasing social and cultural pluralism, and in this vein has tended to favour a degree of devolution from central government to local and regional level. This may partly be seen as a democratic response to the regionalist pressures which began in the late 1960s in states like Britain, France and Spain. It is also often framed in functional terms – some problems are 'too big' for the nation-state while others are more effectively dealt with closer to the ground. But there is no doubt another political agenda at work: namely that, in the context of popular disillusionment with the inability of the nation-state to 'deliver the goods', often reflected in declining support for mainstream parties, there is an attempt to reduce public expectations of what central government can 'deliver' by redirecting certain responsibilities to supra- and sub-national level.

# Nationalism, globalisation and the new Europe

Many of the processes described above are part and parcel of what is now often described as 'globalisation', a concept which refers primarily to the 'global' character of the market economy (see Chapter 9) and the political constraints this allegedly imposes on national governments, but secondarily to a supposed cultural homogenisation often equated with 'Americanisation'. The term has, however, come into its own above all in the aftermath of the collapse of Communist regimes in Central and Eastern Europe in 1989–91. This extraordinary sequence of events itself reflected the inability of the command economies of the Soviet bloc to remain insulated against growing international economic pressures, and especially against a rising tide of popular expectations fuelled by a desire to emulate Western living standards.

The collapse of communism removed the world's sole functioning economic alternative. What socialists used to call 'international capitalism' becomes 'globalisation', not something against which to mobilise resistance but something to be accepted as an inevitable process, announcing the end of socialism in all its forms and paving the way for the integration of the 'Second World' (and its former 'Third World' disciples) into the global market economy. Though apparently neutral, the word is a celebration of ideological victory. And for most West European socialists, however much they despised the Soviet model and welcomed its demise in the interests of political democracy, the event was a defeat none the less because it appeared to demonstrate the invincibility of capitalist market forces. Rather than seeking, as in the past, to distance themselves from Soviet communism as a deformation of their ideals, they have generally found it necessary to accept 'globalisation' and the limits it allegedly sets to the attainment of those ideals.

That socialism is in crisis is undeniable. Some of the West European centre-left is now wary of even using the term, while those who still do are usually seeking to adapt its 'fundamental values' to a radically different kind of programme. However, in the meantime the popular aspirations that socialism has harnessed for more than  century – especially those inspired by the promise of greater economic security and social equality – no longer have a 'natural home'. The resurgence of various forms of nationalism across the continent, an anomalous development if we accept the 'globalisation' thesis, can only be understood in this context. For those who feel most threatened by the competitive rigours of the global market, or who feel their 'identity' undermined by the collapse of traditional collective reference points in an increasingly multicultural and multi-ethnic society, the protective frontiers of the nation-state may appear the last available rampart against the advancing tide.

## The extreme Right and racism

The rise of extreme-Right parties and movements in countries like France, Germany, Belgium, Italy and Austria in the last 10–15 years is a novelty in the post-war period, when such upsurges of support have been rare and of short duration (Hainsworth, 1992). Though each of them builds on a distinctive national tradition and responds to its own particular national environment, and though some of them display 'neo-fascist' characteristics (Cheles *et al.*, 1991), their simultaneous impact displays generic features which relate to the contemporary historical framework outlined above.

Racism towards asylum seekers, immigrants and ethnic minorities is a common theme, and their richest source of support. But this is easily combined with an appeal to all those who feel excluded and neglected in the new consensual politics of mainstream parties, who feel that governments ignore the social costs of economic liberalism and fail to defend the 'national interest' against a variety of threats from 'outside'. A third of France's industrial workers voted for Le Pen in the 1995 presidential elections, and 34 per cent of those who consider themselves 'under-privileged' (*défavorisés*). This alarming statistic indicates the significance of the 'crisis of socialism' in the reviving fortunes of extreme-Right nationalism.

As long as these organisations remain isolated their electoral progress is blocked, but the issue of European integration is one which could provide them with a bridge-head to the electorate (and indeed to some of the politicians of mainstream parties). Economic and monetary union, and the difficulties that may await it, could become a powerful symbol of the outside forces assailing the nation-state, and could produce a situation where the extreme Right became a (dangerous) component of a much wider coalition.

## Nationalism resurgent

The resurgent nationalisms which have redrawn the state map of Eastern Europe (see Maps 2.4 and 2.5) and the former Soviet Union since 1989 are by far the most dramatic and violent manifestation of the phenomenon since the decolonisation struggles of 40 years ago. When the Communist regimes collapsed in domino fashion after the Berlin Wall was breached, few would have predicted this outcome, and it is of course a complex process driven by diverse local circumstances. While world attention has been focused on the horrors of ethnic cleansing in Bosnia and bloody confrontations in Kosovo and Chechnya, the division of Czechoslovakia and the creation of the independent Baltic and other post-Soviet states have been achieved

### Jean-Marie Le Pen (born 1928)

The French National Front was founded in October 1972 out of a somewhat miscellaneous collection of Far-Right groups, and Jean-Marie Le Pen was installed as its leader. He had been a member of parliament in the 1950s for the small business, anti-tax, anti-modernist protest movement led by Pierre Poujade. He had fought as a paratrooper in Indochina and again later in Algeria and remained a staunch defender of Algeria remaining part of France. The National Front remained a very marginal political force until the early 1980s, when the political and economic context, especially recession and unemployment, skilful use of media opportunities presented by local elections, and the proportional representation system of the 1984 European Parliament elections established a national profile for Le Pen and his party, allowing it for a time to overtake the Communist Party. Le Pen has shown great skill in manipulating his populist image and rhetoric. In 1998, however, the party split and his position was markedly weakened. Le Pen denies repeated allegations of anti-Semitism. However, he and his party are very overtly anti-immigrant and racist, linking the presence of immigrants to unemployment and crime, defending proposals to repatriate them, and using slogans such as 'France for the French'.

relatively peacefully, while Poland, Hungary, the Czech Republic and a number of other countries seek admission to the European Union.

However, there are some general features which relate to the framework we have suggested. The first is that once communism collapsed, the successor states faced a crisis of legitimacy. Whatever the democratic thrust of the popular mobilisation which overthrew the Communist regimes, the movement lacked organisational structure, and civil society was insufficiently developed to provide it (except in Poland where Solidarity's ten-year struggle and organised religion offered the rudiments – see Chapter 2). At the same time, popular expectations that imported market capitalism would quickly improve living standards created enormous pressures on the new leaders. Democratisation and adaptation to an alien economic model require time, and in some cases this was not forthcoming.

The second feature is that, in former Yugoslavia and the ex-USSR in particular, lip service had been paid under communism to constituent Republics reflecting the multinational character of the state. In the absence of other collective identities in a stifled civil society, these internal lines of division became salient once the legitimacy of the central state was undermined by the pressures described above (Flenley, 1996; Sofos, 1996). This is not enough to explain the vicious inter-ethnic conflict engendered by some of these nationalisms, but neither is the argument that we are witnessing the resurgence of deep collective animosities that have been suppressed for 50 years or more. The role of embattled and power-hungry leaders, often recycled communists, all too willing to use the dangerous genie of ethnic nationalism to preserve or extend their state territories, cannot be ignored. But the susceptibility of popular opinion to such overtures reflects the ideological vacuum left by communism, and the failure of market capitalism and liberal democracy to provide any credible solutions to their immediate social and economic problems.

## Separatist nationalism

The separatist nationalisms that have emerged in long-established West European states like Britain, France and Spain may seem less amenable to our explanatory framework. Setting aside their longer ancestry, their contemporary resurgence dates

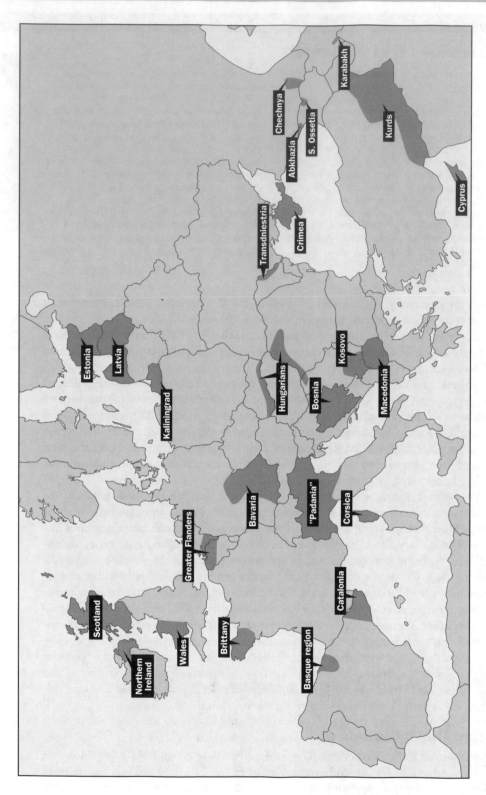

**Map 3.1** Locations of major separatist nationalist movements

from the political radicalism of the late 1960s and early 1970s, much earlier than the context in which we have set the two previous examples. However, as we have indicated earlier, the New Left critique of bureaucratic state socialism (in both its social-democratic and Soviet communist versions) pre-dated the 'New Right' neo-liberal onslaught by a decade, and the so-called 'micro-nationalisms' may be seen as one of the more durable by-products of that era. The New Left's mobilising theme was the democratisation of all spheres of life – workplace (workers' control), gender relations (feminism), political activism ('social movements' rather than traditional 'parties') and political institutions (decentralisation). In this last category, the response in the 1970s was the rise of regionalist movements, with aspirations varying from devolution to autonomy to full independent statehood.

Clearly the emergence of these separatist nationalisms (Basque, Catalan, Breton, Corsican, Flemish and Walloon, Scots, Welsh, the special case of Northern Ireland Republicanism) challenged the legitimacy of what was seen as an unrepresentative central state. The subsequent persistence, growth and indeed relative success of these movements, however, reflect a deepening of these legitimacy problems along the lines suggested earlier. As we have seen, the 'crisis of big government' – the state's inability to support the weight of its growing responsibilities and spiralling costs – led to the collapse of the post-war social-democratic consensus in the wake of the oil crises of the 1970s. If one response to this was the neo-liberalism of the 1980s, another was the demand for the devolution of the state's responsibilities to local and regional level, and the separatist movements fed on this growing support for decentralisation.

Support for the separatists was also strengthened by the fact that most of these regions were decidedly 'Left' in political orientation, while for long periods central government was in the hands of the Right (and a 'centralising' Right to boot!) – in Spain the 40-year Franco regime until 1976 and its conservative aftermath until 1982, in France the Gaullists and their allies from 1958 until 1981, in Britain the Thatcherite Conservatives from 1979 until 1997. These were crucial phases of consolidation for the separatists, and though concessions were made to their demands once left-of-centre parties returned to power at the centre (Gonzalez's autonomy legislation and Mitterrand's decentralisation reforms in the early 1980s, Blair's devolution proposals and the Northern Ireland peace process in 1998), it is far from clear that these will be enough to stem the tide. It is in Spain (especially the Basque region) and in Britain (especially Northern Ireland and now Scotland) that the outcome remains most in doubt. It may well depend on the capacity of the (no longer socialist) metropolitan centre-left parties to make the status quo a more attractive prospect in social and economic terms than the temptations of secession, and on the ability of the nationalists to outflank them on the Left. Here again the 'crisis of socialism' looms large over the fortunes of nationalism.

# Nation and region in the new Europe

The preceding discussion was a necessary preliminary to any attempt to consider how nation and region relate to one another in contemporary Europe. The process of nation-state formation is in constant flux. It never reaches an end-point, is never set in stone. The French historian Ernest Renan (1882) called the nation 'a daily plebiscite'. Notwithstanding the historical, geographical or cultural solidarities on which the nation builds, its aspiration to 'nation-statehood' involves an act of political will, and once established as a nation-state it will only survive as long as its citizens perceive it as 'legitimate'. Many of the states of the former Soviet bloc failed that 'daily plebiscite', and in their disappearance they took with them the 'nations' they claimed to represent. A similar fate is even conceivable for Britain and Spain, two of the longest established states in the modern world, which after centuries of collective existence are forced to acknowledge that their capacity to remain a 'nation', to continue to live together, is possibly at stake.

Many of the nation-states of Europe were once no more than 'regions' within, or straddling across, the frontiers of other territorial units. There are of course many examples where considerations of 'ethnicity' provided the impetus for turning these regions into nation-states (sometimes with disastrous results), but the 'civic' impulse was equally important, and many nation-states were forged politically from ethnic-ally diverse peoples who have been successfully accommodated within a common social value-system. Hobsbawm, while acknowledging the capacity of the State to create national identities after independence, is extraordinarily reluctant to accept that nations may actually be forged by the political struggle for independence itself, insisting instead on the primacy of economic geography and cultural affinities like religion and especially language. He dismisses many contemporary West European separatist movements as no more than 'reactions against centralisation . . . or various other local or sectional discontents capable of being wrapped in coloured banners' (1990, p. 178), not real nationalisms in fact. He may be right that some of these movements do not seriously envisage 'total state independence as their final aim' (1990, p. 179), in which case the validity of the tag 'nationalist' is certainly debatable. But his underlying assumptions about what makes a 'nation' are deterministic, and are contradicted by the pattern of nation-state formation and de-formation in the last two hundred years.

We would agree, rather, with the Welsh Marxist historian Gwyn Williams in his influential essay 'When was Wales?', who wrote 'Wales is now and Wales has always been now . . . it is not a mystical presence ubiquitous through our history. . . . Wales is an artefact which the Welsh produce; the Welsh make and remake Wales day by day and year after year. . . . Wales will not exist unless the Welsh want it' (Williams, 1979). This is not to deny that collective historical myths, a common language, eco-nomic viability, etc. are valuable as mobilising themes and coagulants of identity, and for that reason many 'regions' in the European Union, or indeed in Europe at large, may have little self-awareness as distinctive communities, let alone harbour autonomist or nationalist aspirations. But 'doing' creates a sense of 'being', identities are in a constant state of flux, and the solidarities wrought by the tide of political events may be as durable as those based on 'ethnicity'.

These observations apply equally to other levels of territorial identity, and it is important not to fetishise the 'national' at the expense of the local or regional, or indeed in the contemporary context the 'European'. To the extent that political authority is exercised at all these levels, each is capable of developing a sense of citi-zenship and communal membership, and in the case of certain cities and regions this may be reinforced by apolitical forms of identification – linguistic (including dialect and accent) or cultural (religion, sport, patterns of sociability, etc.). Sovereignty is increasingly diffuse, and in the context of 'globalisation' (or what Hobsbawm calls the 'supra-national restructuring of the globe'; Hobsbawm, 1990, p. 182) nation-statehood no longer offers the same prospects of independence and undiluted self-government which inspired the nationalisms of the nineteenth century, as most of the decolonised nation-states of the 'Third World' could certainly testify. Rogers Brubaker may be right in his claim that 'citizenship is the last bastion of sovereignty' in a globalised world (Brubaker, 1992, p. 180) but citizenship is no longer exclusively the prerogative of the nation-state.

Economic 'globalisation' on the basis of market forces, despite the ideological pretence that it will 'harmonise' global economic conditions through the progressive integration of more 'backward' areas, actually creates disparities and inequalities both between and within nation-states. And cultural 'globalisation', despite its homogenising ('Americanising') dynamics, triggers resistance and a desire to preserve local, regional, national and 'zonal' identities against bland uniformity. We are therefore dealing with a process which, contrary to what its advocates tell us, actually has profound 'disintegrative' effects. This is the challenge that faces Europe. The worst scenario is one in which the aspirations of the European Union, nation-states, and the constituent regions and localities are seen as mutually exclusive, for this leads to recrimination and paralysis. The preferable outcome is a political structure which promotes multiple levels of citizenship, and which allows the multiple territorial identities which structure our social existence to reinforce one another (as they often do!) rather than contradicting one another.

In this context, the various options of decentralisation (administrative or political; local or regional; devolution, autonomy, or full independent statehood) should be seen as points on a continuum rather than as definitive breaks in a chain of sovereignty involving the 'sacrifice' of power at one level and its 'usurpation' at another. In the realities of contemporary Western Europe, it is inconceivable that a newly established small nation-state would sever its multiple economic and cultural ties with its neighbours or invest in all the trappings of nation-statehood that were regarded as *de rigueur* a century ago. If the Scots choose independence, some sort of federation with the other states of the British Isles, themselves also members of the European Union, seems inevitable and would barely affect cross-border transactions in the way alarmists suggest.

What it would represent, however, is the assertion of a new and distinctive framework for *citizenship*, not the *sole* framework of course given the European and indeed local dimensions, but none the less one which was no longer directly shaped by the central government of the United Kingdom. And it should be the responsibility of the European Union to uphold these 'civic' principles of nationhood, based on residency and equal citizen rights, against the 'ethnic' version of nationhood whose traces are only now being expunged from the German nationality code. This problem is all the more salient given the prospect of enlargement of the EU into Eastern Europe, some of whose new nation-states would so clearly and justifiably be disqualified on these grounds.

# A 'Europe of the regions'? The 'hollowing out' of the nation-state

The global market and the new mobility of capital creates economic disparities and inequalities, both within nation-states and across wider territorial entities like the European Union. Traditional state-led policies for addressing such problems, in the

**Federal states:** States in which regional governments have substantial, constitutionally guaranteed powers. The term is often used to describe political systems which are less centralised than unitary states, but without the extreme decentralisation of a confederation. Federal states are often characterised by a complex web of checks and balances between the national government and regional governments. Examples of federal states in Europe are Belgium and Germany.

form of regional development funds, have often suffered the same fate as other expensive interventionist measures associated with the defunct 'social-democratic consensus'. In increasingly liberalised economies, political decentralisation and the devolution of power may thus be seen (in Udo Bullman's words) as a 'means of managing the complexity of problems in the overloaded administrative framework of the nation-state – and perhaps one of the only remaining answers that the latter is still able to give' (Bullman, 1997, p. 9). However, this 'top-down' pressure to off-load burdensome responsibilities is accompanied by 'bottom-up' demands for more leeway to resolve local problems, and in some contexts this dovetails with the political and cultural aspirations of autonomist movements.

Bullman provides a useful typology of EU states (Bullman, 1997, p. 5) which distinguishes four categories (updated here to include recent developments): 'classic unitary', where there is local government, but no regional structure except for centrally-controlled administrative purposes (Denmark, Greece, Ireland, Luxembourg, Sweden); 'devolving unitary', involving reform to establish elected regional authorities with some autonomy and constitutional protection (France, Netherlands, Portugal, and more recently Finland and the UK); 'regionalised', involving a directly-elected tier of regional government with wide autonomy, constitutional status and legislative powers (Italy and Spain); and finally fully **'federal' states**, where powers are shared constitutionally and the regional tier cannot be abolished by central government (Germany, Austria, and now Belgium).

This diversity reflects distinctive national pressures for regionalisation, and distinctive responses on the part of national governments. For example, Germany (as the Federal Republic) and Austria had their federalist structures partly imposed on them by the Allies as the price for their re-establishment as nation-states after the Second World War. Italy, Spain, France, Britain, Belgium and Portugal have all at different times had to cope with internal autonomist pressures. Some have responded by seeking to 'dilute' the problem (Italy's North–South divide, Belgium's linguistic fissure, France's Breton, Basque and Corsican enclaves) by 'regionalising' or (in Belgium's case) 'federalising' across the board. Others have responded more selectively – Spain's profound regionalisation grants special autonomous status to the Basque Country, Catalonia, Galicia, and Andalusia; Portugal restricts devolved government to the Azores and Madeira, while the UK singles out Scotland, Wales and Northern Ireland for special treatment, but begins to move ahead with the regionalisation of England through Regional Development Agencies (RDAs) – a small step to be sure, but a significant one in the context of England's thousand-year history of centralisation.

However, the pressure for regionalisation (or for the strengthening of existing regional structures) is inseparable from the accelerating processes of European integration since the early 1980s, whose free-market logic has reduced the economic autonomy of nation-states and has opened up a field of negotiation which increasingly includes sub-national actors. The increasing proportion of EU structural funds (see Chapter 7) that now have a 'regional' dimension has acted as a catalyst for both cities and regions to lobby the relevant Commission agencies and has fostered both intra- and inter-regional (including transfrontier) co-operation (the Assembly of European Regions, specialist lobbies for border regions, regions in decline, maritime regions etc., regional information offices in Brussels). These channels by-pass the normal structures based on inter-governmentalism and the principles of representation through member states embedded in the Treaty of Rome.

In recognition of these developments the Commission set up the Consultative Council of Local and Regional Authorities in 1988, but without the endorsement of the Council of Ministers. Reluctance on the part of national governments to legitimise sub-national actors no doubt explains their lack of enthusiasm, but at Maastricht four years later the member states found sufficient common ground to reach agreement. The creation of the 'Committee of the Regions' is the first time the EU has given formal recognition in its basic texts to democratic entities at sub-national level (Millan, 1997). However, this was achieved only at the price of allowing national governments to designate their representatives on the new Committee, albeit with the proviso since the Treaty of Amsterdam (1997) that delegates must be chosen from elected local or regional councillors. The Committee of the Regions is therefore set firmly within the *inter-governmental* structures of the EU, and like its predecessor the 'Consultative Council' and its sister institution the Economic and Social Committee, it remains a *consultative* body, and lacks the greater legitimacy conferred on the (admittedly still weak) European Parliament by direct election (see Chapter 7).

However, its lack of formal institutional status is offset by the fact that its very creation reflects the gathering impetus of sub-national interests within the EU. And the constraints imposed on such interests by national governments through the Council of Ministers are offset by the strong pressures towards regionalisation and devolution within each of the member states themselves. While it may not satisfy the partisans of a genuine 'Europe of the Regions' and of a community-wide 'Third Level' of governance, it none the less offers unprecedented recognition to sub-national authorities. This in itself may act as a stimulus to their quest for greater legitimacy and influence, despite the efforts of national governments to contain such aspirations. And while member states are free to decide how to fill their national quota on the Committee (so that currently the 'safer' *local* level authorities supply around half the delegates), national governments will be reluctant to antagonise important lobbies by blatantly under-representing them.

It is commonly assumed that one of the key goals of a centralised regional policy is to reduce territorial inequalities and thereby to safeguard the unity of the state (Artobolevskiy, 1997, p. 1). Political *decentralisation* is often rationalised in similar terms, as a necessary concession to preserve citizen loyalty to the overarching framework of the nation-state. This perspective also implies, of course, that the 'state's' instinct for self-preservation will set limits to the degree of devolution it will tolerate. However, as Gary Marks has argued, it is a mistake to think of the state as actually existing in this way, as if it was a rational thinking agent in its own right, when in reality it is simply a set of institutional norms within which political actors operate (Marks, 1997, pp. 22–3). And these actors have other goals besides defending state centralism (ideological commitments, policy objectives, appeasing **interest groups**, winning elections, maintaining party unity etc.). In this context, these actors may disperse 'authoritative competencies' (Marks, 1997, p. 22) because they wish to shed them, or because their other goals require it, or because they are unable to arrest the process once it has started.

This 'top-down' scenario may be supplemented, as Charlie Jeffery suggests in the same volume (Jeffery, 1997), by a 'bottom-up' perspective based on the notion of 'European domestic policy'. Some strong sub-national actors are claiming the right to intervene in policy areas previously regarded as 'external', as part of the foreign-affairs domain exclusive to the nation-state, on the grounds that these areas should now be regarded as part of the 'internal', 'domestic' affairs of an emerging European

**Interest groups:** Interest groups are more or less formal associations that represent a particular group/clientele or promote collective demands – be they very specific or very general – in the political process, predominantly by public statements, bargaining and lobbying.

**Interdependence:** A condition of great mutual dependence involving exchanges of an economic, social and political nature.

polity. Taken together, both approaches break away from the formal institutional framework of nation-state and EU structures to emphasise the fluid and dynamic politics of an evolving pattern of 'multi-level governance' in which 'authority is scattered and sovereignty shared' (Bullman, 1997, p. 11). In this sense, the 'hollowing-out of the nation-state' is an undoubted reality, though as Loughlin reminds us, nation-states are still 'the most important decision-makers in the European political system' (Loughlin, 1997, p. 147) and the loyalties they continue to engender should not be underestimated.

Multi-level governance should, however, also imply a more relaxed approach to the aspirations of movements seeking territorial autonomy or full statehood, because, as suggested earlier, the lines of demarcation between different levels of sovereignty are increasingly blurred. Such movements once drew sustenance from a romanticised scenario of Third World liberation, and some indeed adopted the thesis of 'internal colonialism'. Now (with the prospect of an end to the Basque and Irish Republican armed struggles) they are more likely to look (selectively and pragmatically) to developments in Central and Eastern Europe and the former USSR, which indicate at least that *size* is no obstacle to nation-statehood, and that *federations* of independent states are an option worth considering. The interest currently being shown by the Council of Europe in a charter of the regions based on the Russian example is perhaps some indication of the evolution of thinking on this issue.

If it is above all their assumption of interventionist economic responsibilities in the globalised market that gives both historic regions and the new city-regions their contemporary dynamism, their legitimacy depends on processes of democratisation and the creation of civic consciousness. This requires the promotion of a modernised political culture based on educated citizenship, and on the recognition that the steering of economic activity today is the prerogative no longer solely of the nation-state but of political actors at diverse levels. The term 'governance' (replacing 'government') emphasises this new **interdependence** of organisations (including non-state actors like the voluntary sector) and the consequent blurring of previously well-defined boundaries.

Winning acceptance of these new realities is a major challenge for the European Union. They make heavy demands on the sophistication of electorates schooled in the unambiguous primacy of the nation-state. Furthermore, while the diffusion of authority and sovereignty may serve to defuse inter-communal tensions, it also raises significant problems of policy co-ordination and accountability. 'Multi-level governance' is no solution unless it can provide a framework for democratisation and, to return to an earlier theme, for social remedies to the effects of the global market. Only then will it represent a genuine barrier against the simplistic populism and ethnic obscurantism which still disfigure certain forms of nationalism in both Eastern and Western Europe.

## ■ Summary

◆ Nations are not 'natural' communities, they are human 'artefacts', socially and ideologically constructed by nationalist movements and more often than not by states.

◆ Nationalism has proved to be a very malleable ideology, capable of being moulded to a variety of different political projects and of appealing to different social constituencies, in response to both domestic and international historical circumstances.

◆ In the contemporary period, while the nation-state form is under increasing pressure from the processes of so-called 'globalisation', nationalism in all its guises has none the less remained a potent force for political mobilisation.

◆ While 'ethnic' versions of nationalism, particularistic and exclusive, are clearly incompatible with attempts to build a consensual value-system (whether liberal or social-democratic) within the European Union, the 'civic' ideal of nationalism (with its emphasis on 'citizenship') is potentially more amenable.

◆ Within this framework, it becomes possible to replace the historic primacy of the nation-state with the more fluid concept of multi-level governance, where Europe, nation, region and locality each offer elements of social identity and democratic accountability in line with their capacity to fulfil popular expectations.

# ■ Questions for discussion

▶ What are the essential differences between so-called 'civic' and 'ethnic' concepts of nationhood?

▶ Why has the nation-state become the main model of political organisation in the modern world?

▶ In what ways do processes of so-called 'globalisation' undermine the nation-state? How, in this context, is it possible to explain the current resurgence of nationalism in many parts of Europe?

▶ Compare and contrast the emergence of autonomist and separatist movements in some Western European nation-states with the new nationalisms in the former Communist bloc.

▶ Is the trend towards devolution and regionalism in many Western European countries compatible with the processes of integration and supra-national decision-making in the European Union?

# ■ Further reading

Brubaker, R. (1992) *Citizenship and Nationhood in France and Germany* (Cambridge, MA: Harvard University Press) usefully explores the differential impact of the 'civic' and 'ethnic' concepts of nationhood on notions of citizenship and nationality in the two countries, whilst acknowledging that these concepts are 'ideal types' and that the historical realities are more complex.

Hobsbawm, E. (1990) *Nations and Nationalism since 1780* (Cambridge: Cambridge University Press) offers an encyclopaedic study of nationalism which examines the range of economic, geographical, political, linguistic and religious factors which have been invoked to explain nation-formation.

Jeffery, C. (ed.) (1997) *The Regional Dimension of the European Union: Towards a Third Level in Europe?* (London: Frank Cass) brings together essays by leading British and American specialists in the field which examine the regional dimension in terms of institutional change, public policy-making, political movements and political culture within the EU.

Jenkins, B. and S. Sofos (eds) (1996) *Nation and Identity in Contemporary Europe* (London: Routledge) examines the specifics of national identity and nationalism in a range of European countries, in the context of external forces shaping contemporary perceptions and reactions (economic globalisation, European supra-nationalism and the end of the Cold War).

Williams, G. A. (1979) 'When was Wales?' (BBC Wales Annual Radio Lecture, 12 November 1979), reproduced in S. Woolf (ed.) *Nationalism in Europe: 1815 to the Present* (London: Routledge, 1996) pp. 203–4, offers a contrasting perspective from Hobsbawm's rather deterministic approach, arguing that 'nations' are created by collective will through political struggle rather than on the basis of historical 'qualifications' for nationhood.

# Social Structure

## William Outhwaite

# CHAPTER 4

'More than other variants of modernity, the European one has been strung between the poles of clear-cut individuality and solidarily-constructed collectivity...'

GÖRAN THERBORN, *European Modernity and Beyond* (1995) p. 15

## Contents

Sociologists have commonly distinguished between 'social structure' and 'social change' and between social structure and culture. We have, however, learned from theorists such as Norbert Elias (1897–1990) and Anthony Giddens (1938– ), among others, that it is more useful to consider social structures as structures-in-transformation and to think of them in terms of their causal effects rather than looking only for their material embodiment. Social structures are not things, like the islands and the sub-continental mass of which Europe is composed, but nor are they just collections of people, like a crowd or the population of a territory. To talk about social structures is to abstract from what is immediately given, as when we talk about the structure of a bridge or the structure of a DNA molecule rather than about just the bridge or the molecule. But social structures are more problematic than structures of the kinds just mentioned, because we rapidly encounter theoretical and even political disagreements about how they should be described.

We are closer, perhaps, to the situation when the structure of DNA was still unknown and alternative models were being advanced, or when structural engineers on vacation get into an argument about the load-bearing structure of a bridge they have just encountered. The situation is, if anything, worse, because we have less reason to expect a lasting consensus about social structures than about those with which biochemists and engineers are concerned. Some social scientists, for example, believe that class structures explain a lot; others that they do not, or that they do not even exist.

We are most likely to find agreement about some of the spatial and demographic aspects of social structure. We can look up the population figures for towns, regions and states in contemporary Europe with reasonable confidence, making estimates to cover under-recording by censuses and other surveys, and note some interesting differences in age structures, birth-rates, and so forth. But this would not get us very far. In discussing population we should perhaps, as Coleman (1996) does, go well beyond this and consider such issues as the values of young adults, as well as their physical living arrangements, or the effects of welfare benefits on families. In other words, structural and cultural processes can be seen to interrelate in all kinds of ways, and any differentiation between the two can only be a matter of temporary convenience. In thinking about social structure we should include not just structural elements in the narrow sense of the term (birth-rates and other demographic variables, spatial distribution, classes, strata and other aspects of social stratification), but also, perhaps, cultural traditions and ways of life and cultural transformations such as those in post-war France described by Kristin Ross (1995).

We must also pay attention to the constant interactions between real processes and their intellectual representations in the media or in the heads of ordinary members of society. As the US sociologist William Thomas (1928, p. 572) put it, 'If men define situations as real, they are real in their consequences.' We are concerned, in other words, not just with 'social facts' but also with 'social representations'.

## ■ Historical background: Europe in its place

The term 'modernity' is both the broadest and the most helpful way in which to describe the form of society which developed in Europe and its settler colonies from around the eighteenth century onwards (see Chapter 1). This form of society has spread, to a greater or lesser extent, across much of the world; as a result, any serious discussion of European culture or social structure has to be primarily concerned with discriminating it from other regional versions of modernity and from modernity in general. Europe can be usefully seen as a crucible in which social and cultural forms, whether indigenous or imported, are warmed up and (re-)exported to other regions of the globe, where they develop in ways which often eclipse their European variants. This can be shown in relation to capitalism, individualism, the nation-state, and so on. The nation-state, for example, rightly seen as somewhat passé in Western Europe, remains the dominant political form on the world stage; the European Union itself, even if it achieves full political union, will only be one (large) state among others. Communism or Marxism–Leninism is another striking example: unsuccessful in the more advanced parts of Europe at the end of the First World War, it gained a foothold on the edge of Europe, in Russia, whence it was imposed on much of the rest of Europe in the aftermath of the Second World War and the substantial Soviet contribution to the defeat of Nazism. Now largely repudiated in Europe, communism remains a significant political force in India and elsewhere.

The numerous critiques of Eurocentrism have reminded us that in studying Europe, even historically, one must constantly keep an eye on the rest of the world. Against this comparative background, however, one can, as Dieter Senghaas (1982) put it, 'learn from Europe' – learn, that is, both from the peculiarities of the European experience and from what certain European states and regions had in common with non-European ones on the eve of modernisation. World history has of course come to the aid of such perspectives, as Europe as a region of the world is increasingly sidelined militarily, politically, economically and to a considerable extent also culturally. The old Eurocentrism now looks not only pernicious, but parochial. And world history is also a world court with Europe in the dock – the image of Europe no longer so much vanguard as vandal, rampaging around the world in a manner which one might describe (in Eurocentric terms) as Hitlerian (see Mazower, 1998). Hostile judgements about Europe often tend to get mixed up with judgements about modernity, industrialism, and so forth – inevitably, because of their original conjunction.

# Contemporary Europe

In the contemporary context, globalisation (see Chapter 9) makes it harder than ever to decide what is specific to the European version of modernity and to European culture and social structure. What in any case should we understand by modernity? The concept has dominated social theorising in the 1980s, replacing the previously fashionable terms 'industrialism' or 'industrial society' in the 1950s and 1960s and 'capitalism' in the 1970s. The underlying rationale of the shift to the term 'modernity' was to move attention away from what in Marxist language would be called the forces of production or the social relations of production, towards more cultural and political dimensions of modern societies. It remains true, however, that one of the defining features of European social structure is the early development (compared with the rest of the world) of capitalism and industrialism, reinforcing and transforming other processes of modernity.

This is not the place to answer the question, raised most insistently by Max Weber (see Portrait 6.1), of 'why it happened here first'. What is clear is that in Europe we are still living with the results, both positive and negative, of having 'started first'. Michael Mann (1986, 1993) may well be right to argue that what counted in Europe was the competition between smallish political units under the unifying umbrella of Christendom. This, and the religious diversification of early modern Europe may, as Weber argued, have contributed to the rise of capitalism. This in turn, for example, reinforced an existing inclination in much of Europe towards nuclear family structures (Laslett, 1971; Seccombe; 1992). As the Swedish sociologist Göran Therborn (1995, p. 24) puts it, 'West of a line from Trieste to St Petersburg, there ... existed, already on the threshold to modernity, a distinctive family type, characterised by late marriages, a considerable number of people never married, and nuclear family households.' This, together with capitalist wage-labour and industrialisation, made Europeans less religious in many ways than other inhabitants of the world. British and then European capitalism enjoyed an early advantage, before being eclipsed (though still not definitively) by North American and then East Asian variants. Similarly, the European nation-state system spread across the world and helped to pull apart the world's remaining big imperial structures, including of course, in the end, those which European countries had established overseas (or, in the Russian/Soviet case, overland). The European states successively and to an increasing degree supervised and shaped the development of capitalism and industrialism on their territories (Barrington Moore, 1966), leaving European capitalism much more regulated than in the USA or Asia (Albert, 1991; Crouch and Streeck, 1997). There are of course exceptions to this tendency in the far west of Europe (the UK) and to some extent, now, the former communist East.

The socialist countries, whose political and cultural version of modernity was strikingly different in the half-century following 1945, appear in retrospect as in many ways simply carrying through many of the same processes by other, more visibly authoritarian means (cf. Therborn, 1995, pp. 121–2). They took control of capitalism to the extent of replacing it with a centrally planned economic system, they pushed through industrialisation policies and got rid of their peasantries, they urbanised in similarly drastic ways, to the point of tragic absurdity in Romania (see Portrait 3.1), and incorporated their populations into (centrally managed) political, educational and media systems. In the USSR and Eastern Europe, however, the modernisation

## Box 4.1

### Max Weber on Europe's universal significance

'A product of modern European civilization, studying any problem of universal history, is bound to ask himself to what combination of circumstances the fact should be attributed that in Western civilization, and in Western civilization only, cultural phenomena have appeared which (as we like to think) lie in a line of development having *universal* significance and value' (Weber, 1920; tr. p. 13).

process gave rise to economic, political and cultural strains which the systems could not control. Unable to innovate successfully in any of these domains, the ruling elites yielded to gentle but compelling external and internal pressures and stepped down into the dustbin of history, where many of them found a lucrative second career recycling the garbage.

The modernisation and industrialisation process produced ultimately (though not really until the 1950s for most of Europe, with the partial liquidation of its independent peasantry and other self-employed people) an 'employment society' or *Arbeitsgesellschaft* (Offe, 1985) whose alleged end is still a matter of controversy. Here again, the socialist countries were simply more radical in abolishing (except in Poland and Yugoslavia) independent peasant agriculture and (again to differing degrees) independent commercial activity. In the capitalist countries of 'Western' Europe, the integration of what Touraine and Ragazzi (1961) called 'workers who started on the land' ('*ouvriers d'origine agricole*') and of independent proprietors was followed by the integration of immigrant workers and, increasingly, their families.

In the course of the 1970s, which one has to see as a crucial turning-point in the development of Western European social structures and ideologies, these two processes of integration began in part to run backwards. The doubling or, in some countries, much worse than doubling of unemployment rates excluded large parts of the populations from labour markets and other forms of social participation, bearing heavily on women, except in the UK and Ireland (Therborn, 1995, p. 63), the old and the young. At the same time, and relatedly, many natives of Western Europe rejected

**Table 4.1**  Structures of employment in Europe: percentages of the employed population by sector

| Country | Sector | 1960 | 1965 | 1975 | 1985 | 1995 |
|---|---|---|---|---|---|---|
| France | Agriculture | 23.2 | 18.3 | 10.3 | 7.6 | 4.7 |
| | Industry | 38.4 | 39.9 | 38.6 | 32 | 27.7 |
| | Services | 38.5 | 41.8 | 51.1 | 60.4 | 64.6 |
| Germany* | Agriculture | 14 | 10.9 | 6.8 | 4.6 | 3.3 |
| | Industry | 47 | 48.4 | 45.4 | 41 | 37.5 |
| | Services | 39.1 | 40.7 | 47.8 | 54.5 | 59.1 |
| Hungary | Agriculture | | | | | 8.1 |
| | Industry | | | | | 33.1 |
| | Services | | | | | 58.8 |
| Poland | Agriculture | | | | | 22.1 |
| | Industry | | | | | 31.7 |
| | Services | | | | | 45.4 |
| Spain | Agriculture | 38.7 | 30.6 | 22.1 | 18.3 | 9.2 |
| | Industry | 30.3 | 34 | 38.4 | 33.9 | 30.1 |
| | Services | 31 | 35.4 | 39.6 | 49.9 | 60.8 |
| United Kingdom | Agriculture | 4.7 | 3.8 | 2.8 | 2.3 | 2.1 |
| | Industry | 47.7 | 48.4 | 40.4 | 34.8 | 27.4 |
| | Services | 47.6 | 49.6 | 55.1 | 63 | 70.5 |

*Figures for 1990 and before relate to West Germany; for 1991 and after to Germany
*Source: OECD Labour Force Statistics, 1965–99* (Paris: OECD) table 7.

**Table 4.2** Residents in selected European countries by nationality in percentages

|  | Non-national Non-EU | Non-national EU | Nationals |
|---|---|---|---|
| EU15 | 2.9 | 1.4 | 95.7 |
| Austria | 8.6 | 1.0 | 93.4 |
| France | 4.0 | 2.3 | 93.7 |
| Germany | 5.2 | 2.1 | 92.7 |
| Spain | 0.5 | 0.4 | 99.1 |
| United Kingdom | 2.1 | 1.4 | 96.5 |

*Source:* 1992 data from Eurostate (1995) *Europe in Figures* (Luxembourg: Office for Official Publications of the European Union) p. 155.

so-called immigrants (though many were second-generation) who were 'here for good' (Castles et al., 1984). Discrimination against ethnic minorities in the labour market could no longer be explained away by language or other difficulties of integration, but racism became more politically entrenched in many countries (see Chapter 3).

It is therefore not surprising that what came to be called social exclusion has become a growing preoccupation in sociological reflection and political discussion, particularly in France, where, as H. Silver and F. Wilkinson put it (in G. Rogers et al., 1995, p. 285), 'In line with the Republican ideology of solidarity, problems like long-term unemployment and rising poverty were construed as manifestations of "social exclusion" or "a rupture of the social bond".' In the UK, which came late to these ideas, the 'New Labour' government which came to power in 1997 briskly inaugurated a 'social exclusion unit'.

The theme of a crisis in the Western European welfare state (Rosanvallon, 1981), and of the work society which underpinned it, is of course a long-standing one. In the German social theorist Jürgen Habermas's early version in 1973, economic crises of capitalism metastasise into the political and cultural sphere, producing irrational state responses or 'crises of crisis-management' (Berger, 1981) and eroding individual motivation. What strikes one in looking comparatively at Western Europe is again the diverse political and cultural responses to socio-economic and social-structural processes which were common to most of the major countries. In Western Europe, it is tempting to offer a state-centred analysis of these differences, rather than the society-centred approaches common to much Marxist and non-Marxist sociology in the 1970s and 1980s. In Eastern Europe, of course, it is inescapable; it was the states which ran most things, and the states which imploded, bringing down the deformed societies they had dominated.

In what follows, I shall examine some of these processes in a bit more detail. Rather than taking traditional structural concepts (family, class, etc.) as the organising principle, I have chosen to use more abstract terms to refer to processes and structures of contemporary Europe. Borrowing from Hermann Schwengel's conception of four 'pillars' of European social structuration, I shall focus, as he has done, on capitalism, constitutionalism, rationalisation and **individualism** (Schwengel, 1999).

**Individualism:** The cluster of doctrines that assert the importance of individual persons and their opinions, rights, welfare, etc. rather than collective structures such as families, churches, states, etc.

## ◼ Capitalism

Europe was the site where capitalism in its modern form first developed, and as it spread through trade, agriculture and what Marx called 'manufacture' into industrial production it transformed European society in all kinds of ways. Note, however, and this is a point that will recur throughout this chapter, that the spread of capitalism was extremely uneven and partial. Reading Marx, who of course was writing in the most advanced corner of Europe, it is easy to get the impression that almost all men, as well as a lot of women and children, were factory workers, and later historians have often encouraged this misapprehension. Barrington Moore (1978) has shown how small was the proportion of the German population in the industrial proletariat, and how small the units in which they mostly worked, right into the twentieth century. France, in comparison with Germany (e.g. Kaelble, 1991), was relatively backward in social-structural terms in the early post-war period. It still had a large peasantry and independent sector. It transformed itself rapidly thereafter in what the French sociologist Henri Mendras (1988) called 'the second French revolution'. And the industrial and productive core of Western Europe, the banana-shaped region centred roughly on the Rhine and running from south-east England to northern Italy and including bits of southern France, northern Spain, and Scandinavia, was very different from the peripheries (Mendras, 1988, ch. 10). Fairly soon bits of the banana rotted, with the decline of traditional industries in Wallonia (the French-speaking province of Belgium), the Ruhr, and so forth, and new centres and types of production came to replace them. The main political axis of the EC/EU remained, however, Paris–Bonn, the UK having joined only in 1973 and thereafter substantially excluding itself from decision-making by its politically irresponsible half-heartedness. Soviet-

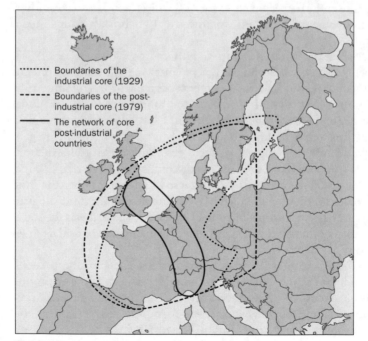

**Map 4.1** Figurations of the core of Europe

dominated Eastern Europe, despite a somewhat standardised development strategy which suited the more backward parts of the empire better than it did East Germany or Czechoslovakia, combined this with a quite substantial degree of sectoral specialisation by country. Here, the postcommunist shake-up and shake-out of the 1990s also shows some states and regions becoming relatively prosperous and others likely to remain disaster areas for decades to come. (On divisions within Europe as a whole, see, for instance, Hudson and Williams, 1999.)

Continental European industrial capitalism developed in tandem with the welfare state, and this continues to give it a different shape from that of other world regions (Albert, 1991; Crouch and Streeck, 1997; Mendras, 1997, ch. 7). Even the UK, where what strategic thinking there is tends to follow the USA rather than the rest of Europe, is still recognisably within a European pattern, and further European integration is likely to sustain and even re-enforce this. On the other hand, Europe is not immune from global pressures and its own internal tendencies away from 'organised' and towards 'disorganised' capitalism (Offe, 1985; Lash and Urry, 1987; Crouch, 1993). Like so many of Europe's contemporary predicaments, this is a mixture of the old and the new. Theorists of capitalism have always been pulled between emphasising its organised, predictable, calculating character and its unpredictable, chaotic aspect, and as **Fordist** mass production gives way to more flexible post-Fordist methods this dualism returns in new forms. Some jobs, for example, become more specialised, skilled and professionalised; others are further down-graded, routinised and casualised into 'McJobs'. Once again, Eastern Europe throws up these issues in a particularly stark form.

Some regions of Europe seem better placed to profit from these developments than others, but it is hard to be confident about predicting developments which often seem to result from happy combinations of luck and entrepreneurship and rapidly become self-sustaining. How far EU policies will follow the imperatives of capitalism itself and encourage regional specialisation, along the lines of a map (see Map 4.2) which attracted some attention in 1999, or pursue more differentiated redistributive strategies, which, however, have largely failed at the level of nation-states, is also an open question.

Capitalism, whatever its virtues (Saunders, 1995), is of course predicated upon inequality and class division, and Europe has been the prime site for anti-capitalist movements based more or less solidly on working-class support. As a general rule, paradoxically, it has been the relatively prosperous North of Europe which had the strongest social-democratic parties, often ruling parties, and trade unions. The South, suffering from greater poverty and more severe strains resulting from industrialisation, has been more fertile ground for minority Communist parties, these however being mostly excluded from power by one means or another. One way or another, Europe developed a characteristic pattern of association between class and voting which has persisted even when class seems to have become merely a variable influencing electoral preferences rather than something directly addressed in political debate. (On class and voting, see Inglehart, 1990; Therborn, 1995, pp. 284–9; see also Chapters 5 and 6.)

In East Central Europe, of course, Communist minorities were able to seize power after the Second World War and establish a version of socialism which was probably doomed by the circumstances of its birth, its association with a generally unpopular (even in Germany and Bulgaria) **hegemonic power**, the USSR, and the means by which it was maintained. Once Stalinised, they could never fully de-Stalinise (see Chapters 2 and 8).

**Fordism:** Named after the early twentieth-century US car-maker Henry Ford, refers to standardised and mechanised mass production: the term 'post-Fordism' has been used since the 1980s to denote more specialised and flexible forms of production, often involving the co-ordination of small-scale producers and catering to small niche markets.

**Hegemonic power:** A state possesses hegemonic power when it is able to create and enforce rules to maintain the international status quo and its own dominance within the existing system.

**Map 4.2** The future of Europe? Where will the jobs be?

© Ian Whadcock 1999

It was in Eastern Europe, once again, that the rise and fall of **social movements** or civil society was most abrupt and striking. The regimes in their final days were mostly confronted by broad coalitions of oppositional forces linked largely by the mere fact of their opposition and an awareness that this was now after all possible. The image of movements of civil society filling the vacuum left by discredited and imploded states was a powerful one on both sides of the falling Iron Curtain. Almost as soon, however, the movements substantially disaggregated, in a fast-forward version of the life-cycle of many Western European movements, into orthodox parties on the one hand and grumpy outsiders on the other. In East Germany, Disneyfied copies of the main West German parties were rapidly cobbled together by ex-Stalinist stooges and Western carpet-baggers; politics in much of the rest of the former bloc took on a vertiginous back-and-forth between neo-liberals on the one hand, sometimes in alliance with clerical conservatives, and rebadged communist parties on the other, benefiting on the rebound from rapid disillusionment with neo-liberal economic policies. And this was in the relatively more fortunate states; elsewhere, the old *nomenklatura* elites have managed to preserve their position, with catastrophic

**Social movements:** Social movements are loosely coupled networks of groups and organisations that, over a considerable period of time, mobilise to achieve or resist social change and/or change society predominantly by means of collective and public protest.

results in, for example, the former Soviet and Yugoslav republics respectively of Belarus and Serbia. This brings us, in a somewhat negative way, to the theme of constitutionalism, which is discussed in the following section.

# Constitutionalism

The constitutional and eventually democratic state is another of those European creations better known in its export model – in this case, the USA. Whatever one thinks about the reality of American democracy, it remains a powerful ideal, deeply entrenched in attitudes and everyday practices, including the defence of free speech in circumstances where even liberal Europeans tend to reach for the penal code. From a North American, and perhaps from an East Asian point of view, Europeans seem somewhat state-centred, waiting for state provision rather than turning to individual or collective self-help. The long-lasting effects of the 1968 protests (see Chapter 2) have, however, sustained a variety of social movements within Europe and increasingly operating on a global scale. Generally, though, we can conclude that twentieth-century Europe produced some of the most decent and attractive states in the world, especially in the north of Europe, but it also provided the two most repellent and destructive ones: Nazi Germany and the Stalinist USSR.

If we take advanced modernity to include not just industrialism and capitalism, urbanism, mass education and so forth, but also certain traditional Euro-American conceptions of citizenship and the public sphere, with roots in the French and American revolutions, then these are not always, at least for the moment, part of the export package when modernity becomes global. There has, for example, been a good deal of debate about whether the state socialism developed in the USSR and imposed on large parts of the rest of Europe should be understood as a variant of modernity, just as it was in previous decades as a variant of industrial society (Aron, 1962), or as in some sense insufficiently, incompletely or unstably modern, in its socio-political structures no less than in its automobile industry. On this view, for example, the 1989 revolutions could be seen as a process of catching-up or rectification (Habermas, 1990; cf. Arnason, 1993).

One of the most important recent social and political transformations in Europe has of course been the destruction of these 'socialist' dictatorships. Whether or not one calls these regimes totalitarian in their practice, it is fairly clear that they pursued an essentially totalitarian ideal of centralised control of economic, political and cultural processes, hidden behind a façade of democratic participation. The rapid democratisation of most of these states is a dramatic instance of a world-wide trend towards democracy in the later twentieth century (Fischer, 1996; Nagle and Mahr, 1999). In the European case, the more or less realistic prospect of accession to the European Union acts as a powerful external stimulus to further democratisation and a brake on possible regression towards authoritarian rule (see Chapter 8).

With the collapse of the 'people's democracies', and the eclipse of revolutionary socialism, the liberal-democratic state, like capitalism, has no obvious practical alternative. If anything, and despite very important elements of disillusionment or political alienation (Budge, Newton et al., 1997; see also Chapter 5), it has acquired stronger roots with the democratisation of everyday life: the growing acceptance, exemplified in spheres as diverse as media interviews with politicians, and child-rearing practices, that all our decisions and ways of life are in principle open to questioning. They become in Habermas's sense 'post-conventional'. In the political context, Habermas himself has, for example, popularised the conception of 'constitutional patriotism' (*Verfassungspatriotismus*) based not on membership of a particular ethnic or national community or *Volk* (see Chapter 3) but on a rational and defensible identification with a decent constitutional state, which may of course be the one whose citizenship one holds as well as the one in which one lives.

But if the liberal-democratic nation-state has few internal enemies, it is increasingly seen as inappropriate to the contemporary reality of global processes and challenges as well as to the desire of many citizens for more local autonomy. In Daniel Bell's classic phrase, it is 'too small for the big problems of life, and too big for the small problems of life' (Bell, 1987, p. 14). In this post-national constellation, as Habermas has called it, the progress of European union, combined as it is with attempts to strengthen regional autonomy under the slogan of 'subsidiarity' (see p. 137), becomes a crucial external determinant of the internal reconfiguration of many European states, notably the UK. Once again, Europe is pioneering a mode of governance, this time transnational rather than national, which gives some practical embodiment to the current extension of democratic thinking into conceptions of cosmopolitan democracy (Held, 1995). This is as important as the earlier extension of liberal democracy into social democracy; it co-exists uneasily, however, with communitarian thinking both in social and political philosophy and in the practice of, for example, Clinton and Blair. The opposition, described by Tönnies (1887), between the large-scale anonymous and formal structures characteristic of modernity and the survival of localised or now sometimes de-localised communities of co-residents or co-thinkers remains a feature of contemporary Europe. This brings us to our next theme, that of rationalisation.

# ■ Rationalisation

Max Weber used the term 'rationalisation' to refer to processes of systematisation in a wide variety of areas of modern societies: the economy, law, bureaucratic organisation, religion and everyday conduct. Entrepreneurs, and increasingly their employees, in early modern Europe began to calculate their economic benefits and losses more precisely and to seek a more predictable environment for their acivity. This meshed in neatly with a trend to the codification of law, notably in the Code Napoléon, which was imposed in the widespread territories he ruled in Europe and elsewhere. State administrations and other large organisations began to rely more on paid officials in complex hierarchies and with clearly defined tasks and routines: the '*fonctionnaire*' or '*Beamte*' in public service and the 'organisation man' in the large corporation (Whyte, 1960; Crozier, 1964). Religious belief became more systematic and streamlined, with the partial displacement, especially in Northern Europe, of the saints and intercession rituals of Catholicism by the more austerely monotheistic and formal Protestant versions of Christianity. With industrialisation and urban migration, religion became increasingly marginalised. Contemporary Europe appears 'modern' in relation to the USA and many other regions of the world in the extent of its secularisation: whatever the difficulties of measurement in this domain, it is clear that religious belief in Europe has mostly ceased to have the kind of importance for social life as a whole which it has retained elsewhere, even in ostensibly secular states like the USA. Scandinavia and East Central Europe have gone furthest in this direction, though France, despite a historically strong Catholic tradition, displays an equally strong secular emphasis in matters of state policy (*laïcité*) and a relatively high level of disbelief in God (Therborn, 1995, p. 275). Individuals, too, have increasingly to 'manage' themselves: their time, their careers, their life-choices and so forth (Beck, 1986). In Eastern Europe, again, this has come as something new to citizens who might have had difficulties in acquiring consumer goods but who were largely cushioned by the state from the bigger risks of life: prolonged illness, unemployment, homelessness and so forth. Women suffered particularly from this shake-up and shake-out (Einhorn, 1993). Many East German victims of the 1997 floods were surprised to find that their new all-German insurance policies left them unprotected.

Once again, the processes Weber described at the beginning of the twentieth century, and whose origins he traced back to the seventeenth and eighteenth, continue in new forms at the dawn of the twenty-first, in management practices of personal appraisal and individual or collective self-management or self-help (Giddens, 1991; Beck, Giddens and Lash, 1994). These are at once liberating, in the way they throw us onto our own resources to define our goals and strategies, and disciplining, in the sense of what Michel Foucault called 'surveillance'. We are constantly under observation, by others and by ourselves. Are you reading this chapter carefully and efficiently? Is it giving you the information and ideas you need? Will it count towards my research output and that of my university? And so on.

Some thinkers have argued that the rationalisation processes characteristic of modernity have given place to a more chaotic postmodern world of disorganised capitalism, franchised welfare services and utilities, unstructured belief, chaotic lives made up of juggling a variety of short-term part-time jobs, and so forth. This seems a mistake. What we find instead in what some people have called a second modernity is an accentuation of many of the same processes under conditions where structures have become more complex and virtual, though no less efficacious. Class structures, thus, remain crucially important determinants of individuals' life-chances, even if they no longer find a direct embodiment in huge working-class occupational communities or mass organisations. The effects of gender, too, have remained pervasive, even as fewer and fewer occupations are explicitly segregated. In this newly rationalised world, issues of individual identity return in new but still recognisable forms.

# Individualism

Asking what is distinctive about European modernity, the French sociologist Henri Mendras (1997, p. 53) offers a historical answer which emphasises the long and slow conquest of Europe (by which he means Western Europe) by a particular ideological model. This model consists of ideological innovations: the individualist notion of the person; the distinction between three types of legitimacy conferred respectively by religion, by politics and by economics; the notion of capital; the conjunction of science and technical progress; the power of the majority; the importance of contractual relationships and the mutual trust they involve; the rule of law; property rights as the law understands them. These are the foundations of Western European civilisation and they are unique in the history of civilisations.

We have encountered these themes already in the previous section, but the first of these deserves special attention. Modernity is, as the German historical sociologist Norbert Elias described it, essentially a 'society of individuals' (Elias, 1988), and, as

Durkheim recognised, individualism has become something of a substitute for religious belief in modern societies. Parents' views on the desirability or otherwise of encouraging independence rather than obedience in their children are, as Therborn notes (Therborn, 1995, p. 292), an interesting marker of differences across Europe. There are striking differences between the value placed on autonomy in the North and Central region (Austria, West Germany, the Netherlands and the Nordic countries) and the emphasis on obedience in the South and West (UK, Ireland, France, Italy, Portugal and Spain), and similarly, between some parts of Eastern Europe (Hungary, East Germany and the former Soviet Baltic republics, but also Bulgaria in the south-east) and others (authoritarian Czechoslovakia, Poland, Belarus and Russia). As in the case of work organisation, discussed below, it is interesting that the traditional stereotype which contrasts a libertarian or anarchic France with a rigid and authoritarian Germany is contradicted by the evidence.

There can be little doubt about the further advance of individualistic values in the late twentieth century (Inglehart, 1977). However, we must remember that an 'ideal type' of modern individualism should not be taken in an exclusive sense. People, particularly women, continue to be defined and to define themselves in relational terms as someone's child, wife or parent. **Patronymics** are widely used both as names and as descriptions in many parts of Europe, and families remain very important, even in the North. In the South, **clientelism** often persists in quasi-familial forms, and in many countries university professors, for example, surround themselves with a small 'family' of assistants.

The important point, however, is that it is increasingly easy for individuals to define themselves in other ways, choosing between a repertoire of identities and foregrounding one or another according to context. (The frequent adoption in internet chat groups of a fictitious identity or the opposite gender is one of the most recent examples.) Here again, we see the inseparable interplay of structural and cultural elements in defining identities. Sexual identity is fairly clear-cut, but its salience in social contexts is highly variable. A homosexual identity may be given a central place by its bearer and his or her associates, or it may be kept in the background by both. Some women may change their names to mark their distinctness from their fathers or parents.

Modernity is characterised, then, by a weakening of traditional identities in the anonymity of cities and individual wage-labour. At the same time, we see a desire to categorise and classify, of which Foucault gave the classic examples in his studies of the emergence of the 'mad', 'sick' or 'homosexual' identity. More particularly, the European nation-states became concerned to count and measure their populations, and to impose a common national identity at the expense of regional ones (Eley and Suny, 1996). Boundary changes throughout the nineteenth and twentieth centuries, and migration flows within and into Europe, have increasingly subverted the latter process, but many European states continue to try to preserve a traditional line. France, in particular, has resisted expressions of cultural difference in public institutions, in particular the wearing of Islamic headscarves in schools, and is currently opposing a European agreement reached in 1992 to support minority languages.

There seems, however, to be an emergent consensus in the multicultural societies of contemporary Europe that it is up to individuals to define their identities, choosing what weight they wish to attach to each, and that 'outing' and 'othering' are unacceptable. Members of ethnic and religious minorities, in particular, have resisted attempts, no doubt well-meaning, to increase their political representation

**Patronymics:** Names derived from a father or other ancestor, for example by suffixes such as -son, -ovich.

**Clientelism:** A structure of relations between powerful patrons such as landlords or political leaders and those dependent on them for services, who reward them by political or other forms of support.

Box 4.2

## Attachments to locality, region, country and Europe

A Eurobarometer survey of people in the 15 EU member states in March and April 1999 showed that a high proportion of respondents felt very or fairly attached to their country, town or village, and region, and over half felt similarly attached to Europe.

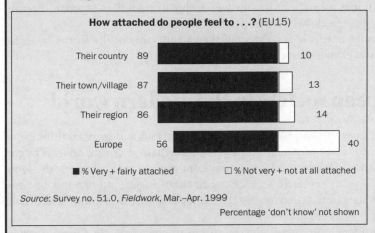

**How attached do people feel to . . . ?** (EU15)

| | % Very + fairly attached | % Not very + not at all attached |
|---|---|---|
| Their country | 89 | 10 |
| Their town/village | 87 | 13 |
| Their region | 86 | 14 |
| Europe | 56 | 40 |

*Source*: Survey no. 51.0, *Fieldwork*, Mar.–Apr. 1999

Percentage 'don't know' not shown

Country-by-country analyses find quite varying levels of attachment to Europe, with the highest proportion of those feeling attached to Europe in Luxembourg and the lowest proportion in the United Kingdom.

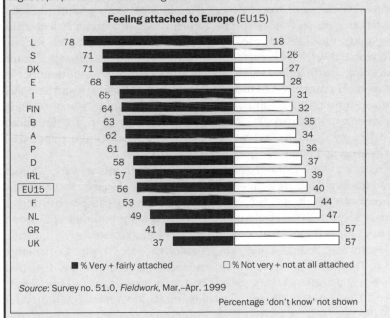

**Feeling attached to Europe** (EU15)

| | % Very + fairly attached | % Not very + not at all attached |
|---|---|---|
| L | 78 | 18 |
| S | 71 | 26 |
| DK | 71 | 27 |
| E | 68 | 28 |
| I | 65 | 31 |
| FIN | 64 | 32 |
| B | 63 | 35 |
| A | 62 | 34 |
| P | 61 | 36 |
| D | 58 | 37 |
| IRL | 57 | 39 |
| EU15 | 56 | 40 |
| F | 53 | 44 |
| NL | 49 | 47 |
| GR | 41 | 57 |
| UK | 37 | 57 |

*Source*: Survey no. 51.0, *Fieldwork*, Mar.–Apr. 1999

Percentage 'don't know' not shown

through the incorporation of traditional elites or 'community leaders'. What seems striking (though see Therborn, 1995, p. 242, for a different point of view) is how relatively hard it has been for Europeans to move to a North American pattern where 'Italian-American', 'African-American' and so on are recognisable identities and where it is understood that the bit before the hyphen will have different degrees of

**Fundamentalism:** Religious believers who see literal meanings in their sacred texts are usually referred to as fundamentalists. Often perceived by outsiders as extremists, fundamentalists usually wish to see their religion playing a bigger role in politics and society.

salience for different individuals. There are of course significant fundamentalist counter-movements, calling forth, in their turn, responses such as that by Samuel Huntington (1993) which manage to be both hysterical and cynical. More seriously, the fundamentalisms of the 'others' are matched by a 'majority' **fundamentalism** which refuses ethnic and cultural difference and for which a black person, say, can never be 'really' British or French. The extent to which a European identity has displaced the traditional primacy of national or regional identities (Scottish, Breton, etc.) is again highly variable between and within states.

In the remainder of this chapter, I shall sketch out some of the forms taken by these processes and elements across European society.

# ■ European society in the modern world

We have learned from thinkers like Elias, Touraine and Giddens to avoid thinking of 'societies' as if they were individuals, capable of thought and action, defined by the boundaries of particular states, and it is no less important to avoid applying the same thinking to 'Europe'. It is clearly an entity with fuzzy edges, and not just because some European states include overseas territories or because Turkey and Russia stretch into Asia.

What can be said in the end about the residual distinctiveness of Europe as a region of the modern world? A familiar theme, invoked even in an advertising series by Shell a few years ago, is diversity, notably the diversity of languages. Compared with the largely anglophone societies of North America or the area sharing Chinese pictograms, or even large regions such as India or the former USSR with an established *lingua franca*, Europe looks rather a mess. We may wonder how far such a perception rests on overlooking linguistic diversity elsewhere in the world, but it is at least true that in the European case a pattern of linguistic variation, largely co-existing with the boundaries of developed modern states, creates powerful entrenched structures and interests which, in turn, act as obstacles to cultural and political integration. (It is obvious, at least to this particular English-speaker, that the official language of the European Union ought to be English, just as it is obvious that its principal institutions should all be centralised in Brussels, but no-one quite dares to say so.)

The contours of Europe's main divisions are shifting in dramatic ways. It is not just that the old political East/West division has now been replaced by an economic one. The cultural North/South divide within Europe remains important, but is changing in many ways, with the modernisation of (parts of the) southern European societies. It is now, for example, Italy, rather than the Protestant northern countries, which (in the absence of adequate child-care provision) apparently puts work before having children. The North–South religious divide remains an important structural principle in Western Europe, as does, further east, that between Orthodox Christianity and Islam. The East–West line also remains crucial, as Germans on both sides (but especially the East) will confirm, and many Central Europeans would also continue to stress the distinctiveness of their societies from 'Eastern' Europe as well as from Russia. There are also many similarities between Scandinavia and parts of East Central Europe, despite their diverse political histories for much of the twentieth century.

Göran Therborn's recent book (1995) is an exceptionally useful attempt to document these and other variations across post-1945 Europe, showing how the country and broader regional groupings vary according to the dimension chosen. The following discussion is heavily indebted to his pioneering work, and I shall be guided by the questions which he poses:

Have the societies of Europe become more similar to others on the globe? More distinctively European? More differentiated or more similar among themselves? (Therborn, 1995, p. 30)

A clear area of difference from most of the rest of the world concerns population. Several European countries have indulged in panics about their low rates of reproduction – France more or less endemically. Europe as a whole has become a low-growth area, an effect mitigated by immigration and the greater fertility of the small immigrant populations. Although these have been relatively small overall, their concentration in particular regions, notably in the larger cities, and in manual occupations, has increased their visibility. In some countries, such as Switzerland, a large proportion of the working class is foreign and unable to vote. Elsewhere, many foreign residents, such as those in Britain from the Irish Republic and the Commonwealth, do have the vote, even if their numbers have not been sufficient to generate substantial ethnic politics of a North American kind.

There has of course been a huge amount of confusion and double-think around issues of immigration and ethnic relations. Many European countries which had not

## Box 4.3

### Europe's population decline

| COUNTRY | 1998 (millions) | Projected 2050 (millions) |
|---|---|---|
| Austria | 8,140 | 7,094 |
| Belgium | 10,141 | 8,918 |
| Bulgaria | 8,336 | 5,673 |
| Croatia | 4,481 | 3,673 |
| Czech Republic | 10,282 | 7,829 |
| Denmark | 5,270 | 4,793 |
| Finland | 5,154 | 4,898 |
| France | 58,847 | 59,883[1] |
| Germany | 82,135 | 73,303 |
| Greece | 10,600 | 8,233 |
| Hungary | 10,116 | 7,488 |
| Italy | 57,369 | 41,197 |
| Lithuania | 3,694 | 2,297 |
| Netherlands | 15,678 | 14,156 |
| Poland | 38,718 | 36,256 |
| Portugal | 9,869 | 8,137 |
| Romania | 22,474 | 16,419 |
| Russian Fed. | 147,434 | 121,256 |
| Slovakia | 5,377 | 4,836 |
| Spain | 39,628 | 30,226 |
| Sweden | 8,875 | 8,661 |
| Switzerland | 7,299 | 6,745 |
| Ukraine | 50,861 | 39,302 |
| UK | 58,649 | 56,667 |
| Yugoslavia | 10,635 | 10,548 |

NETHERLANDS -1.5m

U.K. -2m

RUSSIA -26.2m

GERMANY -8.8m

HUNGARY -2.6m

ITALY -16.2m

SPAIN -9.4m

GREECE -2.4m

[1]Note that France's population is expected to peak at 61 million in 2025 and thereafter to decline.

had substantial colonial empires persisted in the pretence that they were merely receiving temporary 'guest workers' rather than immigrants and that they were not 'countries of immigration'. State policies switched abruptly from active recruitment to attempts to stem the migrant flows; a second wave of immigration occurred in the 1990s with immigrants from the former Communist countries and refugees from there and elsewhere.

The differences between European countries in their labour-force structures are substantially explained by their positions on the historical trajectory from agrarian to industrial and post-industrial society (Therborn, 1995, pp. 65ff). Europe was unique in the thoroughgoing nature of its industrialisation and the primacy for a time, in many countries, of industrial employment. As Therborn (1995, p. 70) notes, 'Sixteen out of . . . twenty-five European countries had a period of (relatively) predominant industrial employment. Outside Europe this has only happened in Taiwan . . .' This to some extent cuts across the East/West divide; some communist and post-communist countries have large agricultural populations and others do not. The gender division of labour is fundamentally shaped by economic factors, in the sense of predominant types of production, but with significant differences between countries which one might expect to be more similar in their structures and attitudes. Conversely, the former state socialist societies of Eastern Europe, though they had much higher rates of female participation in paid work than *most* Western societies, averaged similar rates to Finland and Sweden (Therborn, 1995, p. 63).

Working practices and workplace cultures display considerable diversity in Europe. Broadly speaking, the contrast between corporatist Rhineland capitalism and the neo-liberal British version (Albert, 1991) intersects with that between managerially top-heavy and authoritarian French (and other Latin) enterprises and those in Germany or Scandinavia, where workers have tended to be more skilled, participation more institutionalised and managers less numerous (Therborn, 1995, p. 79; cf. Lane, 1989). How far these differences will persist, against a background of globalisation of both economic structures and managerial cultures, is an open question, as is the future shape of Eastern Europe in the European and world division of labour. Here, of course, EU membership in the short, medium or long term is a crucial factor. But if there is, as Colin Crouch (1993) has suggested, a European model or set of models of industrial relations, this may well appeal to other regions of the world. (In the European context, the UK governments of Thatcher and Major were out on a limb in wanting to abandon some of the benefits of the European system and adopt largely misunderstood Asian models instead.)

Welfare-state structures again display a clear contrast between Scandinavian and Eastern European patterns of state-based provision on the one hand and insurance-based private or semi-private systems in most of the rest of Europe, with the UK, Ireland and Italy in an intermediate position. On the whole, the state-based systems provide more as a proportion of GDP, though the insurance-based systems in France, Belgium and the Netherlands are also major providers. Generally speaking, Europe is characterised by generous welfare states, partly though not exclusively because it tends to be rich. 'In three countries', Therborn (1995, pp. 155–6) notes (the Netherlands, Norway and Sweden, with France close to the same position), 'the welfare state has become more important than private property as a source of household income.' This in turn, of course, relates to broader issues about forms of production, private versus public ownership, and class relations in European states (pp. 123–6). Europe comes out as relatively equal, compared with North America and Australia, but with significant variations between the egalitarian North-west and East and the unequal South (Therborn, 1995, p. 153; see also Bailey, 1992, 1998; Lenoir, 1994).

**Social mobility** has attracted a great deal of often technical social research, though within Europe the differences between countries are not particularly dramatic, with structural changes such as the liquidation of peasantries and the increase in white-collar and service jobs accounting for much of the mobility in European societies. In terms of social openness or fluidity, there are not particularly significant differences between countries. The former socialist countries, which of course actively pursued redistributive policies in the 1950s, have remained rather more open than the capitalist West of Europe, but not dramatically so. Partial exceptions to this trend in their respective camps are Sweden, where mobility is relatively high, and Hungary, where it is relatively low. Japan, the USA and Australia all score higher for openness than any of the major European countries except Czechoslovakia (Therborn, 1995, p. 174; Eriksson and Goldthorpe, 1992, p. 381). Another important parallel between Eastern and Western Europe is the importance of 'cultural capital' in the transmission of advantage. Whereas the children of the traditional European bourgeoisies might hope to inherit land, factories or large amounts of money wealth from their parents, in the twentieth century what has been called the 'service class' of professional and managerial employees in public service and the private sector tend to transmit their advantages through the educational system, by paying for their children to attend exclusive fee-paying schools or by pushing them into and through elite establishments like some of the French *lycées* and the '*Grandes Écoles*', open to all but in practice heavily populated by bourgeois Parisians (Bourdieu, 1970; Marceau, 1977). In Eastern Europe, once again, the threat to traditional forms of inheritance, family succession and educational privilege was more drastic, but old elites often managed to preserve a privileged position through the years of high Stalinism into advanced socialist and then again capitalist conditions (Szelenyi, 1988; Eyal, Szelenyi and Townsley, 1998). With the devaluation in postcommunist societies of many traditional occupations and qualifications, connections with foreigners and an ability to speak foreign languages may be worth years of university or work experience.

Looking more broadly at the cultural sphere, it is clear that Europe's continuing position as a major cultural producer is one of the effects of its previous world hegemony, partly preserved in that of its world languages: English, French, Spanish, Portuguese and to some extent even Dutch. It has also stood up in many ways to the challenge of North American imports. This applies not just to cultural commodities such as films but also to material aspects of life such as the car-based civilisation; despite everything, most European cities remain less car-based and suburbanised than US ones. For a time these might have seemed like cultural lags. Now, however, it appears that in many ways parts of the USA are returning to more 'European' modes of life, including railways and urban mass-transit systems, delicatessen food (even cheese) and niche markets for cult movies in the larger cities.

It is clear that human societies are much more ingenious in their cultural pick-and-mix or *bricolage* than we can predict (see, for example, Gilroy, 1993). It seems fair to expect, however, that despite the Americanising pull of the mass media, reflecting and reinforcing the appeal of North America and to some extent Australia to many young Europeans, Europe will remain culturally distinct from other world regions, with local differences persisting against a background of common European and global systems. The washing powder, for example, may have instructions in

**Social mobility:** The 'upward' or 'downward' movement from one position in a social scale to another, e.g. from 'working class' to 'middle class' – either within an individual's lifetime or from one generation to another.

many languages and contact addresses in half a dozen countries, but the fine detail of domestic work will continue to display interesting differences across the continent. The interrelations between post-conventional post-national identities, themselves competing with more atavistic traditional national identities, and a European identity whose ambivalence Gerard Delanty (1999) has rightly stressed, will form the broader social and cultural background to the ups and downs of the political and economic project of European integration in the early twenty-first century.

## Summary

◆ This chapter has attempted to situate Europe and its distinctive patterns of social structuration in its historical and geographical context, focusing in particular on the specific character of European capitalism, the European constitutional state, the emphasis in many parts of Europe on individualism and the processes of systematisation and calculation summed up in the term 'rationalisation'.

◆ I have tried to bring out the commonalities as well as the differences between the component states and regions of contemporary Europe, which is perhaps not yet 'a society' in the usual sense of the term, but which may be on the way to becoming one.

## Questions for discussion

▶ What is distinctive about modernity in its contemporary European forms?

▶ What are the main distinctive features of European social stuctures?

▶ Have North/South differences within Europe become as important as East/West ones ?

## Further reading

Allum, P. (1995) *State and Society in Western Europe* (Cambridge: Polity). A coherent theoretical analysis with substantial empirical detail on economic systems, civil society (including political parties) and state institutions in France, Germany, Italy and the UK.

Bailey, J. (ed.) (1992; 2nd edn 1998) *Social Europe* (London: Longman). A reliable discussion of some major themes in European social structure and social change.

Hudson, R. and A. M. Williams (eds) (1999) *Divided Europe: Society and Territory* (London: Sage). A creative exploration of economic, political, spatial and social divisions in contemporary Europe.

Therborn, G. (1995) *European Modernity and Beyond: The Trajectory of European Societies, 1945–2000* (London: Sage). A brilliant combination of bold theorising and often surprising empirical documentation.

# Political Participation in Europe

Dieter Rucht

> 'Democracy works towards the self-determination of humankind, and only if the latter materialises does the former become true. Then political participation will be identical to self-determination.'
>
> JÜRGEN HABERMAS et al., *Student und Politik* (1961) p. 15

## Contents

This chapter aims to provide an overview of the extent and forms of political participation in Europe. These terms should be clarified from the outset. First, political participation is understood as a broad category of behaviours that stretch far beyond the conventional and institutionalised forms of citizen activities such as voting (Topf, 1995; Gundelach, 1995; Khan, 1999). Secondly, with the ending of the Cold War, the meaning of Europe as a territorial category has to be broadened. Though in geographical terms Europe always included the territories at least as far East as the Urals, this was less evident before 1989, when Westerners referred to Europe in a political and cultural sense.

We now have to take into account that Europe is a highly differentiated conglomerate with many different states and cultures that each merit individual attention. We lack not only the space for such country-by-country description here, but also information on at least some aspects in some countries. Thus the reader should not expect details on particular countries but rather a rough picture that, at best, highlights some general aspects and trends that would need further elaboration.

This chapter will first discuss the notion of political participation in more general terms, laying out its elementary dimensions and more specific forms of activities. It will then discuss political participation in relation to the organisation of power and the **cleavage** structure in contemporary European countries. Based on these more conceptual reflections and discussions, an empirical picture of four major frameworks of political participation will be drawn, namely those of parties, interest groups, social movements, and mass media. Finally, these frameworks are located in a model of political-interest mediation and some more general conclusions on participation as an asset of democracy are suggested.

## Dimensions and forms of political participation

The term 'participation' implies that an actor – an individual, a group, or an organisation – takes part in something. Not all activities, however, can be called participation.

**Cleavages:** Cleavages separate social or political groups that, having a relatively stable and coherent view on fundamental aspects of society, take opposite stances on issues such as religion, individual liberties and state intervention, social justice, and market economy.

We do not 'participate' in a meal when we are eating alone, but we may participate in a dinner party. We may be nominal members of a religious congregation, but unless we attend its services at least occasionally, let alone play a more active role, we do not participate in this congregation. Thus, participation means taking part in a *collective* endeavour which usually requires some sort of *activity* from several or all of those involved. When talking about *political* participation, this implies that we are not apathetic citizens but take an active role in political life by following events, articulating our demands and opinions, and trying to influence the processes of decision-making that ultimately have binding consequences for larger groups or even the whole of a society (Keim, 1975; Milbrath, 1965; Verba, Nie and Kim, 1978; Pateman, 1970; Parry, Moyer and Day, 1992; van Deth, 1997).

Acting as one among hundreds of citizens in a neighbourhood, tens of thousands in a city, millions in a nation, and hundreds of millions in a still larger community such as the European Union, usually means that our individual impact tends to be extremely marginal. Nevertheless, people do participate in politics at all these levels, in many forms, and sometimes at considerable costs. Participation can be perceived from very different angles. On the one hand, it means the strategic pursuit of individual goals by influencing political processes that affect the achievement of these goals. In its most reduced form, the mechanism by which this influence can and should be sought is the election of political leaders. In economic theories of democracy which put the cost–benefit calculating individual at the centre, this act of choosing between different groups of elites is what democracy is about (Downs, 1957). According to Joseph Schumpeter (1966, p. 252), democracy is nothing other than a 'political method'. Whether or not many citizens participate in this process, and whether or not they engage beyond voting, is of secondary importance. Some political scientists (e.g., Morris Jones), who Bachrach (1967) ascribed to the school of 'democratic elitism', even consider intensive participation as an evil in so far as it seems to indicate widespread dissatisfaction among the populace, which distrusts the political elites, or, worse still, it may deter the elites from making necessary and appropriate decisions. These political scientists perceive a 'democratic dilemma' of 'system effectiveness versus citizen participation' (Dahl, 1994) and therefore want to limit the latter.

On the other hand, as mentioned, some normative theories of democracy consider the range, breadth and intensity of citizen participation as a criterion for a 'good' or, using Benjamin Barber's (1985) term, a 'strong democracy'. Whatever stance one takes in this unresolved debate about what defines and makes democracy work, it should not prevent us from taking an empirical look at political participation as it actually takes place. Such an empirical investigation, however, cannot be undertaken without conceptual tools. A first step in this direction is an identification of four dimensions of political participation.

1   It has already been mentioned that participation can be institutionalised or non-institutionalised. In the former case, participation is defined by explicit rules which, in their most comprehensive form, define who is entitled to do what by using which channel in targeting which person or institution. Such rules, for example, exist for the election of political bodies, **referendums**, appeals to administrative or constitutional courts, and, to a lesser degree, participation in public hearings and inquiries. In other cases, participation is only defined as a right, with no (or only a minimum of) further specification. For example, most modern constitutions guarantee the right of public assembly and free speech regardless of the place and the particular form. In

**Referendum:** An election which allows voters to make a choice between alternative policies on a particular issue. Referendums (**referenda**) are important instruments of direct democracy (see also Box 6.1).

some countries, gatherings and marches in public places have to be announced in advance to local authorities and then permission is subject to certain requirements (della Porta and Reiter, 1998). Similarly, in some countries professional and relatively continuous lobbying is only allowed by groups that are officially registered. Finally, there are forms of political participation that are completely unregulated simply because formal rules are considered to be unnecessary or because the form of action is illegal anyway and therefore cannot become a matter for rules of conduct. An example of the former is an open letter that a group of citizens addresses to the government, or a consumer boycott of an enterprise that is trading with an apartheid regime; examples of illegal forms of political participation are a politically motivated wildcat strike or a blockade of car traffic by environmentalists.

Closely related to the aspects of institutional or non-institutional forms of participation is the particular setting or arena in which participation takes place. Some of these, as already mentioned, are highly institutionalised. On the opposite end of the scale are streets and other public places where many forms of participation can take place, ranging from a collection of signatures to a protest rally to violent action. The mass media provide an important forum for political participation (beyond the fact that they report on many relevant activities, including participation in other settings), particularly because they can potentially reach the whole population. In addition to the kind of setting or arena, we can also distinguish them according to their geographical scope, ranging from the local to the international or even to global levels.

2   A second dimension refers to the kind of actor engaged in participation. In some cases, participation is an individual act, either by choice or by institutional definition. This is true for somebody writing a letter to a Member of Parliament. Also, voting is by definition (secret ballot) an individual act, in spite of the fact that millions may vote on the same day. Because the effect of an individual act is unlikely to have a substantial impact, citizens often unite to engage in collective participation. They create informal groups such as citizen initiatives, join a formal organisation, such as a professional association, political party, trade union, or religious congregation, or they gather on one particular occasion, for example a big demonstration. Participating actors can also be categorised by their socio-demographic and attitudinal characteristics, such as sex, education, political orientation, etc.

3   A third dimension is the material and non-material 'cost' of participation. Signing a petition for animal rights may take only a few seconds and does not involve any risk. Attending a national demonstration in the distant capital may cost us a whole day plus travel expenses. Conducting a hunger strike can be a long, awful and dangerous activity which only a few are prepared to undertake, under exceptional circumstances. Other forms of political participation, e.g. volunteering over many years in a political party, are less spectacular but still require an enormous investment of time and energy.

4   Finally, participation can vary greatly according to its thematic scope and ambition, ranging from moderate attempts to influence political matters to fundamental and radical efforts to change society as a whole. An example of the former is an attempt by a particular social group to prevent an unfavourable new tax regulation. An example of a broad and bold activity is the fight against a Communist regime in spite of the threat of harsh sanctions.

Numerous empirical variations in these four dimensions can be combined in many different ways. Consequently, political participation is extremely multi-faceted. There is a risk of seeing only the trees and missing the wood. Instead of exploring the impressive variety and contingency of countless acts of participation, we should instead look for deeper structures that in many ways underlie and influence the rippling surface of everyday political participation. One way of putting numerous acts of political participation into perspective is by referring to the concept of societal and/or political cleavage structures.

## Power, cleavages and political participation

Solidarity, money and power are probably the most important forces that regulate exchanges between individuals, groups, and organisations in modern societies. Solidarity is a crucial mechanism in holding together, for example, families, self-help groups, neighbourhoods, and ethnic communities. Money is a key mechanism in regulating economic exchanges. Power, according to the famous definition by Max Weber, is the ability to achieve desired ends despite resistance from others.

Modern democratic societies have developed various institutional devices to prevent the concentration and misuse of power in the hands of a few. Most important among these devices are:

(a) the opportunity to replace power-holders via regular elections by the citizens;

(b) the horizontal distribution of power between the legislative, executive and judicial branches of the state, together with the latter's capacity to penalise the illegal use of power; and

(c) the vertical distribution of power between the central state and regional and local authorities.

In more recent times, international governmental bodies have also acquired some formal executive power. However, the means to control these powers democratically still remain underdeveloped, as the example of the European Union demonstrates.

Power relations not only characterise the relationship between the citizenry and the state, and exchanges within the state; they also exist between and within groups of citizens, as a closer look at any political party, trade union, religious congregation, or even an informal citizen initiative would reveal. Particularly in conflictual situations, we can observe that some individuals or bodies do have the ability to pursue their objectives despite the resistance of others, although the use of power may not be as obvious as in the case of policemen or military forces acting against citizens. For example, discrimination against women, based on more or less subtle mechanisms, continues in many spheres of social and political life in spite of legislation granting equal rights (Orloff, 1996).

Since power is unevenly distributed and tends to privilege some interests at the expense of others, power struggles tend to be ubiquitous in politics; but this does not mean that everybody is in conflict with everybody else. There are two reasons why power relations and conflict lines within the citizenry tend to crystallise into relatively stable structures. First, some groups acquire considerable power through their large membership, organisational strength, and critical role for the functioning of society in general. In advanced capitalist societies, the most powerful groups besides the state authorities are the representatives of capital, notably the employer organisations, and the representatives of the workers and employees, i.e., the trade unions. In some Western European states such as Sweden, Norway, the Netherlands, and Austria, these two blocs, together with the state representatives as the third pillar of power, formed a tripartite system of bargaining and decision-making that, because of its formal parallels to a pre-liberal corporatist society, was called **neocorporatism** (Schmitter and Lehmbruch, 1979; Lehmbruch and Schmitter, 1982; Williamson, 1989). This system of decision-making could only work as long as the elites of each of the three pillars could count on the support (or at least the tacit consent) of the broader groups they claimed to represent. In practice this meant that the rank-and-file was not involved in the neocorporatist game, but had to accept the decisions of their leaders. In other words, political participation was a matter for the very few who acted on behalf of the many who remained passive. Over time, however, and due to processes which will be explained in later sections of this chapter, this relatively clear-cut neocorporatist model was weakened and came closer to the pluralist model.

A second reason why power relations tend to crystallise in relatively consistent and stable patterns has to do with the structuration of society in terms of broader social classes and groups. Many people live in similar situations, adopt common world-views, and have common interests. This is true, for example, of farmers, workers, entrepreneurs, and religious people. Because of the commonalities within these groups, and divergent values and interests between them, many concrete conflicts and power struggles are just variants of or derivations from deeper and more general sources of conflict that are relatively stable over time. These general lines of tension and potential conflicts have been called societal cleavages. Cleavages may lead to conflict, but they are not the manifestations of conflict. The latter indicate the former, but cleavages cannot be directly observed. Referring to Western democratic societies, Lipset and Rokkan (1967) have argued that these societies are marked by deeply rooted cleavages that, at least since the end of the First World War, have been 'frozen' in stable constellations of political parties. From this perspective, divisions and alliances between certain types of political parties are organisational representations of underlying social cleavages. The most important cleavages, according to Stein Rokkan (1997), are those between the rural and urban workforces, the political centre and the periphery, religious and secular groups, and between capital and labour. (In political terms, the two latter cleavages are often conceptualised as the right/left cleavage.) More than thirty years after Lipset and Rokkan's analyses of party systems, it has become obvious that the first two cleavages have lost some of their significance, whereas the cleavage between capital and labour is still vital in many countries.

In addition, however, new or renewed cleavages have gained some importance. One is that between Old and New Politics (Hildebrandt and Dalton, 1977) or, in a slightly different formulation, materialism and **postmaterialism** (Inglehart, 1977 and 1981). Old Politics, or materialism, emphasises the values of economic growth and material security, whereas New Politics, or postmaterialism, focuses on aspects of life quality in terms of democratic rights and the integrity of the social and human environment. In party politics, this cleavage was originally marked by the conflict between the established parties (both rightist and leftist) on the one hand and the New Leftist and Green parties on the other. Leftist and postmaterialist values have influenced each other, so that we cannot really speak of a clear distinction between the left vs. right and the materialist vs. postmaterialist cleavage.

**Neocorporatism:**
Neocorporatism is an arrangement in which the leaders of interest groups, together with representatives of the state, jointly make policies and justify these *vis-à-vis* their respective members or clientele.

**Postmaterialism:**
Postmaterialism is a set of values such as freedom of speech and protection of the environment that are supposed to gain relevance after basic material needs (e.g., food and shelter) are satisfied.

Starting in the 1980s, the (re-)emergence of ethnic conflicts seems to indicate a further cleavage. As far as Western Europe is concerned, this became apparent with the increased influx of immigrants and asylum seekers from countries that are culturally distinct from the domestic ethnic majority (see Chapter 3). On the one hand we find a number of parties which, though not *necessarily* nominally liberal parties, pursue a liberal course in dealing with immigrants and asylum seekers; on the other hand we witness the rise of revitalised or newly founded extreme-Right parties with nationalistic and xenophobic undertones. It seems that this constellation not only marks one particular area of conflict, but also has implications in addressing labour-market policy, taxation, attitudes towards European integration, and so forth.

Whereas the concept of cleavage structure was essentially conceived to get a better understanding of party constellations and voter alignments, it appears that cleavage structures have much broader implications. Cleavages also determine the constellation of major interest groups and social movements. This will become clearer when political participation is discussed with respect to these three types of interest mediation in European democracies.

## Party politics and voting behaviour

It is hard to imagine modern politics without political parties. Virtually all official decision-makers are members of parties. Moreover, these decision-makers would not have come into office without the support of parties, which, of course, ultimately depend on voters. Political parties are the main conveyor of people's interests and preferences into the polity. Note that the turn-out in electoral polls is relatively high in Europe (Borg, 1995) when compared with most other forms of political participation. It is, however, important to note that in some Western European countries, for example Belgium, Luxembourg and Greece, voting is compulsory.

As discussed above, people's interests and preferences are not isolated from each other, but cluster along various cleavages, which are mirrored by the constellation of parties – sometimes called the party system – in a given country. Instead of specialising in one single issue, parties usually represent a broader set of beliefs and aims that are influenced by a general perspective on how society and the political order should be. It has been rightly argued that one important function of political parties is to bundle together a great number of particular issues. Although parties directly compete with each other and therefore tend to emphasise differences in their profile, with regard to their own clientele they moderate and balance different demands which, in their original form, would be incompatible. In this perspective, political parties are important mechanisms for pooling, mediating and moderating sets of demands and claims.

By and large, today's parties still mirror the big cleavages that took shape in the last century. Political analysts have identified five major 'party families': the communist, socialist and social-democratic, liberal, conservative, and extreme-Right parties. In addition, a separate farmers' party exists in some countries which still have a significant agricultural sector. In most other countries, this constituency has been absorbed by the more encompassing conservative parties, which also tend to represent the conservative-oriented religious groups. Furthermore, some countries also have ethno-regional parties centred around conflicts between centre and periphery and/or cultural cleavages. Finally, from the 1970s, New Left parties and Green parties have been established in most European countries (Richardson and Rootes, 1994). These additional cleavages have broadened the spectrum of political parties, which had narrowed in the decades after the Second World War.

Whereas Western European countries only gradually tended to broaden the spectrum and number of parties, the fall of the Communist regimes in Eastern Europe has triggered a mushrooming of political parties, which represent not only the full spectrum from the far Left to the far Right, but also very particular social groups (Nagle and Mahr, 1999). On average, the number of parties in Eastern Europe is far greater than in the West (Budge, Newton et al., 1997, p. 231). It is likely that, after a transition period, some of these parties will simply fade away, whereas others will fuse, so that we can expect a concentration process leading to a party spectrum similar to that in the West.

At least in Western Europe, the lines between the (once ideologically more consistent) party families have blurred, so that, for example, Conservative parties now claim to represent the interests of the working class, whereas Social Democrats are no longer focused solely on the working class. This trend towards 'catch-all parties' (Otto Kirchheimer, 1996) not only facilitated the formation of party coalitions but also resulted in a de-alignment of voters. Voting became less and less determined by status and class (Crewe and Denver, 1985).

In the USA and some other countries parties tend to be loose networks without a regular membership, a consistent programme and a coherent body of sections ranging from the local to the national levels; political parties in Europe tend to be clear-cut organisations that are ideologically relatively coherent. As a rule, they are based on a strong apparatus of professionals, but also include a significant number of members ready to volunteer. However, as in many other political organisations, numerous activities are concentrated among minorities that are highly motivated, whereas others remain relatively passive and hardly do more than paying their fees and, at best, occasionally attending a meeting. Overall, parties are crucial forums for political participation, offering many possibilities for playing an active role with varying degrees of involvement. Precisely because party politics becomes more and more dominated by the professionals, and in particular by key players in the 'party machinery' (Michels, 1962), the activity of the rank-and-file is important in exercising some control over the leadership, which otherwise may drift towards transforming the party into a fully fledged oligarchy, as Robert Michels (1962) had predicted early in the twentieth century.

More than the average voter who is an outsider to party politics, the rank-and-file member of a political party is able to recognise the risk of parties degenerating into mere tools for acquiring power against the interests of internal democracy.

In most European countries, parties tend to have a considerable number of members (Katz and Mair, 1992), of whom, as we have seen, only a certain proportion actively takes part in the party's life. Today, the biggest parties in Europe, although they have experienced a drastic loss of membership in some countries, still range between a half to one million members. For example, the Social Democratic Party in Germany had about 818,000 members and its allied conservative counterparts, CDU/CSU, 837,000 members in 1995. The Conservative Party in Great Britain claimed 750,000 members in 1994 and the Labour Party close to 400,000 members in 1998. Membership rates tend to be particularly high in the two countries which have the most pronounced neocorporatist structure, namely Austria and Sweden. Even in the 1980s more than one-fifth of the electorate in these two countries were

### Robert Michels (1876–1936)

A German political sociologist who spent most of his adult life in Italy, Michels was initially a socialist and a proponent of democracy but in his last years sympathised with Italian fascism. In his main book *Political Parties: A Sociological Study of the Oligarchical Tendencies of Modern Democracy*, originally published in 1911, he studied the reason why a full-blown democracy cannot be established. In his answer, he pointed to the structure of political parties and other large associations, taking the German Social Democratic Party as an exemplary case. According to Michels, the party had transformed itself from a socialist movement to a bureaucratic apparatus that was preoccupied in maintaining and enlarging its own power, neglecting the initial goals.

Michels argued that, with continuing existence and growth, informal groups become organised and eventually transform themselves into an oligarchy. The latter is marked by a clear separation between a few leaders and a mainly passive rank and file. The leaders are supported by a bureaucratic apparatus that, with its interest in self-maintenance, loses its zeal for radical change. Though Michels assumed that this trend is inevitable, he still advocated moderating the effects of this 'oligarchical illness' by educating the people. However, he was pessimistic about the chances of broad participation within political organisations, and democratic politics in general.

members of a party (see Table 5.1). By contrast, in West Germany, the UK, and the Netherlands, the rate of party membership was relatively low with 4.2, 3.3 and 2.8 per cent, respectively.

Considering changes over time, we see an overriding trend towards decreasing party membership (see Table 5.1). For Eastern Europe, there is little reliable data available. By and large, the old Communist parties and their direct successors have lost members, while at the same time a plethora of new parties have emerged which, taken together, are unlikely to outnumber the losses of the old parties. For example, the East German Communist Party, SED, had 2.2 million members before 1989, whereas its successor, the PDS, had only around 100,000 ten years later.

**Table 5.1**   Rate of party membership in eleven European countries (as a percentage of all electors per country)

|  | First election in 1960s | Last election in 1980s | Change |
|---|---|---|---|
| Austria | 26.2 | 21.8 | – 4.4 |
| Sweden | 22.0 | 21.2 | – 0.8 |
| Denmark | 21.1 | 6.5 | – 14.6 |
| Finland | 18.9 | 12.9 | – 6.0 |
| Norway | 15.5 | 13.5 | – 2.0 |
| Italy | 12.7 | 9.7 | – 3.0 |
| Netherlands | 9.4 | 2.8 | – 6.6 |
| UK | 9.4 | 3.3 | – 6.1 |
| Belgium | 7.8 | 9.2 | + 1.4 |
| West Germany | 2.5 | 4.2 | + 1.7 |
| Ireland | na | 5.3 | na |

*Source*: Budge et al. (1997) p. 215.

Although party membership is decreasing rather than increasing, and most of those who nominally are party members actually do not play an active role within the organisation, we should acknowledge the fact that a sizeable minority of the population continues to be involved in party politics. Many of them devote much time and energy in support of the party and their wider political beliefs. Just consider tens of thousands of party members who are elected to local and district councils who work, for the most part, not for their personal interest but for the sake of the party and, more generally, the community of citizens.

## Interest-group politics

The term 'interest groups' is used here in a wide sense, covering not only political pressure groups but also the great variety of formal and informal organisations in areas such as welfare, health, sports, education and religion. Many of these organisations are not, or are only occasionally, involved in politics. Since the writings of Alexis de Tocqueville, it has been repeatedly argued that the ensemble of these groups is vital for a working democracy because they express and enhance a sense of community. According to Robert Putnam (1993), these groups embody **social capital** and are crucial in 'making democracy work'. By contrast, societies in which the citizens are not embedded in such associational structures, but rather form a diffuse 'mass', have been perceived as inherently unstable and vulnerable to political alienation, sharp conflict and even dictatorship (Kornhauser, 1959). Other observers have been more sceptical about the flourishing of interest groups – not so much because of the sheer numbers of these groups, but rather because of the asymmetry of interest representation. In contrast to the assumptions of naive versions of pluralist theories, critical observers stress that not every interest in society is represented by a corresponding interest group, nor do the size of the groups and the intensity of their activities reflect the dimension and urgency of the problems that actually exist. Critics point to the fact that it is those interests that can easily be organised and have a great potential for conflict and disruption that dominate the political agenda. They are also likely to be favourably treated in political decision-making. The classic examples of this are the interest groups of employers and workers. In this particular case, because of their inherently conflictual if not antagonistic position, it is unlikely that one side will completely dominate the political game (Marsh, 1983), although studies have shown that the employers tend to be in a stronger position. This is also reflected at the level of EU policy-making (Schmitter and Streeck, 1991).

Another, clearly more problematic, case are the farmers, who, in some countries, have an extremely high organisational membership rate (Sweden nearly 100 per cent, Germany 90 per cent, England and Wales 80 per cent, France 75 per cent; Budge et al., 1997, p. 162) while at the same time lacking a direct and strong opponent representing organised citizens. Consumers' organisations are not in a position to provide this opposition. This has led to a situation where farmers' associations in some countries came close to dictating agricultural policy. No wonder that the agricultural sector was heavily subsidised. In the long run, however, this worked to the detriment of small farmers in particular; but, more generally, it was disadvantageous for entire national agricultural sectors. The constant flow of state subsidies prevented this sector from becoming more competitive. It is no coincidence that even today, and in spite of decades of criticism and many attempts to reform, about 50 per cent of the

**Social capital:** Two different meanings prevail. In the understanding of the French sociologist Pierre Bourdieu, social capital consists of an individual's intangible resources based on personal ties with other people – resources that can be used to enhance the individual's social status and career. The US political scientist David Putnam means by 'social capital' the associational life of a society that creates bonds of solidarity and a sense of responsibility for the common good and the functioning of democracy.

European Union's budget is devoted to financing agriculture, including the storage and destruction of overproduced goods. In a similar vein, the German coal industry was and still is heavily subsidised owing to the pressure of the mining industry. It produces at costs that are more than double world market prices.

While, as we have seen, some interests are powerfully represented and fiercely protected, others remain virtually invisible. This tends to be the case when the underlying problems are broad and diffuse, thus not fitting the relatively short perspective of electoral periods. An example of such a diffuse interest is the call to 'save the planet Earth' for future generations. Also, the interests of individuals who are structurally isolated from each other tend to be under-represented, such as those of consumers, women, and the unemployed. Finally, the same applies to the interests of those groups which are numerically and/or socially marginal and therefore have difficulties in getting a voice, such as asylum seekers and political prisoners. The situation worsens when the two latter criteria come together, as in the case of poor single mothers. In these situations, there is only hope if other, more central and more articulate, groups act as advocates for those who lack organisation and voice.

Broadly speaking, the field of interest groups is structured along the same societal cleavages as are expressed in the political party systems. Thus we find groups situated along the cleavages of the religious vs. the secular, centre vs. periphery, dominant vs. minority ethnic groups, and, most important, Left vs. Right. In contrast to the party system, which in most Western European states includes a very limited number of parties that claim competence in many if not all policy domains, the spectrum of interest groups comprises much more, and more specialised actors. Thus, in contrast to the political parties, interest groups tend to focus on a limited set of related issues. As a result, we find an amazing variety of interest groups, some of them consisting of many millions of people (e.g., automobile clubs), others gathering just a few dozen; some groups having a broad agenda, others being extremely specialised; some being close or even affiliated to an existing party, others carefully trying to remain independent from any party; some acting mainly in closed circles of lobbying, counselling and negotiating, others seeking public visibility and support.

Size of membership is one, but not always the most important, organisational resource to make an impact on public policy. If it were the most important, automobile clubs would have a tremendous say in politics. In practice, other often much smaller groups such as employer associations and trade organisations are likely to be of more importance when it comes to policy impacts. Bowles and Gintis (1986, p. 90), referring to the employers' liberty to invest or not invest, and to hire and fire, stress that the 'presumed sovereignty of the democratic citizenry fails in the presence of a capital strike' by potential investors.

Due to their distinct national traditions and economic and social structures, the relative size and importance of various kinds of interest group varies greatly from country to country – although countries akin to each other such as the Nordic states or Mediterranean states tend to show similar patterns. But we should also note that the aggregate membership in interest groups may vary greatly from country to country, and likewise the comparison of the same kinds of interest groups across countries.

The scattered data now available – ongoing research may soon produce rather better figures – suggests that many more people are engaged in interest groups than in political parties. This probably still holds when we take into account that an individual can be a member of only one political party but have multiple memberships in various interest groups. Based on the World Values Survey, we have rough indica-

**Table 5.2**   Organisational membership in interest groups (in percentages)

|  | Religious or church organisations | Trade unions | Political parties or groups | Professional associations | Sports or recreation |
|---|---|---|---|---|---|
| Belgium | 12.2 | 14.4 | 5.8 | 6.7 | 19.5 |
| Denmark | 6.7 | 49.0 | 6.5 | 12.1 | 33.5 |
| France | 6.2 | 5.2 | 2.7 | 5.0 | 15.7 |
| Germany | 15.9 | 15.7 | 7.5 | 8.9 | 32.3 |
| Great Britain | 16.6 | 14.4 | 4.9 | 9.8 | 16.9 |
| Ireland | 13.9 | 8.8 | 15.1 | 5.0 | 23.7 |
| Italy | 8.0 | 5.9 | 5.0 | 3.9 | 11.3 |
| Netherlands | 34.9 | 19.1 | 9.4 | 13.1 | 40.4 |
| Norway | 11.2 | 41.7 | 13.9 | 16.3 | 32.8 |
| Portugal | 10.5 | 4.5 | 4.0 | 3.5 | 11.5 |
| Spain | 5.2 | 2.7 | 1.8 | 2.7 | 4.9 |
| Sweden | 10.3 | 59.1 | 10.0 | 12.0 | 31.8 |
| USA | 48.7 | 8.9 | 14.5 | 15.2 | 20.3 |

*Sources*: Budge et al. (1997) p. 163; data from *European Values Study*, 1990.

tors of organisational membership in many countries of the western hemisphere. More recent data are also available for Eastern Europe which show a great variation in organisational membership across countries (Barnes, 1998). Table 5.2 shows the percentages of those belonging to different organisations in selected Western countries. Religious organisations, trade unions, sports or recreational groups, and professional organisations tend to outnumber party membership.

Though not all these groups are concerned with politics, and some only occasionally so, we can conclude that there exists an extremely rich and multi-faceted associational spectrum which creates both needs and opportunities for political participation. For the most part, participation in this context does not mean directly engaging in professional politics, but rather, taking part in societal activities, which, however, may have an indirect impact on policy-making. For example, the many voluntary associations active in matters of social welfare and health reduce the load and cost of state activities in these areas; successful strikes for higher wages in industry may increase production costs and thereby reduce the export of goods, which in turn decreases income from certain taxes and thus puts pressure on state finances. So even seemingly non-political activities are likely to have political consequences. Moreover, the sheer number and size of associations in one policy area may impress politicians so that they tend to take the claims of these associations into account.

Unfortunately, with a few exceptions, we do not yet know the precise international comparative data on trends in associational membership, so the current debate about an alleged decrease of 'social capital', that is, the positive effect of a rich associational life for the overall quality of democracy, cannot be settled. Based on somewhat sketchy and unsystematic data from the USA, the argument has been made that the sense of community and social responsibility, as indicated by participation in associ-

**Table 5.3**   Unionisation in Western and Eastern countries

**Trade union membership as per cent of the dependent labour force**

**Western European countries**

| | | | |
|---|---|---|---|
| Belgium | 47 | Ireland | 42 |
| Denmark | 87 | Italy | 39 |
| Germany (West) | 32 | Netherlands | 33 |
| France | 11 | Norway | 61 |
| Great Britain | 39 | Portugal | 25 |
| Greece | 17 | Spain | 15 |

**Eastern European countries**

| | | | |
|---|---|---|---|
| Albania | 61 | Latvia | 58 |
| Armenia | 34 | Lithuania | 14 |
| Belarus | 93 | Macedonia | 41 |
| Bulgaria | 48 | Moldova | 78 |
| Estonia | 44 | Poland | 23 |
| Euro-Russia | 80 | Romania | 46 |
| Georgia | 46 | Slovenia | 55 |
| Germany (East) | 39 | Ukraine | 82 |
| Hungary | 39 | | |

*Sources*: Budge et al. (1997) p. 170; data from *Eurobarometer*, 39 (Spring 1993); *Central and Eastern Eurobarometer* (Fall 1992).

ational life, is diminishing (Putnam, 1995). The decrease of party membership in most European countries, as well as the decrease of unionisation, suggests this argument may apply outside the USA. Unionisation in the former Communist regimes in Eastern Europe was traditionally high, particularly because it tended to be associated with certain privileges. With the fall of communism, union membership in Eastern Europe has drastically decreased, though it still tends to be higher than in Western Europe (see Table 5.3).

Union membership declined in most parts of Western Europe, including economically strong countries such as Great Britain, France, Italy, and the Netherlands (Budge, Newton et al., 1997, p. 172). With the exceptions of Finland, Sweden, Norway and Spain, membership was stable (Denmark) or decreasing across Western Europe between 1985 and 1995 (see Figure 5.1). In some countries, e.g. Italy, France and Great Britain, the considerable decline in union membership had already begun during the 1970s. In Great Britain, admittedly during the period of aggressive anti-union politics by the Thatcher government, the unions lost 2 million members (16.4 per cent) between 1979 and 1983 (Visser, 1986).

It would be risky, however, to use trends of party and union membership to draw more general conclusions about associational life. First, some associational sectors, such as nature conservation and environmentalism, have experienced significant growth in the last three decades. Secondly, new branches of associations are probably growing to a greater extent than some of the older branches are shrinking. Thirdly, the nature of associational life may be under-reported because membership, the category usually asked about in surveys, has a special meaning that does not necessarily

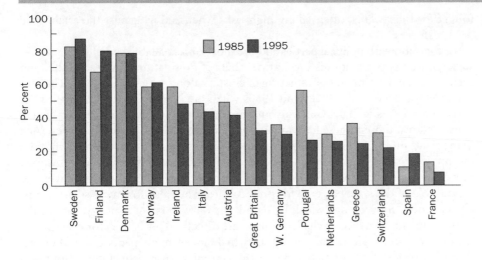

**Fig. 5.1** Union membership in Western Europe

fit the more informal adherence to, and type of, associations which seems to have become more common in recent decades. These associations, very similar to the social movements to be discussed next, tend to be networks of communication and action rather than formal interest groups. Let us now take a look at social movements and protest politics.

# Social movements and protest politics

In singling out social movements as a particular form of collective behaviour, we should not ignore the fact that they overlap with interest groups and political parties. In contrast to interest groups and parties, however, social movements tend to form loose networks without a clear-cut membership, a definite programme and statutes, and elected bodies. Social movements may incorporate organisations (such as parties and interest groups), but as a whole they do not form an organisation.

Major social movements may have a considerable life-span and attract large numbers of people, though these large numbers are typically only mobilised for distinct protest events and do not take part in the other less spectacular activities of such groups. Protest, of course, is not a privilege of social movements. Even well-established interest groups and political parties, sometimes even those in power, may engage occasionally in protest activities. However, in contrast to such established groups who usually have either institutionalised or other ways of access to the polity, social movements typically rely on protest because other channels of influence and pressure are not available.

As emphasised earlier in the chapter, the activities of social movements and protest groups (henceforth social movements) constitute an important, though often neglected, part of political participation. Social movements have brought about major changes in history, for example, the abolition of feudalism and slavery, the breakthrough of liberal democracy, the ending of colonial exploitation, the granting of full citizenship to women, and the fall of some Communist regimes in Eastern Europe. All this became possible only because millions of people stood up and fought for their rights, often taking high risks when acting against the established political forces.

In common with political parties and the more or less established interest groups, social movements are not distinct entities that act in isolation from each other and their wider environment, but rather form clusters along societal cleavages. This, for instance, was true in the 1920s and 1930s when fascist movements challenged the leftist movements in Italy, Germany and Spain. Today, we find similar conflictual constellations, though these tend to be more focused around particular issues, such as the rights of immigrants and asylum seekers, abortion, law and order, etc. Besides the opposition between movements and counter-movements, more often we see movements targeting the state, in particular the political elites in power. Given the central role of the state not only for political order but also for many societal conditions, social movements, which by definition want to change society, can hardly avoid trying to influence or challenge the state directly. This is true, for example, in conflicts around regional autonomy, in which social movements quite often act alongside regionalist parties to oppose the central government. Other groupings such as the women's movement also have to target the power-holders if they want to change the public policies which, taken together, have a great influence on women's condition of life (equal opportunity, equal pay, paternal leave, provision of child-care, opposition to rape and other forms of violence, and abortion).

How relevant in quantitative terms is participation in social movements when compared with political parties and interest groups? Large movement organisations, which come close to being regular interest groups, may comprise more than 100,000 regular supporters and many more sympathisers and/or donors. Greenpeace in Germany, for example, had more than 500,000 regular donors throughout the late 1980s and the 1990s. The activity of those donors, however, hardly goes beyond signing an annual cheque, so we may question whether this 'credit card participation' (Richardson, 1995) can be counted as true political participation. At the opposite end of the scale, we find numerous citizens' groups which, taken together over the full spectrum of political areas, may number as many as tens of thousands in the large European countries. A study on 'Left-alternative groups' in West Berlin identified more than 1,000 groups in 1993, focusing on new social movement issues such as peace, the environment, women, gay and lesbian rights, nuclear power, civil rights, and development in Third World countries (Rucht, Blattert and Rink, 1997).

A second source for identifying the activities of social movements is surveys. The Political Action Study (Barnes, Kaase et al., 1979), its follow-up study (Jennings, van Deth et al., 1990) and analyses based on the World Values Survey (Roller and Weßels, 1996) shed some light on the relevance of protest activities in various countries. The two main findings were that in all countries under investigation: (1) a sizeable minority of the population actually participated in various kinds of unconventional activities; and (2) many of the participants tended to combine conventional and unconventional forms, with very few (admitting to) having been involved in illegal activities. Over the period between 1974–5 and 1990–1, it was found that the proportion of people participating in unconventional activities continued to increase (Topf, 1995) (see Table 5.4).

Several surveys of the then EC countries in the 1980s also showed surprisingly high levels of support for various kinds of movements (conservation, environment, anti-nuclear, peace) in the Netherlands, Germany, France, Italy and Great Britain (Fuchs and Rucht, 1994). Some countries, in particular those which are economic-

**Table 5.4** Unconventional political participation (in percentages)

|  | United States | | | Great Britain | | | Germany | | | France | |
| --- | --- | --- | --- | --- | --- | --- | --- | --- | --- | --- | --- |
|  | 1975 | 1981 | 1990 | 1974 | 1981 | 1990 | 1974 | 1981 | 1990 | 1981 | 1990 |
| Sign a petition | 58 | 61 | 70 | 22 | 63 | 75 | 30 | 46 | 55 | 44 | 51 |
| Participate in lawful demonstration | 11 | 12 | 15 | 6 | 10 | 13 | 9 | 14 | 25 | 26 | 31 |
| Join in boycott | 14 | 14 | 17 | 5 | 7 | 14 | 4 | 7 | 9 | 11 | 11 |
| Participate in unofficial strike | 2 | 3 | 4 | 5 | 7 | 8 | 1 | 2 | 2 | 10 | 9 |
| Occupy building | 2 | 2 | 2 | 1 | 2 | 2 | * | 1 | 1 | 7 | 7 |
| Damage property | 1 | 1 | N.A. | 1 | 2 | N.A. | * | 1 | N.A. | 1 | N.A, |
| Personal violence | 1 | 2 | N.A. | * | 1 | N.A. | * | 1 | N.A. | 1 | N.A. |

*Sources*: 1974–5 Political Action Study; 1981 World Values Survey; 1990–91 World Values Survey. Drawn from Dalton (1996) p. 76.
*Note*: Table entries are the percentages who say they have participated in the activity. An asterisk denotes less than 1 per cent; N.A. denotes the question was not asked in this study.

ally least advanced, are almost consistently at the bottom (Portugal, Spain, Ireland) (see Table 5.5).

Probably the best indicator of the strength and development of various social movements is their actual protest activities as reported in daily newspapers. A comparative study on protest movements in France, Germany, the Netherlands, and Switzerland in the period from 1975 to 1989 found significant differences in the levels and thematic distribution of protests (Kriesi et al., 1995). The mobilisation in

**Table 5.5** Organisational membership in various groups and movements by country (in percentages)

|  | Third world development | Conservation, environment, ecology | Women's groups | Peace movement | Animal rights | Voluntary organisation concerned with health |
| --- | --- | --- | --- | --- | --- | --- |
| Belgium | 5.6 | 6.5 | 9.7 | 1.9 | 7.5 | 4.2 |
| Denmark | 2.8 | 7.6 | 1.7 | 2.1 | 4.1 | 5.8 |
| France | 2.6 | 2.3 | 1.0 | 0.5 | 2.3 | 2.8 |
| Germany | 2.2 | 4.6 | 5.6 | 2.0 | 4.8 | 4.4 |
| Great Britain | 2.0 | 5.6 | 4.8 | 1.1 | 1.9 | 3.5 |
| Ireland | 1.6 | 2.3 | 4.6 | 0.6 | 1.0 | 3.2 |
| Italy | 1.1 | 3.3 | 0.4 | 1.2 | 1.7 | 2.6 |
| Netherlands | 14.3 | 23.8 | 7.3 | 2.9 | 12.5 | 19.8 |
| Norway | 5.1 | 4.1 | 2.9 | 1.5 | 1.8 | 12.3 |
| Portugal | 0.5 | 0.8 | 0.2 | 0.4 | 0.8 | 2.7 |
| Spain | 1.0 | 1.4 | 0.7 | 0.7 | 0.9 | 1.6 |
| Sweden | 9.4 | 10.5 | 3.0 | 3.2 | 7.0 | 2.2 |
| USA | 2.0 | 8.4 | 8.4 | 2.0 | 5.5 | 7.4 |

*Sources*: Budge et al. (1997) p. 163; data from *European Values Study*, 1990.

**Table 5.6**   Volume of participation in four West European countries, 1975–89 (in 1000s per million inhabitants)

|  | France | Germany | Netherlands | Switzerland |
|---|---|---|---|---|
| 1. Nuclear weapons | 0.4 | 11.6 | 11.8 | 0.7 |
| 2. Other peace movement | 4.0 | 7.1 | 5.1 | 5.3 |
| 3. Nuclear energy | 12.8 | 12.8 | 5.1 | 7.2 |
| 4. Ecology movement | 4.4 | 11.3 | 8.0 | 10.6 |
| 5. Anti-racism | 4.8 | 8.7 | 4.5 | 0.8 |
| 6. Other solidarity movement | 4.4 | 6.3 | 13.2 | 15.2 |
| 7. Squatters' movement | 0.3 | 6.7 | 10.4 | 7.9 |
| 8. Other countercultural | 2.7 | 6.7 | 3.7 | 10.5 |
| 9. Homosexual movement | 0.8 | 0.3 | 2.0 | 0.7 |
| 10. Women's movement | 1.5 | 1.7 | 1.6 | 2.1 |
| **Total NSMs** | **36.1** | **73.2** | **65.4** | **61.0** |
| 11. Student movement | 4.8 | 1.5 | 2.2 | 0.2 |
| 12. Civil rights movement | 1.5 | 1.3 | 0.6 | 2.7 |
| 13. Foreigners | 2.5 | 4.2 | 7.1 | 8.5 |
| 14. Regionalist movement | 16.6 | 0.1 | 0.0 | 10.6 |
| 15. Education | 4.0 | 1.5 | 1.0 | 0.2 |
| 16. Farmers | 6.6 | 0.3 | 1.3 | 0.8 |
| 17. Labour movement | 10.1 | 4.3 | 9.2 | 3.7 |
| 18. Other Left | 2.0 | 3.9 | 2.4 | 2.4 |
| 19. Countermobilisation | 0.9 | 1.3 | 3.0 | 0.9 |
| 20. Right-wing extremism | 3.3 | 3.8 | 0.7 | 0.6 |
| 21. Other Right mobilisation | 2.6 | 1.9 | 1.0 | 2.0 |
| 22. Other mobilisation | 8.8 | 2.7 | 6.2 | 6.6 |
| **Total not-NSMs** | **63.9** | **26.8** | **34.6** | **39.0** |
| All mobilisation | 100.0% | 100.0% | 100.0% | 100.0% |
| N (number of events) | (2,132) | (2,343) | (1,319) | (1,215) |

*Note*: The squatters' movement includes actions for autonomous youth centres, mainly to be found in Switzerland. The category 'other countercultural' includes actions by groups like the Autonomen or terrorist organisations that are not directed at the goals of any of the other NSMs. 'Countermobilisation' refers to all actions directed against the new social movements listed in the table. Examples are demonstrations against abortion or in favour of nuclear energy. The category 'civil rights' includes actions against repression and state control to the extent that they are not part of the campaigns of the other movements. The category 'foreigners' refers to actions by residents of foreign origin, against both the regime in their country of origin and their treatment in the country of residence. The figures for the labour movement do not include strikes, but they include any other actions that may take place around strikes (for instance, factory occupations or demonstrations).

'unconventional' protest (such as collections of signatures, demonstrations, strikes, blockades, violent attacks) per million inhabitants was strongest in Germany (211,000), followed by the Netherlands (198,000), France (178,000) and Switzerland (156,000). When strikes are included, the volume of participation is highest in France, followed by Germany, the Netherlands and Switzerland (Kriesi et al., 1995, p. 22). If the issues of the new social movements are grouped together, they account for 73.2 per cent of all identified protests in West Germany but only 36.1 per cent in France. In measuring mobilisation, striking differences across the four countries can be seen (see Table 5.6).

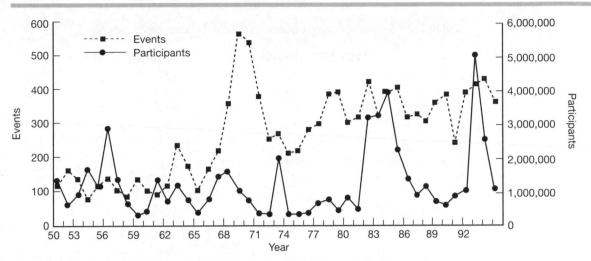

**Fig. 5.2** Protest events and participants in West Germany, 1950–94
*Source*: Prodat/Rucht.

In contrast to France, the peace movements in Germany and the Netherlands attracted many protesters. However, the student movement, the area of education, the labour movement and the anti-racist movement had most participants in France. Switzerland takes the lead for the solidarity and regionalist movements, whereas Germany ranks highest in mobilisation against nuclear-energy installations.

More detailed data covering the period from 1950 to 1994 for West Germany (including East Germany from 1989) show that the number of protests has increased each decade, while mobilisation in these protests followed a more discontinuous pattern, with the largest mobilisation during the 1980s (see Figure 5.2). The structure of protest in West Germany has changed considerably over these 45 years. The average size of protest was highest in the 1950s and lowest in the 1960s. Whereas protests in the 1950s were predominantly organised by single, national, interest groups, in later periods both informal groups and alliances of different kinds of groups moved into the foreground. Overall, issues of democracy and citizen participation, labour, and peace were most important, though their relative weight changed over time. While during the 1970s and 1980s most protests centred around new social-movement issues, in the 1990s 'bread-and-butter issues' (unemployment, housing, welfare) and – partly related to that – conflicts around right-wing extremism and immigrants became important in East Germany and, to a lesser extent, in West Germany where new social-movement issues continued to be significant. The distribution of forms of protest activities has also changed over time. Most importantly, the proportion of violent events increased (see Table 5.7). The extraordinary rise in the 1990s is almost exclusively due to right-wing extremism and xenophobia. We should also note, however, that compared with the other activities, very few people participated in all kinds of violent events and, moreover, mobilisation *against* right-wing extremism and xenophobia by far outnumbered the opposite forces.

The growing relevance of movement and protest politics, sometimes perceived as a result of the failure of political parties (Lawson, 1988; Kitschelt, 1990; Richardson, 1995), has raised the question of whether some countries are on their way to becoming 'movement societies' (Neidhardt and Rucht, 1993; Tarrow, 1994; Meyer and Tarrow, 1997). It seems that protest that previously was more concentrated in

**Table 5.7**   Types of protest activities in West Germany (per cent)

|                | 1950–59 | 1960–69 | 1970–79 | 1980–89 | 1990–94 |
|----------------|---------|---------|---------|---------|---------|
| Appeal         | 29.5    | 44.4    | 36.4    | 16.9    | 13.7    |
| Procedural     | 5.2     | 5.1     | 6.1     | 2.9     | 2.2     |
| Demonstrative  | 55.0    | 36.7    | 43.5    | 55.8    | 57.2    |
| Confrontational| 7.4     | 9.2     | 9.8     | 14.4    | 11.9    |
| Violent        | 2.9     | 4.6     | 4.3     | 10.0    | 15.1    |
| **Total**      | **100** | **100** | **100** | **100** | **100** |
| N              | 1,133   | 2,544   | 2,990   | 3,512   | 1,847   |

*Source*: Prodat/Rucht.

particular social strata has spread out to many groups in society, including even re-latively privileged groups such as teachers, dentists, and airline pilots. Obviously, the threshold for engagement in protest politics has lowered. At the same time, distinct forms of protest are no longer bound to particular issues and social groups. Sit-ins and blockades that used to be the tactics of civil-rights groups are also practised by conservative protesters. Previously unconventional forms of protest have become 'normalised' (Fuchs, 1991) so that the distinction between conventional and un-conventional participation is gradually becoming meaningless. Modern means of communication have contributed to diffuse protest within and across national boundaries and some groups, most notably Greenpeace, have become professionals in the staging of protests and, through their sophisticated public-relations work, are widely known. Moreover, these groups tend to be more trusted by the populace than established political forces. Overall it seems that protest politics has become a com-mon practice that complements rather than competes with the more established forms of political participation.

# Mass media

Modern politics, including most forms of political participation, is strongly shaped by the mass media (Lichtenberg, 1990). Clearly the mass media are in a different position from parties, interest groups and social movements because they are not primarily created to influence political decisions, let alone to achieve political power. However, most of our information about political issues, players, and activities and decisions comes from, or is transmitted by, the media. Protest, for example, is prac-tically non-existent for those who are not participants or bystanders unless it is reported in the media. It follows that most political activities are geared to receiving (positive) media coverage.

As many studies have shown, the media do not just mirror but also shape de-velopments. In other words, they select, comment, evaluate, take part and are some-times partisan in political matters. Thus, at least in some instances, the media participate in political matters in very similar ways to, say, interest groups. This is most obvious when the media are directly concerned, for example, when it comes to defending the freedom of the press and access to information. But they also play a political role in many other instances: they may more or less openly favour a political candidate or party during an electoral campaign, as was the case with the UK tabloid newspaper *The Sun*, which bluntly supported the Conservative Margaret Thatcher in the late 1970s but Tony Blair's New Labour in the late 1990s – as long as he did not stray too far from the owner's (Rupert Murdoch) views on Europe.

A second reason why the media have implications for political participation is that they can provide a crucial forum for various kinds of political actors. Although the mass media establish a structural asymmetry between the few who are audible and visible and the millions who merely read, listen or watch, the media can choose whether or not to accept advertisements from political groups, and can give a voice to protest groups or individual citizens as well as to key figures, invite letters to the editors, organise debates and political talk-shows, etc. Thus the media themselves can contribute to strengthening the idea of active citizenship or, alternatively, rely mainly on prefabricated statements issued by the professional public relations units of the established players.

Compared with the early decades of the twentieth century when most mass media were closely bound to, if not directly controlled by, particular political groups, the mass media have become more independent and probably more balanced in their views *in so far as they follow an ethos of professional journalism*. Related to this, it also appears that relevant parts of the mass media put more emphasis on their role in providing a forum for information, debate and deliberation rather than perceiving themselves as educators, tutors, agitators or entertainers of the 'masses'. This complements a perception of citizens as not restricted merely to the role of selecting between competing sets of political elites. By and large it seems that the mass media mirror and shape the trend towards a more active citizenship, though we should not forget the existence of segments that are deplorable if our ideal is to encourage an informed and active citizenship.

## ■ Towards a participatory society

1  How high a value is placed on political participation depends on the view we take about what democracy ought to be like. On the one hand, proponents of a purely representative model tend to reduce the political activity of the ordinary citizen to the act of voting. In this perspective, the citizen has the right and duty to select the political leadership which, to judge by its professionalism, expertise, and relative detachment from any particular social group, is likely to take the best decisions. Hence intensive participation should be reserved for a relatively small elite. On the other hand, proponents of an 'associative' (Hirst, 1994), 'strong' (Barber, 1985), and **participatory democracy** (Pateman, 1970) tend to perceive high levels of participation as an expression of a healthy democracy. In this perspective, participation is not only a means to reach certain goals but a goal in itself, that is, a desirable form of political life. Although it has been argued that low levels of participation may indicate high levels of satisfaction among the citizenry, this is not substantiated by empirical evidence (Dalton, 1996). In fact low participation seems to indicate disappointment, apathy and political alienation among those who stand aside from the political process. Typically, these are the people who are less privileged, educated, and articulate, so their interests are further marginalised by their low voice (Key, 1958; pp. 642–3; see also Lijphart, 1997). Based on his secondary analysis of various

**Participatory democracy:** This connotes decentralisation of power for the direct involvement of amateurs in authoritative decision-making.

surveys, Dalton (1996, p. 79) concluded that 'protest is more common among the better educated'. Hence both high and socially broad levels of participation should be considered as a strength rather than disregarded. An active and informed citizenry is an asset for the quality and stability of democracy. It may prevent elites from pursuing essentially their own interests, and it may contribute to a more balanced sharing of responsibility within the community – from the local to the international levels.

Looking back over history, the evolution of modern democracy can be interpreted as a process of the progressive inclusion of groups that were initially perceived as not worthy and/or not capable of taking part in the political process (Dryzek, 1996). Having reached a stage where, with the exception of a few borderline cases, all social groups in the Western World have acquired the right to vote, we should encourage people to broaden and intensify political participation so that we come closer to the meaning of democracy as 'the rule of the people by the people for the people'.

2   Historically, modern political parties, interest groups and social movements have emerged and developed largely in parallel to each other, so that their development has not been a 'zero sum game' in which one player can only gain at the expense of the others. We have no reasons to assume that the growth of one type of actor is inherently bound to the stagnation or decline of another. Moreover, it seems that many people tend to combine participation in these different structures according to their strategic assessments of their situation and needs. Finally, it appears that the borderlines between these three forms are blurring – thus, parties and interest groups tend to adopt forms of protest politics, whereas protest groups tend to seek close alliances with parties and interest groups. Also, we should not forget that many established parties and interest groups are outgrowths of social movements.

3   Parties, interest groups, movements, and the mass media are located in the public sphere, where they mediate between individual citizens and the political decision-makers. Though these systems of interest may empirically overlap, they have distinct functions and properties and so cannot replace each other. Therefore, from an analytical perspective, they should be conceived as distinct entities. With regard to the politically oriented segments of the mass media, this seems to be relatively clear. They are, for the most part, commercial enterprises whose main function is to report and comment on news. In contrast to the three other systems, the mass media relatively rarely act politically to further their own interests.

We can conceptualise the structural location of parties, interest groups and movements in a model of interest mediation as illustrated in Figure 5.3. At the centre of the model is the public domain, to which, in principle, every actor has access. The non-public environment of this domain is composed of two spheres that form separate worlds and have to be bridged by the four systems of interest mediation. One sphere is that of the private life-world of the citizens; the other is composed of the segments of the political–administrative system that are kept apart from the public, in particular the state bureaucracies. Other parts of the state, most notably parliament and the courts, are to a large extent part of the public domain.

The systems of interest mediation which are more or less centred in the public domain have differential reaches in each domain. Parties tend to be less strongly anchored in the social milieux of citizens, but reach far into the realm of the state, including its non-public institutional settings. In some countries, such as Austria and Sweden, there are even fears that parties have achieved a quasi-statist role. Parties are also distinct in that they not only transfer the demands of the citizens into the

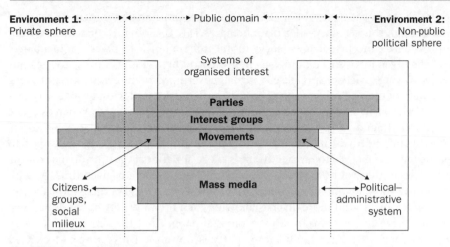

**Fig. 5.3** A model of interest mediation
*Source*: adapted from Rucht (1995) p. 108.

decision-making systems but, at least as governmental parties, they also try to legit-imise political decisions and, quite often, to defend the state's interest *vis-à-vis* challenging groups. Thus there is a two-way process of interest mediation.

Interest groups tend to be more symmetrically centred in the public domain, having both roots in the social milieux of the citizens and some leverage within the state institutions, though not to the same extent as political parties (for example, associations are not officially represented in parliaments).

Social movements are probably the most strongly embedded in the life-world of the citizens, and claim to be their most authentic voice, but have hardly any access to state institutions.

Finally, the mass media certainly have links to both environments of the public sphere, but do not tend to have significant overlaps with them. Instead, the mass media concentrate on reporting what is going on in the public sphere and therefore attentively watch the other systems of interest mediation, including the public parts of the political–administrative system.

4    As far as empirical data are available, they suggest that political participation is increasing rather than decreasing in most European countries. Moreover, it seems plausible that political participation is unlikely to recede even though we have witnessed, more recently, decreasing participation in some groups and some areas. First, according to survey data, interest in politics is stable or even tending to increase. In addition, more and more people are drawn into higher education. We know that there exists a strong correlation between education, interest in politics, and political participation.

Secondly, the technical means and the facilities both to follow and to intervene in political matters are becoming more easily available, cheaper and more efficient. Given modern techniques of communication, it is not difficult to organise a group, to produce a newsletter, and to reach people by other channels of communication. Not surprisingly, the fax and, more recently, the internet are becoming important tools for mobilisation among protest groups.

Last, but not least, we have witnessed a diversification of social groups and group-specific needs and claims which cannot easily be adopted and promoted at an aggregated level. Today, it is very difficult to identify the common denominator of a social class. Though this category is far from being useless, it is obvious that we also need more specific concepts such as 'socio-moral milieux' or 'life-styles' to adequately cover the diversity of social positions, interests and behaviours. Similar to the constantly growing variety of specialised journals covering virtually every aspect of social life, we also witness a proliferation of groups, both outside and within broader associations, which articulate very specific political demands and critiques. Whereas in the late nineteenth and early twentieth centuries political activism was usually closely bound to embeddedness in a distinct ideological camp, which, in turn, was bound to a particular social class, today's activism is more situational and contingent on the specificities of the groups to which we currently feel close at any given time. As with the growing volatility of rational voters, other forms of political participation also become more flexible and more diverse, allowing for a broad variety of combinations.

Considering these trends, it also becomes apparent that the act of voting every few years for a particular candidate or party is not an effective way to feed very specific interests into the political process. Firstly, we can only vote for parties as a whole, whereas ideally we would wish to combine some aspects from one manifesto with other aspects from other manifestos. Secondly, voting results at best only vaguely indicate a certain direction in which the majority wants to see things move – they are certainly not a clear instruction regarding the whole variety of policy matters at stake. Because the act of voting closely resembles signing a blank sheet of paper whose text will only take shape afterwards, other forms of participation in concrete policies in particular settings and at critical points of time become more and more important.

5　Even though societal conditions for increased political participation in Europe may be favourable today and in the foreseeable future, it is clear that participation has its limits for several reasons. First, the time an individual can spend on political participation is restricted to the extent that people have to work and fulfil their other daily duties. Secondly, participation in modern policy-making requires one to have specific knowledge and skills in order to be recognised as a serious player and eventually become influential in specific policy areas. Thus, even when better equipped than ever, we may restrict participation to those questions we are most familiar and/or concerned with, while in many other areas we tend to rely on some sort of representatives, not necessarily elected politicians, who supposedly express and promote our interests without our explicit instructions. Closely related to this is the fact that many political matters are influenced by non-local and even international factors beyond our immediate field of vision and control. At these higher levels, however, it becomes more difficult to participate. Although some groups, particularly international non-governmental actors, try to follow and adapt to this shift towards higher levels of decision-making (Greenwood and Aspinwall, 1998; della Porta, Kriesi and Rucht, 1999), they tend to do so as small circles of political entrepreneurs acting on behalf of a diffuse audience of supporters who may or may not applaud but have no real say within the organisation, as the case of environmentalists suggests (Rootes, 1999). A striking example of this is Greenpeace – a highly professional organisation supported by many donors but essentially lacking the rank-and-file that would represent the organisation below the national level. These difficulties in participating as a lay-person in national and international politics probably also account for the fact that, in spite of the fashionable talk about globalisation, the cross-national co-operation of

### Jürgen Habermas (born 1927)

Born in Germany, a philosopher, sociologist and political commentator in the tradition of leftist Critical Theory. He is preoccupied with two concerns: first, the analysis and critique of modern capitalist societies; secondly, the study of the normative, legal and empirical foundations of modern democracy. Inspired by the principles underlying an 'ideal speech situation', that is a discourse ruled by nothing else than the 'power of the better argument', Habermas, in political terms, advocates an enlightened citizenry that actively takes part in public life and political decisions, and a procedural rationality of political decision-making that, on crucial issues, is ultimately based on universal values instead of a mere compromise between conflicting interests. In his two-volume book *The Theory of Communicative Action*, originally published in 1981, Habermas argues that societal systems such as the economy (ruled by money) and the state (ruled by power) tend to colonise and undermine the 'life-world', which is geared towards 'communicative' as opposed to instrumental and strategic action. In his more recent work, Habermas acknowledges the role of associational groups at the periphery of the political system as critics and challengers of those groups who are essentially power-oriented.

many political groups is still very moderate and, as the German case demonstrates, protest activity continues to concentrate on sub-national levels. Also EU-related protest has increased to a much smaller degree than one might expect (Tarrow, 1995).

6   Sceptics such as the German sociologist Niklas Luhmann (1969) have argued that demanding intense participation for everybody in every political decision would mean installing frustration as a principle. Others, such as Jürgen Habermas (1992; see also the epigraph at the beginning of the chapter), without denying the advantages of the division of labour in economy and politics, advocate broad participation at least in those matters which are crucial for an order that deserves to be called democratic.

## ■ Summary

◆ Political participation needs to be defined broadly. Power and political cleavages are significant dimensions and forms of participation.

◆ There are three major frameworks for political participation: party politics and voting behaviour, interest group politics, and social movement and protest politics.

◆ Political participation in Europe varies considerably in form and degree, ranging from voting to violent protest, concentrating in some countries mainly on institutionalised participation while in other countries also including substantial elements of protest politics.

◆ The activities of these frameworks of participation, as well as parliamentary and governmental actions, are presented to a wider public via the mass media. These, though not allowing for much citizen participation, play a crucial role in providing information about the political process and linking the citizens with the state.

◆ The complex interplay between various political actors can be represented in a model of interest representation that puts the activities in the public sphere at the centre of the political process.

◆ Extensive use of different forms of participation is an asset rather than a danger to viable democracies.

## Questions for discussion

▶ What are the characteristics of political parties, interests groups and social movements?

▶ What are the main political cleavages in modern European democracies?

▶ In which respects do patterns of political participation in Eastern and Western Europe differ?

▶ Are political parties sufficient to make democracy work?

▶ Why are the mass media important for the political process?

▶ Is broad political participation a danger to democracy?

## Further reading

Budge, Ian, Kenneth Newton et al. (1997) *The Politics of the New Europe: Atlantic to Urals* (London and New York: Longman). A solid and encompassing introduction with many empirical data, including aspects of political participation.

Dalton, Russell J. (1996) *Citizen Politics: Public Opinion and Political Parties in Advanced Industrial Democracies*, 2nd edition (Chatham, NJ: Chatham House). A comprehensive discussion of the involvement of citizens in the political process, including the politics of parties and social movements.

Greenwood, Justin and Mark Aspinwall (eds) (1998) *Collective Action in the European Union* (London and New York: Routledge). An up-to-date collection of essays on various aspects of collective political participation in the EU.

Marsh, Allan, Samuel H. Barnes and Max Kaase (1990) *Political Action in Europe and the USA* (London: Macmillan). A shortened version of the Political Action Study whose first results were published in 1979.

Roller, Edeltraud and Berhard Weßels (1996) 'Contexts of Political Protest in Western Democracies: Political Organization and Modernity', pp. 91–134, in Frederick Weil et al. (eds), *Extremism, Protest, Social Movements, and Democracy: Research on Democracy and Society*, vol. 3 (Greenwich/London: JAI Press). A broad cross-national comparison of the extent and underlying factors of political protest.

van Deth, Jan (ed.) (1997) *Private Groups and Public Life: Social Participation and Political Involvement in Representative Democracies* (London: Routledge). A collection of informative articles covering a broad range of aspects of political participation with special emphasis on European countries.

# Government and Politics

Thomas Saalfeld

'In framing a government to be administered by men over men, the great difficulty lies in this: you must first enable the government to control the governed; and in the next place oblige it to control itself.'

JAMES MADISON, *Federalist Papers*, 51

## Contents

## Introduction: government and politics in a changing world

Our perceptions of the state and the political institutions governing states are changing. Phenomena such as globalised economic competition, the expanding role of world financial markets, the growing importance of multinational corporations, the activities of transnational social movements, regional co-operation across national borders, European integration and the growing importance of international organisations appear to undermine the power of nation-states and national governments. In addition to such challenges from the supra-national level, the nation state and national governments are challenged by the growing demands of actors at the sub-national level such as regions or particular linguistic or ethnic communities. New social movements have challenged the monopoly of 'conventional' politics and politicians (see Chapter 5). National political institutions are increasingly locked into the role of one actor amongst many in a number of networks made up of interest-group representatives and bureaucrats. Elected governments in Europe may seem to be no longer fully 'in charge'. Their role often seems to be no more than that of a co-ordinator in a multitude of overlapping networks.

Such developments challenge both the legitimacy and the efficiency of government institutions at the national level. Nevertheless, the national governments of Europe continue to dominate policy-making at the domestic level and have remained important actors on the international stage. They participate in the shaping of the rules of international politics. Their legislation continues to shape policy at the national level. They still have tremendous powers to raise revenue and redistribute resources. Figures 6.1 and 6.2 illustrate the share of **gross domestic product (GDP)** various European governments raised (mainly through taxation) and spent in 1997. Figure 6.1 shows that in 1997 European governments were able to extract substantial shares of the national GDP through taxation. The highest levels of taxation occurred in

**Gross domestic product (GDP):** Common indicator of the level of a country's economic activity. It represents the total value of the goods and services produced by a country's economy during a specified period of time excluding the income of the country's residents from investment abroad.

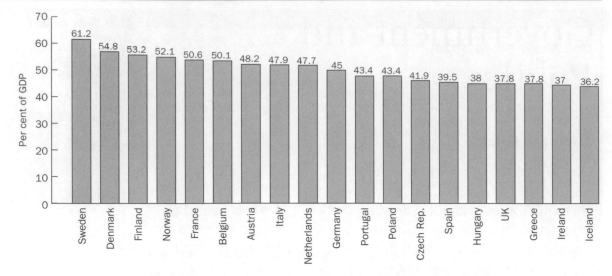

**Fig. 6.1** General government current receipts in 19 European states, 1997

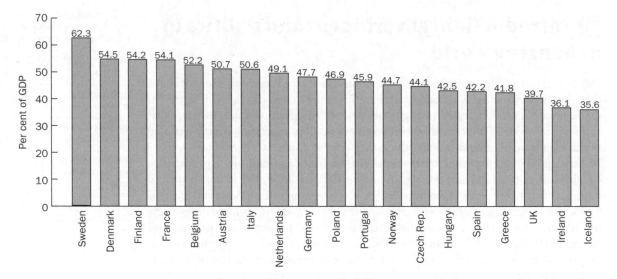

**Fig. 6.2** General government total outlays in 19 European states, 1997

Sweden where the government raised revenues and undertook expenditure (outlays) worth over 60 per cent of that nation's GDP. The lowest level occurred in Iceland but revenue still accounted for over one-third of GDP (36.2 per cent) and government spending in proportion to GDP amounted to over 35 per cent. Although the extent of government involvement in the economy varies considerably across European countries, it is substantial everywhere.

Although national governments continue to influence their citizens' lives, national political institutions are deeply affected by the developments mentioned above. The nature of governing has changed. It has become more complex and less hierarchical. Governments are less able to impose policies 'from above' as in the 1950s. They have

## Max Weber (1864–1920)

German sociologist and political economist who is best known for his thesis of the 'Protestant ethic', relating Protestantism to capitalism, and for his studies of bureaucracy. Through his insistence on an objective and value-free approach to scholarship and his analysis of social action in terms of individual perceptions and meanings, Weber profoundly influenced sociological theory. Apart from his academic work he played an important role in German public debate between 1916 and 1918 when he argued in favour of a strengthening of parliament and assisted in the drafting of the German constitution of 1919. His most influential academic works include *The Protestant Ethic and the Spirit of Capitalism* (1902) and *Economy and Society* (published posthumously in 1922).

'become more coordinating bodies, seeking to ensure that their country's firms and people (or most of them) can prosper in an era of global competition' (Hague et al., 1998, p. 39).

Elected politicians find it increasingly difficult to understand and influence, let alone control, the complex bargaining processes between governments, bureaucracies, regulatory agencies and interest groups at the national, sub-national and supra-national levels ('multi-level bargaining'). Citizens find these processes even more opaque. This raises the serious question of whether, and how, citizens can learn what they need to know in order to participate meaningfully in democratic politics in an increasingly complex political environment (Lupia and McCubbins, 1998). To whom are government agencies politically accountable? How can a degree of demo-cratic 'control', accountability and responsiveness be maintained under such circum-stances? How can Madison's 'dilemma', expressed in the epigraph at the beginning of this chapter, be 'solved' under such circumstances?

In many ways this raises a fundamental political question that was posed by Max Weber (see Portrait 6.1) a century ago. He observed the growing importance of experts, technocrats and bureaucrats in the modern world and considered this a challenge for democracy. He recognised the tension between the efficiency of bureaucratic rule on the one hand, and popular political participation on the other. Modern democracies cannot be run efficiently without delegating powers to experts in political and bureaucratic organisations. Bureaucratic organisations in his sense include not only public administration and government agencies, but also major in-terest groups and political parties. Weber predicted a growing tendency for politics to be dominated by bureaucrats rather than by publicly accountable politicians. There have been many valid criticisms of aspects of Weber's work on bureaucracy. Nevertheless, the fundamental problem remains a perennial one for students of government and politics and has been severely compounded by developments such as the ones sketched above.

How serious are these challenges to modern European democracies? What insti-tutional arrangements do different political systems use to cope with these problems – and to what effect? The aim of this chapter is to compare and analyse the main features of European governments from this important perspective: to what extent do different political systems offer solutions to Madison's problem of **accountability** and Weber's related problem of bureaucratic rule? To what extent are they responsive

**Accountability:** The requirement for agents (or representatives) to answer to the principals (or represented) on the exercise of their powers and duties. Political systems typically employ certain institutional arrangements ('mechanisms' such as parliamentary investigations, public inquiries, ministerial responsibility, collective responsibility, etc.) to ensure at least a degree of accountability.

**Technocratic rule:** A tendency in complex, modern states to delegate more and more powers to bureaucratic experts rather than elected politicians, who cannot match the former's expertise.

to popular preferences? What scope is there for democratic political leadership (rather than bureaucratic or **'technocratic' rule**) and how effectively are political leaders held to account? What are the costs and benefits of different forms of political delegation and accountability?

The citizens of European states do not govern themselves. All European countries are representative democracies, albeit with varying degrees of direct popular participation. In all European countries, citizens delegate political authority to representatives, whose task it is to act on behalf and in the best interest of 'their' citizens. In most European states they elect parliamentary assemblies which then choose a head of government. Heads of government delegate authority to individual cabinet ministers who are in charge of specialised departments of state. Together with the members of parliament and the heads of governments, these ministers make political decisions. Yet they usually transfer the authority to carry out these decisions to appointed officials: civil servants and executive agencies.

The processes of delegation do not end with a transfer of authority. Those who delegate power and authority want to make sure that it is used in their best interest. They want to hold those on whom they confer authority accountable. Yet, accountability is highly problematic. Certainly, voters can choose not to re-elect a member of parliament who is perceived not to have represented their local interests faithfully. How do voters know whether or not their representative has done a good job? Many of them do not have enough time and expertise, and most do not have access to detailed information about their representative's performance. If they did have the resources they might not wish to concentrate them on monitoring their elected representatives. The same problem occurs at other levels of the political process: members of parliament delegating authority to a prime minister and a cabinet do not have the expertise and resources to obtain sufficiently accurate information on their behaviour. Ministers will find it almost impossible to monitor the behaviour of civil servants and executive agencies in charge of carrying out their policies. In fact they depend on civil servants to formulate their policies in the first place. In this chapter we follow through the whole chain of democratic delegation and accountability and look at the nature of delegation and its implications for democratic accountability at each stage.

## How citizens express their political preferences: direct versus representative democracy

Democracy, as one textbook author (Heywood, 1997, p. 66) remarks, 'links government to the people' and he adds that 'this link can be forged in a number of ways: government of, by and for the people'. It is clear that most modern democracies in Western Europe are not governed directly by the people themselves. There are obvious practical reasons for this: many citizens do not have the time, expertise, experience and political judgement to make political decisions on complex issues themselves. In politics as in all other organisations, delegation of powers to specialists (e.g., elected politicians or civil servants) can be highly beneficial for the citizens. Although there is considerable variation between individual democracies, only a handful of European constitutions allow 'the people' to participate directly and continuously in decisions over public policy, usually in the form of referendums (see below). All European democracies are representative democracies where elected officials act as 'agents' who 'represent' the interests of a 'principal', namely the citizens. 'In **representative government**', as Hague, Harrop and Breslin (1998, p. 22) point out, 'decisions are reached by politicians elected to act on behalf of the voters.'

## Direct participation through referendums

Nevertheless, most European democracies do allow some elements of direct popular participation in issues of public policy. The extent to which this is the case varies considerably. There is a great variety of different forms of popular participation in public policy, such as referendums and popular initiatives (see Box 6.1). Referendums may allow voters to decide on public policy and other important issues directly.

---

### Box 6.1

### Referendums and popular initiatives

*Referendums* and *popular initiatives* are the most important mechanisms by which voters may participate directly in public policy-making and make choices between alternative policy proposals.

In a *referendum* the initiative to put a question to the voters does not rest with the voters themselves. A referendum

- may be initiated by the government or the parliamentary majority (as in the United Kingdom),
- may be initiated by a constitutionally specified parliamentary minority, or
- may be mandatory on certain specified issues such as constitutional amendments or major international treaties (as in Denmark).

In the case of *popular initiatives*, the right to initiate a popular vote on a matter of public policy rests with a specified number of *voters*. An issue will be put before the electorate if a specified number or percentage of signatures can be obtained from voters in a specified time period.

Referendums and popular initiatives can be called 'decisive', if the result of the vote binds the government. They are 'advisory' if it is up to the government or the parliamentary majority to decide whether or not it will accept the expressed will of the people (Möckli, 1998, p. 91).

---

Referendums have a number of advantages:

- They allow citizens to decide a political issue directly.
- They may ensure that elected politicians do not lose touch with voters' preferences.
- They may enhance democratic accountability: campaigns conducted in the context of referendums can be an important device for informing citizens about major issues of public policy.
- Some forms of referendum can be an important institutional check on the power of elected governments and can increase the government's political accountability to the people.

On the other hand, referendums as instruments of **direct democracy** also have a number of disadvantages:

- If the electorate decides an issue, this is usually at the expense of other constitutional bodies such as parliaments. Parliamentary minorities may use the referendum to

**Representative government:** A form of government where a legislature with significant decision-making power is freely elected. Political decisions are made by elected representatives on behalf of the represented.

**Direct democracy:** A form of government where those entitled to decide do so directly in sovereign assemblies or referendums.

**First-past-the-post electoral system** A way of describing simple-plurality electoral systems. They are commonly used to allocate seats in single-member districts. In order to win a seat, a candidate is required to get more votes than each of the others (plurality). The candidate is not required to have the vote of a majority of those voting in the constituency. In Europe, the simple-plurality system is used only in the United Kingdom. Its main advantage is its simplicity. Its main disadvantage is that it is likely to produce disproportionate outcomes.

**Second ballot systems:** A form of plurality or majority electoral system requiring a winning candidate to get a majority of the votes cast (50 per cent of the vote in a constituency plus 1) in a first round. If no candidate gains a majority of the votes in the first round, a second ballot is held for the strongest of the first-round candidates. This system is used in France. The candidate with the plurality of votes wins this second ballot.

**Alternative vote (AV):** Electoral system where voters rank the candidates in single-member districts according to their preferences. In a first step, all first preferences are counted, and any candidate with more than half of the votes is elected. If no candidate achieves half of the vote, the candidate with fewest first preferences is eliminated and their second preferences are redistributed. This is repeated with third, fourth, etc. preferences as often as required until a candidate wins more than half of the valid votes. AV is used in elections to the Australian parliament.

**Proportional representation (PR):** Electoral systems with multi-member districts, in which parties are represented in an assembly in proportion to their overall electoral strength. Most continental West European electoral systems (except France and Italy) are more or less pure systems of proportional representation.

**Party list systems:** A proportional electoral system which distributes the seats on a national (such as in Russia and the Netherlands) or regional

overturn a legitimate decision taken by the parliamentary majority or destabilize the government. It is often said that in the first German republic, the 'Weimar Republic', extremist parties used referendums to destabilise democracy, for example.

- Frequently referendums acquire the character of a general popular vote of confidence or no-confidence in the government rather than the expression of a political preference on a specific policy issue.

- The parliamentary majority only has an incentive to use a referendum if it expects political benefits from it. If it is in political difficulties, a successful referendum may give it renewed popular legitimacy and respect at home and abroad. It will then find it difficult to resist the temptation to 'secure the desired result of referendums by controlling their timing and wording' (Hague, Harrop and Breslin, 1998, p. 108).

- Where it is easy for minorities to request a referendum, or the support required to initiate a popular initiative is low, governing may become a very difficult and time-consuming process. It may be difficult to make vital but unpopular decisions at all, and governments may find it difficult to pursue coherent policies.

For these reasons, referendums and popular initiatives usually supplement representative forms of government in exceptional circumstances rather than replacing them. All modern democracies are representative democracies: they are systems of government in which – at least ideally – 'the popular majority, through its elected representatives in the legislative branch, effectively controls public policy' (Strøm, 1995, p. 53).

## Electoral systems

In representative democracies, competitive, free and fair elections are the most important way for voters to express their political preferences and delegate their right to make public policy to elected politicians for a specified period of time. Elections are the most important mechanisms for citizens to choose politicians as their agents and to hold them to account. The citizens' opportunities to influence the selection and election of persons who represent them are constrained by the nature of the electoral system, that is, the way in which votes for a candidate or party are 'translated' into parliamentary seats.

There are a number of basic requirements for a democratic electoral process: for elections to be competitive, citizens must have a choice between several parties or candidates, and their vote must potentially have an influence on the composition of the parliamentary assembly. The 'unity lists' used in most 'people's democracies' of Eastern Europe before 1989/90 would not qualify as competitive elections as the percentage of seats for each party was largely predetermined. For elections to be free, certain civil liberties must be guaranteed: freedom of speech, freedom of association, freedom to register as a voter, party or candidate, freedom from coercion, freedom of access to the polls, confidentiality of the vote, and the freedom to complain. For elections to be fair they must be administered in a non-partisan fashion. There must be universal suffrage. Reporting by the media (especially electronic media) must be balanced, the counting of the vote must be open and transparent and parties must be treated equitably both by the government and by other public authorities. Fraud and vote-rigging are not permissible (Hague, Harrop and Breslin, 1998, p. 99; Taagepera and Shugart, 1989, pp. 11–18). In Western Europe, the freedom and fairness of elections

**Portrait 6.2**

## Maurice Duverger (born 1917)

A French political scientist who is best known for his work on French politics and his comparative work on party organisation and party systems, especially the link between electoral systems and the shape of party systems. His thesis that the plurality vote strongly favours the development of a two-party system while proportional systems of representation (PR) favour the development of a multi-party system is sometimes referred to as 'Duverger's law'. Duverger is Professor

Emeritus of Political Sociology and Economics at the Sorbonne, University of Paris I. He has also been a member of the European Parliament. His most influential academic works include *Political Parties: Their Organization and Activity in the Modern State* (English translation, 1954), a classic of modern party theory.

has been guaranteed since 1945. It remains to some extent problematic, however, in some eastern and south-eastern European countries, which – after the collapse of communism in the Soviet Union and its former satellites – are still in a transition to liberal democracy.

Even if elections are free and fair, as they now are in most European countries, there may be considerable differences in the specific way votes are translated into seats, in particular the proportionality between votes and seats. Rules governing this process have a strong influence on which party or parties govern, which ones are in opposition, which ones are not represented at all, and even, some argue (see Portrait 6.2), on how many parties exist. What electoral systems structure the delegation process between voters and politicians in Europe? We can distinguish between (a) plurality and majority systems, on the one hand, and (b) proportional representations (PR) systems on the other. There are three main types of plurality and majority systems: the simple plurality vote (also known as the **first-past-the-post-system**), the **second ballot** and the **alternative vote (AV)**. The main types of **proportional representation** are: **party list systems**, the **single transferable vote (STV)** and **additional and compensatory member systems (AMS)**.

Three key characteristics determine the proportionality of seat allocation:

- The *district magnitude*, that is, the number of seats allocated in a district. Some systems use single-member districts where each district elects one Member of Parliament. Others use multi-member districts where several MPs are elected for each district. In extreme cases (like the Netherlands and for half the seats in the Russian Duma), the whole country is treated as one large multi-member district. In general, it is possible to say that the larger the districts, the more proportional the electoral system tends to be.

- The *allocation formula*, that is, the specific mathematical procedure by which votes are translated into seats. In single-member districts such as those traditionally used in British general elections, no complex formula is required. The candidate with the largest number of votes is awarded the seat. In multi-member districts, certain mathematical formulas are used (for a description, see Lijphart, 1994).

- There may be *thresholds* specifying a minimum-number share of the vote a party must gain in order to be represented in the parliamentary assembly. Such rules may reduce proportionality as they may exclude smaller parties whose share of

basis (for example, in Germany or Italy). This order is often determined by party bodies. Once the parties' share of the vote is established, the parliamentary seats are filled using the party lists. Seats are allocated to candidates, starting from the top of the lists. Such lists can be 'open' (that is, the voters may change the ranking on the lists by indicating preferences for certain candidates) or 'closed' (the voters can only accept or reject the list as drawn up by the parties, as in the 1999 European Parliament elections in Britain). Party list systems are used in most countries of continental Western Europe, with varying degrees of party control over the ranking of candidates and openness to changes through the voters.

**Single transferable vote (STV):** A system of proportional representation for multi-member districts. It is used in the Irish Republic and Malta. Each voter lists a number of candidates in order of preference. In a first step, first preferences are counted. Those candidates who have achieved at least a certain quota of votes (usually the 'Droop quota' [named after a Belgian mathematician] of the number of total votes divided by the number of available seats plus 1) are elected. Their 'surplus votes', i.e., the number of votes by which they exceed the quota, are transferred to the next candidate on those voters' lists. When no further candidates can be elected by this route, the candidate with the fewest first preferences is eliminated and their second preferences are transferred. The process continues until all seats in a district are filled.

**Additional and compensatory member systems (AMS):** Electoral systems with at least two tiers of electoral districts, used, for example, in Germany as well as in the elections for the Scottish Parliament and the Welsh Assembly. They involve a lower-level local constituency, with which a representative can maintain personal contact, and a higher-level regional or even national district in which minority interests can be proportionately represented. Voters have two votes, one for each district. The party vote at the upper level (e.g., the national level) is used to calculate the percentage of parliamentary seats a party will receive. The mandates won in the lower-level constituency contests are then deducted from this total. Thus, parties winning a less-than-proportional share of seats at the lower level are compensated with a higher number of seats from the party lists at the higher level.

**Plurality (or majority) systems:** Electoral systems which emphasise the powers of political candidates or parties backed by an absolute or relative majority (plurality) of the voters. The winner in elections 'takes all' in such systems. Normatively such systems are based on the belief that a government formed this way offers the most effective and accountable form of government.

**Presidential system of government:** A system of government in which the head of government is a president whose office is politically and constitutionally separate from the legislature.

**Parliamentary system of government:** In a general sense any system of government which operates through a popularly elected parliament. In a more specific sense, 'parliamentary systems of government' are systems in which the heads of government are selected by the assembly and govern through a majority in the assembly.

the vote is below the threshold. Thresholds serve to avoid a strong fragmentation of the party system in parliament by barring small splinter parties and regional parties from parliamentary representation. They are used in a large number of European countries such as Albania, Bulgaria, Croatia, the Czech Republic, Denmark, Estonia, Germany, Greece, Hungary, Italy (for the lower house), Latvia, Lithuania, Moldova, the Netherlands, Norway, Poland, Romania, Russia, Slovakia, Spain and Sweden. They vary from 0.67 per cent in the Netherlands and Norway to 12 per cent in Sweden (Budge et al., 1997, p. 236).

There has been a long debate about the advantages and disadvantages of different electoral systems for the quality of a democracy, especially in countries where electoral reform has been an important issue (such as in France, Italy and Britain) and in the new democracies of Central and Eastern Europe. **Plurality (or majority) systems** are often criticised as being unfair to smaller parties or as benefiting parties whose support is concentrated in certain electoral districts. On the positive side, plurality systems, usually based on one-member constituencies, are believed to discourage voters from supporting minor parties and to favour the development of a two-party system with a one-party majority. This is believed to make for stable government and frequent alternation of the two major parties in power.

## ▉ Parliamentary democracy, presidential democracy, hybrids and other forms

The link between voters and elected deputies is only the start of a whole chain of further delegation processes. In the following sections, we shall follow these processes through and analyse the institutional arrangements structuring them. Before we do that, it is useful to look briefly at a number of fundamental ways of organising representative government: parliamentary government, presidential government and several hybrid forms. The key differences between these systems lie in the different relationships between voters, head of state and head of government on the one hand, and the head of state's and head of government's relationship with the parliamentary assembly on the other.

Pure **presidential systems of government,** found in only three European countries (see Table 6.2), have the following main characteristics:

- The head of government – usually called a president – is popularly elected, that is, the voters determine in practice directly who leads the government (although an electoral college may be used, as in the United States of America).

- The president 'is always constitutionally the head of government, *regardless of the party composition of the legislature*' (Budge et al., 1997, p. 239, emphasis added). He or she names and directs the composition of the government and has some constitutionally granted law-making authority (e.g., the right to introduce legislation, or a legislative veto, that is, to block the assembly's legislative proposals).

- Both the president and the legislature are elected independently of each other for a fixed, constitutionally prescribed term.

The key characteristics of a pure **parliamentary system of government**, like the British political system, are that:

**Table 6. 1** Parliamentary and presidential systems of government (according to Verney)

| Parliamentary system | Presidential system |
|---|---|
| 1. The assembly becomes a parliament | 1. The assembly remains an assembly only |
| 2. The executive is divided into two parts | 2. The executive is not divided but is a president elected by the people for a definite term at the time of assembly elections |
| 3. The head of state appoints the head of government | 3. The head of the government is head of state |
| 4. The head of government appoints the ministry | 4. The president appoints heads of departments who are his or her subordinates |
| 5. The ministry (or government) is a collective body | 5. The president is sole executive |
| 6. Ministers are usually members of parliament | 6. Members of the assembly are not eligible for office in the administration and vice versa |
| 7. The government is politically responsible to the assembly | 7. The executive is responsible to the constitution |
| 8. The head of government may advise the head of state to dissolve parliament | 8. The president cannot disolve or coerce the assembly |
| 9. Parliament as a whole is supreme over its constituent parts, government and assembly, neither of which may dominate the other | 9. The assembly is ultimately supreme over the other branches of government and there is no fusion of the executive and legislative branches as in a parliament |
| 10. The government as a whole is only indirectly responsible to the electorate | 10. The executive is directly responsible to the electorate |
| 11. Parliament is the focus of power in the political system | 11. There is no focus of power in the political system |

*Source*: D. Verney, 'Parliamentary Government and Presidential Government', pp. 31–47, in A. Lijphart (ed.), *Parliamentary versus Presidential Government* (Routledge, 1992).

- 'The head of the government – for whom there are various different official titles such as prime minister, premier, chancellor, minister-president, and taoiseach – and his or her cabinet are dependent on the confidence of the legislature and can be dismissed from office by a legislative vote of no confidence or censure' (Lijphart, 1992, p. 2).

- There is 'no popularly elected president with real political powers' (Budge et al., 1997, p. 238). In some European democracies, the monarch still serves as a ceremonial head of state; in others this function is exercised by a president who is elected by parliament or some other form of electoral college.

- The heads of government are selected by the legislature. The political scientist Arend Lijphart (1992, p. 3) uses the term 'selected' rather than 'elected' because 'the process of selection can range widely from formal election to the informal emergence from inter-party bargaining in the legislature followed by an official appointment by the head of state'.

The diagrams in Figure 6.3 summarise the above and characterise the primary links of delegation and accountability between different actors in pure presidential and

**Presidential systems**

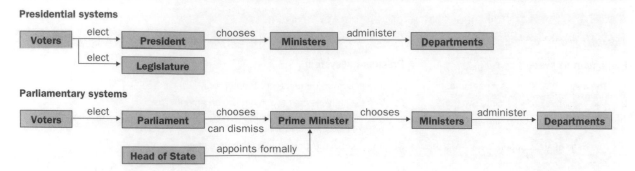

**Fig. 6.3** The logic of delegation and accountability in presidential and parliamentary systems of government

parliamentary systems of government. To what extent does the distinction between presidential and parliamentary systems of government cover the systems of government in Europe? Table 6.2 is an attempt to classify European parliaments according to the above criteria. Out of 33 states listed in the table, only 15 fit the model of a (more or less) pure parliamentary, 3 the model of a pure presidential system of government. The remaining 15 regimes are not well represented by the traditional classification of parliamentary versus presidential systems of government. Many of them are mixed or 'hybrid' types with a relatively powerful, popularly elected president and a confidence relationship between cabinet and parliament (which, as we saw above, is untypical of presidential systems of government). The political system of Switzerland with its rotating presidency and the lack of a confidence relationship

**Table 6.2** Classification of executive–legislative relations in Europe, 1997, according to Shugart and Carey's (1992) scheme

| Parliamentary | Presidential | Premier–presidential | President–parliamentary | Assembly–independent |
|---|---|---|---|---|
| Belgium | Belarus | Austria | Armenia | Switzerland |
| Bulgaria | Cyprus | Finland | Croatia | |
| Denmark | Georgia | France | Russia | |
| Germany | | Iceland | Ukraine | |
| Greece | | Lithuania | | |
| Ireland | | Macedonia | | |
| Italy | | Moldova | | |
| Luxembourg | | Poland | | |
| Malta | | Portugal | | |
| Netherlands | | Romania | | |
| Norway | | | | |
| Slovenia | | | | |
| Spain | | | | |
| Sweden | | | | |
| UK | | | | |

*Sources*: M. S. Shugart and J. M. Carey, *Presidents and Assemblies: Constitutional Design and Electoral Dynamics* (Cambridge: Cambridge University Press, 1992) p. 41; I. Budge et al., *The Politics of the New Europe: Atlantic to Urals* (London and New York: Longman, 1997) p. 241 (figure 10.2).

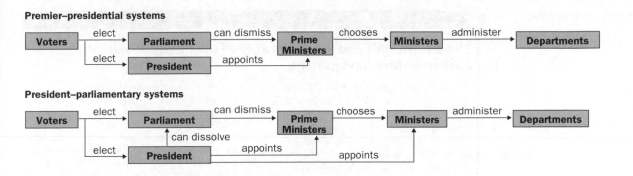

**Fig. 6.4** The logic of delegation and accountability in hybrid systems of government

between parliament and government escapes convenient classification altogether. Shugart and Carey (1992) have therefore suggested a more elaborate classification, which uses two fundamental dimensions:

- The president's or head of state's authority over the prime minister and/or the cabinet (strong in presidential systems and weak in parliamentary systems); and

- The separation of assembly and cabinet survival, which is maximal when the president or head of state cannot dissolve parliament and parliament cannot terminate a president's term before it reaches its constitutionally prescribed limit (except in the unusual case of a successful impeachment). The separation of assembly and cabinet survival is minimal in parliamentary systems where a government's loss of parliamentary confidence may lead to a new government or to new elections, i.e., a new parliament, or both.

According to Shugart and Carey's typology, the French system, for example, would be a mixed type, which they call 'premier–presidential' (sometimes also called 'semi-presidential') system .

The president in such a system has ultimately no strong authority over the cabinet (as in a parliamentary system of government), because the latter ultimately depends for its survival on parliamentary support. At the same time, parliamentary and presidential survival are closely tied together as the president can dismiss the prime minister and his or her cabinet at will. The example of the Fifth French Republic underlines that the character of a 'premier–presidential' system depends on whether the assembly is dominated by the president's party. If this is the case, the president is in a particularly strong position, almost like the President of a presidential system. If the assembly is dominated by a party which is opposed to the president's, the president may have to share power with a prime minister from a different party ('cohabitation'). When this happens, the French system looks much more like a parliamentary system.

A further mixed type is the 'president–parliamentary system', where:

- The president is popularly elected and has therefore considerable democratic legitimacy;

- The president appoints and dismisses cabinet ministers;

- Cabinet ministers are, in addition, subject to parliamentary confidence; and

- The president has the power to dissolve parliament, or legislative powers, or both (Shugart and Carey, 1992, p. 24).

Box 6.2

## The advantages and disadvantages of presidential and parliamentary government

*The main advantages of presidential systems and the main disadvantages of parliamentary systems of government are said to be:*

- Presidential systems of government are believed to guarantee executive stability, because the president's term of office is fixed, whereas executive stability in parliamentary systems of government may be threatened by the cabinet's loss of majority support in the assembly.
- Presidential systems can be said to command a higher degree of democratic legitimacy as the chief executive (usually called the president) is directly elected. This contrasts with the indirect election or selection of the executive by parliament in parliamentary systems of government.
- Presidential systems are often believed to have a more effective system of checks and balances, because executive and legislative powers are clearly separated. In parliamentary systems of government, by contrast, executive and legislative powers are 'fused' as long as the cabinet enjoys parliamentary majority support, because the government usually controls the majority in the legislature. Presidential systems are taken to be characterised by more limited government.

*The main disadvantages of presidential systems and the main advantages of parliamentary systems of government are often considered to be:*

- The separation of powers between the president and the executive on the one hand and the legislature on the other may turn into 'deadlock' when disagreement between the two bodies occurs. Unlike in parliamentary systems with party discipline and the possibility of a vote of no confidence, presidential systems of government often do not have any effective mechanisms for resolving such disagreements.
- Presidential systems are often said to suffer from 'temporal rigidity'. The president's fixed term in office 'breaks the political process into discontinuous, rigidly demarcated periods, leaving no room for the continuous readjustments that events may demand' (Linz, 1992, p. 120). Under parliamentary systems of government, by contrast, 'myriad actors' may at any time between elections adopt basic changes, cause realignments, and above all, make or break prime ministers' (ibid., p. 124). The possibility for parliament to remove a head of government in the middle of a legislative term or for the head of government to dissolve parliament prematurely, if he or she loses parliamentary confidence, gives parliamentary systems of government more flexibility to respond to political change.
- Presidential government is said to operate on a 'winner-take-all' basis. 'In a presidential election, only one candidate and one party can win; everybody else loses. Moreover, the concentration of power in the president's hands gives him or her very little incentive to form coalitions or other power-sharing arrangements. Especially in an already divided and polarized nation, winner-take-all is highly likely to create even more division and polarization' (Lijphart, 1992, pp. 18–19). This criticism has often been levelled against the presidential systems of Latin America, but could also be applied to the ethnically and/or socially divided new democracies of Central and Eastern Europe.

In this system, the president's powers over the prime minister and his or her cabinet are maximal, whereas the separation of assembly and cabinet survival is minimal as the president can dissolve the chamber without serious restrictions. This system comes close to the highly unstable system of the Weimar Republic and is currently used in Armenia. Russia and Ukraine come close to this system.

The final category in Shugart and Carey's typology (with no presidential control over cabinet and maximum separation of assembly and cabinet survival) can be termed 'assembly–independent' systems of government. The only European system of government that fits this description is that of Switzerland, which does not have an elected president as head of state and where the (collegial) government is chosen by the assembly, but cannot be removed by it.

There has been a long-standing and contentious debate in politics and political science about the merits of presidential, parliamentary and hybrid systems of government (see Box 6.2). It is characteristic of this debate that the advantages of presidential systems are simultaneously seen as the disadvantages of the parliamentary system and vice versa (Lijphart, 1992). The increase in the number of hybrid systems in Europe since 1989 can be seen as an attempt by constitutional 'designers' to combine the advantages and avoid the disadvantages of both systems. It could be argued that hybrid forms combine 'the advantages of direct democratic election and stable tenure associated with a presidential executive and the flexibility of a parliamentary cabinet and prime minister' (Lijphart, 1992, p. 20). In hybrid systems deadlock can be avoided and the president can potentially function as an arbitrator between the executive and legislative branches of government. They can, however, also compound legislative instability, as the experiences of the 'Weimar Republic' or the Russian system of government show.

Despite the manifold institutional differences, it can be argued that most European systems of government are fundamentally different from a pure presidential system and share one central characteristic: they conform to Strøm's definition of parliamentary government as 'a system of government in which the prime minister and his or her cabinet are accountable to any majority of the members of parliament and can be voted out of office by the latter . . . through an ordinary or constructive vote of no confidence. What characterizes parliamentary democracies is that the cabinet must be tolerated by the parliamentary majority, not that the latter actually plays any direct role in the selection of the former. . . . The definition . . . provides an effective operational tool whereby we can classify political regimes. Thus, France V is a parliamentary system (which also happens to have a powerful president), whereas Switzerland is not' (Strøm, 2000). We shall therefore pay particular attention to the crucial relationship between parliaments and governments. Before we reach this step, we must discuss briefly the **co-ordination** processes within government and the possibilities for governments to control the implementation of their policies via executive agencies and civil servants.

# Prime ministers and cabinets

Most voters and members of parliament expect the government of the day to have a coherent policy and to be able to implement it. If a minimum of coherence were not achieved and ministers had no control over their departments, the idea of democratic accountability to the voters would be in question. Coherence is important, because accountability depends on our being able to identify and attribute political responsibility. If political decisions 'emerge' as a result of a chaotic interplay of various actors, it is difficult for voters to identify those responsible for them. Coherence is also a prerequisite of effective and efficient policy-making as decisions in different policy areas may interact with one another. Decisions in one ministry may affect a policy area for which another ministry is responsible. For example, decisions in a ministry of education may have serious implications for the ministry of social security or the ministry of labour.

Coherence and 'identifiability' of political responsibility are, however, highly problematic in modern politics. Despite the constitutional powers and political resources many heads of governments enjoy, departmental ministers and their government

**Co-ordination, positive and negative:** 'Positive coordination is an attempt to maximize the overall effectiveness and efficiency of government policy by exploring and utilizing the joint strategy options of several ministerial portfolios. . . . Negative coordination, by contrast, is associated with more limited aspirations. Its goal is to assure that any new policy initiative designed by a specialized subunit within the ministerial organization will not interfere with the established policies and the interests of other ministerial units. . . . Procedurally, positive coordination is associated with multilateral negotiations in intra- or interministerial task forces. . . . By contrast, negative coordination is more likely to take the form of bilateral "clearance" negotiations between the initiating department and other units whose portfolios might be affected – but whose own policy options are not actively considered' (Scharpf, 1993, pp. 143–4).

departments are, on the whole, quite independent. Even where a head of government is relatively dominant, he or she will have to rely on the expertise of the departments, especially the civil servants in the departments. They co-operate intensively and regularly with experts in interest groups and in the scientific community. Such 'policy communities' around ministries are crucial for the preparation and implementation of policies and tend to resist centralised co-ordination.

Conflicts between ministries are often avoided rather than resolved through a coherent, common policy. There is a tendency for ministers to be reluctant to interfere in their ministerial colleagues' portfolios as they expect, in turn, their ministerial colleagues to respect their control over their 'own' ministries. This may lead to what is often referred to as 'negative co-ordination' which operates solely to ensure that any new policy initiative will not interfere with established patterns of policy and organisation (Scharpf, 1993, pp.143–4).

Negative co-ordination may help to control conflicts between ministries and establish a degree of unity, but has the disadvantage of a reduction in the scope for policy innovation: it is a conflict-avoidance rather than a problem-solving strategy (Scharpf, 1993, p. 144). There are various institutional mechanisms by which coherence can be facilitated. It is possible to distinguish between *hierarchical* and *collective mechanisms* (Andeweg, 2000).

Hierarchical mechanisms include:

- *Prime ministerial government*, where the head of government enjoys a privileged role vis-à-vis individual ministers, and powers to appoint and dismiss ministers, or the right to formulate general policy guidelines for the government as a whole which are binding on individual ministries. Some prime ministers, such as the German Federal Chancellor, have a full-blown department (Chancellor's Office) with specialised sections monitoring the activities of each department of government. The effectiveness of such resources depends on the political circumstances: departmental ministers with a strong position in the prime minister's party, or ministries controlled by a coalition party, are difficult for a head of government to control. Other hierarchical mechanisms are, therefore, frequently used.

- *Inner cabinets* usually contain the political 'heavyweights' in a cabinet. Inner cabinets consist of the head of government and a number of important key ministers. They usually meet regularly and attempt to co-ordinate the government's overall policies. Inner cabinets are smaller, more flexible decision-making bodies than the cabinet. The political weight of the ministers involved may help to establish a degree of coherence and resist departmental particularism.

- Inner cabinets have one drawback if the government is a coalition cabinet: although they may contain some party-political 'heavyweights', they do not comprehensively involve the wider parliamentary and extra-parliamentary leaderships of all coalition parties. Consent of all parties inside and outside parliament is more problematic in coalition governments than in single-party governments as ministers from different parties may have fundamentally different policy preferences. Therefore, coalition governments often use *coalition committees* and *party summits*, which frequently include non-governmental party leaders. These bodies may prepare decisions, which are then carried out by cabinet and parliamentary majority.

Collective mechanisms are based more strongly on the equal status of ministers and include:

- *Cabinet government*: if the cabinet meets frequently and makes significant collective decisions, it can limit the extent of 'departmentalism', that is, a lack of co-ordination between the individual government departments. In most contemporary European countries, however, the cabinet's role as a policy co-ordinator has never been very strong, or is diminishing. The growth of government responsibilities means that cabinets are no longer able to co-ordinate and prepare all major government decisions. The initiative has shifted 'downwards' to the individual departments and inter-ministerial negotiations and 'upwards' to the head of government. Cabinets are often left with the task of ratifying decisions that were made elsewhere.

- *Overlapping jurisdictions* between ministries can improve inter-departmental co-ordination and overall coherence. Ministries of Finance such as the British Treasury often have overall responsibility for government spending and may have the statutory right, indeed duty, to interfere in the autonomy of so-called 'spending departments'. Another example is the German Ministry of Justice, which screens government bills from all departments in order to ensure their compatibility with the constitution and other laws. Bilateral or multilateral inter-ministerial co-ordination involving a large number of expert civil servants have replaced the cabinet as the dominant collective mechanism to ensure coherence.

- *Cabinet committees* are another, related, collective mechanism that aids co-operation and co-ordination between different ministries. They may be permanent or *ad hoc* and are usually comprised of a number of cabinet ministers (often represented by high-ranking civil servants, or shadowed by parallel committees consisting of civil servants) in a policy area wider than the remit of individual ministries (e.g., foreign and defence policy, home and social affairs). To the extent that the head of government controls the composition and chairmanship of such committees, they can be an important power resource of the head of government.

Most governments employ a mixture of these and other co-ordination mechanisms to ensure coherence and to control the co-ordination problems caused by 'departmentalism' and coalition government. However, an equally important relationship is that between elected politicians, government ministers in particular, and civil servants, those officials who advise government ministers and are in charge of policy implementation. This crucial link in the democratic chain of delegation and accountability will be dealt with in the following section.

## Ministers and civil servants

The traditional institutional device to ensure the compliance of unelected civil servants with the decisions of elected politicians has been the hierarchical organisation of government departments. Government departments can be compared to a pyramid where formal power is concentrated in the hands of very few politicians at the top. Ministers are at the apex of a government department and can give orders to civil servants.

This constitutional position is common to all modern democracies. In reality, however, ministers depend very much on the advice of their civil servants. Insisting on a distinction between ministerial policy-making on the one hand and administration and implementation of this policy by civil servants on the other is unrealistic. Civil servants often have more specialised knowledge of the policy area in question than the supposedly superior minister. Ministers rely on them for advice on policy development. As a result, the formal constitutional position of a minister as an elected – and therefore democratically legitimate and accountable – head of a department who controls the civil servants further down the hierarchy is often a fiction. Even if ministers are determined to stamp their political authority on their department, they depend on the advice of highly knowledgeable experts from the civil service. Some governments (e.g., the Thatcher government in Britain in 1979–90) have attempted to gain more independence from bureaucratic expertise by making use of outside advisers and think-tanks. Nevertheless, the problem remains a significant one.

Another problem for the coherence of government policy is the tendency for ministers to 'go native', that is, they gradually begin to identify with predominant, often long-established norms and 'views' held by the majority of senior civil servants in their departments. They may acquire what could be called the norms of a departmental 'culture'. The extent to which elected politicians are absorbed into a department's 'culture' depends to some extent on the individual minister's personal convictions and strength. There are, however, *institutional safeguards* that help to tackle the problem:

- In some governments, *frequent ministerial reshuffles* are partly aimed at preventing ministers from 'going native'. The disadvantage of this approach is that departmental ministers spend relatively short periods of time in a department and are never able to acquire at least some expertise in the policy matter concerned. The dependence on civil servants for information and expertise remains considerable.

- In some countries such as Belgium, France or Sweden, ministers have their own *ministerial cabinets*. Members of such *cabinets* are often either policy experts from outside the civil service or expert civil servants politically loyal to the minister. They advise the minister on key decisions.

- In some other countries such as Germany, ministers have powers to appoint a certain number of loyal supporters to key civil service positions (*political appointees*). The minister will still be dependent on civil service advice, but high-ranking civil servants are chosen because they share his or her political views.

Some Western European countries have witnessed a massive privatisation and restructuring of their central bureaucracies since the 1980s. In Britain, for example, the Thatcher and Major governments (1979–97) considered the size of the British bureaucracy to be one of the causes of low economic growth. Many tasks carried out by bureaucracies, it was thought, could be carried out more efficiently by the private sector. The size of the public sector, therefore, was to be reduced and the financial accountability of the remainder to be increased. Many nationalised industries, such as steel, coal, oil, water, electricity, gas and rail transport, were partly or completely privatised. Many government services were opened up to private-sector competition. Private business could be contracted to run a service to certain standards for an agreed price (including, for example, prisons). Government ministries were radically restructured. Government agencies were carved out of the old ministries to run specific services. Such agencies had an almost contractual relationship, with their sponsor department specifying the extent of public funding and the expected level of services. Wherever possible, public agencies were encouraged to compete with each other for the supply of services. The intention was to set up an 'internal market' even where a free market in the real sense could not be created, as in the National Health Service (NHS).

The reforms of the public sector in Britain were emulated in the Netherlands and Sweden. The British experience shows that the devolution of public services to the private sector may lead to a reduction of public expenditure and a more efficient provision of certain services, although the success of the British programmes of the 1980s and 1990s has been variable. The incoming 1997 Labour government, for example, clearly realised that the **internal market** in the National Health Service and local government had been problematic both in the generation of unnecessary bureaucracy and in the quality of provision. The privatisations and creation of 'internal markets' in Britain have created *new problems of oversight and accountability* as new techniques such as contracting and franchising were introduced into the management of public services. One of the main problems is that 'Public servants are becoming more responsive downwards, to their users, and less accountable upwards, to their political masters' (Hague et al., 1998, p. 231).

# Legislative–executive relations

To what extent are elected members of parliament able to hold government ministers and civil servants accountable? According to a popular view, parliaments have declined in the past century. It is often argued that the growth of government responsibilities over the last century has overpowered traditional parliamentarism, that governments dominate the legislative process via disciplined parliamentary parties, that backbenchers are powerless, and that the main instruments of parliamentary scrutiny, such as Question Time, are ineffective. Although it is undeniable that governments dominate parliamentary business in most chambers, there are considerable differences between countries, and parliaments do exercise important powers and functions.

At a general level, all parliaments continue to fulfil important linkage functions between voters and government. Not only do members of parliament articulate their constituents' interests and preferences in parliament, they also inform their constituents about political events and decisions. Members of parliament are also an important feedback channel for ministers. They are better able than overworked ministers to maintain close contacts with their constituents and can convey information on the effects and administration of their policies to government ministers, who – as a result of their workload – often suffer from an increasing degree of isolation from voters. Members of Parliament, alerted by voters, function almost like a 'fire alarm' that voters may use to inform ministers about the local implementation of policy (McCubbins and Schwartz 1984). This may help ministers to monitor the effects of their policies and the activity of civil servants.

In this section we shall examine in what specific way parliaments can scrutinise governments and hold them to account, and in what way they contribute to a better exchange of information between voters and government. Members of parliament have two main types of controls vis-à-vis governments: **ex-ante controls**, which are effective before a government takes office, and ongoing controls (or **ex-post controls**), which become effective after a government has been appointed. We shall look at some of those controls, concentrating on the elected lower houses of parliament.

**Internal market:** A concept from the field of New Public Management (NPM), which has come to dominate debates about the reform of the public sector in the United States of America, the United Kingdom, New Zealand and Sweden in the 1980s. Traditional state functions are increasingly 'contracted out' to external providers competing for a contract from government as a service 'purchaser'. Even within the public sector, funders are systematically separated from providers of services. For example, public health authorities contract with providers – such as hospitals – to supply health care on agreed terms. Public providers compete with other outside providers for the award of a contract.

**Ex-ante/ex-post controls:** When political authority is delegated from a principal (for example, a government minister) to an agent (for example, a civil servant), the principal has two fundamental ways of controlling the agent. *Ex-ante* controls apply before the delegation takes place. Principals may screen agents for their suitability or set out the agents' duties in contracts. *Ex-post* controls apply after the delegation has taken place. Principals may monitor their agents' performance by requiring them to report on their activities or by using independent bodies to audit agent performance.

## Ex-ante controls

One of the key characteristics of parliamentary democracies is that members of the government, including the head of government, usually come from the ranks of the parliamentary parties. Although they may have to give up their parliamentary mandates once they assume government office (as in the Netherlands), they usually become government members after having risen through the ranks of their parliamentary parties, gaining the respect of their fellow members of parliament. In systems where cabinet ministers go through a long parliamentary 'apprenticeship' or, alternatively, gradually rise within their parties, fellow party members and members of parliament have the opportunity to gather information on prospective ministers and (as 'selectorate') exert influence on their political careers.

On average, 75 per cent of all West European cabinet ministers between the end of the Second World War and the end of 1984 were members of parliament at the time of their appointment. There are considerable national variations, with Ireland, the United Kingdom and Italy displaying the highest shares, of around 95 per cent, and at the other extreme, more than four out of ten Dutch and Norwegian cabinet ministers having no parliamentary experience prior to their appointment (see Figure 6.6). A similar variation can be discerned in the data on average seniority (Figure 6.5). At the one extreme, the average British cabinet minister looks back at a parliamentary career of more than 12 years before he or she gets appointed to the cabinet. At the other extreme, the parliamentary apprenticeships of Belgian, Dutch, French and German cabinet ministers prior to their appointment last only between seven and eight years.

A further ex-ante control refers to the process by which governments take office. Parliaments may be closely involved in the formal investiture or election of governments. In some countries an incoming government must win an 'investiture vote' before it can assume power. This is the case in Belgium, Germany, Ireland, Italy, the Netherlands and Spain. Parliaments in which governments are formally voted in have a stronger say in the delegation process (and stronger ex-ante control) than parliaments where this is not the case.

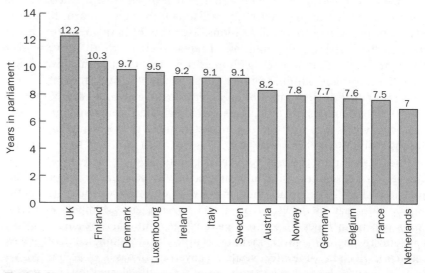

**Fig. 6.5** Average seniority of ministers in 13 European countries, 1945–84
*Source*: Cotta (1991).

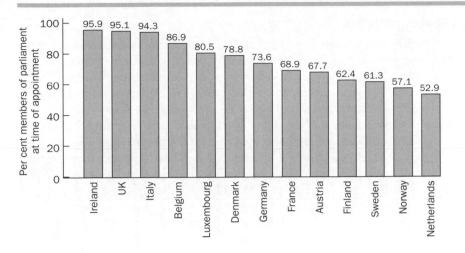

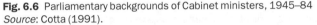

**Fig. 6.6**  Parliamentary backgrounds of Cabinet ministers, 1945–84
*Source*: Cotta (1991).

Another constraint in executive–legislative relations is what is often referred to as 'recognition rules'. Such rules specify 'who will be asked to form governments, and in what order' (Strøm, 1995, p. 76). In countries with a plurality electoral system and/or countries without coalition government, such as Greece, Spain and the United Kingdom, the formation of government is a relatively straightforward process. In countries where elections do not produce a single party controlling a majority of seats in parliament, however, the formation process is usually more complex. Parliament's role in the process of government formation will be strong if the election result gives parliamentary actors a choice (usually, in multi-party systems where no single party achieves an absolute majority of seats). Parliamentary ex-ante controls will be greatly reduced in (near) two-party systems with one-party governments. To a lesser extent, parliaments will be strengthened if parliamentary actors control the process of coalition formation or are consulted in the process.

The controls discussed in this section are constraints on the government *before* it assumes office. They do not guarantee, however, parliamentary accountability after a government has been appointed. A parliament's ability to exert scrutiny and influence vis-à-vis the government *after* the latter's formal appointment depends on the strength of ongoing or ex-post controls. We shall deal with such mechanisms in the following section.

## Ongoing (ex-post) Controls

There are a number of ways governments may be required to report on and justify their activities in parliament. Plenary debates in which government ministers have to report their decisions and justify them in the face of criticism by the opposition are the most important device. Transmitted by the media, such debates are particularly important to inform the ultimate democratic principals, the voters, on the government's record and the political alternatives. As Figure 6.7 shows, parliaments vary greatly in the time they spend on debates. The Greek parliament with 224 plenary meetings and the British House of Commons with 167 per year (in the mid-1980s) are to a large extent 'debating chambers'. The Bundestag, the lower house of the

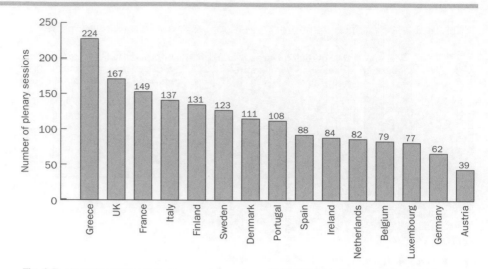

**Fig. 6.7** Average number of plenary sessions per year (mid-1980s) in the parliaments of 15 European countries

German parliament, where more parliamentary activity takes place in committees than on the floor of the chamber, has often been called a 'committee chamber' or a 'working chamber' rather than a 'debating chamber' or an 'arena parliament' such as the British House of Commons.

Usually it is his or her party membership that defines the nature of a member's oversight activities. The government, for example, will generally be more willing to share information with members of the governing parties as long as sensitive information is not disclosed to the public. Some of the processes that are relevant in this context have been labelled the 'intra-party mode' of executive–legislative relations by the political scientist Anthony King (1976). The monitoring carried out by the parliamentary majority party or parties can be very effective as the government depends on their votes and other forms of support. Yet these monitoring activities are usually conducted behind closed doors.

A further key dimension of executive–legislative relations is what King (1976, pp. 17–18) calls the 'opposition mode' which is 'characterized by, indeed defined by, conflict' (King, 1976, p. 18). The public confrontation between government and opposition in parliament and the media may not always be popular with the electorate, yet it is crucially important for the information of voters. It prevents the government from monopolising the political agenda, presents voters with political alternatives to government policy, reveals strengths and weaknesses of government policy, indicates the government's and opposition's competence in answering critical questions, and forces the government to justify decisions in public. Opposition parties usually (except in the case of minority governments) lack the necessary parliamentary votes to block government policy or to unseat the government, but their main aim is to appeal to the public in a permanent election campaign (Crick, 1970). This permanent election campaign is of great importance as a source of information for voters and crucial for public government accountability. A forceful opposition may also influence the government's policy choices indirectly, especially if its criticism is (quietly) shared by members of the majority parties.

Oppositions in parliamentary democracies have a whole 'arsenal' of different

**Table 6.3**   Forms of parliamentary questioning in west European parliaments

| | Written question | Oral question (question hour/time) | Urgent question | Topical hour | Interpellation with censure motion | Interpellation without censure motion |
|---|---|---|---|---|---|---|
| Austria | Yes | Yes | Yes | Yes | Yes | No |
| Belgium | Yes | Yes | Yes | No | Yes | Yes |
| Denmark | Yes | Yes | No | No | Yes | Yes |
| Finland | Yes | Yes | No | No | Yes | Yes |
| France | Yes | Yes | No | No | Yes | Yes |
| Germany | Yes | Yes | Yes | Yes | No | Yes |
| Greece | Yes | Yes | Yes | No | Yes | Yes |
| Iceland | Yes | Yes | No | Yes | No | No |
| Ireland | Yes | Yes | Yes | No | No | No |
| Italy | Yes | Yes | No | Yes | Yes | Yes |
| Luxembourg | Yes | Yes | Yes | No | Yes | Yes |
| Netherlands | Yes | Yes | No | No | Yes | No |
| Norway | No | Yes | Yes | No | Yes | No |
| Portugal | Yes | Yes | No | No | Yes | No |
| Spain | Yes | Yes | No | No | Yes | Yes |
| Sweden | No | Yes | No | No | No | Yes |
| Switzerland | Yes | Yes | Yes | Yes | No | Yes |
| UK | Yes | Yes | Yes | No | No | No |

*Source*: M. Wiberg, 'Parliamentary Questioning: Control by Communication?' pp. 187–8, in H. Döring (ed.), *Parliaments and Majority Rule in Western Europe* (Frankfurt am Main/New York: Campus/St Martin's Press, 1995).

tools to extract information from governments and monitor their activities including parliamentary questions (see Table 6.3) and debates on problems of particular current interest.

In most parliaments, committees are the single most important monitoring device. Strong committees 'can provide legislators with the information that they need to participate effectively with the executive across a wide range of policy areas' (Mezey, 1998, p. 783). European parliaments vary greatly in the extent to which they allow committees specialisation and give them a powerful role in the scrutiny of government policy.

Finally, unlike presidential systems of government, the elected chambers in parliamentary systems of government have the power to dismiss a government for political reasons. A government that does not enjoy the confidence of the elected lower house of parliament has to resign. Yet, resignation rules vary across countries. In Denmark, Sweden, Finland and Ireland a government will usually step down after a defeat on a major bill, even if it is constitutionally not obliged to do so. The government resigns as a result of a constitutional convention. In other countries (such as Britain), conventions and rules are more restrictive and protect governments more strongly: a government only has to resign after a defeat on an important bill if it has explicitly declared the vote to be a matter of confidence. In Germany, Spain and (since 1995)

Belgium, the rules are even more restrictive: only a constructive vote of no-confidence will bring a government down; that is, a government only has to resign if an absolute majority dismisses it by simultaneously electing an alternative government. The threat of removal serves as the ultimate sanction, a 'threat' that parliament, especially disaffected parts of the majority, can use against an unco-operative government.

The diagnosis of a universal 'decline' of parliaments is usually based on a number of misconceptions. First, it is usually based on an unrealistic fiction of an alleged 'golden age' of parliaments in the nineteenth century, which is used as a benchmark for comparisons. It is true that party discipline and hence government control over parliaments was not as strong in the mid-nineteenth century as a century later. Yet, mid-nineteenth-century parliaments (such as the British House of Commons in its 'golden age' between 1832 and 1867) were not democratically elected chambers as a considerable part of the population was excluded from voting. In many European countries (for example, in the German Empire of 1871–1918) they were in fact utterly powerless. Secondly, the diagnosis of a decline is usually based on a narrow notion of the powers of parliament vis-à-vis the government. While this may be a useful starting point for analysing the relationship between parliament and president in a presidential system, it is completely misconceived for the study of systems with a 'fusion' of the executive and legislative branches of government, as is the case in all parliamentary and most hybrid systems of government. In such systems, a realistic judgement only emerges if we look at the informal ex-ante and ex-post controls and the role parliamentary parties play in this context.

## Institutional checks

In many West European countries, parliament and government operate under a system of powerful 'institutional checks' or 'external constraints'. In some countries there are a large number of more or less independent agents with the authority to challenge, veto or delay actions decided on by government and parliament.

Constitutional courts with far-reaching powers of judicial review can be serious constraints on parliamentary majorities and governments. They may protect parliamentary minorities against unconstitutional government legislation. In the German case, for example, the federal government, a state government or a group of at least one-third of the Members of the Bundestag may challenge the constitutionality of any federal or state law even if it does not involve a particular case arising from the implementation of a specific act (Goetz, 1996, pp. 97–8). In Germany, for example, the court is not only an external check on the government, its deliberations and hearings are also important sources of public information. The court also has the authority to force the government to disclose information on its policy. It can therefore help parliamentary minorities in their attempt to monitor government activities. The same applies to independent public inquiries of the type used in the United Kingdom.

In federal systems, sub-national territorial units and their governments may enjoy considerable veto powers and act as institutional checks. In the German case, for example, it is not unusual for the opposition to seek to reduce the government's information advantage through the assistance of 'friendly' state (*Länder*) governments.

Executive responsibilities may be delegated to *nearly autonomous* or *semi-autonomous bodies* such as, in Germany, the central bank (*Bundesbank*), the Federal Employment Office (*Bundesanstalt für Arbeit*) and numerous other bodies which are organised under public law and carry out important federal policy functions. One of the first acts of the new Labour government in the United Kingdom in 1997 was to make the Bank of England independent. Since 1 January 1999 the European Central Bank has fulfilled a similar function for those member states of the European Union which have joined the European Monetary Union.

Not least because the point is often overlooked, it is important to mention the benefits for democratic accountability of the independence of the *Bundesbank* and other parapolitical bodies. An independent central bank reduces the advantages governments can derive from their easy and privileged access to information in the domain of economic policy. An independent central bank is an important source of

**Table 6.4**  Strength of institutional checks in western European countries

| Country | 'Schmidt Index' | 'Huber/Ragin/ Stephens Index' | 'Colomer Index' | Strength of institutional checks (summary indicator) |
|---|---|---|---|---|
| Austria | 3 | 1 | 3 | Medium |
| Belgium | 3 | 1 | 3 | Medium |
| Denmark | 2 | 0 | 2 | Low |
| Finland | 1 | 1 | | Low |
| France | 1 | 2 | 3 | Low |
| Germany | 5 | 4 | 4 | High |
| Greece | 1 | | 0 | Low |
| Iceland | 1 | | 2 | Low |
| Ireland | 2 | 0 | 2 | Low |
| Italy | 3 | 1 | 4 | Medium |
| Luxembourg | 2 | | | Low |
| Netherlands | 1 | 1 | 2 | Low |
| Norway | 2 | 0 | 1 | Low |
| Portugal | 1 | | 2 | Low |
| Spain | 2 | | 3 | Medium |
| Sweden | 1 | 0 | 1 | Low |
| Switzerland | 5 | 6 | 6 | High |
| UK | 1 | 2 | 1 | Low |

*Notes:*
- The 'Schmidt Index' expresses the extent of institutional constraints facing the executive branch of government. It ranges from '0' ('no constraints') to '6' ('executive branch severely constrained'). The coding is as follows: (1) executive constrained by EU membership (0 = no; 1 = yes); (2) federal system (0 = no; 1 = yes); (3) high threshold for constitutional amendments (0 = no; 1 = yes); (4) influential second parliamentary chamber (0 = no; 1 = yes); (5) autonomous central bank (0 = no; 1 = yes); (6) frequent use of referendums (0 = no; 1 = yes). The data refer to the period 1960–89 and were updated by the author of the present chapter to include the accession of Austria, Finland and Sweden to the European Union (the codings for these countries were increased by 1).
- The 'Huber/Ragin/Stephens Index' ('constitutional structure index') is also an additive index using the following variables: (1) federalism (0 = no, 1 = weak, 2 = strong); (2) parliamentary/presidential government (0 = parliamentary, 1 = presidential or collegial executive); proportional representation/ single-member districts (0 = proportional representation, 1 = modified proportional representation, 2 = single-member, simple plurality systems); bicameralism (0 = no second chamber or second chamber with very weak powers, 1 = weak bicameralism, 2 = strong bicameralism); referendum (0 = none or infrequent, 1 = frequent).
- The 'Colomer Index' of 'institutional pluralism' ranges from 0 to 7. It codes the effective number of parties in parliament, bicameralism, elected president and decentralisation (according to intensity from 0 to 2 except for the variable 'elected president').

*Source:* M. G. Schmidt (1997, p. 252); Huber, Ragin and Stephens (1993, p. 728).

information on the direction and consequences of government economic policy. Similarly, in Germany, the monthly reports of the Federal Employment Office on the labour-market situation and the annual reports of the Committee of Economic Advisers provide the public with an enormous amount of information on key areas of economic policy.

Supra-national or transnational bodies such as the European Union (EU) are increasingly becoming institutional checks on national parliamentary majorities. The making of EU decisions through inter-governmental bargaining is often criticised for the inevitable loss of parliamentary accountability. National governments enjoy much better and more up-to-date information on EU matters than national parliaments. Nevertheless, the EU is an external check on national governments, a source of information and a potential ally for parliamentary minorities.

The extent to which national governments are constrained by institutional checks in their 'environment' varies considerably. Table 6.4 uses a few indexes developed in the comparative literature to 'measure' the degree of constitutional 'shackles' national governments are constrained by in (Western) Europe. Taken together these indexes suggest that the governments of Switzerland and Germany face the most far-reaching institutional checks in Western Europe. In a number of countries (Italy, Spain, Belgium and Austria) governments have to deal with intermediate levels of institutional constraints. In all other countries, governments operate under considerably fewer and less severe institutional checks. Overall, the governments of Greece and Sweden are subject to the lowest levels of institutional checks in Western Europe – that is, national governments in these countries are relatively free to carry out their policies independent of other actors and institutions in the political system.

# ■ The costs and risks of democratic decision-making

Some national governments (such as the Swiss or German governments) operate in a highly constrained institutional 'environment' at the national level. In other countries (such as Greece, Sweden or the United Kingdom) elected governments are less constrained by formal institutional checks. From one point of view about what is desirable, the less constrained versions of government are very attractive: democracy is partly defined by majority rule. The party winning the majority (or plurality) of votes in a general election forms a government and ought to have as many political and administrative means as possible at its disposal to implement the promises it made in its election manifesto. Other bodies with lower levels of direct democratic legitimacy ought not to be able to block the execution of the popular will. The ultimate judge will be the electorate at the next general election. The British 'Westminster model' has often been seen as an 'ideal type' of political system in which the will of the majority prevails in this way (Lijphart, 1984). Yet this 'majoritarian' model has also had its critics. Lord Hailsham (1976) called it an 'elective dictatorship'. Others have argued that democracy is only partly defined by majority rule. It is also defined by an equal chance for all to participate in decision-making either directly (see Chapter 5) or through chosen representatives, and by the protection of minorities. A different point of view about what is desirable therefore sees relatively unbridled majority rule and liberal democracy as being compatible only on two conditions:

first, the effective exclusion of the minority from the policy process is mitigated if majorities and minorities alternate in government; secondly, majority rule is less problematic if a country is relatively homogeneous and does not have any significant ethnic, linguistic, religious or other minorities whose demands would be permanently excluded or neglected under unfettered majority rule (Lijphart, 1984, p. 22). If such minorities exist, a less 'majoritarian' system with more institutional checks on the majority and stronger incentives for the government of the day to seek consensus by consulting minorities is more suitable. One of the main drawbacks is that such a 'consensus model' makes governing more difficult and complex. Decision-making 'costs' are high in such systems (see below).

Yet, governing has become more complex in all democracies. The Central and Eastern European states of the former Soviet empire have embarked on far-reaching programmes of democratisation, decentralisation and privatisation. The Western European states are facing other problems that make governing more complex. Globalisation, European integration, the growing assertiveness of regions and regional governments, privatisation and 'marketisation' in the traditional public sector, the growing importance of **policy communities** and the growing demand on the part of citizens to participate directly in political decisions are but a few examples.

As a result, political decision-making costs have increased in most countries. The political scientist Giovanni Sartori (1987) argues that political decisions always involve a trade-off between two variables: (a) 'decision-making costs' such as the time and other resources, which are required to arrive at a certain decision, and (b) 'external risks' such as the risk of incompetent decisions, oppression and similar problems (see Figure 6.8). One of the solutions he offers to the dilemma posed by this trade-off is political representation or, in the language of this chapter, delegation. Delegation reduces the number of decision-makers and hence decision-making costs, as long as agents act in the best interest of, and are accountable to, their principals. Mechanisms ensuring accountability in representative democracies have been one of the main themes of this chapter.

Applying this theory to the figures in Table 6.4 shows that governments in countries with high levels of institutional constraints (Switzerland, Germany) face high decision-making costs, because they operate in relatively decentralised systems with a relatively large number of other political actors (such as federal-state governments, a constitutional court, an independent central bank and the like) with real veto powers. Negotiating compromises amongst such actors may be a cumbersome and time-consuming task. For governments of countries with low levels of institutional constraints it is much easier to reach political decisions without protracted bargaining.

**Policy communities:** Networks of government ministries, executive agencies, interest groups and other non-government actors in a particular policy area. These networks cut across the formal divide between governmental and non-governmental actors and are 'communities' in so far as they share expertise and a common definition of the problems in a particular area. A great deal of public policy, especially uncontroversial and routine legislation, is typically made in such 'communities'.

**Fig. 6.8** External risks and decision-making costs
*Source*: Sartori (1987) p. 219.

### Giovanni Sartori (born 1924)

The Italian-born Albert Schweitzer Professor Emeritus in Humanities at the University of Columbia has been one of the most influential political scientists since the Second World War. He has made major contributions to the comparative study of politics, the empirical theory of democracy, and party theory. His most important academic works include

*Parties and Party Systems* (1976), *The Theory of Democracy Revisited* (1987) and *Comparative Constitutional Engineering* (1994).

However, the involvement of more actors in the decision-making process also diminishes the external risk in countries such as Switzerland and Germany, because representatives of those affected by a decision have more 'access points' to the political process and more opportunities to 'veto' or delay decisions, that is, to force the government to think again. The reverse is the case in countries where national governments face only minimal institutional checks.

We might, however, suggest that the processes of globalisation, the growing importance of regionalism and the increasing demands citizens make for direct influence on public policy (for example, through the use of referendums) have increased decision-making costs in all European democracies. Governing has become a more time-consuming, multi-level bargaining process in which governments are agenda setters and co-ordinators, but often do not have the resources and expertise to impose a policy 'from above'. They need the co-operation of other actors both at the national as well as at the sub-national and supra-national level. These difficulties can be seen as undermining the ability of any government to run its country well, but they also open up opportunities. We could argue, from the perspective of Sartori's decision-making model of democracy, that we are witnessing the emergence of political systems with more opportunities for minorities to influence policy. For example, environmental pressure groups which fail to make their voice heard at the national level may attempt to pursue a different route and use the level of the European Union to achieve their goals. Nevertheless, the problems are equally evident: if consensus is difficult to reach, the veto and delaying powers of minorities may slow down decision-making, lead to irrational decision-making or prevent necessary decisions altogether. Trade-offs seem to be inevitable in politics.

## ■ Summary

◆ Modern democratic politics in Europe is largely based on representative government where citizens delegate political authority to representatives. Political accountability is usually achieved indirectly, by a chain of further delegation processes from elected parliamentarians via government ministers to civil servants. The nature of these representative institutions shapes the extent to which those who delegate (principals) are able to hold those to whom authority is delegated (agents) accountable.

◆ The possibility of using referendums and the nature of electoral systems shape the possibilities for citizens to influence policy and the recruitment of political elites (members of parliament, ministers, prime ministers and/or presidents).

◆ The relationship between members of parliament, heads of government and heads of state is strongly influenced by particular institutional arrangements: there are systematic variations between presidential systems of government, parliamentary systems of government and a number of hybrid systems. In all cases members of parliament find themselves in a very difficult position vis-à-vis the government: the government's level of expertise and information-processing capacity is vastly superior. Parliaments, however, influence the selection of ministers and employ a number of instruments to obtain information and hold the government accountable. Their ability to do so is generally underestimated.

◆ There is a natural tendency for governments to develop elements of 'departmentalism'. Heads of government employ a number of devices to counter these tendencies and ensure the coherence of government policy. We can distinguish hierarchical mechanisms such as prime ministerial government, inner cabinets or coalition committees, or more horizontal instruments such as cabinet government or cabinet committees.

◆ Like all other delegation processes, the relationship between departmental ministers and civil servants is characterised by information asymmetry. Ministers can employ a number of institutional devices to reduce the asymmetry (ministerial cabinets, politically appointed civil servants, outside think-tanks).

◆ There is considerable variation in the extent to which governments in Europe are subject to external institutional checks such as constitutional courts, federal systems of government, independent central banks or supra-national bodies such as the European Union.

◆ The more institutional checks, the higher the decision-making costs. The fewer institutional checks, the higher the external risk faced by actors that are affected by, but not involved in, government decisions.

◆ The decision-making costs in the process of delegation have increased with phenomena such as globalisation and regionalisation.

# ■ Questions for discussion

▶ What are the most important types of referendums? What are the main advantages and disadvantages of referendums?

▶ What are the most important differences between the various electoral systems used in Europe? What are the implications of each electoral system for the ability of voters to hold elected politicians accountable?

▶ What are the comparative advantages and disadvantages of parliamentary, presidential and hybrid systems of government?

▶ How can ministers hold civil servants accountable?

▶ To what extent are parliaments nowadays reactive and marginal political actors?

▶ What are the main differences between majoritarian and consensual democracies in terms of the protection of minority interests and decision-making costs?

# ■ Further reading

Budge, I. et al. (1997) *The Politics of the New Europe: Atlantic to Urals* (London and New York: Longman). This textbook was written mainly for undergraduate students and provides a vast amount of important factual information and comparative interpretations of European political systems.

Gallagher, M., M. Laver and P. Mair (1995) *Representative Government in Modern Europe*, 2nd edn (New York: McGraw-Hill). This text was written mainly for undergraduate students of European comparative government and politics and provides readers with a great deal of important factual information and interpretation.

Lijphart, A. (1984) *Democracies: Patterns of Majoritarian and Consensus Government in Twenty-One Countries* (New Haven and London: Yale University Press). The book contrasts the 'Westminster model' as almost an ideal type of a 'majoritarian' system of government with more consensual forms of democracy. Although it is now a little dated, the book still provides important insights into some of the basic 'mechanisms' of government and politics in Europe.

Lijphart, A. (ed.) (1992) *Parliamentary versus Presidential Government* (Oxford: Oxford University Press). A reader containing excerpts from a number of classic texts on the comparative advantages and disadvantages of presidential and parliamentary systems of government.

Page, E. C. (1992) *Political Authority and Bureaucratic Power: A Comparative Analysis*, 2nd edn (Hemel Hempstead: Harvester Wheatsheaf). An accessible comparative study of bureaucracies and questions of political accountability from a Weberian perspective with a focus on Britain, France, Germany and the United States of America.

Shugart, M. S. and J. M. Carey (1992) *Presidents and Assemblies: Constitutional Design and Electoral Dynamics* (Cambridge: Cambridge University Press). Although the book's focus is not exclusively on Europe and is slightly more advanced than the texts above, it is one of the most important comparisons between parliamentary and presidential systems of government.

# Ever-Closer Union: European Co-operation and the European Dimension

Anne Stevens

'RECALLING the historic importance of the ending of the division of the European continent, and the need to create firm bases for the construction of the future Europe ...

RESOLVED to continue the process of creating an ever closer union among the peoples of Europe, in which decisions are taken as closely as possible to the citizen in accordance with the principle of subsidiarity ...

HAVE DECIDED to establish a European Union ...'

> Preamble to the Treaty of European Union (Maastricht Treaty) which came into force 1 November 1993

The context and content of the idea of 'Europe' have changed markedly in the 1980s and 1990s. The major developments of the two decades have pulled many of the nation states more closely together but the configuration of the links and institutions which bind them has changed. The 'European dimension' with which this chapter is concerned is the process of closer integration between European nation states. This is one of the most remarkable and distinctive features of contemporary Europe. The states, nations and societies of much of Europe have come to work together and cooperate in a large number of ways. This has created a new dimension to many of their activities that can be called the 'European dimension'. The links between states in Europe are closer and more dense than those between states in other regions of the world, and, as Chapter 8 demonstrates, with the ending of the sharp division of Europe, more states are being incorporated into what was previously the West European network. The discussion in this chapter will focus upon the processes of ever-closer union that increasingly link European states multilaterally. The European dimension is not simple or uniform, nor can it be regarded as simply involving a steady expansion of the European Union. But (see below) the advent of economic and monetary union, the formal recognition of **subsidiarity** and flexibility and the need to manage the enlargement process all point to complex and varied patterns of relationships within the European Union. The defence and security dimension (see Chapter 10) adds another layer of complexity. This chapter sets out some of the major aspects of the (non-military) European dimension and the reasons that underlie it, as well as the current state of the institution, the European Union, which principally embodies it, and the policies it conducts.

**Subsidiarity:** The principle, developed from Roman Catholic social thought, that public policy decisions should be made, and action taken, at as low a level and as close to the citizen as possible. It is enshrined in the Treaty of European Union, which requires that the Community act only if, and in so far as, the desired objectives cannot be sufficiently achieved by the member states. Some argue that the principle also requires devolution from central to local government.

**New World Order:** A term used by President Bush at the end of the Cold War which called for a world governed by international law, the respect of human rights and the renewed authority of the United Nations.

# Integration: how and why?

In the 1990s relationships within Europe, compared with those of the Cold War period, became more fragmented, more problematic, more uncertain. The problems of ethnic and territorial conflict, suppressed so often in Eastern Europe by the repressive ideological and political straitjacket of Marxism–Leninism, came so rapidly onto the scene that after 1990, despite the rhetoric about a **New World Order**, any easy euphoria about the changes was quite promptly dispelled (see Chapters 3 and 10). The rationale for integration now became one of managing the new relationships. Ever-closer union as a process, however ill-defined its goal, locked existing and potential member states into regular mutual interaction, discussion, negotiation and decision-making.

## The changed context

The need to manage new relationships was urgent because so much had changed. As late as the end of the 1970s it could still be argued that it was precisely its division which ensured peace within Europe, and hence Western European prosperity (De Porte, 1979). Soviet President Gorbachev himself, while advocating, as part of his policy of reconstruction (*perestroika*), renewed and improved relationships between the European Community and the states of the Council for Mutual Economic Assistance (CMEA or Comecon) within a 'common European home', thought that this could and would be accompanied by 'the attachment of European States to different systems of society' (speech to the Council of Europe, July 1989, quoted in Mayhew (1998).

The disappearance of the formal divisions that had shaped Europe and relationships between the European states since the late 1940s meant that there was an urgent need to reappraise the situation. The unification of Germany on 3 October 1990 was the most important development. It ended the division which had, in a largely unintended but crucial way, banished the spectre of a repeat of the resurgence of German dominance such as had occurred between the wars. It created a very large and populous single state at the geographical centre of Europe. The organisational and economic effort which it required placed considerable strains upon German resources, both public and private. The speed and completeness of the unification upon the West German model, and Chancellor Kohl's leadership of the unified state until 1998, ensured a continued commitment to co-operation and integration. Nevertheless, the balance had been altered.

*Obstacle*

*\* crossed*

## Frameworks for integration

The radical changes that occurred during the 1990s took place in a context shaped by existing networks of institutions and relationships. The division of Europe had produced frameworks for co-operation in both East and West Europe, but very few which spanned the divide. The major civilian organisations are considered below, while the European dimension in security and defence is discussed in Chapter 10 (see also Box 10.2 on the Organisation for Security and Co-operation in Europe). The East European framework for economic co-operation – the Council for Mutual Economic Assistance – disintegrated rapidly with the break-up of the Soviet Union and its empire. A more pragmatic and functional inter-state co-operation has since developed. Poland, Hungary, the Czech Republic and Slovakia constitute the so-called Visegrad forum, named after the town where they met in 1991. Out of this grew the Central European Free Trade Association, which now includes Slovenia and Romania. Bulgaria, Ukraine, Latvia and Lithuania all hope to join this free trade area (Hyde-Pryce, 1998a, p. 262). In the north, the Council of Baltic Sea States has brought together the Scandinavian countries, Germany, Poland, the Baltic Republics and Russia. One of the priorities of the Finnish presidency of the EU in the second half of 1999 was to develop this 'northern dimension'.

In the West, the Council of Europe, founded in 1948, brought together all the West European states to work together through a framework of intergovernmental conventions, which are binding only upon those states which actually ratify them, and come into force only when a quorum of states have done so. These conventions cover areas such as educational and cultural exchanges and developments, and the conservation of the environment. They deal 'with low key issues that facilitate public policy-making', and the conventions of the 1980s and 1990s have concerned matters such as football hooliganism (Laffan, 1992, p. 47).

By far the most important of these conventions is the European Convention on Human Rights. An enforcement mechanism, with a European Court of Human Rights, which is binding on those states that have accepted it, considers complaints which allege that the Convention has been breached. The Council of Europe co-operates with the EU and in 1989 the EC was for the first time a signatory to a Council of Europe convention (on the elaboration of a European Pharmacopoeia) (Laffan, 1992, p. 47). The European Court of Justice accepts that the European Convention on Human Rights sets out the general principles of human rights, which ought to obtain in the cases that it tries. It is important to note that the European Court of Human Rights is quite separate from the European Court of Justice. The Council of Europe was one of the first West European organisations that the East European countries sought to join as they emerged from under the shadow of the Soviet Union, and the Council was particularly active in promoting democratisation. Although the expansion in the scope of the activity of the European Union means that in some areas its work is now overshadowed, it remains an important forum for wider patterns of co-operation.

The Organisation for Economic Co-operation and Development is the successor to the body that was set up on the demand of the United States to oversee the distribution of the 'Marshall aid' reconstruction funds that the USA made available in the 1940s to the West European states (under Soviet influence the Central and East European states turned the offer down). Its membership now extends well beyond Europe, and it can be seen as having transformed itself into a body for the developed world as a whole (see Chapter 9).

The European dimension is also expressed through a number of smaller and more specialised agencies that promote cross-border co-operation. To take an example from the area of transport, the European Civil Aviation Conference, which until the early 1990s comprised only West European states, now has an expanded membership, which means that for the purposes of technical discussions on civilian air-transport matters Europe now extends from Reykjavik to Vladivostok. The EUREKA programme – 'an umbrella mechanism for mostly small R[esearch] and D[evelopment] projects' (Peterson and Sharp, 1998, p. 7) – grew between 1992 and 1997 from 20 (18 West European States plus the European Commission and Turkey) to 26 members, with links to many more. Similar developments can be observed in many other sectors.

The European Union itself was also a product of the Cold War context. The first of the founding treaties of what is now the European Union was the European Coal and Steel Community Treaty of 1951, between six states (Belgium, France, Germany, Italy, Luxembourg and the Netherlands). This was followed in 1957 by the Treaties, between the same six states, which created a European Economic Community (EEC) and a European Atomic Energy Community (Euratom). Out of those beginnings the 15-member European Union of the start of the new century has evolved, with a dense and complex treaty framework which effectively forms its constitutional basis. It is considered in much more detail below. In the changing context it rapidly became clear that the institutions that had been developed by the 1990s to provide a framework of co-operation among Western European states in the context of the Cold War, including the European Union, now provided a basis on which to manage the new links and networks.

## The interests of the nation-state

Many member states continue to have a paradoxical relationship with the European Union, and the rationale of membership of the Union as contributing to the protection, indeed advancement, of vital national, as opposed to collective, interests remains a powerful one. For example, France has consistently, until very recently, in both policy-making structures and approach (Guyomarch et al., 1998), assumed that the EC and now the EU provides a mechanism 'constructed on the idea that a larger economic entity would be more capable of defending itself against external economic aggression' (Picq, 1995, p. 145) for the expression of French ideas and the protection of French interests on a wider stage – that is, that it is traditional French **protectionism** writ large.

Such approaches to the rationale for EU membership continue to have a particular resonance in relation to the desire for membership of certain nation-states. In the case of the Mediterranean enlargement of the 1980s (Spain, Portugal and Greece joined what was then the European Community) the states involved had all fairly recently emerged from a period of non-democratic government. Membership of the EU provided a confirmation of their status as fully-fledged democracies, and an external constraint on any tendency to revert to **autocracy**. Thus their engagement in the process of integration constituted an affirmation of their identity as autonomous nation-states. Much the same logic applies to the applicant states of the former Soviet bloc, for whom membership of NATO and the EU symbolises autonomy and a move 'back to Europe' (Henderson, 1999).

## The dynamics of trade

The realisation that new technologies, new patterns of economic activity and new trading patterns were posing serious economic challenges constituted a further rationale for integration in the post-Cold War world (see also Chapter 9). In the context of globalisation, the development of effective trading patterns, and wide possibilities for the development and diffusion of innovation and for the maintenance of competitivity, help to constitute a national rationale for integration, even if at the level of the firm the approach must be global. Governments may perceive this as being best achieved through integration.

It was the logic and dynamics of trading and economic relationships, in particular, which prompted the developments that resulted in the 1995 enlargement of the

**Protectionism:** The use of trade barriers such as tariffs, taxes, technical rules and invisible barriers in order to protect a state's economy from imports.

**Autocracy:** Government by a single person having unlimited power.

EU to include Austria, Sweden and Finland. These members of the European Free Trade Association felt that they risked economic marginalisation if the advent of the single market and the EU's developments in technology projects resulted in greater dynamism within the EU from which they would be excluded (Dinan, 1994, p. 446). The EU equally valued its trading partnership with the EFTA countries. The initial response was the negotiation of the European Economic Area (EEA), but the disparities in power and influence within this – the EFTA countries were bound to adopt EU regulations, which they could not be involved in shaping – led Austria, Finland and Sweden to seek and gain membership.

## An ongoing process

Ever-closer union can be viewed as an ongoing process with a momentum of its own. The process was given particular impetus by the relaunch of the European Community in the mid-1980s. By then a number of essentially institutional issues that had proved to be major obstacles to policy development within the EC had been removed. The Mediterranean enlargement (Spain, Portugal and Greece) had been agreed.

A solution, involving a substantial rebate negotiated by Mrs Thatcher, had been found, at the Fontainebleau summit of 1984, to the long-running dispute over the size of the British contribution to the EC budget. Very shortly after Jacques Delors took office as President of Commission in 1985, a sense of frustration with the institutional patterns that seemed to have thwarted progress came together with a call for the elimination of all frontiers within the Community. At the Milan European Council meeting of June 1985 the Commission *White Paper on the Completion of the Internal Market* (the so-called 1992 programme) was approved, and agreement was reached on the calling of an Intergovernmental Conference (IGC) to draft a treaty that would amend the institutional framework. The outcome of the negotiations within the Intergovernmental Conference was the Single European Act (SEA), which came into force in 1987. It was a single act both in the sense that it amended all the three founding treaties that formed the bases of the ECSC, the EEC and Euratom, and in that it brought into the treaty framework the machinery that had developed on the margins of the European Community for political (foreign policy) co-operation between the member states.

One interpretation of the SEA, associated with Delors, saw it as resulting from a determination on the part of the member states to increase the scope and pace of integration. From a rather different angle, that of Mrs Thatcher for example, it is possible to see the SEA as little more than the necessary framework for the achievement of an open, competitive, liberalised and deregulated European market. As Urwin points out, 'the difference [between the two views] was that one was looking beyond 1992 to some kind of political union, while the other would be content with the internal market flanked by heightened cooperation among the member states on a host of other issues' (Urwin, 1991, p. 240).

Within a short time after the implementation of the SEA the European context had changed dramatically. The European Community was steadily putting into place the measures needed to implement the single market and this was producing a greater level of public awareness of the issues and challenges. For Delors, however, the single market formed only one part of a much bigger whole. Social policy measures which, it was hoped, would secure the support of the electorate for integration by ensuring

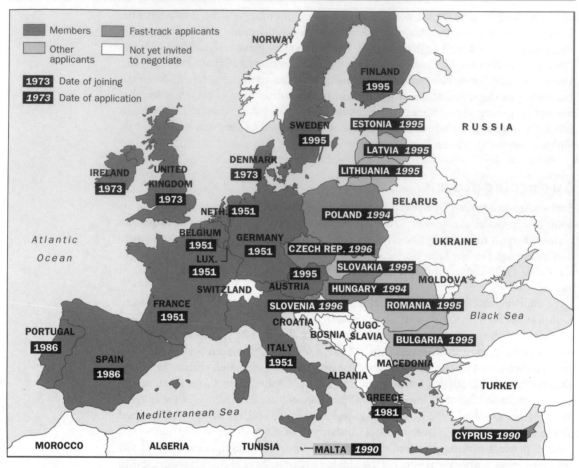

**Map 7.1** The enlargements of the European Union (ECSU in 1951; EU for later dates)
*Source*: *The Economist* (London), 23 October 1999.

at least that market-driven developments did not damage their social benefits constituted one part of this larger picture. In December 1989 a Community Charter of the Fundamental Rights of Workers was accepted at the Strasbourg European Council. Economic and monetary union was a still higher priority, and the Madrid European Council of June 1989 agreed to the launching of the first stage of progress towards economic and monetary union in 1990. These decisions coincided with the upheavals in Eastern Europe and launched a fierce debate about whether it was preferable to 'widen' or to 'deepen' the European Community. The debate was epitomised by the gulf between Mrs Thatcher, whose 'vociferous support for an immediate widening of the Community's membership barely disguised her determination to prevent deepening at all costs' (Dinan, 1994, p. 163) and Delors who called for a major strengthening of the Community in the face of the evolving situation.

The decision to hold an Intergovernmental Conference to negotiate the treaty amendments which would be needed to implement economic and monetary union, and the slightly later decision to hold a simultaneous and parallel Intergovernmental Conference on political union, provided some resolution to this debate and resulted in the Treaty of European Union (TEU), often known as the Maastricht Treaty, which came into force in November 1993. The TEU both created the European Union and contained a timetable for economic and monetary union. This Treaty marked a decisive step away from most visions of the European Community as no more than an enhanced and efficient single market. In the context of the end of the Cold War this step, although debatable and contested, marked a recognition that the future must indeed be based on both the widening and the deepening of the 'ever-closer union' to which the founding treaties aspired. It was in part the recognition of the need for sustained and steady progress that motivated the agreement that a further treaty would be needed five years on, and the Treaty of Amsterdam, ratified on 1 May 1999, was the result.

At the level of relationships between states the European dimension thus enmeshes them in a plethora of networks and institutions, with the European Union as a particularly dynamic and dominant part of the pattern. However, as the quotation from the Maastricht Treaty at the head of this chapter indicates, integration is intended to be the ever-closer union of peoples. There is a 'European dimension' to the way in which governments, groups within civil society, and individuals behave in contemporary Europe.

# The impact of 'Europe'

The fact of being enmeshed in a network of European institutions has inevitably affected the behaviour and reactions of the national governments involved. The rather dense pattern of contacts and interactions ranges from those in which decision-making is fairly informal, such as regular bilateral meetings between heads of government, through the more formalised arenas of the intergovernmental organisations, to the European Union, with its complex structures and procedures that can make laws which apply directly to every citizen.

The processes of negotiation, co-ordination and often compromise which are involved in such policy-making have had a number of effects to which governments have had to adapt. One governmental reaction has been to attempt to use the scope offered by the European level to extend national policies into a wider field. This was for a long time a notable feature of French policy towards the European Union, which it saw partly as a means of translating traditional French protectionist policies to a broader arena. The British support for the Single European Act is another example. A second effect has been to force politicians to confront and agree to actions and decisions that they might not otherwise have taken. An example of this is the changes introduced to Italian budgetary and financial policy so that Italy could fulfil the conditions for participation in the single currency. In a country where achieving sufficient agreement between a multiplicity of political parties and factions to achieve radical reform is often well-nigh impossible, civil servants and experts could appeal to rationality and necessity since the overall aim of maintaining Italy's position in 'Europe' was accepted by all (Radaelli, 1999a, pp. 2–3). At both its creation in the late 1950s and its relaunch in the 1980s governments looked to the European Community to have a galvanising effect upon industry and commerce and to induce necessary modernisation. Equally, however, 'Europe' can become an umbrella, which politicians use to deflect blame or criticism when things seem not to be going well, or policies turn out to be unpopular.

As a consequence of the policy implications of engagement within the network of European institutions political parties have also been affected by increasing

**Box 7.1**

## Parties in the European Parliament, September 1999

| | EPP/ED | PES | ELDR | GREENS/ EFA | EUL/ NLG | UEN | EDD | IND | Total |
|---|---|---|---|---|---|---|---|---|---|
| Belgium | 6 | 5 | 5 | 7 | | | | 2 | 25 |
| Denmark | 1 | 3 | 6 | | 1 | 1 | 4 | | 16 |
| Germany | 53 | 33 | | 7 | 6 | | | | 99 |
| Greece | 9 | 9 | | | 7 | | | | 25 |
| Spain | 28 | 24 | 3 | 4 | 4 | | | 1 | 64 |
| France | 21 | 22 | | 9 | 11 | 12 | 6 | 6 | 87 |
| Ireland | 5 | 1 | 1 | 2 | | 6 | | | 15 |
| Italy | 34 | 17 | 7 | 2 | 6 | 9 | | 12 | 87 |
| Luxembourg | 2 | 2 | 1 | 1 | | | | | 6 |
| Netherlands | 9 | 6 | 8 | 4 | 1 | | 3 | | 31 |
| Austria | 7 | 7 | | 2 | | | | 5 | 21 |
| Portugal | 9 | 12 | | | 2 | 2 | | | 25 |
| Finland | 5 | 3 | 5 | 2 | 1 | | | | 16 |
| Sweden | 7 | 6 | 4 | 2 | 3 | | | | 22 |
| UK | 37 | 30 | 10 | 6 | | | 3 | 1 | 87 |
| Total | 233 | 180 | 50 | 48 | 42 | 30 | 16 | 27 | 626 |

| | |
|---|---|
| EPP/ED | European People's Party/European Democrats: includes Christian Democrats, British Conservatives, and mainstream French Gaullist (RPR) members |
| PES | Party of European Socialists |
| ELDR | European Liberal, Democratic and Reformist Party |
| GREENS/EFA | Green Group of the European Parliament/European Free Alliance: includes Greens and various regionalist/home rule parties |
| EUL/NLG | Confederal Group of the United European Left/Nordic Left |
| UEN | Union for a Europe of the Nations: includes dissident Gaullists |
| EDD | Europe of Democracies and Diversities: includes French members of Chasse Pêche Nature Tradition (Hunting, Fishing, Nature, Tradition) and Eurosceptics from the UK, Denmark and the Netherlands |
| IND | Independent and non-attached |

*Note:* After the elections a Technical Group of Independents (TGI) brought together MEPs from parties of different political persuasions to enable them to benefit from group privileges. At the September 1999 plenary session, MEPs endorsed a recommendation from the Affairs Committee that the TGI Group should be disbanded on the grounds that it was in breach of the Rules of Procedure because it did not have a political complexion.

*Source:* http://www.macmillan-press.co.uk:80/politics/eu/euparlelections.htm  Adapted from European Parliament Directorate-General for Information and Public Relations, *Session News*, 28 September 1999.

integration. Many, for example the Christian Democratic parties of much of Western Europe, have consistently favoured closer union. Others have been more hostile – the extreme Left and the extreme Right have generally opposed increased integration – or, as is the case of the Gaullists in France and both the British Labour and Conservative Parties, have shifted in their attitudes. But even those parties which oppose integration fight the elections for the European Parliament, even though the campaigns are invariably rather nationally based, and there is still only very limited transnational co-operation and organisation amongst parties, although they do form cross-national groups within the European Parliament (see Box 7.1).

The growing weight of the European Union as a regulator in economic, commercial and industrial matters, and its role as a provider of grants and funds for various purposes, has resulted in an increased awareness among businesses and interest groups of the European dimension of their activities and interests. For many firms this has coincided with the steady implementation of the policies designed to create the single market and with the huge increase in global flows described in Chapter 9. One consequence has been a mushrooming of lobbyists, and of local offices for public and private bodies, groups and enterprises in Brussels – by 1992 there were 3,000 special interest groups there (Mazey and Richardson, 1993, p. 108).

## A contested rationale: popular support and the growth of Euroscepticism

Ministers, officials, politicians, business people and the leaders of interest and pressure groups have adapted their behaviour and policies to the existence of a European dimension. The governing elites in Europe are by and large supportive of the process of integration. 'National elites had shared interests in promoting European integration yet preventing the erosion of national interests that provided their own legitimacy . . . The result was the so-called "permissive consensus", whereby Europe's publics were content to delegate responsibility to their leaders to tackle the European integration project' (Hix, 1999, p. 164). However, the 1990s have demonstrated that the rationale for integration, which seems compelling to governments, may be contested by citizens and the electorate. In 1990–1 the Eurobarometer public opinion surveys in the member states of the EU showed that 72 per cent of those surveyed were in favour of their country's membership of the European Union and 82 per cent were generally 'for' the 'efforts being made to unify Western Europe' (Hix, 1999, pp. 135–6). These figures have since fallen markedly.

The process of ratification of the Maastricht Treaty opened up the issues surrounding integration to widespread debates across the member states in an unprecedented way. Maastricht ratification produced referenda in Denmark, Ireland and France, and fierce political controversy in the United Kingdom, as Prime Minister John Major battled to carry through the necessary parliamentary process against not only the Labour opposition, which was happy to use it to discomfit the government, albeit on the argument of objection to the UK opt-out from the Social Chapter of the Treaty, but also the 'Eurosceptic' rebels in his own party. The consequence was that the nature and rationale for integration became a topic of widespread discussion and controversy. The referenda on membership in the applicant countries in 1994 revealed far from universal support, although only Norway (again) rejected membership.

The divisions in the support for the process of integration, and over what sort of outcome should emerge from it, are related to a wide variety of cultural, political and economic factors, including a decline since the mid-1980s in the willingness of people to support integration simply because they believe that a united Europe would be 'a good thing'. The perception of being a 'winner' or a 'loser' as a consequence of the policies of the EU seems in the late 1990s to be more crucial as a determinant of support for integration. The divisions which result from these complex factors cut across traditional party divides, have a considerable impact on the internal politics of the countries of Western Europe and result in complex and fragmented political competition (Hix, 1999, pp. 133–65). Any self-evident rationale for integration can no longer be taken for granted but instead the case has to be made and fought for.

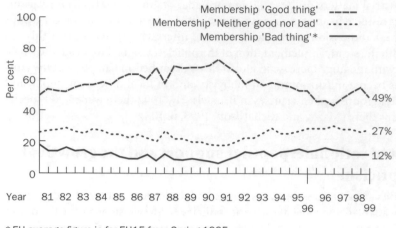

* EU average figure is for EU15 from Spring 1995.

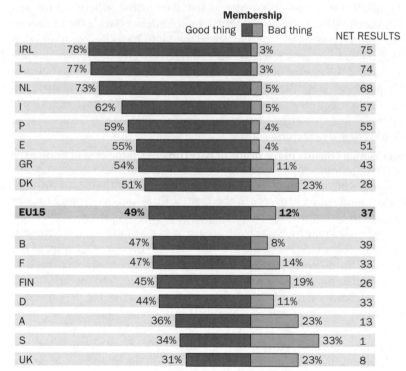

**Fig. 7.1** Support for European Union membership
*Source*: European Commission (1999) *Eurobarometer*, 51, p. 25.

In Eastern Europe there was, after 1989, a high level of support for a 'return to Europe', in the sense of a desire to escape from the Communist model (Mayhew, 1998, p. 10; Hyde-Pryce, 1998b, pp. 264–5), to be incorporated within the network of international organisations which link West European countries, and above all to symbolise a return to Europe by joining an EU which, at the beginning of the 1990s, seemed to be achieving its targets – prosperity, growth and the completion of the single market – and moving forward. But this enthusiasm was not necessarily matched on the EU side, and it became obvious both that great difficulties and changes would be involved, and that not all the applicant countries would be able to move forward together. The 'slow-track' applicants were appeased by a start to the process of assessing of their ability to conform to the EU's legislation (the *acquis communautaire*) and annual progress reviews. Moreover, the existing member states were not disposed to be particularly generous or to sacrifice their own key interests (for example, the protection of their textile industries or agriculture) to facilitate the process. So some disillusion has grown and there is a recognition that, despite continued majority support for accession in the candidate countries, governments will need to provide extensive information and also to woo sensitive groups such as trade unions and farmers (Mayhew, 1998, pp. 380 and 388).

# The structure of the European Union

The European Union occupies a key and central position within the processes of ever-closer union. A series of treaties have shaped its structures, and resulted in a complex set of institutions. Its current shape was fashioned by the TEU, which created the European Union and profoundly altered the constitutional architecture of Western European integration.

The European Union comprises not only the long-standing European Community (EC) as 'Pillar I' of the Union, but also two new, differently structured 'pillars', one for justice and home affairs ( Pillar III) and one for a common foreign and security policy (Pillar II).

## The institutions of the EU

The European Council consists of the heads of government (in the case of France the President, who is head of state) of the member states. Its main role is to guide the development of the EU and its policies and to resolve, at the highest level, disputes which cannot be settled elsewhere. It considers issues that arise in relation to any or all of the areas with which the European Union is concerned. The role of the other institutions is to formulate policy, to express it in legislation, and to oversee

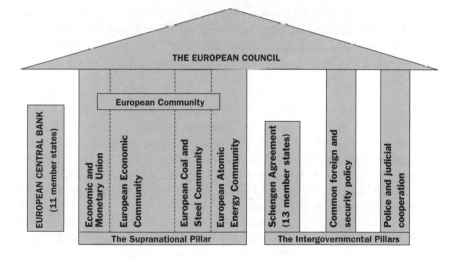

**Fig. 7.2** The architecture of the European Union

the implementation of the legislation and the identification, and where necessary punishment, of breaches of the law. The Council of Ministers is a body which, although legally a single institution, takes a large variety of different forms, since it may meet as a specialised group of ministers from each of the member states dealing with any specific policy area. The senior grouping is the General Affairs Council consisting of foreign ministers, which acts as the decision-maker for Pillar II as well as for major issues and general co-ordination for Pillar I. There is a Justice and Home Affairs Council of the relevant national ministers for Pillar III. The Council of Ministers meetings are presided over by a minister from the member state that at the time holds the six-month rotating presidency of the Council.

The other institutions are the European Commission (see below), the European Parliament, and the European Court of Justice. The Commission elaborates policy and proposes the necessary legislation, and in some fields, such as agriculture and coal and steel, has important powers of secondary legislation and implementation. The Parliament debates, considers and advises, and exercises some powers of veto and decision, and the Council of Ministers decides, usually by voting through a system of weighted votes (qualified majority voting – QMV), though legislation in some policy areas requires unanimous agreement. The Court of Justice, along with the Court of Auditors, has an essentially supervisory role. In Pillars II and III the outcome of the decisions taken does not normally involve Community Law and the Court does not have powers to review those decisions. Through its interpretation and application of legislation, the Court of Justice has, however, at times played a major role in the development of the EC's scope and powers and the balance of its institutions. The Economic and Social Committee and the Committee of the Regions have an advisory role.

The creation of the European Union with its pillarised structure greatly increased the complexity of structures and processes. The central structures remain those of the EC. The 'community' method of decision-making involves interaction between at least three parties – the Council of Ministers, the Commission and the Parliament – and is hence already complex. The other pillars overlap with Pillar I. The TEU formally separated the decision-making processes, but utilised common structural frameworks. Thus it provided that in Common Foreign and Security Policy the General Affairs Council, acting unanimously, could agree on 'joint actions' and could then, by QMV as in Pillar I, agree how these joint actions should be implemented. The Commission has the right (though not, as in Pillar I, an exclusive right) to propose actions. And in some cases the actions can only work well if European Community means – trade policy, and funding for aid or collaboration – are utilised to further them (Peterson and Bomberg, 1999, p. 244). The coming into force of the Amsterdam Treaty on 1 May 1999 resulted in a marked reduction of the scope of Pillar III, with matters relating to the crossing of internal and external borders, immigration policy, and visas and asylum being transferred to Pillar I (the EC). There is a certain logic in ensuring that all provisions for the movement of persons are dealt with by similar mechanisms. There had been dissatisfaction with the complex results of the Maastricht arrangements (Uçarer, 1999). The new title of the EC treaty created by Amsterdam does provide that such decisions shall be taken by unanimity and that the Commission shall share the right of initiative with the member states, so the move does not represent a major shift in approach.

At the same time Pillar II (the common foreign and security policy) was given an extended institutional framework (Peterson and Bomberg, 1999, pp. 228–46). This was at least partly in response to its perceived inadequacies, since it had been be-devilled by disagreements not so much about policy as about decision-making mechanisms. Pillars II and III of the EU operate primarily through agreement be-tween the member states, but since the EU as such has no legal right to sign treaties or pass binding legislation (Lintner and Church, forthcoming), its policies are largely embodied in legal acts of the EC. Policies may also be expressed through, for example, international agreements with non-member states or groups of states.

## Amsterdam and flexibility

During the 1990s the EU adopted a pragmatic but complex political response to the challenges presented by some of the broader variations in the political and economic circumstances of member states stretching from north of the Arctic Circle to the Mediterranean and constituting a European Union of ever-increasing scope. This was the introduction of greater complexity and flexibility. By creating two pillars with an essentially intergovernmental structure alongside the more supra-national pillar of the EC, the EU recognised that identical decision-making procedures and methods need not apply to all areas of EU policy. By permitting the United Kingdom to exclude itself from the operation of the social policy chapter attached to the TEU, the other member states, tacitly acknowledging irreconcilable ideological differences (which disappeared after the Labour victory in the UK election of 1997, so that the opt-out was abandoned), deserted the principle of the uniform application of EU legislation, which had been one of the main features of its nature and originality since the beginning. Economic and Monetary Union (EMU) does not embrace all the member states (see below). Nor is it simply a matter of opting out. The Treaty of Amsterdam envisages that 'member states which intend to establish closer coopera-tion between them may make use of the institutions, procedures and mechanisms laid down by the Treaties' to achieve such co-operation in both the EC and the Justice and Home Affairs pillars, provided, amongst other conditions, that at least a majority of all the member states are involved, and the others are entitled to join in later if they can take on board what has been done.

With the ratification of the Treaty of Amsterdam, co-operation based on the EU institutions and methods (perhaps between a 'core' group of EU member states and resulting in a union of concentric or perhaps overlapping circles of integration) can in theory commence. It relates only to future developments, so will not allow member states to 'pick and mix' within existing policy provisions, and 'it will be very difficult for flexibility to be practised in the EU's core policy areas' (Nugent, 1999, p. 89). According to the Treaties this kind of flexibility will operate alongside the principle of subsidiarity, defined more fully by a protocol attached to the Treaty of Amster-dam than it was in the TEU, which requires the EU to justify any action it undertakes on the bases both that it cannot be done by member states acting alone, and that it can be better done by the EU. Combined with the prospect of enlargement, these features of the EU's evolving constitution provide no reason to suppose that the evolution of the EU will be simple or straightforward.

## The role of the European Commission

The European Commission is central to the decision-making processes of the Euro-pean Union and hence at the heart of the European Integration dimension of con-temporary Europe. For matters covered by Pillar I of the EU structure (the European

Community) it alone has the right to lay before the Council of Ministers the text that, if agreed, will become European Union law. Ideas and proposals for such laws come from many sources, including the European Council, the Council of Ministers and the European Parliament, and not just within the Commission and its adminis-trative services, but they are worked up by the services of the Commission, and the Commission controls their priority and progress. So it can be described as an 'agenda-setter'. The Commission has also been described as a 'broker of interests' and as a 'purposeful opportunist' (Cram, 1999, p. 48), its purpose frequently being to extend its scope for action and increase the range of matters dealt with through the pro-cesses of integration. In the Common Foreign and Security Policy (CFSP) it has fewer powers, and the 'High Representative' for CFSP provided for by the Amster-dam Treaty (Javier Solana) is a senior official of the Council of Ministers, not part of the Commission. However, the Commission is a participant in the discussions and decision-making and through the EC external relations, trade and development policies in which its role is substantial, it does play an important role (Holland, 1999, p. 232). In Justice and Home Affairs the Amsterdam Treaty has resulted in the Com-mission gaining increased rights in some areas (Uçarer, 1999).

The Commission can trace its antecedents back to the High Authority of the European Coal and Steel Community, the body that was given executive respons-ibility by the Treaty of Paris to propose and implement policy for the coal and steel sector. Given the restricted and relatively technical policy area in which the High Authority operated it was feasible for it to be designed as a body of selected experts (Radaelli, 1999b, p. 4) who would be able to discern the 'best' policy. As Jean Monnet, who designed the system, perceived it (Peterson and Bomberg, 1999, p. 232), they would gradually draw the affected groups in society into involvement in making the 'right' decisions. Once this system was seen to be working well in one sector there would be pressure for it to be applied also to other areas, and in this way integration would gradually spread outwards, through the processes known as *engrenage* (enmesh-

---

**Box 7.2**

### The 'empty chair' crisis

General de Gaulle (see Portrait 2.5) came to power in France in May 1958, shortly after the creation of the European Economic Community. He had, while out of power, been opposed to the process of European integration. However, he acknowledged the benefits likely to accrue both to the French economy and the scope for French leadership amongst the nation-states of Europe. Although his attempts to shift the EEC into directions which he thought more likely to reinforce France's position failed he was able, in 1963, to veto the British application for membership, at least partly to avoid the advent of a rival for leadership. He became concerned at growing attempts by the Commission to assert the supra-national powers of the EEC and its own status. He did not wish to see the EEC given increased powers to raise its own resources, nor a concomitant increase in the powers of the European Parliament. In 1965 he used a dispute over agricultural policy decisions as an excuse to withdraw from the major decision-making processes of the Community, thus leaving an 'empty chair'. The problems were resolved by the Luxembourg Compromise of 1966, a statement which had no legal status but considerable moral and political force, noting the French view that in cases of disagreement, discussion should, when member states felt that their vital national interests were affected, continue until unanimity was achieved. This 'Luxembourg veto' reinforced the inter-governmental aspects of the Community. The compromise also involved agreement by the member states to rein in aspects of the Commission's behaviour where it was acting too much like a government (for example, in receiving ambassadors).

ing) and spill-over. In such a system political visions and choices become almost irrelevant, and the Council of Ministers something of an afterthought.

The creation of the European Economic Community and Euratom, the widening of the spheres of policy-making and the perception that a major step forward in integration was occurring resulted in a somewhat different perception of both Commission and Council of Ministers, although any pretensions to grandeur the Commission entertained were dashed by the 1965 'empty chair' crisis (see Box 7.2).

The term 'the European Commission' refers both to the College of Commissioners – the 20 Commissioners, one from each of the smaller states and two each from the five larger states (see Box 7.3) – and to the administrative staff who support them. It is divided into departments, known as Directorates-General, each looking after a specific policy area, plus a number of specialised services, such as the interpreting and conference service and the statistical service. Each Commissioner has responsibility for one or more of these areas and is supported in his or her tasks by an extended private office (cabinet). The role of the College of Commissioners and its president again acquired a high profile under the charismatic leadership of Jacques Delors between 1985 and 1994. Jacques Santer was chosen by the member states to replace him on the basis that the Commission should do less, but do it better.

However, allegations of corruption and poor administration forced the resignation of the whole College in early 1999. The former Commissioners continued on an acting basis until a new team took office in September 1999. The episode illustrated some of the strengths and limitations of the collective nature of the College of Commissioners. There was no mechanism by which the Commission President, the

## Box 7.3

### Commissioners of the European Union, 1999

| | |
|---|---|
| Romano Prodi (Italy) | President |
| Neil Kinnock (UK) | Vice-President, Administrative Reform |
| Loyola de Palacio (Spain) | Vice-President, Relations with the European Parliament, Transport and Energy |
| Mario Monti (Italy) | Competition |
| Franz Fischler (Austria) | Agriculture, Rural Development and Fisheries |
| Erkki Liikanen (Finland) | Enterprise and Information Society |
| Frits Bolkestein (Netherlands) | Internal Market |
| Philippe Busquin (Belgium) | Research |
| Pedro Solbes Mira (Spain) | Economic and Monetary Affairs |
| Poul Nielson (Denmark) | Development and Humanitarian Aid |
| Günter Verheugen (Germany) | Enlargement |
| Chris Patten (UK) | External Relations |
| Pascal Lamy (France) | Trade |
| David Byrne (Ireland) | Health and Consumer Protection |
| Michel Barnier (France) | Regional Policy (also responsible ad personam for the Inter-Governmental Conference) |
| Viviane Reding (Luxembourg) | Education and Culture |
| Michaele Schreyer (Germany) | Budget |
| Margot Wallström (Sweden) | Environment |
| Antonio Vitorino (Portugal) | Justice and Home Affairs |
| Anna Diamantopoulou (Greece) | Employment and Social Affairs |

member states or the Parliament could require the resignation of a single com-missioner. In picking former Italian Prime Minister Romano Prodi to preside over the next College of Commissioners the member states indicated their desire for a president who would be in a position to impose his leadership on the team, and who was able to require written guarantees of individual resignation if he demanded it before accepting the nominations (*The Guardian/The Independent*, 7/8 July 1999). It was not entirely a team of his own choosing, however. Commissioners are nomi-nated by the individual member states, and Prodi engaged in determined, but not entirely successful, negotiation with them to obtain the balance he sought, both of gender and of political orientation. While some 80 per cent of the members of the post-1967 European Commissioners have been career politicians before their appointment to the College (Hix, 1999, pp. 35–6) they have come from a broad spectrum of the mainstream political parties from Left to Right, including, in the Prodi Commission, the German Greens. The College thus does not come into office on the basis of any defined or agreed political programme. Although the Commission is responsible for proposing policy developments and detailed policy measures, some-times at the behest of either the European Council or the Council of Ministers, it is not like a national government, even a coalition government, in terms of programme or ideology.

Nor is it like a national government in terms of accountability. The President's appointment and those of the individual Commissioners have to be confirmed by the Parliament, after hearings, and the Parliament can force the collective dismissal of the whole college, though when the Santer Commission resigned it was in re-sponse to a highly critical report from a committee of independent experts set up by the Parliament, rather than a vote of no-confidence. The MEPs can ask Commissioners questions. But the College of Commissioners never has to face the electorate, its priorities and programmes are not the outcome of a popular mandate, and it can seem remote from democratic processes and public opinion.

The scandals that emerged in early 1999 highlighted some of the weaknesses of the Commission, both the College of Commissioners and their services. It was re-vealed as fragmented, under-resourced to confront the demands placed upon it, with an inadequate ethos of responsibility and accountability and poor management and control. Many of these weaknesses had long been recognised and the Santer Commission had been undertaking a number of initiatives to try to tackle some of them. The incoming President, Romano Prodi, vigorously supported the continua-tion of reform, which he allocated to Commission Vice-President Neil Kinnock.

However, the central bodies of the European Union face fundamental challenges in the first years of the new century. The organisation of the Commission and the processes of decision-making are already unwieldy and complex. The current organ-isation, with the presence in the Commission of nominees from every member state, and two from the largest, each with specific and separate functional responsibilities, cannot survive the enlargement of the EU to the six front-runner states, still less the second-stage applicants. This was recognised as early as 1992, but as the Treaty of Amsterdam was drafted the issue was fudged and put off until at least a year before the membership of the EU exceeds 20.

## Enlargement: challenges and prospects

In retrospect, as Irene Brennan suggests in Chapter 8, the Copenhagen Council of June 1993 may be seen as a crucial moment in determining the long-term scope and nature of relationships between states within Europe as a whole. The EU can no longer be envisaged, at least in the long term, as a club of West European states. New ways will have to be found of determining where the boundaries of the Union should lie and managing relationships between states that are actual or potential members of the Union and those that are not and are not likely to become so.

The process of the expansion of the European Union to (potentially) at least 26 member states through the accession of 10 Central and East European countries and Cyprus, and possibly Malta, will be a prolonged one. The process began with a meeting in March 1998 of the 'European Conference', which is intended to meet annually and bring together all the Union's member states with all the applicants. Turkey, a very long-standing applicant, was invited to the conference, but on the basis that it was not yet in a position to enter the enlargement process. This approach so angered the Turkish government that it stayed away.

For the other applicants the process involves individual pre-accession partnerships covering their commitments to move towards adoption of the Union's laws and policies (the *acquis communautaire*) and the provision of financial and technical assistance by the Union. Negotiations began with the first six applicants in mid-1998.

The timetable for the process is still far from clear and 'the talks are sure to be lengthy and difficult' (Baun, 1999, p. 280). It is generally thought that accession for the first group of countries will not occur before 2003 and more probably not until 2005 or later. Whilst there may seem to be a degree of inevitability about the process, there are undoubtedly formidable difficulties to be overcome (see Chapter 8). On the EU side, enlargement will involve

- institutional reform;
- a shift in geographical balance;
- reform or adaptation of a number of existing policies;
- agreement over the extent and directions in which the EU budget should redistribute resources;
- a willingness on the part of the existing member states to prefer enlargement to the pursuit of their own national interests and to avoid disruptive linkages of consent to enlargement to other issues. (Mayhew, 1998, p. 353)

The challenges to the candidate states are even more formidable (see Chapter 8). In the face of these challenges, and the protracted time-scale over which progress to a Union of at least 26 will emerge, there is no room for complacency or comfortable assumptions. Nothing can be taken for granted.

## Euroland

The challenges of enlargement are being faced at the same time as those of another profound change in the relationships between the countries of Europe. On 1 January 1999 the currencies of eleven member states of the European Union became locked together with fixed exchange rates. The Euro came into existence as the common unit of currency in all these countries. It was at first a virtual unit of currency: while many transactions and amounts were expressed in Euros, there were not as yet any Euro banknotes and coins, and travellers moving from one country into another still needed to exchange their cash, albeit at fixed rates. The notes and coins will be introduced in 2002 and will replace the national notes and coins over a period of a few months.

For countries both inside and outside what was quickly dubbed 'Euroland' the importance of these developments is immense. The arrival in paypackets, shops and streets of the new currency will be the outward and visible sign of a lengthy and complex process. The desirability and possibility of an economic and monetary union as a necessary accompaniment to, indeed the next stage of, common policies on agriculture, competition and trade had been under discussion since the end of the 1960s; 1979 saw the creation of a European monetary system including an exchange rate mechanism that limited the scope of exchange rate fluctuations. French dissatisfaction with what they saw as domination of the system by the German Mark and West German Central Bank (the *Bundesbank*), a developing understanding of the possible consequences of the implementation of the single market programme, and the personal commitment of Jacques Delors to a project which he saw as central to deeper integration, led to the Delors Report of 1989, written by a committee which included the governors of the central banks of the EU member states, chaired by Delors. In some respects the timing was opportune: although progress was not rapid, Economic and Monetary Union, as advocated by the Delors Report, came to be seen as one of the main ways in which a newly unified Germany, the emergence of which risked altering the political balance of the integration process in unpredictable ways, could be more closely linked to West European partners. The linkage was clearly articulated from November 1989 onwards.

The timetable for movement through the second and third stages of Economic and Monetary Union, and the criteria to be used to assess the fitness of each member state for inclusion within the common currency zone, were settled, after difficult negotiations, in the Maastricht Treaty. The most distinctive feature of the system adopted within the treaty was its explicit recognition that the Economic and Monetary Union, despite being seen as a key stage in the achievement of integration, would not involve all the member states. It was recognised that 'not every country would be economically able, and no country would be politically forced, to join the currency union at the outset' (Dinan, 1994, p. 177).

In the event, four of the sixteen member states were outside 'Euroland' when it was created on 1 January 1999. Denmark, Sweden and the United Kingdom decided

---

**Box 7.4**

### The 'Maastricht criteria' for membership of the common European currency

- An average inflation rate not exceeding by more than 1.5 per cent that of the three member states with the lowest inflation rates.

- A budget deficit of less than 3 per cent of GDP.

- A public debt ratio of not more than 60 per cent of GDP.

- Exchange rates within the 2.5 per cent margins of the Exchange Rate Mechanism for at least two years 'without severe tensions' and without devaluations.

- An average long-term nominal interest rate not exceeding by more than 2 per cent that of the three member states with the lowest rates.

These criteria were mitigated by a number of qualifications – for example, government debt could exceed 60 per cent of GDP if it were diminishing steadily and fast enough. The final decision on eligibility was both a political and an economic one. All member states except Greece were held to be eligible when the decision about membership of the Euro was made in the Spring of 1998, but Denmark, Sweden and the United Kingdom opted not to join. The euro was introduced on 1 January 1999. In 2002 Euro banknotes and coins will replace national ones in the participating countries.

to stay outside despite being adjudged economically eligible to join. Greece was found to be too far outside the criteria. Fulfilment of the criteria had placed the economies of a number of the member states under considerable economic and political strain. The perceived difficulties of maintaining a common currency across such diverse economic structures were certainly reflected in the initial fortunes of the Euro, which fell quite sharply against both the dollar and the pound Sterling over the first six months of its existence. Maintaining monetary discipline was likely to continue to pose problems and difficulties: for example, Italy, which had managed to gain acceptance of the view that it was sufficiently close to fulfilling the criteria to be allowed to enter, only by the imposition of special taxes, and the production of a plan to reduce its debts sharply by 2002, announced a few months into 1999 that its budget deficit would be well above the maximum allowed under the stability pact which was designed to prevent the currency being weakened by just such deficits. The consequence should have been a large fine; but the German desire for automatic disciplinary measures had been tempered by French insistence that such decisions must be political (Hix, 1999, p. 288). No fine was imposed.

Managing the Euro is now the task of the European Central Bank. This, along with organising the introduction of the new banknotes and coins and, above all, maintaining appropriate fiscal and monetary discipline and a reasonable balance between the participating economies – in 1999 Ireland was growing very rapidly while Germany continued to stagnate – will be major challenges for the countries of Euroland and for the system. Managing the relationships within the EU between those states that do participate in EMU and those that do not will be equally challenging. The Euro may prove to be a stable and successful currency and Sweden, Denmark and the United Kingdom might move to adopting it, despite formidable domestic political difficulties. Greece is expected to join within about three years from the launch. However, it is very unlikely that the countries of Eastern and Central Europe will be in a position to join at the point of enlargement, or for some considerable time thereafter. So the European dimension will for the foreseeable future involve both an extensive common currency zone, with a currency that may become a major world currency (Hix, 1999, p. 305), and an important array of states outside this zone.

# The policy impact of the European dimension

The policies of nation-states may be classified into three types, and the same classification can be applied to the policies of the EU. The three types are *constitutive* policies, concerned with the establishment and maintenance of the formal rules for the government of society and for dealing with conflict; *redistributive* policies, involving taxation and the provision of services; and *regulatory* policies, which control the way in which economic and social activities are carried out, with the objective of preventing harm, or promoting outcomes regarded as desirable. This section looks at some of the major policies of the European Union under the two latter headings.

## Regulatory policies

Many observers of the EU (Majone, 1996) have argued that it is primarily a regulatory state. Central to its activities are policies on internal and external trade, market competition, and the social and environmental consequences of economic activity. The *Single Market Policy*, launched in 1985, was a particularly high-profile regulatory policy. It was intended to relaunch and complete the moves begun in the 1960s to sweep away barriers to trade and commerce between the member states. This meant underpinning the free movement of goods, services, capital and people throughout the EU by the removal of technical, physical and fiscal (taxation) barriers to such movement. The programme was given urgency by the adoption of a deadline – the end of 1992 – and by the specification, in the White Paper which launched the programme, of the pieces of legislation that would be needed to carry it out. While the programme is often regarded as a success, in that the target for the making of the laws was largely achieved, implementing it equally and fully in all the member states is a much slower and much less sure process. The impact of the ongoing process of creating free movement in a single market is an enormous and very varied one, involving activities ranging from services such as air transport and banking to manufacturing and purchasing. The abolition of 'duty free' sales for travellers within the EU on 1 July 1999 was a visible example of the consequences of this policy.

*Competition Policy* is very closely linked to the single market policies, for it is intended to ensure that suppliers of goods and services have equal and fair access to the market. This involves preventing companies colluding or acting, together or separately, in unfair ways to impede or eliminate competition for their products. It also provides controls over the merger or take-over of large companies which might then be able to monopolise, or at least dominate, the market for particular goods or services, and it also prevents member states from assisting their own industries with subsidies that give them an unfair advantage over competitors.

*Environmental Policy* has grown steadily in scope and importance since the 1970s. It can be seen as an instance of positive integration, concerned not with preventing barriers, but with improving conditions. The policy is largely concerned with the environmental impact of industry and agriculture, covering areas such as air and water pollution, waste disposal, and the protection of nature, particularly natural habitats. It also has some elements that seek to promote environmentally sensitive behaviour by citizens, for example through the labelling of environmentally friendly products. A particularly contentious issue has been the prohibition of the shooting for sport of a number of species of birds, especially migrants. Feeling against what was seen as an attack on traditional ways of life and pastimes in the South of France has been so strong that in 1999 a number of MEPs were returned to the European Parliament to represent the 'Hunting, Fishing, Nature, Tradition' Party dedicated to fighting these provisions.

The *Social Policy* of the EU is also a largely regulatory policy, concerned with the position of people as employees and workers. Health and safety, equality of opportunity for men and women, working time (limiting the number of hours' work that employers may demand) and the rights of employees to be consulted about their companies' decisions all figure within this policy. For Jacques Delors the development of better working conditions and the reduction of unemployment were crucial to accompany single market and Economic and Monetary Union policies. Workers should not pay the price of those policies, but should rather directly perceive that they benefited from increased integration. The impact has, however, been limited. The EU has been able to do very little directly to influence unemployment levels. And a largely regulatory policy with its emphasis upon people as workers does not cover the issues that are at the heart of national governments' social policies – housing, health care, and education for example.

## Redistributive policies

The budget of the EU takes up only a very small proportion of the wealth of its members. In 1999 it was about 1.11 per cent of the Gross National Product of the member states. Only about 2.5 per cent of the public expenditure of the member states is spent through the EU budget (Nugent, 1999, p. 190). It is apparent that there is very little redistribution of resources through the EU. The two main areas in which spending occurs are agricultural policy and what are known as the structural and cohesion funds.

*Agricultural Policy* was the first common policy to be developed by the EU and still accounts for about 50 per cent of budget expenditure. It is designed to ensure stable and adequate food supplies and to reduce undue dependence on imports. Its creators could remember the bitter hunger suffered by many European citizens during wartime. It also has social and – slowly but increasingly – environmental objectives. It is seen as desirable that rural communities should be enabled to subsist, and that the land should be cultivated and cared for. These objectives have come at a high cost, for the policy has involved mechanisms for supporting the prices of agricultural products, which have often resulted in distorted, unbalanced and over production. The Commission recognised that the extension of such price-support policies to the large and more backward agricultural sectors of the Central and East European applicant countries as a consequence of enlargement would be very costly indeed, and in its *Agenda 2000* programme sought to reform the policy, to limit the expenditure, and to shift some of the financial support to subsidising farmers directly rather than paying inflated prices for their produce. The proposals were softened at the last minute, largely due to the insistence of French President Jacques Chirac at the Berlin European Council in March 1999, but progress is slowly being made towards reform of the policy.

The diversity of the member states of the European Union, and the divergences in economic prosperity between the different regions, means that the various policies may have different impacts in different places. In particular, both the single market policy and Economic and Monetary Union could mean that capital, investment and employment flow to well-endowed regions, increasing their prosperity even more, while regions with less developed infrastructure, less skilled and educated workforces,

---

**Box 7.5**

### The objectives of the Common Agricultural Policy

The objectives of the Common Agricultural Policy have remained unchanged since they were set out in Article 39 of the Treaty of Rome (renumbered by the Amsterdam Treaty as Article 33). They are:

• To increase agricultural productivity by promoting technical progress and by ensuring the rational development of agricultural production and the optimum usage of factors of production, especially labour.

• To ensure a fair standard of living for the agricultural community, in particular by increasing the individual earnings of persons engaged in agriculture.

• To stabilise markets.

• To ensure the availability of supplies.

• To ensure that supplies reach consumers at reasonable prices.

and less modern industry may suffer even more. The EU treaties set out 'harmonious development' as one of the treaty objectives, and this is the objective that the *structural* and *cohesion funds* seek to address.

The *structural funds* are aimed at specific regions of the EU that are regarded as being relatively deprived; or at specific objectives – promoting employment, assisting the adaptation of workers to industrial change (for example, retraining, skills development) and assisting change in agriculture and fisheries. The *cohesion funds* were set up by the Maastricht Treaty and aimed at the four poorest countries (Ireland, Spain, Greece and Portugal) with the objective of assisting them to move towards the level of economic convergence required for participation in Economic and Monetary Union. Both these policies redistribute resources from the richer to the poorer regions of the Union, or from flourishing to more deprived sectors of the economy. The prospect of enlargement to East and Central Europe called these policies into question: their extension to the applicant countries was likely to result in the loss of funds by current recipients, and quite large transfers to the new member states. *Agenda 2000* proposes reducing the number of regions eligible for structural fund assistance and emphasising the need to improve competitiveness and economic diversification. Some of the countries that have been major recipients of these funds – particularly Ireland – have seen substantial economic growth in the late 1990s. Nevertheless, shifting patterns of redistribution, even on the relatively modest scale that the EU budget makes possible, are likely to have important political effects on the process of closer integration across more of Europe, as people perceive themselves as winners or losers, and as economic interests shift.

## Rights, obligations and relationships

Although other regions of the world are developing networks of connections in both the military and civilian (especially trading) areas, Europe is distinguished by the extent of the co-operation which has developed. This co-operation takes place in a variety of ways and for various reasons. With the ending of the Cold War the dual structures of the previous forty years have been superseded by more all-embracing networks, modelled on the West European patterns.

Involvement in these networks affects contemporary Europe at all levels. Individuals have acquired new rights and new obligations as a result of aspects of this involvement, including the applicability of European law directly within the member states. For example, The European Convention on Human Rights allows individuals to require their governments to recognise certain rights, while equal rights between working men and working women have been much enhanced in a number of countries as a result of the development of European Union law. Equally, however, citizens of the Union find themselves under an obligation not to hunt and shoot migratory birds, an obligation much resented by those, for example in the south of France, who see it as disturbing traditional habits and lifestyles. This has resulted in political protest and the rise of social movements. So the European dimension also affects groups, associations and political parties. And at the highest levels it constrains the behaviour of national governments, which, as the crisis over bovine spongiform encephalopathy (BSE, or mad cow disease) amply demonstrated, are linked to other governments and to the European Union as a whole in ways that involve policy, regulation and funding.

The European Union is the most visible and dominant feature in this network, as its geographical extent and the scope of its interests continue to expand. It is a crucial factor of political life not only for those European states that are actual or potential members of the Union, but also for those that are not. The EU is, however, not moving inexorably towards union in the form of a centralised, all-embracing or even uniform federation. It is becoming an ever more complex, interconnected, overlapping system of rights, obligations and relationships. The increased emphasis now placed upon flexibility and subsidiarity, and the arrangements that will certainly have to be made for post-accession transition periods for the East European candidate states, all support this view. The undoing of the multiple functional co-operations that have grown up is not a credible scenario. There will be a need for long-term management of relationships between the Union and its member states, and those states – some of them large and potentially, if not actually, powerful, such as Russia, Ukraine, even Turkey – where membership is either not likely at all, or likely to be substantially delayed. The challenges and pressures are considerable, but must be viewed in the context of the fifty years since the last pan-European civil war and the ten years since the end of the division of Europe. The web of co-operation and integration that constitutes the European Dimension has withstood substantial pressures. It will certainly evolve and change: much of Europe's prosperity and peace depends upon its survival.

## ◾ Summary

◆ An interlocking web of relationships links the nation-states of Europe and provides a 'European dimension' to the activities of individuals, groups, political parties and governments. Since the end of the Cold War the Central and East European states have largely been assimilated into the pattern developed in Western Europe.

◆ The interests of the nation-states, the dynamics of trade and the impetus of the ongoing process all underpin the rationale for the increasing density of the web of relationships. Although largely supported by elites, popular support for ever-closer union within the European Union can no longer be taken for granted.

◆ The European Union, the dominant institution of this European dimension, has a complex structure, with three pillars, and increasing provision for flexibility. It is faced with particular challenges in defining the role of the European Commission, in handling enlargement and with the advent of Economic and Monetary Union. Its principal policies, both regulatory and redistributive, continue to evolve, but it is increasingly unlikely to turn into a European superstate analogous to existing nation-states.

## ◾ Questions for discussion

▶ Is ever-closer union to be interpreted as a 'loss' or a 'pooling' of national sovereignty?

▶ How crucial is the European dimension to the internal politics of the nation-states?

▶ In what ways can or should the European Union be 'doing less but doing it better'?

▶ Does the 'European dimension' imply a convergence of national policies and/or cultures?

▶ What are the economic and political advantages and disadvantages of the Euro for the states in 'Euroland' and those outside it?

## Further reading

Henderson, Karen (1999) *Back to Europe: Central and Eastern Europe and the European Union* (London: UCL Press) discusses eastward enlargement.

The Macmillan European Union series contains a growing number of detailed studies of aspects of the European Union: McCormick, John (1999) *Understanding the European Union* (London: Macmillan) is a very useful concise introduction.

Nugent, Neill (1999) *The Government and Politics of the European Union*, 4th edn (London: Macmillan) is the authoritative and comprehensive guide to the institutions of the Union.

Peterson, John and Elizabeth Bomberg (1999) *Decision-Making in the European Union* (London: Macmillan) provides extensive insight into the dynamics of policy-making.

Urwin, Derek (1991) *The Community of Europe: A History of European Integration since 1945* (London: Longman), and Laffan, Brigid (1992) *Integration and Cooperation in Europe* (London: Routledge), both provide valuable historical overviews of the process of ever closer union.

For an up-to-date survey of current developments, see Cram, Laura, Desmond Dinan and Neill Nugent (1999) *Developments in European Union Politics* (London: Macmillan).

# The Challenge of the East

# CHAPTER 8

Irene Brennan

> '*There is a tide in the affairs of men*
> *Which, taken at the flood, leads on to fortune;*
> *Omitted, all the voyage of their life*
> *Is bound in shallows and in miseries.*'
>
> WILLIAM SHAKESPEARE, *Julius Caesar*

The European Union (EU) at the Copenhagen European Council meeting of June 1993 made the momentous decision to commit itself to an enlargement process to the East. It decided to allow accession by those Central and East European countries (CEEC) with which it had Europe (Association) Agreements (see Box 8.1), provided they were able to meet the economic and political conditions laid down (EU Council, 1993).

The process moved forward decisively in 1997 when the EU Council adopted the proposals for enlargement set out in a document prepared by the European

## Contents

---

### Box 8.1

### The Europe (Association) Agreements between the EU and the Central and East European countries

The first of the Europe (Association) Agreements were signed in December 1991 between the EU and the 'Visegrad Group' – Hungary, Poland and Czechoslovakia. Later in 1993, agreements were signed with Bulgaria and Romania and subsequently with the three Baltic States and Slovenia. There are also similar agreements with Cyprus and Malta. These agreements have provided a legal framework for the work towards accession by the candidate states and the EU. The overall thrust of each Agreement is to work towards the accession to the EU of the partner. The economic principles of the Association Agreements aim to establish capitalist market relations:

• to move towards free trade;

• to promote harmonious economic relations;

• to promote the economic prosperity of the partner state.

The Europe (Association) Agreements prepared the ground for the accession strategy that was to be developed during the rest of the 1990s. They have created in each case three institutions: the Association Council, the Association Committee and the Association Parliamentary Committee. The Association Committee is the main vehicle for step-by-step negotiation, producing an 'asymmetric' agreement where concessions are first to be implemented by the Community (Avery and Cameron, 1998, p. 16).

Commission (see Chapter 7), entitled *Agenda 2000* (European Commission, 1997) (see Box 8.2). This proposed enlargement will be qualitatively different from earlier ones, because, if it is successfully completed, it will create a new European order, not just in Western Europe but across the whole European continent; for it will have an impact not only on the actual and potential members of the EU, but also on the Russian Federation, the Commonwealth of Independent States (CIS), and Turkey. The EU will cease to be simply Western European in character; it will be much more diverse and its political and economic core will gradually move closer to Central Europe. More than one hundred million new citizens will contribute to its growing political and economic strength. This ambitious project has the support of both the Russian Federation and the United States; they see it as helping to ensure European political stability and security, so creating a more peaceful international system.

---

## Box 8.2

### *Agenda 2000* criteria for EU membership

**FIRST PILLAR ISSUES** (The European Community)

*First pillar political requirements:*

- stable democratic institutions
- independent and well-trained judiciary
- stable constitution
- a constitutional authority/court
- free and fair elections
- possibility of transfer of power to the opposition
- a role for the opposition in parliamentary proceedings
- rule of law
- adequate and well-trained police forces
- autonomy (relative) of local government
- free media
- safety of journalists
- respect for human-rights conventions
- respect for minorities

*First pillar economic requirements:*

- a functioning market economy
- capacity to deal with the competitive forces within the EU

assessed by:

- liberalisation of prices
- liberalisation of trade
- stabilisation of the economy
- reform of the financial sector
- patterns of ownership
- quality of capital – human and physical
- quality of infrastructure

and, according to the Europe agreements:

- harmonious trade relations
- the establishment of free trade

**LEGISLATIVE REQUIREMENTS: ADOPTION OF THE *ACQUIS***

- legislation on key single market directives
- legislation on other key areas, e.g. industry; energy
- legislation on First/Third Pillar issues

**SECOND PILLAR REQUIREMENTS** (COMMON FOREIGN AND SECURITY POLICY)

- adoption of common positions by the candidates with the EU Council
- establishment of continuous joint consultation between the EU and the candidate states

**THIRD PILLAR REQUIREMENTS** (POLICE AND JUDICIAL CO-OPERATION)
(as designated in the TEU, Article 29)

Co-ordination of policies with those of the EU on

- asylum policy
- movement of people across borders
- immigration policy
- combating drug addiction
- combating international fraud
- judicial co-operation
- police and customs co-operation

However, this proposed enlargement (or, more correctly, series of enlargements), both now and in the future, is, and will be, a critical test of the EU's capacity to maintain, extend and deepen its integration processes. To achieve the political and economic restructuring which will transform their societies from planned economies and non-pluralist political systems to capitalist markets and pluralist democracies, the candidate states must establish new institutions, introduce new laws, and encourage the formation of appropriate socio-economic relations and political processes. They have already discovered that the requirements of a capitalist market will, at times, conflict with the democratically expressed expectations of Central and Eastern European (CEE) electorates. This can result in popular alienation and demoralisation; attitudes which will intensify if the enlargement process is seen as unnecessarily slow.

EU policy-makers are closely monitoring these changes and offering assistance and guidance; they are deeply involved in policy decisions and are jointly responsible with the CEE candidate governments for the movement towards enlargement. In the worlds of private industry and finance, the controllers of EU capital flows must assess how much of these should be invested in the CEEC and under what conditions. EU producers, traders, bankers, as well as EU officials, grapple with problems of protectionism and anti-dumping policies, and confront the implications, negative as well as positive, of a free market with the East. The backward and under-invested sector of CEE agriculture, particularly in Poland, presents a special challenge to the EU. The cost of funding it under present Common Agricultural Policy (CAP) rules is perceived as prohibitive, and this is creating further pressure on EU agriculture to move towards the free markets envisaged by the World Trade Organisation (WTO; see Box 9.3) and generates considerable political opposition in the EU. Somewhat similar problems exist in the field of cohesion and structural funding; the enlargement process is forcing the pace of policy change in both the EU (see Chapter 7) and the CEECs.

As well as overseeing the extension and strengthening of Western democracy in the former Soviet states of Central and Eastern Europe and their integration into the capitalist international economic system, the EU must also undertake the transformation which is demanded of it by the enlargement process. The movement towards widening is also accelerating the pace of a deepening internal EU integration. The majority of member states that have committed themselves to Economic and Monetary Union (EMU) have kept to a very rigorous and demanding timetable in order to achieve the necessary structural changes before the accession of any of the CEECs. Similar commitments will have to be made to change the institutions of the Union, the Common Agricultural Policy and Community Budget allocations, if the EU is to expand to 20, 25, or even more states (see Chapter 7).

Finally, the EU is confronted by the necessity of preserving good relations with important bordering states, while moving through the various stages of enlargement to the East. In this chapter we are concentrating upon CEE issues, but we should mention that Malta, Cyprus and Turkey are also candidate states. The Turkish government's stance could block Cypriot accession by linking it to Turkey's own troubled candidature. The Russian government, while accepting in principle the proposed accession of the Baltic states, wishes the EU to join with it to put pressure on them to end perceived discrimination against ethnic Russians, especially in Latvia (see Box 8.3). It is also very concerned about proposed NATO enlargement to this region, its impact on Russian security, and how the EU sees this issue in the light of the development of a European Security and Defence Identity (ESDI) (see Chapter 10).

Box 8.3

### Latvia

In Latvia in 1991, ethnic Russians comprised about half of the population. The question in Latvia on independence was whether a civic form of citizenship would be adopted (Latvia for all those living in Latvia, regardless of ethnicity), or a more exclusive ethnicised form (Latvia for Latvians). In the event, Latvia, like Estonia, placed linguistic conditions on ethnic Russians that have made it very difficult for many adults to exercise their political rights and left children born of ethnic Russians after 1991 stateless. Since 1991, the more educated Russians have emigrated or managed to satisfy the linguistic requirements for citizenship, but many others have not (about 34 per cent of the total population). The EU initially refused to place Latvia on the 'fast track' for accession, in part because its record on human and civic rights was deemed unsatisfactory. Under the pressure of the Council of Europe and other international organisations, Latvia has gradually relaxed its citizenship laws, allowing greater opportunities for different ethnic groups living in the republic to adopt Latvian citizenship. The actions of both the Russian government and the EU Council appear to have influenced Latvia's policies on these issues. Therefore the EU has felt able to congratulate Latvia on the adoption of a 'windows' system and the granting of citizenship to Russian children born after 1991, but a number of problems remain.

## The challenge of diversity

If the present candidates for accession are eventually successful, the EU will stretch from the Arctic to Cyprus and from Ireland to Estonia (see Map 7.1). The considerable diversity between candidates, economically, politically and culturally, presents the EU with major strategic problems. The CEECs do not form a bloc; not all of them were in the former Soviet system: Romania was under the dictatorship of Ceauşescu, and Slovenia was part of what was then Yugoslavia. Even between the former CEE Soviet states there are considerable contrasts. During the late Soviet era, Hungary had a much more relaxed political environment than Czechoslovakia or the German Democratic Republic, and has found it easier to democratise.

The economic disparities between the CEECs are also marked. Slovenia, in 1996, had a Gross Domestic Product per capita purchasing power parity (ppp), in ECUs, of E10,110, while Latvia's was E3160; the Czech Republic's was E9410, while Poland's was E5320 (Table 8.1). It is to be expected that these disparities will increase; those CEECs not in the first enlargement will find it more difficult to attract investment. This uneven and unequal development will characterise Europe for the foreseeable future (Amin and Tomaney, 1995); the pace and direction of the way forward will be determined by states' present circumstances and history (Dunford, 1998; Pickles and Smith, 1998).

The EU has decided that the enlargement process will proceed in stages and that the candidate states will be put into two categories. The European Commission document *Agenda 2000* (1997) identified five CEECs for the so-called 'fast track' process of enlargement, and direct negotiations on accession have been opened between the EU and the Czech Republic, Estonia, Hungary, Poland and Slovenia. The other CEE candidate states, the so-called *pre-ins* – Bulgaria, Latvia, Lithuania, Romania, Slovakia – were seen as still in the process but not, at that time, as candidates for the first wave. However, individual rankings have changed; for example, Slovakia moved onto the fast track as there appeared to be decisive progress in the development of

**Table 8.1** Economic indicators for Central and East European EU candidate states

| | A | B | C | D % | E % | F |
|---|---|---|---|---|---|---|
| Bulgaria | −7.2 | −3.3 | 68 | 13.7 | 82 | 1049 |
| Czech Rep | −4.8 | 3.4 | 89 | 5.2 | 11.1 | 9.5 |
| Estonia | −10.0 | 3.3 | 69 | 4.6 | 1076 | 11 |
| Hungary | −5.3 | 2.1 | 86 | 10.4 | 23 | 18 |
| Latvia | −20.9 | 1.5 | 52 | 6.7 | 951 | 8 |
| Lithuania | −25.8 | 3.0 | 42 | 6.7 | 1021 | 9 |
| Poland | −0.03 | 5.9 | 104 | 10.5 | 43 | 16 |
| Romania | −6.9 | 3.4 | 88 | 8.8 | 210 | 145 |
| Slovak Rep | −8.3 | 5.8 | 90 | 12.5 | 10.1 | 6.5 |
| Slovenia | −4.0 | 4.1 | 96 | 14.8 | 201 | 9 |

A. Gross Domestic Product: average change in dollars, 1990–3
B. Gross Domestic Product: average change in dollars, 1993–7
C. % of 1989 Gross Domestic Product in 1996
D. % of workforce unemployed
   (*Source*: ECE, 1998.)
E. % consumer price change annual average, 1992
F. % consumer price change annual average, 1997
   (*Source*: EBRD, 1997.)

democracy in that country. Others might be dropped if they fail to meet expectations. This strategy is contentious: there are worries that the *pre-ins* may fall into a limbo of stagnation and despair.

Albania and the republics of former Yugoslavia, with the exception of Slovenia, are not seen as immediate candidates for accession, although Croatia began to meet the conditions for membership (see Box 8.2) following the death of President Franjo Tudjman in December 1999. Apart from the Baltic States, the EU does not see former Soviet Union republics as candidates for accession. Instead, Russia, Ukraine, Belarus and Moldova have been given Partnership and Co-operation Agreements.

Following the 1993 decision of the EU regarding enlargement, there was some concern that the EU was dealing with the candidate states only on a one-to-one basis. However, what Baldwin (1994) calls the 'hub and spoke' approach was modified by the introduction of multilateral negotiations; the candidate states were allowed to attend certain meetings of the EU Council and the Council of Foreign Ministers. At Luxembourg (European Council, 1997) it was decided to establish a *European Conference* for all candidates, together with EU member states.

# Political challenges: the development of democracy

All of the candidate states have now begun the introduction of the reforms stipulated as the minimum requirement for accession (see Box 8.2). These should lead to a

**Oligarchy:** Rule or government by a small group or a few people.

pluralist democracy with stable institutions; independent judiciaries, police forces and media; and a political system open to the introduction of capitalist market-isation. While accepting the reality of diversity by adopting its multi-track approach to the enlargement process, the EU has certain policy aims that establish the *sine qua non* of accession for any candidate. All the CEECs face problems of political restruc-turing. These arise out of two main historical features of the CEECs: only in the twentieth century did they build modern nation-states and they all have societies formed in part by socialist systems adopted after the Second World War.

## The political legacy of the Cold War era

For CEECs in the Soviet system, the political process was dominated by the *Nomen-klatura* of the Communist elite. The system possessed institutions that underpinned this. However, it differed somewhat from state to state (Glenny, 1990). In some, the elite operated through a number of compliant parties dominated by one Workers' Party (German Democratic Republic); in others, through one Communist Party (Soviet Union). Trade unions were seen as channels for the implementation of government policy; the media were expected to support official positions.

Although the Soviet states tended to function with relatively closed **oligarchies**, there was some measure of political (non-pluralist) participation, in spite of the violent repressions that occurred. In Central Europe, from the 1960s onwards, Hungary developed a more flexible, pragmatic system which, by the 1980s, was moving decisively towards the West and quietly co-operating with the Ostpolitik of the Federal Republic of Germany. Poland had the strongest movement of popular dissent and the greatest sense of its own national identity. Czechoslovakia suffered the greatest political repression; the regime unsuccessfully sought support by ensur-ing that living standards were the highest in the Soviet bloc, but its 'velvet revolution' in 1989 was supported by the overwhelming mass of the population.

During the 1980s, internal economic weaknesses, together with substantial external debt, created an environment that led to a growth in mafia networks throughout the CEECs. This intensified the vulnerability of the judiciary and police to criminal interference; they were already much more dependent on state control than their counterparts in the West (although this should be seen as relative, as the case of Italy reminds us).

In some states (Czechoslovakia, Romania) the judiciary, police and secret police operated under the more or less direct control of the state in matters of perceived political importance; in others a more open discussion was allowed (as in Hungary). Slovenia belonged to former Yugoslavia, which had a more decentralised system than the Soviet model, but was very repressive towards nationalist revanchism; and Romania was under the idiosyncratic and highly autocratic rule of Ceauşescu, which was more politically repressive than that in any neighbouring state except for Albania.

## The curbing of nationalist ambitions and ethnic rivalries

At the beginning of the twentieth century, the long-standing nation-state system of Central and North-east Europe was still in place. What is now Hungary, the Czech Republic, Slovakia, Slovenia and the Galicia region of Poland were part of the Austro-Hungarian Empire; the western part of Poland was part of Germany, and the eastern part under the Russian Tsar, as were the Baltic States. In South-east Europe, Bulgaria and Romania had recently freed themselves from the domination of the Ottoman Empire. The various treaties of Versailles created a number of new nation-states: Yugoslavia, Czechoslovakia, the Baltic States, a much larger Romania and a much reduced Hungary, and re-established Poland. However, when Hungary lost two-thirds of its territory by the Treaty of Trianon, in 1920 soon after the Treaty of Versailles, this left large Hungarian minorities in the newly created nation-states of Czechoslovakia, Romania and Yugoslavia. Poland had large communities of Jews, Russians and Ukrainians; the Baltic States, Russians. For all of these states, nation-state building relied upon a nationalist ideology (Bugajski, 1993). This fuelled tensions between states, especially those having large minorities ethnically related to populations in neighbouring countries. The moves to authoritarian, ultra-Right policies during the inter war period opened the door for later CEE collaboration with the Nazi plan to eradicate Jewish, Roma (gypsy) and Slav minorities. After the Second World War most of the region was incorporated into the Soviet bloc, which was not sympathetic to nationalist politics.

There are now, in addition to the Hungarian minorities in countries bordering Hungary, communities of Albanians throughout the Balkans, Turks in Bulgaria, Germans in Poland and substantial minorities of Roma people throughout Eastern and Central Europe. The collapse of the Soviet system found many ethnic Russians in the Baltic States; in Latvia they comprised about half of the population (see Box 8.3). And in spite of the destruction of most of the CEE Jewish community during the Holocaust, the region still shows clear signs of tensions in relations with Jews.

Since 1989 there has been some concern that the CEECs might be destabilised by ethnic tensions (Bollerup and Christensen, 1997). Because the severe economic problems of nearly all CEE economies have led to a decline in living standards and a disappointment of initial expectations, this has, at times, produced a reaction of the 'tyrannical majority' against the minorities, to use Agh's phrase (1998, p. 13). There has been some evidence that candidate states with large minorities have been allowing, or even pursuing, discriminatory practices, especially against Roma and Russian populations. There have been migrations, related to such practices, from some of the CEECs, such as Slovakia and the Czech Republic. This issue has complicated the development of full co-operation between the CEECs and the EU in the area of Justice and Home Affairs (see Box 8.2).

However, the situation in the candidate states is generally much better than might have been expected. The 1995 Pact for Stability, first proposed by the French government, has built on intra-regional co-operation and uses the Organisation for Security and Co-operation in Europe (OSCE; see Box 10.2) as a monitoring agent. It has led to agreements between the candidate CEECs on the treatment of ethnic minorities – for example, that between Romania and Hungary. They have been made aware that accession depends upon the acceptance of EU positions on respect for minorities, as well as conformity with the decisions and policies on human rights of other European institutions, such as the Council of Europe and the OSCE itself. Unfortunately the necessary categorisation of CEE candidates into the 'fast track' and the rest – necessary because of their diversity – may result in ethnic populations being left straddling the EU border after the first wave of enlargement. For example, it is possible that the Hungarians in Slovakia and Romania may be cut off from those in Hungary.

## The introduction of political pluralism

The CEE candidate states are now trying to facilitate democratisation. According to Rustow (1970), democracy needs consolidation after the period of initial crisis. This is no easy task (Elster, Offe and Preuss, 1998, pp. 30–1) and the changes needed cannot be introduced overnight; a transition period is inevitable. As a further complication, the CEECs face the problem of parallel restructuring; political changes are taking place at the same time as profound changes in the economic system.

Nevertheless, the democratisation of the CEECs is not proceeding in a vacuum; it benefits from the supporting role of the EU. As Pridham (1995) has shown, the successful transition from authoritarianism to democracy for the Southern Mediterranean states was helped greatly by the centripetal attraction of the EU and its supportive accession strategy.

Since 1989, the 'fast track' states have had political systems in which presidential power is relatively weak and executives are responsible to parliaments (see Chapter 6). Parliaments are crucial to the pluralist, democratic, political process (Leibert and Cotta, 1990). Even when inexperienced, they are the arenas in which political conflicts are manifested and, in some instances, resolved. Progress towards participatory democracy in these states has been substantive. In contrast, in south-east Europe and most of the Baltic States, there are free and fair elections with basic civil liberties, but parliamentary power is limited.

Even in the more advanced states, such as Hungary and Poland, the democratisation process has suffered because of a number of factors that militate against a truly consolidated political system. There is a tendency to make frequent changes in electoral rules. Most parties (except for the reformed Communists) have weak organisational capabilities, fragment easily and are dominated by short-term programmes and personalities. At the moment, the links between sections of the electorates and political parties are somewhat tenuous, because of the lack of perceived socio-economic differences in strategy between the parties: that is to say, there is insufficient class politics for firmly consolidated democracy. Within the CEE parliaments, there are a number of related problems: the inexperience of parliamentarians; lack of government support for parliamentary committees; the rapid changeover of politicians as many drop out of political life for personal and not just for electoral reasons (Agh, 1998).

However, in contrast to the 'fast track' CEECs that benefit from the centripetal dynamic noted above, many *pre-in* CEE states (notably Bulgaria) are still in political and economic turmoil. Slovakia, which under the leadership of Vladimir Meciar between 1991 and 1998 developed a nationalist and autocratic government, has had to undergo a second transition, and now has moved quickly onto the fast track. However, Bulgaria, Latvia, Lithuania, and probably Romania, are certainly far from accession and not subject to the same, strong, supportive, centripetal EU attraction.

# ■ The politico-economic challenge: democracy vs. the market?

The strategy of the EU since Copenhagen has been to encourage the CEECs to pursue both democratisation and the 'free' market. This rules out a democratic system based upon, say, a social market, as envisaged by Gorbachev (White, 1991). In the

CEECs, there is a growing tension between democratisation and marketisation; electors in the CEECs are beginning to realise that policies that they frequently dislike, because they are associated with falling living standards, are driven by the EU accession strategy. All CEE politicians, committed to winning EU membership, will continue to implement marketisation: it is a non-debatable given. Because the needs and wants of ordinary citizens are not seen by the elites as part of the primary political agenda, the latter tend to fall back into a state of undemocratic oligarchy. There is, therefore, a widespread popular cynicism about democratic processes and institutions. As for the pre-ins, democracy for them becomes more and more formalised and elite-managed, as is the case in many Latin American countries (Pridham, 1995).

It is clear that the EU priority has been economic reform, even at the expense of disillusionment and cynicism among the CEE electorates. However, among Western leaders there were reservations about the imposition of the so-called 'shock therapy' on the CEE states. In January 1990 French President Mitterrand, with the support of the German commercial banking sector – which had a high CEE debt exposure – proposed that continuing economic integration between the CEECs should be supported, and argued for a slow economic transition with democratisation as a priority (Gowan, 1995a). However, the view that prevailed was that of most of the leading economists in the United States (Sachs, 1995) and the United Kingdom (Rollo et al., 1990). They were supported by their respective governments and had the enthusiastic backing of the new political elites in the CEECs. What was initiated was a rapid move to capitalist market economies, the dismantling of the integrative structures and the turning of the CEE economies to the West. To achieve this transition quickly a 'shock therapy' of reforms was introduced: price liberalisation; privatisation and stabilisation of the currency; and severe cuts in public expenditure.

The effect of this strategy, together with the loss of CMEA markets and Soviet subsidisation, was an economic implosion (see Table 8.2). In 1996, of the CEECs,

**Table 8.2** Living standard indicators in selected Central and East European EU candidate states

|  | A | B | C | D | E |
|---|---|---|---|---|---|
| Hungary | 4120 | 28.9 | 23.8 | 0.7 | 70 |
| Bulgaria | 1350 | 23.4 | 16.6 | 2.6 | 71 |
| Romania | 1480 | 22.2 | 16.2 | 17.7 | 70 |
| Lithuania | 1900 | 25.2 | 15.3 | 2.1 | 69 |
| Latvia | 2270 | 24.5 | 12.5 | – | 69 |
| Poland | 2790 | 21.5 | 20.0 | 6.8 | 70 |
| Estonia | 2860 | 25.5 | 15.6 | 6.0 | 70 |
| Slovakia | 2950 | 17.6 | 13.4 | 12.8 | 72 |
| Czech Rep | 3870 | 44.9 | 36.2 | 3.1 | 73 |

A. GDP per capita 1995 $
B. GDP per capita purchasing power parity 1981 (PPP is defined as the path of the nominal exchange rate that would keep the real exchange rate with other currencies, e.g. the dollar, constant over a given period)
C. GDP per capita purchasing power parity, 1995
D. % of population on less than one dollar a day
E. life expectancy, 1995
*Source*: World Bank, 1997.

**Autarchy:** Strictly, autarchy means rule or government by a single person. The word is also sometimes used as an alternative spelling of autarky, which means a policy of being economically self-sufficient as a nation or community. Such self-sufficiency is often protected by various measures to hamper or discourage cross-border trade.

only Poland had recovered its 1989 level of GDP; for political reasons it had been given a considerable amount of support through substantial debt forgiveness and had received more than average Foreign Direct Investment (FDI). Every other CEE economy was in severe recession or even collapse.

# ■ Economic challenges: the road to the market

## The inherited problems of the CEE economies

All of the CEE candidate states, apart from Romania, belonged to the former Soviet system, which had a considerable amount of economic **autarchy** (protected separation from the international economic system). On its collapse the CEECs were faced with substantial restructuring. All of them, except Czechoslovakia, had industrialised only after the Second World War and, in the initial stages, the Soviet strategy of state planning was very successful. However, by the late sixties certain economic problems had become pressing. The individual national economies had developed in parallel: there was no proper international division of labour. Protectionism, as well as a too slow assimilation of new technology, and an extensive rather than intensive production strategy, slowed development. The Comprehensive Programme of Integration, adopted in 1975 by the Council for Mutual Economic Assistance (CMEA), was an attempt to overcome some of these difficulties. But there was no overall supra-national regulation of the market in the CMEA, nor did it have a fully convertible currency or goods convertibility; it was neither a customs union nor a common market (Csaba, 1995).

With the collapse of the Soviet system, the CMEA started to disintegrate in 1990. Its formal dissolution in 1991 had a profoundly disruptive impact upon CEE regional trade and therefore on the former Soviet states' economies (Gowan, 1995a). The Soviet subsidisation of CEE economies through cheap energy transfers, high product prices, hard-currency surpluses and loans had been considerable (Zloch-Christy, 1987). The former Soviet states of Central and Eastern Europe (CEECs) had produced for the large Soviet market, whose demand for consumer goods, industrial equipment and materials, agricultural and transport products had been well nigh insatiable and which had been willing to pay higher than world prices for somewhat inferior products. In return, the CEECs had had access to energy and other raw materials at as much as 50 per cent below market prices; the CEECs had expanding markets and relatively low production costs. The Comprehensive Integration Programme had established very large plants in the CEECs to supply the whole of the Soviet market; when the CMEA disintegrated the CEE economies were left with huge enterprises and no buyers for their products. In addition, there was a high level of debt; during the debt crisis of the early eighties, the Union of Soviet Socialist Republics (USSR) had provided hard-currency funds to meet debt repayments; it had also allowed hard-currency surpluses to be maintained with itself by the CEECs. This ended when the CMEA was dissolved.

Intra-regional trade between the CEECs had collapsed by 1993. The trade between Czechoslovakia (and its later component parts), Hungary, Poland, Bulgaria and Romania fell from $37,000 million in 1989 to $3,000 million in 1993 (Mayhew, 1998, p. 87). Throughout the CEECs the services originally supplied by the state sector have not been fully replaced by the private sector; most new investment has been in industrial production The problems in agriculture will be discussed below.

The effect on living standards and quality of life for the majority of the CEE populations has been marked (see Table 8.2). The fall in standards of living has been acute, with Estonia, Bulgaria and Romania having a drop of about a third while Latvia (with Russia) is down nearly 50 per cent. Even in Poland, there has been a fall in purchasing power parity (PPP). Slovakia, Romania, Poland and Estonia have high figures (for European states) of those living on less than 1 dollar per day. Most of these unfortunates are Roma people, the unemployed, or others dependent on social security networks: 'Everywhere the social cost of transition turned out to be considerable and much higher than expected' (Elster, Offe and Preuss, 1998, p. 245).

# Meeting the challenge of economic restructuring

The CEECs were hoping for a type of Marshall Plan to aid them in transition. However, the EU states, not having the large surpluses enjoyed by the United States after the Second World War, have opted for much more limited interventions.

## 1 Programmes of assistance

The EU has tried to help the CEECs to meet the challenge of restructuring, in part, by programmes of assistance. The first, in 1989, was PHARE, an acronym for Polish and Hungarian Economic Restructuring. This assistance was later extended to the other CEECs (including some which are not candidates) and will be extended to former Yugoslavia and Croatia when they are able to meet the criteria. Although the sums concerned have been substantial, they amount to only ECU10 per annum for each person in the CEECs (Mayhew, 1998, p. 17). This programme is now being driven by the needs of accession through 'accession partnerships', in which the EU (through the Commission) has a major role in deciding how PHARE monies should be allocated. Community loans have also been available. And recently the vast majority of the funds of the European Investment Bank have been used in Poland, Hungary and the Czech Republic. They have been used for infrastructural projects, such as in transport, where trans-European network links (TENs) will benefit the EU as well as the CEECs. It is possible that PHARE and Community loans will be synthesised into a form that is close to structural funding, at least for those candidates on 'fast track'.

## 2 The introduction of competition

The primary consideration for economic policy-makers after the collapse of the Soviet system was to oversee the transition to a market economy in the CEECs. To this end there has been a concentration on developing a competition policy, in order to eradicate monopolies created by state planning. Severe cuts in state subsidies have also been imposed (except, be it noted, in the areas of agriculture, fisheries or the ECSC sector because of parallel supports within the EU itself). However, the implementation of competition policy is politically sensitive in the CEECs because it threatens local industries that are incapable of withstanding international competition. These are frequently very large, monopolistic firms that are seen as important to the national economy. EU-supported policies that lead to their break-up, a reduction of industrial capacity and a development of so-called capital- (not labour-) intensive methods, are interpreted, within the CEECs, as attacks on national assets and on the workforce, as well as an attempt by EU producers to protect themselves from competition (Gowan, 1995a). In any case, CEE firms tend to have co-operative rather than competitive relations between themselves; this approach is seen by many in the CEECs as necessary for economic survival in Eastern Europe, where barter and *blat* (personal influence) arrangements are common. However, although there have been some changes (Fingleton et al., 1996), much needs to be done to conform to EU requirements on competition law.

### 3    Trade issues

The major problems in this area are:

- punitive anti-dumping policies by the EU;
- structural resistance within the EU to CEE imports;
- negative CEE balance of trade with the EU;
- low levels of regional trade between the CEECs.

Most CEE trade has been conducted with the EU and this is carried forward in the framework of the Association Agreements (see Box 8.1). These are, in principle at least, based on the guiding principles of the Treaty of Rome (1957) implemented through the 1986 Single European Act (SEA): freedom of goods, services, capital and labour. The movement of goods has been addressed by a number of measures in the areas of industrial policy. It has now been established that there is (limited) free trade in industrial goods from the CEE partners into the Union, except in the areas of clothing, textiles, coal and steel products, where punitive restrictions apply.

Unfortunately the strength of the CEECs is precisely in those areas that are seen as sensitive by the EU producers, so the economic restructuring of the CEECs is dependent upon overcoming resistance within the EU towards CEE imports. In contrast, in the CEECs the level of EU imports in the areas of industrial equipment and investment goods is high. This is leading to an imbalance in trade, which causes social as well as economic difficulties (Csaba, 1995) but this protectionist EU culture is not sufficiently challenged.

The World Trade Organisation (WTO) (see Box 9.3) policies have been used as a guide on the issue of intellectual property rights and there has been a very substantial liberalisation of capital movements in line with the rules of the Organisation for Economic Co-operation and Development (OECD). However, flows of foreign direct investment (FDI) are not as high as Western economists had anticipated in the early 1990s; they failed to take into account the depressive impact on the CEE economies of 'shock therapy' reforms; the demands on German capital of the German unification; and the attraction of China and the Pacific Rim economies for US capital. The Russian crisis of August 1998 impacted fairly severely on some EU financial sectors. Moreover, punitive commercial policy instruments by the EU against the CEE economies also deters foreign direct investment.

## ■ Meeting the challenge of agricultural reform

The major challenge in this area is the development of appropriate policies to rationalise and modernise CEE agriculture, which has suffered, in the main, from under-investment and lack of infrastructural support, while at the same time carrying forward a parallel restructuring of the EU sector. Both CEE and EU agriculture are becoming more and more subject to the pressures of GATT agreements that are directed towards more open markets and governed by WTO rules (see Box 9.3).

Most of the CEE countries, except for Czechoslovakia, were industrialised after the Second World War, but the proportions of the workforce in agriculture have remained relatively high: for example, in 1996, in Poland nearly 27% and in Romania over 34% of workers were in agriculture. While for the EU as a whole it is less than 6%, in contrast the average figure for the CEECs is a little under 25%. And since the implosion of the CEE economies in the early 1990s, there has been a continuing increase of farm workers in a number of the CEECs. For example, in Romania they have risen from 29% to 39% of the total workforce. However, CEE agriculture has had declining levels of production because of the difficulty of paying for fertilisers and farm equipment as farm-gate prices have plummeted (OECD, 1997).

During the Soviet era, although intensive investment was made in CEE manufacturing industry, in most of the CEECs farming was seen as relatively unimportant and badly neglected. Poland, which has one of the largest agricultural sectors, has some very serious problems. Before 1989, most agriculture in the CEECs was collectivised and therefore, to some extent, rationalised, but in Poland a stubborn resistance, led by the Church, was successful in maintaining private ownership. However, most of the private farms were very small and hardly mechanised at all, so levels of agricultural production have been correspondingly low (OECD, 1997). As Poland is by far the largest of the CEECs, the problems of its agriculture are of considerable political and economic significance.

Since 1990, throughout the CEECs, the disintegration of the CMEA has depressed demand for agricultural products and a further decline in investment has increased the problems of CEE farmers. Privatisation, carried out in the majority of CEECs where agriculture was collectivised, has further fragmented and weakened the agricultural sector.

## CEE agriculture, the EU and GATT provisions

Net trade with the EU is much in the latter's favour because EU agriculture benefits from the CAP supports. CEE privatised agriculture, when exporting its products, has found itself confronting EU (and US) protectionist restriction in a number of areas, while at the same time being undermined by their imports (OECD, 1997). In addition, in many of the CEECs it is difficult for their food-processing industries to compete in EU, US and other international markets. In spite of this, it is anticipated by the EU policy-makers that CEE farm-gate prices will slowly rise, coming nearer to those of the EU. But this may well push up domestic prices in the CEECs to what might be regarded as politically intolerable levels. International investment flows into CEE agriculture, moreover, have been minimal.

But the EU is also faced with a dilemma. Under GATT rules, the CAP is gradually being modified and EU farmers are subjected to market pressures. However, if enlargement is to proceed then there must be either a radical extension of the existing CAP reform programmes (Tangermann and Josling, 1994), which would be unacceptable to the WTO, or an acceleration of reform, which is very unpalatable to those EU member states that benefit from the CAP. The European Commission's proposals for initial steps in this direction were watered down by the Berlin European Council (spring 1999). The states concerned may derail the enlargement process, if they feel that their worries are not addressed.

These problems indicate that a longer pre-accession period may well be thought desirable for the CEECs, in order to bring their farm prices slowly up to EU levels, to rationalise their food-processing industries and to give more time to EU agricultural interests. Because of the agreements made in the Uruguay Round of GATT, it will be difficult for the EU to offer direct help – the so-called 'Aggregate Measure of Support' – to the CEECs during the coming period of transition; export subsidies are even more problematic.

# ■ Meeting the challenge in the EU of reform of the structural funds and the community budget

The cost of the enlargement process is considerable for both the CEECs and the EU, so there is some difficulty in finding sufficient resources for it. The amount of investment required will require EU funds as well as national and private-sector contributions (*Agenda 2000*, European Commission, 1997). In addition to the economic demands made on both by the introduction of an EU-compatible market economy and the dilemmas of agricultural restructuring, there are other important reforms that must be implemented in the CEECs if integration is to proceed. These include the implementation of effective programmes of nuclear safety and environmental protection (see below).

The Western powers have preferred to pursue NATO enlargement before EU enlargement, which has meant that resources have had to be directed first to security expenditure rather than to preparation for EU enlargement. Most importantly, it should not be forgotten that, in addition, the costs of NATO enlargement (see Box 1.1) will be considerable for both the EU and the CEE states. Estimates differ; the comparatively low estimate of the Rand Corporation is that it will cost $42 billion over the next ten years. If we accept this figure, this would mean that, leaving aside internal modernisation costs of $10 billion, the *additional* cost of making the systems of the CEE and the western powers compatible will be at least $32 billion, of which the EU member states will pay 50 per cent and the USA 15 per cent. The CEECs are thus being asked to find 35 per cent of this sum (i.e. about $10 billion). Although the cost to existing NATO and EU member states will be considerable, the burden is heaviest on the relatively poor CEE NATO members; Poland, Hungary and the Czech Republic joined NATO in 1999.

NATO hostilities against the Federal Republic of Yugoslavia inflicted $60 billion of damage on that country alone (Economist Intelligence Unit report, 1999) as well as seriously affecting other states in the region. This has left the EU member states with the problem of deciding the extent to which existing funds should be diverted to humanitarian assistance and reconstruction programmes in the Balkans.

As a response to all of these factors, EU policy-makers are trying to evolve a strategy that will enable CEE enlargement to be carried forward without too much cost to member states, and in such a way as to avoid alienating the present net contributors to the EU, particularly Germany. Therefore the financial ceiling of EU budgetary contributions will not be raised. But the present major EU beneficiaries of cohesion and structural funds – Greece, Portugal, Spain, Italy, France and Ireland – would resist a straightforward transfer of funds to the CEECs from monies now allocated to them, so that solution is not available.

## A new approach to cohesion policy

A similar problem exists in the allocation of structural and other funds. If the subsidies provided by the structural and cohesion funding programmes of the EU (see Chapter 7) were to be maintained after enlargement, and CEE states also had access to them on comparable terms, the cost to the EU would be very considerable indeed. Enlargement might well be seen as prohibitively expensive for the present net contributor states. But if the present overall budget levels were adhered to, and existing criteria applied, that would mean a net transfer of 85 per cent of available structural funds to the CEECs, with only Greece of the present members being left with some support (Mayhew, 1998, p. 291). This is not a feasible option for enlargement because the present beneficiaries of funding would then have very little interest in its achievement.

But it is argued (Mayhew, 1998) that very few, if any, of the CEE economies would be able to absorb massive transfers quickly: the necessary institutional, economic and legislative mechanisms have not yet been put in place. Therefore, it is envisaged that a new form of structural funding will be introduced that takes into account the needs and expectations – to some extent – of the present beneficiaries. Transfer of funds to the CEECs will take place slowly, following the adage, 'To him who hath, it shall be given him'. In spite of probable disappointment at the level of structural funds being offered, the CEECs' need for accession will almost certainly keep them in the negotiations, however long drawn out and initially disappointing.

# ■ The challenge of environmental hazard in the CEECs

## Industrial pollution

There are a number of serious problems concerning the environment that confront the EU in the East. During the period of rapid industrialisation after the Second World War, parts of Central Europe relied on inferior brown coal as one of their sources of energy. This has resulted in severe pollution that has been exacerbated by the failure, found throughout the CEECs, to institute sufficient safeguards against other forms of chemical industrial pollution of water, air and earth. The massive investment needed to remedy this situation should be introduced over a period of ten or more years and will be in accord with EU directives. With perhaps misplaced optimism, the private sector is being called upon to contribute towards the cost of this transformation (Avery and Cameron, 1998, p. 110).

## Nuclear safety

Nuclear safety is of great importance for the whole of Europe. The disaster at Chernobyl in April 1986 demonstrated that nuclear fall-out knows no frontiers. In order to achieve the necessary safety standards in nuclear power stations in the next ten years, there needs to be co-operation between the CEECs, the EU, the EBRD and the World Bank, because the costs are too heavy for the CEE states to carry alone, and the situation too dangerous to be left unremedied.

# New borders, new opportunities, new problems?

## Movement of people

Movement of people is an issue with considerable political implications and importance for relations between the CEECs and the EU; it has highlighted political differences about migration and accession policy. The drive to achieve economic convergence in order to meet the requirements for economic and monetary union has sharply increased unemployment in EU member states. This process has been intensified by the impact of so-called globalisation processes on employment. There is therefore a resistance to substantial CEE inward migration from both EU governments and workers. As a result of political pressure, it is becoming more difficult for workers from candidate states to enter the EU, unless they belong to clearly identifiable categories such as 'key personnel' and are deemed necessary in order to facilitate the movement of services, goods and capital. Once within the EU such CEE workers do, however, have recognised legal rights. But it is not at all clear how the political transition can be made from the present tight policies to the free flow of labour within an enlarged EU.

## Co-ordinated CEE and EU policy on refugees and asylum seekers

Refugees and asylum seekers constitute two groups that have internationally recognised rights to enter the EU and CEECs. The conflicts in former Yugoslavia have generated large flows of refugees into the CEECs and the EU. Refugees from this and other conflict zones, and those claiming political asylum, frequently approach the EU from a CEE state. In addition there have been flows of such migrants from within the CEECs themselves; hostile attitudes in the CEECs towards minorities, such as the Roma in the Czech Republic and Slovakia, have produced a large increase in legal and illegal migration to the EU. This has heightened EU Council concern about co-operation on border controls and immigration.

For many non-European refugees, the CEE states operate as quasi-border areas for the EU. In some EU states, such as Germany, entrants designated illegal immigrants are returned to the CEE state which was their last port of call. So the CEECs in turn are adopting more stringent measures that may have an effect on CEE domestic attitudes. As for CEE citizens, those in some 'fast track' states feel themselves in danger of being cut off from their own ethnic minorities in *pre-in* states. Also, citizens of CEE candidate states will in future find it more difficult to have access to their traditional CIS markets.

## Combating crime

Since the collapse of the Soviet system there has been a very substantial rise in international crime in the CEECs. This impacts on the EU, and includes smuggling by Russian, CEE, Italian, other EU and non-EU mafias, of drugs, arms and radioactive material; the illicit trafficking of women, young people and children for prostitution and pornography; money laundering and international fraud networks; and car-theft networks. The economic implosion of Russia, Belarus, Ukraine, Central Asia and South-east Europe has generated more problems of this kind and created incentives for increased criminal activity, made easier by the destruction of the 'iron curtain'.

### Co-operation on justice and home affairs (the Third Pillar) and the position of the CEECs

As part of the continuing process of integration around Third Pillar issues (see Box 8.2), Europol has been established to combat crime within the EU and across its borders. EU co-operation on these matters is rudimentary and lacking in appropriate institutional support, so progress is slow. The CEECs are involved in joint working groups with the EU states in this area. However, because the discussions about Third Pillar issues have been almost entirely intergovernmental in character, the CEECs have found it difficult to be clear about the precise nature of EU policy and possible future developments. Moreover, the effort to adopt and implement Third and related First Pillar acquis has placed a heavy burden on the CEE candidate states, who are frequently short of the skilled personnel and material resources needed to implement those measures adopted.

### New borders – relations with Russia

The peace and security of the European continent rests, to a very considerable extent, on the preservation of good relations between the European Union and Russia, as EU strategy documents have recognised (European Union Council of Ministers, 1995). The Russian government has made it clear that it is in favour of EU enlargement but has serious concerns about NATO enlargement (see Chapter 10). It sees the former as creating a framework of stability in Central and Eastern Europe that will facilitate trade and co-operative activity. To this end it has supported the collaboration of Gazprom, the Russian natural gas exporter, with EU multinationals, in the distribution of natural gas in the EU and in the proposed building of a new gas pipeline through Belarus and Poland. It has also welcomed the accession candidatures of the Baltic States; it sees these countries as conduits for EU–Russian trade, including the most important: energy.

The Russian Federation has welcomed EU, but not NATO, enlargement. However, the relation between these two processes is becoming closer, as NATO is seen not only as the foremost defence organisation in Europe, but also as the framework which will help support the creation of a European Security and Defence Identity. However, Kaliningrad, the large, decaying Russian military base wedged between Lithuania and Poland, will, if both gain accession to the Union, be surrounded by EU territory. If there were to be a parallel enlargement of NATO that would isolate Kaliningrad, a situation would arise that would be of deep concern to Russia.

## ■ Widening, deepening or both?

There has been a considerable debate among policy-makers in the EU about the effect of enlargement on the Union and its institutions and processes (Ehlermann,

1995). The enlargement to the East is frequently described in terms of a 'widening' of the Union. At times there have been fears that this might be achieved at the expense of the continuing process of 'deepening' integration.

There are two minimalist strategies on the enlargement. As an example of the first, former prime minister John Major gave support, just after the collapse of the Soviet system, to a strategy of rapid EU enlargement to the East, in the hope the EU would be transformed into a deregulated single market operating, in the main, through intergovernmental co-operation. This is sometimes described as *Europe à la carte*.

In contrast, some of those committed to a federalist project of EU integration have feared, at times, what they consider might be a too precipitate accession strategy. They emphasise the importance of a *core Europe*; the pursuit of the federalist project at the expense of enlargement. With the prospect of enlargement to the East, some have fallen back on the arguments of Huntington (1993), also used by some Eurosceptics, that there are fundamental divisions in Europe between the civilisations of the East and West.

These views: *Europe à la carte* and *core Europe*, have been rejected by the vast majority of EU policy-makers and analysts. Their consensus is that widening is necessary and will be of benefit to the Union, but must be pursued around a core, and with flexibility (see Chapter 7). Those who support the federalist project believe that a *federal state* would have a balance of centralised and decentralised decision-making (*subsidiarity*) with all members committed to policies adopted at the centre. Some, having Eurosceptical tendencies, have argued instead for 'advanced groups' being allowed to create an EU *variable geometry* without a fixed core. However, then it would be more than likely that the EU would be faced with the danger of states not opting out, but being left out of various *ad hoc* arrangements. Instead, most EU policy-makers argue for *flexible, open partnerships with a common core of policies*. This structure would satisfy not only those who wish to preserve a strong core, but also those who believe that open partnerships between groups of EU states, on less important issues, would avoid the dangers of a *multi-tiered* EU. Even those states who have reservations about federalism in the long term see such partnerships as a viable option. Therefore it is probable that this is the form EU integration will take in the medium term.

## The timetable for accession

Although optimists in the EU and the CEECs have hoped that the first wave of enlargement will be achieved shortly after the millennium, say 2002, more pessimistic assessments put it somewhere between 2004 and 2008. (See Box 8.4 for *Agenda 2000* assessments of the candidate states' preparedness.) The member states of the EU are in agreement that the accession processes cannot move to completion until the EU has successfully achieved Economic and Monetary Union (EMU); the EU must have secured a stable financial and economic integration before proceeding to the next wave of enlargement, if the dynamic of integration is to be maintained. Candidate states are being asked to prepare themselves to enter EMU on accession; no opt-outs are contemplated. This must mean a longer rather than a shorter period of preparation for accession.

The vexed questions of structural and cohesion funding and of agriculture reform will be easier to handle (within the Union) if the pre-accession period is longer rather

Box 8.4

## *Agenda 2000* assessments of the candidate states

In the EU forward programme known as *Agenda 2000*, prepared by the European Commission in 1997, the original Copenhagen criteria were amplified. The Commission's opinions on the extent of conformity to the criteria by the candidate countries for accession to the EU were accepted by the EU at the Luxembourg Council, December 1997. Viewed against the political criteria (see Box 8.2), Poland, Hungary, the Czech Republic, the Baltic States and Slovenia were all assessed as having properly functioning political institutions that respected one another's competencies. However, Romania and Bulgaria were seen as having some difficulties with respect for the rule of law at all levels of administration. Although Hungary, Estonia, the Czech Republic, Slovenia and Poland received a favourable assessment from the Commission, their levels of corruption were noted adversely, as were those of all the applicants. There were some gaps in the operation of human-rights conventions in Bulgaria and Romania and a number of states were assessed as having problems in dealing with their minorities according to EU criteria. These included the Czech Republic (Roma), Romania (Roma and Hungarians), Estonia (Russians), Latvia (Russians), Slovakia (Hungarians and Roma) and Bulgaria (Roma and Turks). Poland and the Czech Republic were criticised for placing some restrictions on the freedom of the press. In addition, in Bulgaria, the police were also judged to operate outside the law at times, and the judiciary to be not fully independent. Slovakia was assessed most negatively of all the candidate states because it failed to establish stable democratic institutions operating according to a constitution. It also had a secret police force not operating under democratic control and had not established a fully independent judiciary.

In assessing the performance of the candidate countries against the economic criteria (see Box 8.2) the Commission recognised in its document that the second criterion (capacity to deal with competitive forces) is very difficult to apply, as it depends on assessments of future performance. It came to the conclusion that the five 'fast track' candidates had (more or less) functioning market economies, as did Slovakia. However, of them, only Poland and Hungary were thought able to withstand competitive EU pressures (if they pursue present policies); the Czech Republic, Slovenia and Slovakia must improve their performance to be able to do so. Estonia was thought to be the weakest among the 'fast track'. Poland and Slovenia were criticised for dragging their feet on property restitution, although all candidate states failed on that to a greater or lesser extent. Of the non-fast track candidates, Bulgaria was assessed as not having even started seriously to implement a reform programme. Romania, and also to some extent Latvia and Lithuania, were thought to have problems of industrial obsolescence, large loss-making state-owned firms, a slow privatisation process, and low energy prices. They were all seen as requiring financial-sector reform, especially Romania, which, in addition, suffered from low levels of skill among the workforce.

---

than shorter. Similarly, the free movement of workers within the EU will be difficult to achieve within a short time-frame in conditions of high unemployment in the EU states bordering the CEECs, such as Germany. The compromise solution – the CEECs to be admitted to EU membership, but with restrictions still placed upon their citizens' right of EU entry – is opposed by EU Commission policy-makers.

The CEECs also, as noted above, face considerable challenges as they adopt the EU *acquis* in advance of accession. One of these is the establishment and consolidation of the necessary institutional frameworks and mechanisms to oversee structural changes. During the early and mid-1990s, there was a failure in the CEECs to introduce the structural changes necessary for accession. There appears to have been a resistance from the free-marketeers towards state intervention and from national bureaucrats towards the dismantling and replacement of inadequate, existing state regulation (Smith and Swain, 1998). In the economic arena, there have been insufficient institutional supports put in place to ensure long-term capital accumulation, the regulation of the market through the rule of law, and the maximising of profit by state co-ordination (Amsden et al., 1994). Hungary has made more progress with these reforms than other CEECs (Mayhew, 1998) but is an honourable exception that proves the rule; even other 'fast track' candidates have much to do in this area.

For the CEECs that are not part of the first enlargement, the pre-accession period will be both long and difficult. These states will almost certainly include Bulgaria, Lithuania, Latvia and, possibly, Romania. Slovakia, if it satisfies the political criteria,

**Anarchy:** A term frequently used in International Relations theory. It refers to the fact that no legitimate world government exists, a fact which is perceived by realists and idealists alike as inherently dangerous and destabilising.

will probably move to 'fast track' status. For most of the present *pre-ins*, the pre-accession process will probably take fifteen or more years. This has considerable implications for their domestic politics and they will need to receive substantial support from the EU if they are not to fall into **anarchy** or authoritarianism. While there is no danger of the Latin Americanisation of 'fast track' candidate states, it is a fate that hangs over the rest, unless firm measures are adopted.

# ■ Summary

◆ Enlargement of the European Union to the Central and East European countries which have association agreements with the EU will pose substantial challenges both for the candidate countries and for the EU.

◆ For the candidate states, whose starting points are very diverse despite a shared history of Soviet domination, the challenges include political re-structuring; a resolution of the tensions caused by the need to pursue marketisation policies which are widely unpopular while developing democratic institutions and habits; and substantial economic reform.

◆ The EU also faces the challenges of providing assistance to the candidate states in a number of areas, and of structuring policies so as to accommodate their accession.

# ■ Questions for discussion

▶ Why is there tension between the processes of marketisation and democratisation in the states of the former Soviet system?

▶ How should the EU handle the diversity between the candidate states? What are the problems of designating some candidate states as *pre-ins* or 'slow track' rather than 'fast track'?

▶ 'Enlarging the European Union demands a deepening of its integration.' Do you agree?

▶ Why do the reforms of the EU Common Agricultural Policy and the EU Community Budget present such a challenge to the European Union and why are they essential prerequisites for EU enlargement to the East?

▶ The major EU member states have accepted the policy of introducing expansion of the North Atlantic Treaty Organisation (NATO) to Central Europe before proceeding with EU enlargement. Why have they adopted this strategy?

# ■ Further reading

For the position of the European Union and an outline of its strategy, see:

European Commission (COM) (1997) *Agenda 2000: For a Stronger and Wider Union* (Brussels: Bulletin of the European Union).

For a good introduction to the major issues and debates, see:

Mayhew, A. (1998) *Recreating Europe: The European Union's Policy towards Central and Eastern Europe* (Cambridge: Cambridge University Press).

Sperling, J., and E. Kirchner (1997) *Recasting the European Order* (Manchester: Manchester University Press).

On the politics of Central and Eastern Europe and some of the issues arising in the political sphere, see:

Agh, A. (1998) *The Politics of Central and Eastern Europe* (London: Sage).

Elster, J., C. Offe and U. K. Preuss (1998) *Institutional Design in Post-Communist Societies* (Cambridge: Cambridge University Press).

For an exploration of theories of transition, see:

Pickles, A. and A. Smith (eds) (1998) *Theorising Transition: The Political Economy of Post-Communist Transformations* (London: Routledge).

# Europe and the World: The Impact of Globalisation

Ian Manners

## Contents

'We must think about an interdependent world and how to co-operate in this Europe, and in this world.'

MIKHAIL GORBACHEV, speech to the University of Bristol (1993)

Europe's relationships with the rest of the world have been, and will be, of crucial importance to understanding the changing nature of global politics and Europe's place on a globalising planet. In this chapter we will attempt to explore and explain these relationships from a variety of viewpoints as we consider the links between Europe and the world from fifteenth-century sea travel to twenty-first-century internet.

The relationship between Europe and the world is one which can be approached from several directions and one which has been, and continues to be, full of tensions. It is worth acknowledging the impact of Europe's colonial past. European states (including Russia) have, over the past 500 years, conquered and colonised virtually every single corner of the world in one form or another. These different experiences of conquerors and vanquished, exploiters and exploited, 'old world' and 'new world', act as a distinguishing factor in the contemporary relations between Europe and the world. West European states make up 18 of the world's 30 wealthiest states with an average annual Gross National Product (GNP) measured at Purchasing Power Parity (PPP) of around $20,000 per person. In contrast, former West European colonies, mainly in Africa and South Asia, make up 27 of the world's 30 poorest states with an average annual GNP measured at PPP of around $1,000 per person (World Bank, 1999). From this perspective Europe can be seen to be the exploiter of the world, with its relations being characterised by a combination of colonial legacy, predominance in international institutions, and continued exploitation through the forces of globalisation.

In thinking about how best to analyse Europe's relations we need to consider the question of perspective and how this shapes our view of the world. The analysis presented in this chapter attempts to combine three different approaches in order to gain a better overview of Europe's relationships. The three types of approach used here are those based on historical experience, multilateral institutionalised relationships, and the impact of globalisation. The first section looks at the historical experience of Europe's relationship with the rest of the world over roughly the past 500 years from the 'discovery' of the 'new world' at the beginning of the sixteenth century to the end of the 'Cold War' at the end of the twentieth century. The second section looks at the

## Globalisation in question

It is by no means accepted whether globalisation really exists and what it actually is – to put it bluntly, globalisation itself is in question. Whilst some argue that globalisation is a radical transformation of the global economy through advances in the movement of capital, the means of production and the movement of trade, others argue that globalisation is simply an extension of modernisation or liberalisation in another form: 'The processes of modernisation which provided the foundation for the rise of the centralised European nation-state in the late nineteenth century now make for globalisation, sweeping across the boundaries of the densely populated and geographically concentrated states of western Europe.'

Hirst and Thompson (1996) sum up this disagreement by contrasting a globalised economy (one that has been radically transformed) with an international economy (one that is largely an extension of existing national practices):

A globalized economy [is one in which] distinct national economies are subsumed and rearticulated into the system by international processes and transactions.

compared with

An international economy is one in which the principal entities are national economies.

In parallel to this contention over whether globalisation actually exists, is the argument over what globalisation actually is. Some argue that globalisation is primarily the result of global flows of capital such as money and finance, foreign direct investment and portfolio investments. Others argue that globalisation involves a much broader spectrum of global flows, including capital, such as technology, knowledge, people and culture, as Amin and Thrift (1994) explain:

At work, then, is a multi-faceted process of global integration guided by, but not always made in the image of, the most powerful transnational firms, institutions, actors, and cultural hegemonies of the capitalist world economy.

rise of multilateral institutionalised relationships throughout the world in the post-Cold War period, including Europe's role in the United Nations (UN), the World Trade Organisation (WTO), and its progress in European integration. The third section looks at the impact of globalisation (see Box 9.1) on Europe's relations with the world, including a consideration of the different forces of globalisation, as well as the contrasting moves towards regionalisation and local forces. The concluding section looks at the dynamics of change in Europe's relations with the world and then summarises the main insights of this chapter as Europe moves into the twenty-first century.

# Structure of relations

As well as considering the choice of analysis when contemplating Europe's relations with the world, it is also useful to view the range of these relations as falling into five very broad types: socio-cultural, economic, environmental, political and security. These different types of relationships are very closely interrelated and cannot truly be considered separately. Socio-cultural relations involve social contact through the media of transport, tourism or telecommunications. Economic relations involve the exchange of value through trade, investment, ownership, loans and aid. Environmental relations involve the impact of human activity on the global environment through pollution, over-use of natural resources, and the exchange and reduction of biodiversity. Political relations involve contact between politicians, states and international organisations through diplomacy, international law, and institutions such as

**Table 9.1**   Richest and poorest: Ranked PPP measures of GNP per capita, 1997

| Richest | | Poorest | |
|---|---|---|---|
| 1. Singapore | $29,000 | 123. Sierra Leone | $510 |
| 2. United States | $28,740 | 122. Ethiopia | $510 |
| 3. Switzerland | $26,320 | 121. Mozambique | $520 |
| 4. Hong Kong | $24,540 | 120. Burundi | $590 |
| 5. Norway | $23,940 | 119. Rwanda | $630 |
| 6. Japan | $23,400 | 118. Malawi | $700 |
| 7. Denmark | $22,740 | 117. Yemen, Rep. | $720 |
| 8. Belgium | $22,370 | 116. Mali | $740 |
| 9. Austria | $21,980 | 115. Congo, Dem. Rep. | $790 |
| 10. Canada | $21,860 | 114. Nigeria | $880 |
| 11. France | $21,860 | 113. Zambia | $890 |
| 12. Netherlands | $21,340 | 112. Madagascar | $910 |
| 13. Germany | $21,300 | 111. Niger | $920 |
| 14. United Kingdom | $20,520 | 110. Tajikistan | $930 |
| 15. Australia | $20,170 | 109. Angola | $940 |
| 16. Italy | $20,060 | 108. Burkina Faso | $990 |
| 17. Sweden | $19,030 | 107. Uganda | $1,050 |
| 18. Finland | $18,980 | 106. Bangladesh | $1,050 |
| 19. Israel | $16,960 | 105. Guinea-Bissau | $1,070 |
| 20. Ireland | $16,740 | 104. Chad | $1,070 |
| 21. New Zealand | $16,600 | 103. Nepal | $1,090 |
| 22. Spain | $15,720 | 102. Kenya | $1,110 |
| 23. Portugal | $13,840 | 101. Haiti | $1,150 |
| 24. Korea, Rep. | $13,500 | 100. Benin | $1,260 |
| 25. Greece | $13,080 | 99. Lao PDR | $1,290 |
| 26. Slovenia | $12,520 | 98. Congo, Rep. | $1,380 |
| 27. Chile | $12,080 | 97. Turkmenistan | $1,410 |
| 28. Czech Rep. | $11,380 | 96. Azerbaijan | $1,520 |
| 29. Malaysia | $10,920 | 95. Central African Rep. | $1,530 |
| 30. Argentina | $9,950 | 94. Pakistan | $1,590 |

**Developed world:** Those parts of the world which can be considered to have undergone industrialisation and have developed primary, secondary and tertiary sectors of their economy. Also termed the 'first world' or the 'north', it includes most of Europe.

**Developing world:** Those parts of the world which have not undergone industrialisation and usually rely on their primary economic sector. Also termed the 'Third World' or the 'south', this includes most of the former European colonies.

the UN. Security relations involve co-operation and conflict between peoples and states in order to deal with perceived threats, and involve military co-operation, military conflict, attempts to maintain peace, and the exchange of weaponry. All five types of relationships are part of an increasingly dense web of linkages between peoples and states on a global scale.

In each of these five types of relationships it is also worth considering the degree to which they picture an unequal relationship between Europe and the world. For most of the past 500 years Europe has been the pre-eminent exporter of cultural values, pollution, economic goods, political institutions, and military conflict. The late-comers to this formerly European 'club' of unequal partners have, in the past 50 to 100 years, been the USA, Japan, Canada, Australia and New Zealand, and more recently, Singapore, Hong Kong, South Korea and Taiwan. These states, together with Europe, make up the World Bank's group of 'high-income economies' which dominate most of the structure of global relations. This domination of the structure of global relations by the rich **developed world** is seen by many in the **developing world** as an extension of colonial patterns of exploitation in the post-colonial period through other means.

The approach adopted will condition our thinking about Europe's relations with the rest of the world. However, it is clear that Europe's relations are multi-faceted and play both positive and negative roles in shaping contemporary viewpoints. Thus, it seems sensible to adopt a combination of approaches which will allow us to examine the historical, institutional and globalised views of the relationship.

# █ History – from the age of empires to the new world order

The history of the past 500 years of Europe's relations with the world can, broadly speaking, be seen to consist of three distinctive periods. The first period was characterised by the spread of European influence and involvement throughout the world from the late fifteenth century to the early twentieth century. The second period was characterised by the transformation of influence through the world wars in the early to mid-twentieth century. The final period was characterised by the retreat from global domination in the mid- to late twentieth century.

## Mercantilism, colonialism and empires, 1492–1914

Europe's relationship with the rest of the world began in the late fifteenth century through the rise of sea-borne trade by the maritime states of Portugal, Spain, the Netherlands, France and England. Although ancient European history is centred on the Mediterranean and North Africa, its relationship with the world beyond its near neighbours only became truly global with the arrival of its ships in the Americas in the 1490s. From the 1490s to the 1770s European economic and trade influence spread around the world, largely based on the **mercantilism** of its companies, which developed into the practice of **colonialism**. From the 1870s to the 1900s influence was renewed through **Imperialism**, spurred by the impetus of the industrial revolution and the European rivalries this spawned.

Until the 1450s Europe's relations with the world were largely confined to sea journeys across the Mediterranean and around the North African coast, as well as land journeys along the Silk Road to China and southwards via Byzantium/Constantinople towards the eastern Mediterranean. During the second half of the fifteenth century advances in sea travel made it possible for European ships to travel beyond the relative safety of the coastlines of Europe and Africa. The first half of the sixteenth century saw a swift progression by the Spanish and Portuguese from the 'discovery' of the Americas to the subjugation of its peoples by the European monarchs and church.

The expansion of European domination of world trade during the period from 1450 to 1640 has been described as the 'long sixteenth century', in which a **World System** of modern capitalism was created (Wallerstein, 1972). This trade expansion was actively pursued by European states, based on the practice of mercantilism in order to ensure that economic power was increased through exports and domination of trade routes. Portuguese and Dutch traders were particularly important in opening trade routes around the coast of Africa, South Asia and South-East Asia. British and French traders sought to pursue trade routes across the Atlantic towards

**Mercantilism:** The pursuit of trade surpluses in order to increase the wealth of a state. It emphasised the importance of exports and decreasing imports as well as attempting to accumulate wealth in the form of precious metals.

**Colonialism:** The practice of holding land as a form of colony in order to increase the wealth of a colonial state. The colonies had little political independence and primarily served an economic purpose.

**Imperialism:** The seizing of territory by military means involving the subjugation of its peoples. The empires created were based on hostility and conflict for political and economic gain.

**World System:** Immanuel Wallerstein's description of a single world arrangement of economic and political relations which expanded from Europe in the sixteenth century to encompass the globe.

North America. Such trade routes were regulated by state-supported trading companies such as the Dutch East India Company and the British Hudson Bay Company. However, during the second half of the eighteenth century the European role in trade began to change with the decline of Spanish rule in the Americas, the declaration of independence of Britain's American colonies, and the decline of the mercantilist philosophy. The argument developed by Adam Smith in the 1770s favoured free trade rather than mercantilist trade as leading the way to economic prosperity (Smith, 1784). By the end of the 1830s most Latin American colonies had gained independence from their European rulers.

From the 1870s onwards the industrial revolution in Europe led to a 'scramble for Africa' as the western European states sought to seize provinces for their empires. This outbreak of empire-building originated in the advances in technology which allowed for improved transportation and increased specialisation of production. However, the primary cause was the need for economic resources to feed the growing industrial economies of Europe, compounded by the fierce rivalries between these powers. By 1900 the European imperial powers of Britain, France, Germany, Portugal, Belgium, Italy and Spain ruled all of Africa except Abyssinia/Ethiopia. These seven European states, together with the remnants of the Dutch colonies, also ruled over South and South-East Asia as well as the Pacific and most of the Caribbean. Foremost amongst these European empires was that of Britain, which, after the end of the Napoleonic Wars in 1815, maintained an empire on which 'the sun never set'. The British Empire was sustained by naval superiority and helped maintain a global economic system, based on the gold–sterling standard from 1870 onwards, termed a *Pax Britannica* during the period 1815 to 1914. However, from the 1880s onwards the other European powers, in particular France and Germany, attempted to change this British hegemony, which eventually led to the collapse into war in 1914.

## Thirty years' crisis, 1914–44

The outbreak of war in Europe in 1914 marked the beginning of the end for European dominance of the rest of the world. The thirty years' crisis of European states from 1914 to 1944 was eventually to lead to the end of European empires, first through the League of Nations, then through the UN and eventual independence. The periods prior to, and following, the thirty years' crisis were characterised by relatively free international trade, which had been growing evenly since the 1870s. However, the thirty years' crisis differs from the rest of the twentieth century in that it was a period largely characterised by economic protectionism, which was partially responsible for the length and depth of the crisis.

The combination of industrialisation, imperial ambitions and nationalism led the European empires of Germany, Austria–Hungary, France, Britain and Russia to war against each other in 1914. The war immediately spread beyond Europe to include its colonies around the world, in particular Africa and the Middle East. After three years of futile trench warfare, the entry of the USA into the war in 1917 led to the defeat of the Central Powers a year and a half later. Following the war reparations extracted in the Treaty of Versailles in 1919, Germany and the Ottomans lost their empires to League of Nations mandates held by Britain, France, South Africa, Australia, Japan and New Zealand. More importantly, the US President Woodrow Wilson insisted that the principle of **national self-determination** form part of the basis for the settlement of the war (see Box 3.3). Although applied only in Europe

**National self-determination:** The possibility for any nation to determine for itself by whom and how it should be governed. The implications are that the nation is sovereign and that government should be both independent and democratic.

after the First World War, the principle of national self-determination was to play a far more important role after the end of the Second World War.

The Treaty of Versailles solved none of the problems which had led to war in 1914, and partially led to the world economic depression of the 1930s as it failed to bring stability to the global economy. In reality the First World War had seriously disrupted the growing global trade of the previous fifty years and significantly reduced the role of Britain, France and Germany within it. By the time of the Wall Street stock market crash in 1929 it had become apparent that the global economy was actually very interdependent and that the fate of European economies was tied to those of the US economy and of the colonies, as well as of states in Asia and South America. As world trade continued to shrink in the 1930s the combination of protectionism, unemployment and inflation all contributed to global depression and political instability.

Although the Depression of the 1930s did not alone lead to the Second World War, it was a significant factor in sowing the seeds of political instability and extremism in Europe. To a greater extent than the war of 1914–18, the Second World War did engulf most of the world, and was truly global in its legacy. Despite three acts of aggression – by Japan in Manchuria, Italy in Abyssinia/Ethiopia, and Germany in Europe during the 1930s – it was Adolf Hitler's invasion of Poland in 1939 which provoked the Second World War. The war itself had three main effects on Europe and its relations with the rest of the world: ensuring that the USA would be forced to ascend to global hegemony; inspiring independence movements in its colonies; and inducing moves to integration in its aftermath.

# Cold War and independence, 1947–89

The Second World War altered the relationship between Europe and the world beyond all recognition, causing a shift in power away from the European empires of the previous 500 years and towards the global domination of the new superpowers – the United States of America and the Soviet Union. The war also precipitated the process of decolonisation by Europe's exhausted powers as the winds of change swept across the world and liberated over one hundred states between 1946 and 1984. In addition, the impact of the Depression and the failure of the League of Nations during the interwar years led to the creation of the United Nations in 1945 as an umbrella organisation for all states, old and new.

During the war the Axis powers of Germany, Italy and Japan were defeated by a precarious alliance of Britain, the Soviet Union and the USA, but the Allied powers began to fall out almost as soon as the war was over. At the end of the war, Europe became divided as the invading forces of the Allies from the eastern and western fronts met on the Elbe in Germany. Although few foresaw it at the time, this division of Germany between east and west in 1945 was to be reflected in Europe and most of the world for the next four decades. The hot conflict between 1939 and 1945 rapidly froze into a Cold War between the two victorious armies of the United States and the Soviet Union in a condition known as **bipolarity**. The emergence of two superpowers, married to opposing ideologies, was to be the conditioning factor in Europe's relations with the world from 1945 to 1989. It is interesting to consider that during this period the peace and security of Western Europe was secured by the co-operation and guarantees of two former British colonies, the USA and Canada – such was the reversal of fortune after 1945.

At the same time as the Cold War was reducing European states to secondary

**Bipolarity:** An arrangement of international relations in which two actors or 'poles' are each vying for dominance over the other. Often refers to the division of the world into roughly equal military blocs. In the Cold War period, the two superpowers leading these two blocs were the USA and the USSR

Box 9.2

## Europe and decolonisation

| Year | Empire | Colony |
|------|--------|--------|
| 1946 | Britain | Jordan |
| 1946 | France | Syria |
| 1947 | Britain | India, Pakistan and Bhutan |
| 1948 | Britain | Burma, Sri Lanka and Palestine |
| 1949 | Netherlands | Indonesia |
| 1951 | Italy | Libya |
| 1954 | France | Cambodia, Laos and Vietnam |
| 1956 | France | Morocco and Tunisia |
|      | Britain | Sudan |
| 1957 | Britain | Ghana and Malaysia |
| 1958 | France | Guinea |
| 1960 | France | sixteen West African colonies |
| 1961 to 1962 | Belgium | three Central African colonies |
| 1960 to 1984 | Britain | fifty-one colonies around the world |
| 1974 to 1975 | Portugal | seven coastal colonies around the world |

roles in support of the superpowers, so the process of decolonisation was rapidly granting independence to their former dominions (see Box 9.2). In 1945 there were seven European states with colonies scattered around the world, some of them big, as with Britain and France, and some of them small, as with Spain. Although the granting of independence began in the Middle East during 1946, it was to be another thirty years before the Portuguese gave up their colonies, and there are still some colonial possessions maintained by European states today.

Britain granted independence to its South Asian colonies in 1947–8 and to another fifty-one colonies around the world between 1960 (Nigeria) and 1984 (Brunei). The final remnant of empire left by the British was Hong Kong in 1997. Independence for most French colonies came between 1954 (French Indochina) and 1962 (Algeria). The two remaining Dutch colonies of Indonesia and Surinam gained independence in 1949 and 1975, respectively. Libya and Somalia, the two Italian colonies, became independent in 1951 and 1960. The Belgian central African empire of the Congo, Burundi and Rwanda was late to gain its freedom, in 1961–2. The last act of European decolonisation came with the arrival of democracy in Portugal and the gaining of independence for some of the oldest colonies in the world in 1974–5.

It is worth remembering that Part Four of the European Community (EC) Treaty refers specifically to twenty-one 'overseas countries and territories' through which member states still maintain some form of special relationship with their colonies. These include such far-flung territories as French Polynesia, the Netherlands Antilles, the British Caribbean islands, and Danish Greenland. Also interesting is the fact that the European Community includes the French overseas departments of French Guiana, Guadeloupe, Martinique and Réunion.

## Economic boom, 1950–70, depression, 1973–9, and transition, 1980–9

During the period of decolonisation in the 1950s and 1960s global trade returned to levels seen prior to the First World War, encouraged by the resurgence of free trade and the role of the USA in world politics. Between 1959 and 1971 the USA maintained the gold–dollar standard as the stabilising factor in international trade, and as a symbol of a period of *Pax Americana* in the post-Second World War period. As Europe's imperial role disappeared during this period its focus turned inward towards attempts at integration, culminating in the Treaty of Rome establishing the European Communities in 1957. The economies of the European states boomed during the 1950s and 1960s, especially those of the six EC states (France, West Germany, Italy, the Netherlands, Belgium and Luxembourg) whose Gross Domestic Product (GDP) grew by 5 per cent per annum on average. But this export-led economic boom was not merely a North American and European phenomenon as countries in the rest of the world also benefited, for example those in South America and East and South-East Asia.

By the end of the 1960s a number of factors combined to bring to an end the economic boom, which led to a world-wide depression during the 1970s and into the 1980s. The first indications that the post-war period of stability was over came with the student-led social unrest of 1968, precipitated by a combination of ideology, protest and social militancy (see Chapter 2). Secondly, the USA's declining hegemony in world trade, combined with the costs of waging war in Vietnam, led to the collapse of the gold–dollar standard (see Box 2.2) in 1971, with the arrival of floating exchange rates and their associated instability from 1972 onwards. Thirdly, the products of **newly industrialising countries** were increasingly displacing European and North American goods in global markets. In particular, European manufacturing, such as motorbikes, cars, ships, and consumer products, was beginning to become uncompetitive against products built and assembled elsewhere in the world. During the 1970s the economy of Japan surpassed those of the European states and outperformed that of the USA. Finally, the oil shock of 1973–4 threw the economies of Europe and North America into an economic depression characterised by a combination of stagflation and high levels of unemployment.

The decade of the 1980s was to be one of both enormous instability and transition for Europe's relations with the rest of the world. The economic depression of the 1970s deepened with the second oil shock caused by the revolutionary overthrow of the Shah of Iran in 1979. The Soviet Union's military intervention in Afghanistan, compounded by the deployment of new nuclear missiles by both the superpowers during 1979, led to increased tension in Europe. In 1982 the global financial system received a shock with the news that Mexico was about to default on the significant loans it had accepted during the 1970s. This led the way for a global debt crisis which shook European lenders, both public and private. Although the IMF was able to overcome the short-term problem by rescheduling Latin American debts, the longer-term debts of the world's **highly indebted poor countries** in Africa, Asia and Central America hangs around their necks to this day. Until 1986 it looked as though Europe was continuing to sink deeper into economic depression, with the new freeze in superpower relations showing few signs of thawing. In an attempt to revive their ailing economies the members of the European Community decided to complete the single market by 1992, and, in the Single European Act of 1986, gave the EC the powers to do so. In Eastern Europe the Soviet President Mikhail Gorbachev attempted to revive the Communist economies by introducing both domestic and foreign-policy reforms from 1985 onwards. After 1987 Europe's economy began to revive as a result of a combination of domestic economic reforms, renewed financial confidence, and the push towards the single market. A far greater impact came when Gorbachev's

**Newly industrialising countries:** Those countries which have recently undergone industrialisation and do not have to rely on their primary economic sector. These countries are currently found only in South-East Asia.

**Highly indebted poor countries:** The world's most indebted countries and the plan to reduce their outstanding debt to 'sustainable' levels, assuming they adopt 'good' economic policies.

**Neo-colonialism:** The continued exploitation of former colonies through other means, usually involving aid, technical assistance and foreign direct investment.

**Multilateralism** International relations involving more than two participants in an attempt to achieve common goals.

foreign-policy reforms led to the revolutions of 1989 as the satellite countries of Eastern Europe rejected communism and chose capitalism instead.

Our historical analysis allows us to portray Europe's relations with the world as being dominated by European states and empires. This tends to underplay the changing role of other factors, such as movements of people and capital, as well as the increasing prominence of international law and institutions. However, we do need to be aware that from the perspective of most of the world's population, Europe's (and now the developed world's) role in their lives has appeared to involve exploitation, through colonies, empires, Cold War conflict and now through multinational companies and debt burdens in a form of **neo-colonialism**.

# ■ Multilateralism – the structure of global relations

In taking a historical approach we can appreciate how Europe's relations with the world have developed. However, in order to gain a contemporary view of these relations it is useful to look at the way in which they are currently organised through international arrangements. In the post-Cold War world, international relations are increasingly structured and organised through multilateral agreements, such as the General Agreement on Tariffs and Trade (GATT) (see Box 9.3), and international institutions such as the United Nations (UN). This structure of Europe's relationship with the rest of the world may be seen as consisting of three components: the notion of polarity in the post-Cold War world; the arrangements of international institutions; and finally, the role of European integration in shaping these relations.

## Post-Cold War world

During 1990 the events in Eastern Europe and increasing problems in the Soviet Union made it clear that the world was left with only one superpower – the United

---

**Box 9.3**

### The General Agreement on Tariffs and Trade and the World Trade Organisation

Following the achievement of fixed exchange rates, with competitive devaluations prevented by the IMF, the USA led negotiations to further liberalise trade, which led to the General Agreement on Tariffs and Trade (GATT) signed by 23 countries in 1947. From 1947 to 1993 the members of GATT participated in eight rounds of multilateral talks which sought steadily to reduce discriminatory trade practices, remove non-tariff barriers, and broaden the scope of the products covered. In 1994 the Uruguay round of GATT talks succeeded in creating a new, powerful World Trade Organisation (WTO) with a dispute-settlement mechanism capable of dealing with

the ever-increasing demands of world trade regulation in the post-Cold War era. The World Trade Organisation, with headquarters in Geneva, sets out for its members a framework of rules designed to provide unrestricted access to markets, but also to prevent predatory behaviour such as 'dumping' – exporting goods at less than cost price in order to drive competitors out of business. In 1999, agreement was reached that China would join the organisation. If the agreement is ratified by the existing member states the territory covered by World Trade Organisation rules will be substantially expanded.

States of America. The successful liberation of Kuwait by a US-led co
in February 1992 led to the observation that a move from a bipolar
world had taken place. This view was reinforced by the US-led UN ¡
troops which were sent to Somalia in December 1992 to protect food aid
number of events in 1993 indicated that the unipolar moment, if it had ev
had passed with the collapse into civil war in Yugoslavia, the announced re
US marines from Somalia, and the increasing coolness of Russian relation
events indicated that the post-Cold War world would not be one based on a re
US hegemony leading its European allies and the UN in the pursuit of global ¡
instead it would involve many more actors with divergent opinions.

The post-Cold War world is one which some might describe as **multipolar** in t
it is not dominated by two superpowers, as in the Cold War; neither is it dominate
by a hegemon, such as the United States. Instead a multipolar world is one in which
there are many states that are unable or unwilling to dominate each other, and, more
importantly, have nothing to gain from doing so. This is a world in which the real
gains are to be achieved through co-operation rather than the competition which
has characterised most of the past century. In this multipolar situation the world's
more significant poles share international trade, investment, and agreements, which
make them far more interdependent than ever.

**Table 9.2** The ties that bind – trading economies (world's twenty largest economies, 1997/98)

| Country | GNP (billion) | Merchandise trade (billion) | Services trade (billion) | Trade as proportion of GNP |
|---|---|---|---|---|
| USA | $7,690 | $1,628 | $396 | 26% |
| Japan | $4,772 | $669 | $171 | 18% |
| **Germany** | $2,319 | $1,007 | $198 | 52% |
| **France** | $1,526 | $594 | $142 | 48% |
| **Britain** | $1,220 | $589 | $176 | 63% |
| **Italy** | $1,155 | $455 | $139 | 51% |
| China | $1,055 | $323 | $52 | 36% |
| Brazil | $773 | $112 | $27 | 18% |
| Canada | $584 | $419 | $64 | 83% |
| **Spain** | $570 | $242 | $75 | 56% |
| Korea, Rep. | $485 | $226 | $47 | 56% |
| **Russia** | $403 | $101 | $31 | 33% |
| **Netherlands** | $403 | $382 | $93 | 118% |
| Australia | $380 | $121 | $33 | 40% |
| India | $374 | $76 | $25 | 27% |
| Mexico | $349 | $247 | $25 | 78% |
| **Switzerland** | $313 | $159 | $41 | 64% |
| Argentina | $306 | $56 | $9 | 21% |
| **Belgium** | $268 | $329 | $69 | 148% |
| **Sweden** | $232 | $152 | $38 | 82% |

*Source:* World Bank and World Trade Organisation.

This is particularly true for European states, whose wealth and well-being are increasingly the result of closer integration and movement towards mutual interdependence. But the multipolar world is not just one dominated by the 'old' powers – the United States, Japan, Germany, France, Britain, Italy, Canada and Russia. Many 'new' actors are increasingly entering the world stage. In the multipolar world these 'new' actors take the form of emerging economies, such as China, Brazil, Mexico and India, or they take non-state forms such as international organisations and non-governmental organisations, which play an increasingly important role.

# International institutions

The post-Cold War world, and Europe's role within it, is increasingly shaped by a preponderance of international institutions created to provide some semblance of global order. The precise nature of these institutions is somewhat debatable. It is arguable whether they represent the beginnings of a world government or whether they are little more than international agreements to co-operate. There are three broad groups of international institutions and organisations considered important, all of which feature European participation, whose extent and influence varies, depending on the origins, role and size of the institution.

## United Nations

The first group is that of the United Nations system of international organisations created at the end of the Second World War. Since 1945 the United Nations (UN) has grown from 51 members to185 in 1999 and it is the most inclusive of all the categories presented here. The UN consists of a central system of organs mostly based in New York, and a large array of specialised agencies and programmes spread around the world. Although the General Assembly is the main body for the debate of issues by all 185 delegates, guaranteeing global peace the most important organ is the Security Council. The Security Council consists of fifteen members, five of whom are permanent, and these five, unlike the other ten, have the right of veto over the Council's decisions. The post-war origins of the Council are demonstrated by the fact that the five permanent members are the USA, Russia, China, Britain and France – the five victorious powers at the end of the Second World War. With a majority of European veto states sitting in the Security Council many have argued that this gives the Council a bias towards a European perspective. Outside the UN's central system there are a number of organs playing important roles in helping economic and social development across the world. These include the UN Children's Emergency Fund (UNICEF), the UN Development Programme (UNDP), the UN Fund for Population Activities (UNFPA), the World Food Programme (WFP) and the World Health Organisation (WHO). European countries, especially those of the Nordic region, have always played important roles in these specialised agencies through funding, staffing and providing political support.

## Bretton Woods

The second group of international institutions has its origins in the 1944 International Monetary and Financial Conference held at Bretton Woods, New Hampshire, towards the end of the Second World War (see Box 2.2). The creation of the International Monetary Fund (IMF) and the International Bank for Reconstruction and Development (known as the World Bank) was followed in 1947 by the General

Agreement on Tariffs and Trade (GATT) (see Box 9.3). During its first 16 years, membership of GATT was limited to more developed countries, particularly from Europe, but this began to change during the Tokyo round (1973–9) with 99 countries participating. By the time the Uruguay round began in 1986 many countries opposed to its free-market rationale were changing their position and by 1999 it had 134 members distributed more evenly around the world.

## Developed world

The third group of international arrangements consists of those of the developed or industrialised world, which are far more selective in their membership than either the UN (open to all) or the institutions of Bretton Woods (open to all who agree to the rules). First among these is the Organisation for Economic Co-operation and Development (OECD) comprising the world's 29 most developed states, 22 of which are European. The Organisation for European Economic Co-operation (OEEC) was created in 1948, at the insistence of the USA, as the multilateral institution responsible for co-ordinating and organising the distribution of Marshall Aid to Europe. By 1960 the OEEC had increased in size from 16 to 20 members, including Canada and the USA, but the creation of the European Economic Community in 1957 (see Chapters 2 and 7) had provided six of its core members with an alternative forum for co-operation. In order to adapt to these events the OEEC was renamed the OECD in 1961 and given the task of co-ordinating members' economic development policies as well as acting as a forum for discussion and a source of information. The OECD is seen by some as a symbol of continued economic domination of European and developed states over the rest of the world. The fact that it has recently admitted Mexico (1994) and Korea (1996) weakens some of this argument, but not all. Beginning in Rambouillet, France, in 1975, the heads of government of the seven leading OECD states began meeting annually to discuss the world's economic problems. The group of seven (G7) consisted of the leaders of the USA, Japan, Germany, France, Britain, Italy and Canada, until 1977 when the President of the EC Commission began to attend. In Birmingham, Great Britain, in 1998, the group was joined by Russia, when it became known as the group of eight (G8) for the first time. Although it is a summit meeting and not an institution, the G8 is evidence of the multipolar structure of international economic organisation, led by the USA but with a disproportionate voice for European states and including the European Union.

## Integration and global relations

In addition to Europe's relations being shaped by international developments such as the changing nature of the multipolar world and the rise of international institutions, discussed above, there is also a continent-based form of integration which is equally important. Since its origins in the European Coal and Steel Community of 1951, through the Treaty of Rome creating the European Communities in 1957, to the Single European Act significantly reviving the European Community in 1987, the process of integration had been one situated in a Cold War environment, with an internal focus to its activities. Since the end of the Cold War in the early 1990s, the European Community has transformed itself into the European Union through the Treaty of Maastricht in 1991, and further adapted itself in the Treaty of Amsterdam in 1997 (see Chapter 7). This transformation has shifted the emphasis of the European Union away from the internal dynamics of creating common policies and a single market to a broader role on a more global scale.

**Multipolarity:** Refers to the division of the world into three or more power blocs.

During the Cold War the European Community developed an array of policies to deal with its external relations, including a commercial policy with the developed world; a development policy with the developing world; an overseas territories policy to deal with the remnants of its member states' empires; and a range of more general provisions for institutionalising its relations with international organisations (such as GATT and the UN), with nearby states (through trade or association agreements), and through admitting other European states to become members. The transformation of the European Community to the European Union at the end of the Cold War has accelerated a desire to play a more global role and has led to the extension of foreign policy activities through the creation of a common foreign and security policy (CFSP). These foreign policy provisions have provided the framework, if not the willingness, for the EU to engage in a far broader range of activities from joint actions to peacekeeping missions, both of which were considered 'taboo' subjects in the Cold War world.

By taking an institutional approach we are able to consider the way in which Europe's relations in the post-Cold War world are structured by **multipolarity**, by the role of international institutions, and finally by European integration. All three of these types of arrangements continue to focus on the role of the state as being the agent of action in some kind of 'international system'. However, it now seems appropriate to ask whether Europe's relations with the world are actually shaped by this state-focused activity at all. Perhaps we should now consider global relations which go beyond the state, but which possibly play a far more important role in shaping Europe's relations with the world.

# Globalisation – global forces and Europe

The third and final way of looking at Europe's relations with the world is to consider the role which the multi-faceted forces of globalisation are playing in shaping the links between the lives of Europeans and those of the peoples of the rest of the world. The reality is that these relations are increasingly determined by global factors that go beyond the historical patterns and international relations analysed in the two previous sections and which make it necessary for us to consider a far more complex reordering of European interactions in a post-Cold War, post-international world. In order to achieve this far-reaching vision of Europe's rapidly changing relations with the world it is useful to consider the nature of globalisation (see Box 9.1), the role of regionalisation, and the counter-forces of localisation.

## Global flows

Globalisation is a process involving the increasing irrelevance of barriers such as borders, distances and states, to global flows of both tangible and abstract commodities such as goods, services, technology, people and ideas. There are no set definitions or limits to what form these types of global flows take, but it might be useful to talk of at least seven categories of global flows. The *first global flow* is that of production, found in the increasingly mobile economic activities of multinational companies (MNCs) which now serve as the world's main conduit for the manufacturing, distribution and retailing of goods and services. MNCs of European origin play a significant role in the global flow of production, in particular through oil companies (such as Royal Dutch Shell), motorcar companies (such as Daimler-Benz), electronics companies (such as Philips), and consumer goods companies (such as Unilever).

The *second global flow* is of finance, through billions of dollars, Euros and yen crossing the globe in the form of currency speculation, stock ownership, inter-institutional borrowing, and foreign direct investment. In terms of stock exchanges New York and Tokyo lead the way with over 57 per cent of the global value of stocks, followed by the European exchanges of London, Frankfurt and Paris, having 16 per cent of the global stock value between them (Buckley, 1999, p. 3).

The *third global flow* is that of information and knowledge, through media such as television, telecommunications, satellite communications and the rapid spread of the internet. This flow of information is based on advances in technology, which is increasing the means for communicating and disseminating knowledge. Although the flow of information originates largely in the USA and uses English as the language of communication, the European role is more than merely secondary. It is based on the impact of European companies such as Deutsche Telekom, France Telecom and British Telecom as well as media corporations such as Philips, Bertelsmann, Fininvest and Canal Plus, and uses other European languages as well as English.

The *fourth global flow*, of people through migration (long and short term), travel and tourism, is another feature driving globalisation. Global migration is observable in the increasing number and diversity of non-indigenous people living and working in other countries. This trend is particularly noticeable in Europe and the other OECD countries, which receive and send migrants from and to the rest of the world. During the 1990s this flow into European countries increased from 1.3 million to 1.5 million people (approximately) per year, partially reflecting the impact of the end of the division of Europe and wars in the Balkans (World Bank, 1999, p. 364).

Alongside these increasing flows of information and peoples has been the *fifth global flow*, of culture. Although what actually constitutes 'culture' is notoriously difficult to define, it is largely accepted that flows of cultural attributes such as art, language, music, film and other socially constructed forms of communication are increasing, although not on an even basis. It has been observed that the flow of culture is neither two-way nor is it affecting the globe to the same degree as other global flows. It would be simple to argue that global flows of culture are leading to an 'Americanisation' of popular culture, but the impact is a little more complex than that. Four of the world's ten most widely spoken languages come from Europe. The extent to which the language in which cultural products are conveyed is understood across the world has an impact on the flow of culture in the spoken and the written form. The four languages of European origin are English, comprehended by 7% of the world's speakers, Spanish with 6%, Russian with 4% and Portuguese with 3%, although easily the world's most spoken language is Mandarin with 16% (Buckley, 1999, p. 8; and Meadows, 1996, pp. 4–5).

The *sixth global flow* is that of geography, which is being changed and shaped by the speed and ease with which borders and boundaries of a physical and political nature are being crossed. Global geography is being reformed by the combination of advances in transport, communications, technology and the liberalisation of trade. This global flow allows families, groups and communities to maintain and develop contact to an extent not possible even a generation ago. The impact in Europe can be seen through the desire to create a single market in the 1980s and the improvement of transport infrastructures found in trans-European networks linking Europeans together through rail, roads, tunnels and bridges.

The *final global flow* is that found in the increasing pluralism of structures of authority and governance. This flow is leading to a multiplicity of international authorities responsible for global regulation of trade in everything from services to endangered species. In addition, increasing demands for local autonomy compete with regional attempts to create supra-national structures as the state's hold on sovereignty is questioned. In the case of Europe, at the same time as the region is integrating into the EU, some of its states are also decentralising as in Belgium and the UK, or fragmenting as in Czechoslovakia and Yugoslavia.

## Regionalisation

At the same time as Europe's relationship with the world is being shaped by the forces of globalisation discussed above, it is also part of a trend towards creating regional trading blocks known, in world politics, as regionalisation. Since the 1970s world trade has come to be increasingly dominated by regional trading blocks or regional integration arrangements (RIAs), which themselves have become the focus for patterns of trade amongst their members. The world's eight largest regional trade blocs in the 1990s were the Asia-Pacific Economic Co-operation (APEC) Forum (with 45% of world exports), the European Union (40%), the North American Free Trade Area (17%), the Association of South-East Asian Nations (6%), the Latin American Integration Association (4%), the Gulf Co-operation Council (2%), the Andean Group (1%) and the Southern African Development Community (1%) (World Bank, 1998, pp. 326–9). As will be discussed below, this pattern of regionalisation leads to two observations about Europe's trading relations with the world. First, these relations are primarily focused on a very small group of developed countries, led by the USA and Japan, who are themselves involved in creating RIAs. Secondly, in the next 30 years these regionalised relations may be transformed by the economic development of other large non-European states, in particular China.

Europe's trading relations with the world are dominated by the 'triadic' nature of world trade. **The Triad** consists of the world's three largest economic entities – the European Union, the United States, and Japan (see Table 9.3). Between them they account for approximately 50% of all world trade and 50% of the world's GDP. All three Triad powers are engaged in extending regional and inter-regional trading arrangements through the negotiation of free trade agreements. While Japan has developed its relations with its ASEAN neighbours, in particular through foreign direct investment (FDI), the United States has negotiated a North American Free Trade Agreement (NAFTA) with Canada and Mexico, and the EU has created a European Economic Area (EEA) with Norway, Iceland and Liechtenstein as well as

**The Triad:** Kenichi Ohmae's 1985 description of the world's three economic giants – the United States of America, the European Union and Japan.

**Table 9.3**  Triadic dominance of trade (% of total world trade)

|      | EU | | USA | | Japan | |
|------|---------|---------|---------|---------|---------|---------|
|      | exports | imports | exports | imports | exports | imports |
| 1960 | 20%     | 22%     | 16%     | 11%     | 3%      | 4%      |
| 1970 | 17%     | 19%     | 14%     | 12%     | 6%      | 6%      |
| 1980 | 15%     | 19%     | 11%     | 12%     | 7%      | 7%      |
| 1990 | 16%     | 17%     | 12%     | 15%     | 8%      | 7%      |
| 2000 | 15%     | 14%     | 12%     | 16%     | 8%      | 6%      |

negotiating the Europe Agreements with ten Central and Eastern European countries (see Box 8.1 and Chapter 8). The only Western or Central European state that
has not negotiated a free-trade agreement with the EU is Switzerland, which rejected
joining the EEA in a referendum in 1994. The USA and Japan have led the way
towards bringing NAFTA and ASEAN together in the APEC in order to further free
trade. The EU and USA have formalised their relations through the 1990 Transatlantic
Declaration and the 1995 New Transatlantic Agenda. The weakest side of the trian-
gle linking these Triad powers is that between Japan and the EU, although a series of
Asian–Europe Meetings (ASEM) in Bangkok in 1996 and London in 1998 have started
to address this imbalance. However, the continuing violation of human rights in
Burma by its illegitimate government continues to sour EU–ASEAN relations. As the
focus on the Triadic dominance of world trade indicates, despite the global economic
changes of the past four decades, these three economic 'superpowers' have consistently accounted for between 52% and 61% of all merchandise trade, even though
they only constitute 13% of the world's population.

This pattern of Europe's economic relations being shaped by the Triadic dominance of trade looks set to change in the next 20 years with the anticipated rise of a
fourth global economic superpower – China – and the arrival of the Quad. During
the 1980s and 1990s the value of Chinese merchandise trade grew by an average of
13% and 17% per year for each decade respectively. This explosion of Chinese trade,
together with the increasing liberalisation of its economy, has led many to conclude
that its economy will soon grow to match that of the industrial economies of the
Triad. An extension of these figures provided by the World Bank has led it to predict
that the Chinese economy could surpass that of the Triad countries in the next 20
years. However, such continued high levels of economic development are predicated
on the prior achievement of broader economic, democratic and human-rights freedoms. Although China does currently have the world's seventh largest economy because of its population of 1,200 million, its average citizen only ranks 65th in the
world in terms of relative wealth. In terms of quality of life, China comes nowhere
near the standards achieved by the Triad, as its **Human Development Index** rating
places it 106th in the world, far behind Canada (1st), France (2nd), the USA (4th)
and Japan (8th) (UN Development Program, 1998, p. 1). Similarly, China's poor
record on human-rights abuses places it 10th out of the world's worst. Its **Human
Rights Index** rating demonstrates its lack of political freedoms over the past ten years
since the brutal repression of pro-democracy demonstrators in Tiananmen Square
in June 1989 (*Observer*, 28 June 1998, p. 10). All these factors, together with the precarious nature of its economic boom, look likely to make Europe's relations with
China far more unsettled in the future than those with practically any other country
in the world.

## Localisation

'What . . . European societies are trying to come to terms with is how to enter new
forms of globalisation. . . . It goes global and local at the same moment. Global and
local are the two faces of the same movement from one epoch of globalization, the
one which has been dominated by the nation-state, the national economies, the
national cultural identities, to something new' (Hall, 1997, pp. 26–7).

As Stuart Hall suggests above, new forms of globalisation have both a global and a
local component to them, both of which are changing Europe's relations with the

**Human Development Index:** A
means used by the United
Nations Development Program
for rating the quality of life,
based on life expectancy,
education and real GDP per
capita.

**Human Rights Index:** An index
developed by the *Observer*
newspaper as a means of
drawing attention to the worst
human rights abusers in the
world.

world. Thus, in addition to the forces of globalisation and regionalisation, there is a third pattern of global change which is shaping the way Europe interacts with the world. This pattern is somewhat different from the previous two in that instead of contributing to the increasing sameness or homogeneity of the world, it is leading to increasing differences or heterogeneity. Thus, to a certain degree, localisation can be seen as a contrasting force to those of globalisation and regionalisation in presenting particular patterns of behaviour with a local dimension. These trends towards particular local patterns can be seen in increasing claims to distinctiveness through culture, economics and politics. To take examples from Europe to illustrate this point, we can see that at the same time as globalisation and regionalisation is taking place, so are demands for increased regional autonomy in most European states. Increasingly, local authorities in countries around Europe, from Britain to Germany and from Belgium to Spain, are seeking greater autonomy as a political right (see Chapter 3). This process of localisation tends to become even more politicised when based on linguistic or cultural differences, as can be seen throughout Europe.

At the end of this consideration of Europe and globalisation it is worth asking ourselves whether all three of the forces discussed above are not in fact part of the same process. What we are observing at the beginning of the twenty-first century is a Europe situated in an increasingly interconnected world which is both globalising and fragmenting at the same time. It is globalising through the increasing flows of products, people, ideas and culture but this is not leading to a simple homogenisation of Europe and the world. In contrast, the combination of globalisation, regionalisation and localisation are actually part of a process of going beyond simple economic explanations of the world towards more complex social explanations of Europe's relations with the world.

## The dynamics of change

In conclusion it is worth looking at the dynamics of change in order to gain a sense of where the relationship between Europe and the world is going. The dynamics of change present us with a mixed picture of Europe's relations with the world. This picture consists of five broad patterns in the twenty-first century. First among these is the pattern of Europe's relations with the former British colonies of the United States, Canada, Australia and New Zealand. All four of these states have developed into strong economies based on mixed patterns of production reinforced by liberal forms of government and multicultural societies. All four have surpassed, or are likely to surpass, the levels of development found in Britain. If democratic consolidation succeeds in South Africa, it is likely that this former British colony will also join the first group in the future.

The second developmental pattern is that demonstrated by the former communist-bloc countries of Central and Eastern Europe and Russia. The triple transformation of the post-Cold War period in most of these countries is beginning to lead to their membership of some very selective clubs such as the OECD and NATO (for Poland, the Czech Republic and Hungary) and membership of the European Union.

The third developmental pattern is that seen in the NICs of East Asia led by the Japanese economic miracle, but also including the 'tiger' economies of South Korea, Taiwan, Singapore and Hong Kong. Since the end of the Second World War, and particularly in the 1980s and 1990s, these states have achieved the distinction of moving from the developing world to that of the developed. Demonstrations of this achievement can be seen in the fact that Singapore, Hong Kong and Japan now have some of the richest citizens in the world, whilst Japan and South Korea are members of the OECD club of the world's developed economies. It is likely that these NICs will soon be matched by levels of development in Malaysia and Thailand. Although China is predicted to become the world's largest economy by 2020, the wealth of its average citizen will still be slight and its continued development will depend on successful political transformation.

The fourth developmental pattern is that of the large former Iberian colonies of Latin America, in particular Chile, Argentina, Venezuela, Uruguay, Mexico, Colombia and Brazil. Since partially overcoming the dual challenge of the 1980s debt crisis and the transformation to democracy in the 1980s and 1990s, these states have achieved impressive levels of development. The continued success of this progression will depend in part on reducing levels of economic disparity within the countries in order to consolidate democracy, as well as reversing the trend of reduced trade with Europe. However, some Central American states have not benefited to the same extent. Despite sharing similar patterns of colonisation and exploitation with the rest of Latin America, countries such as Haiti, Nicaragua and Honduras have suffered greatly from the regional impact of Cold War rivalry between the United States and the Soviet Union.

The final developmental pattern is that of the former European colonies of Africa and South Asia, which on average have found it difficult to improve the living standards of their peoples significantly since the achievement of political independence in the 1950s and 1960s. To a certain degree North Africa and a few exceptions such as South Africa, Gabon, Botswana and Namibia have been able to avoid this pattern. But the vast majority of Africans, and some South Asians, find their living conditions similar to or worse than those found at independence. It seems that at the end of the twentieth century international organisations and globalisation have failed to bring

**Table 9.4** The world's poorest – debt and aid (16 worst cases)

| Country | External debt (% of GNP 1996) | Overseas development aid (% of GNP 1996) |
|---|---|---|
| Mozambique | 411% | 60% |
| Nicaragua | 322% | 57% |
| Angola | 310% | 16% |
| Congo, Rep. | 260% | 23% |
| Guinea-Bissau | 248% | 67% |
| Côte d'Ivoire | 171% | 10% |
| Zambia | 161% | 19% |
| Mauritania | 157% | 26% |
| Ethiopia | 149% | 14% |
| Congo, Dem. Rep. | 127% | 3% |
| Vietnam | 123% | 4% |
| Syria | 120% | 1% |
| Nigeria | 114% | 1% |
| Tanzania | 114% | 17% |
| Jordan | 110% | 7% |
| Cameroon | 106% | 5% |

benefits for a great number of the world's poorest people, as they pay more interest on debt than they receive as aid and their standards of living continue to fall.

'Is it true – as Franz Fanon claimed – that since its development has required the spoliation of the non-European world, "Europe is literally the creation of the Third World"?' (Waites, 1995, p. 13). It is undoubtedly true that, over the past 500 years of history, Europe has transformed the world in every sense through trade, travel, empires, industrialisation, and wars. It seems sensible to argue that, through the creation of international institutions, multinational companies, regional trading blocs, and globalised patterns of exchange, the world is now transforming Europe.

## ■ Summary

◆ In order to understand the complexity of the relations between Europe and the world it is necessary to go beyond simple explanations of contemporary analyses. A more comprehensive analysis would need to take into account the insights provided by complementary approaches including the role of historical ties, the institutional structure of international relations, and processes of globalisation.

◆ Europe's relations with the world have been significantly shaped by its historical experience of mercantilism, colonialism, world wars, Cold War, economic depression and interdependence. On the one hand this history has led to close relations with those states around the world who have shared the benefits of this relationship, such as the USA, Canada and Japan. On the other hand, this variety of experiences has made many of the world's poorest states extremely wary of their relations with Europe.

◆ Since the end of the Second World War a series of international organisations and agreements have increasingly shaped the interplay between Europe and the world. With the end of the Cold War this institutionalised structure of global relations has come to assume greater importance, particularly since the USA repeatedly attaches significance to them.

◆ European states play privileged roles in many of the bodies of the United Nations, the IMF and World Bank, as well as the OECD and Group of Eight. The European Union also institutionalises a number of relationships with the world through its external and foreign policies.

◆ The past five decades have seen the acceleration of a process which has been ongoing for the previous five centuries – the increasing integration of the world's economic, social and political activities. What is different about the post-Second World War period is that non-European states such as the USA and Japan, international organisations such as the WTO, and non-state actors such as MNCs, have played a far more important role than ever before.

◆ In the post-Cold War world of the twenty-first century the European Union, European states, European companies and European peoples will increasingly form closer relationships with the rest of the world.

## ■ Questions for discussion

▶ What role has Europe played in the development of world trade?

▶ What impact did Europe's empires have on its international role?

► Did the Cold War make any real difference to Europe's relations?

► Is the post-Cold War era significantly different from the previous century?

► What role does Europe play in international organisations?

► Is the Triad of any real importance in a globalising world?

► Has Europe benefited from globalisation? Has the rest of the world?

# ◼ Further reading

Axtmann, Roland (ed.) (1998) *Globalisation and Europe: Theoretical and Empirical Investigations* (London: Pinter). A multidisciplinary collection of more advanced articles on the relationships between European states and the processes of globalisation.

Bretherton, Charlotte and John Vogler (1999) *The European Union as a Global Actor* (London: Routledge). A broad survey of the European Union's role in global politics which challenges traditional assumptions about international behaviour.

Dent, Christopher (1997) *The European Economy: The Global Context* (London: Routledge). A general introduction to the economic dimension of Europe's relations with the world.

Fieldhouse, David (1999) *The West and the Third World* (Oxford: Blackwell). A rich historical survey of Europe's relations with the third world, focusing in particular on its colonial heritage.

Waites, Bernard (ed.) (1995) *Europe and the Wider World* (Milton Keynes: Open University Press). A very basic introduction to Europe's relations with the world.

# CHAPTER 10

# European Security

Mike Bowker

## Contents

'States ... face risks and dangers, rather than enemies. ...'

ANTHONY GIDDENS, *The Third Way: The Renewal of Social Democracy*
(1998) p. 137

This chapter will examine the issue of European security. It will first consider security in the Cold War period. How dangerous was the Cold War? How close were we to a major war on the continent? The chapter then moves on to look at how far Europe and the world have changed since the Cold War ended, before considering what the main threats to security are in Europe today. Finally, the chapter looks at the possible means of reducing these threats. Is the state still the primary unit for security? Or do regional institutions, such as NATO, the EU/WEU and the OSCE, have an increasingly important role to play?

## European security in the Cold War period

Keith Krause has offered a useful definition of security, arguing that security is primarily about reducing the risk of organised violence in public life. This allows us to look at security issues at three different levels: the threats states pose to each other; the threats institutions of organised violence (both formal and informal) pose to states and regimes; and the threat those that hold the means of violence pose to citizens and society. These threats may or may not be physical, according to Krause, and therefore the means of preventing security threats will involve measures which include the military, but not exclusively (Krause, 1998). This seems a useful definition, the basis of which will underpin the discussion that follows.

In the Cold War era, thinking on European security was dominated by **realist**, rather than **idealist** concepts. This was scarcely surprising. To many, peace and stability in Europe looked precarious – particularly in the immediate post-war period. Europe was a divided continent, Germany a divided country, and Berlin a divided city. Divisions of this kind have a tendency to lead to tension and often to war. In the case of post-war Europe, fears were heightened owing to the ideological differences on either side of the divide, which resulted in Europe becoming the most heavily armed region of the globe. In many respects, the Cold War was a uniquely dangerous time. If a war started in Europe, few doubted that it would quickly escalate into all-out nuclear war involving both of the superpowers – the United States and the

**Realist:** Realist thinkers argue that states always pursue their own national interests in the world, both to maximise their own power and to defend their own territory.

**Idealism:** A normative International Relations theory which accepts the problems and dangers of anarchy in the international system but, unlike realist theories, seeks to overcome them through the creation of an international community based on international organisations and a greater emphasis on international law.

USSR. Even a more limited nuclear exchange would leave millions of casualties whilst the survivors faced an uncertain future due to the devastating ecological effects of nuclear war (see box 10.1).

A number of crises in Europe might conceivably have escalated into nuclear war during the Cold War period. Most of these started in Eastern Europe and were the result of Moscow's inability to gain legitimacy for its dominance over the region. Uprisings against Moscow took place on a fairly regular basis – in the GDR (East Germany) in 1953, in Hungary in 1956, in Czechoslovakia in 1968, and in Poland at frequent intervals after 1956, culminating in the Solidarity rebellion of 1980–1. On each of the above occasions, the Communist authorities were able to suppress the uprisings by force and restore order. The West, for its part, had soon come to accept that these countries were in the Soviet sphere of influence, and made little attempt beyond diplomatic representations to give support to the rebels. On the whole, the West did not wish to encourage rebellion in Eastern Europe. Stability in Europe, based on the recognition of a divided continent and a bipolar balance of power, appeared to be nothing more than a sensible acceptance of post-war realities.

The one area where the lines of division in Europe remained unclear into the 1960s was Berlin. As a result, Berlin became the main point of East–West tension in Europe in the early years of the Cold War. Berlin was an embarrassment to Moscow, and not only because it was a visible island of Western opulence within the Soviet bloc. Situated approximately 100 miles inside the former GDR, the divided capital city was used by the West as a spying centre and military base, whilst the open border between the two parts of the city was a convenient escape-hatch to the West for disgruntled East Germans. Stalin and Khrushchev both put pressure on the West to withdraw from its sector of Berlin at various times, but without success. Finally, Khrushchev decided to resolve the issue in 1961 by building the Berlin Wall. The Wall came as a considerable shock to the Germans at the time, but it was regarded by many others around the world as a reasonable compromise. The West maintained its position in West Berlin, whilst the Soviets ended the immediate threat, to the East German state, of mass emigration – three million people, or a fifth of the total population of the GDR, had fled the country from its inception in 1949 to the time when the Berlin Wall was built in 1961.

The Wall also contributed to the stabilisation of Europe through the *de facto* recognition of the political status quo on the continent. Stability was further ensured when this unwritten understanding was formalised through Willy Brandt's *Ostpolitik* (Eastern policy) of the early 1970s and the Helsinki Final Act of 1975 (see Box 10.2). Brandt's *Ostpolitik* was made up of a series of bilateral agreements signed by Bonn with the USSR and its East European neighbours which, *de facto* if not *de jure*, accepted the division of the German state and the post-war German borders. Helsinki, in many respects, was a multilateral version of Brandt's *Ostpolitik*. All of Europe (with the exception of Albania) plus the USA and Canada (because of their membership of NATO) signed the Helsinki Final Act, which, in practice, also accepted the geopolitical status quo in Europe and, therefore, the existence of a Soviet-dominated Communist bloc in Eastern Europe. Opponents of these agreements characterised Helsinki and *Ostpolitik* as the Western equivalent of the Brezhnev Doctrine, in appearing to accept communist dictatorship in the Soviet bloc for the perceived greater good of stability in Europe. Although this criticism was valid to a certain extent, both Helsinki and *Ostpolitik* contained subversive elements. Thus, Brandt never formally abandoned the ultimate goal of German unification, and indeed argued

## Box 10.1

### Nuclear winter

An article written in 1993 outlined the possible long-term ecological problems of even a limited nuclear war in Europe. The pollution caused would obscure the sun and lower temperatures over a wide area by as much as 20 degrees centigrade. Such effects would darken the skies sufficiently to endanger plant life and produce dangerous levels of chemical and radioactive poisons. It was estimated that the missiles on board a single US SLBM (submarine-launched ballistic missile) would be sufficient to initiate nuclear winter (Kegley and Wittkopf, 1999, p. 431).

Box 10.2

## The Conference on Security and Co-operation in Europe, the Helsinki Final Act, the Charter of Paris and the Organisation for Security and Co-operation in Europe

In 1973 a Conference on Security and Co-operation in Europe (CSCE) first met in Helsinki, attended by the representatives of 35 states – all those in Europe except Albania together with Canada and the United States. The Conference arose from the possibility, in a new climate created by the willingness of West Germany to recognise the existence of East Germany as a separate state, and by the desire for détente and disarmament, of conducting multilateral negotiations to settle some of the issues that had remained outstanding since 1945, and to improve economic relationships. The Soviet Union had long been keen for such negotiations, seeking especially to get international confirmation of its post-war borders and status. It thus sponsored the CSCE. The outcome of the first meetings of the CSCE was the conclusion, in August 1975, of the Helsinki Final Act, divided into three 'baskets'. The first re-confirmed the frontiers settled after the war. The second was concerned with economic issues. The Soviet Union, in its eagerness to achieve the formal ratification of post-war borders and other security and economic advantages in the first two 'baskets' was willing, with its communist allies, to sign up to a third 'basket' dealing with a number of issues subsumed under the rubric of human rights (Mastny, 1993, pp. 421–42). The document was not a legally binding treaty, but rather a declaration of intent. It nevertheless proved one of the more significant catalysts for the fall of the communist systems, in that it gave the populations an official document to cite, signed by all the communist states, promising to defend free speech, freedom of movement and many other aspects.

The Helsinki Final Act thus set the stage for the transcendence of communism, first *ratifying* Yalta (the borders agreed at the Yalta summit in the Crimea between Stalin, Roosevelt and Churchill, in effect allowing Soviet dominance of Eastern Europe) and then *transcending* it by formalising the agenda of international public law (sovereign equality of states, territorial integrity, non-intervention in internal affairs, and inviolability of frontiers) to cover relations between states, but at the same introduced human rights and fundamental freedoms as part of European inter-state relations, including the idea of equal rights and the self-determination of peoples. The CSCE played a crucial part in the final days of communism, above all at its Vienna follow-up meeting in November 1986. The concluding document of the Vienna conference set out a far-reaching agenda of human rights and civil society and by 1989 Gorbachev had adopted this. He did not regard this is incompatible with the socialism he was seeking to maintain, but it proved to be so.

At its Paris meeting in November 1990 after the collapse of communism the CSCE created, in a document known as the Paris Charter, a number of institutions designed to give it a more permanent form and to make it a more effective instrument of democratisation: (i) a Council made up of foreign ministers; (ii) a Permanent Secretariat in Vienna; (iii) a Conflict Prevention Centre in Vienna; (iv) an Office of Democratic Institutions and Human Rights in Warsaw; and (v) a Parliamentary Assembly. The informal relationships of the Conference became more formalised at the Budapest summit in 1994 when it became an Organisation (the OSCE). By then it had 53 members and there were high hopes for its role in the settlement of territorial conflicts. However, the wars in the Balkans starkly revealed its inadequacies. Above all, the tension between the core OSCE principles of national self-determination and the inviolability of borders has still to be reconciled. Russia hoped to make the OSCE the main security body in Europe to replace NATO, but these aspirations have not been fulfilled.

that the *raison d'être* for the political division of Germany would fade as *Ostpolitik* encouraged closer economic, cultural, social and personal ties between the two German states. The Helsinki Final Act, for its part, acknowledged the divisions in Europe but it also contained explicit commitments to human rights throughout the continent. This aspect of Helsinki was increasingly taken up by dissidents in Eastern Europe as they demanded that their governments, at a minimum, abide by international agreements freely entered into. Although the West was initially reluctant to embarrass Moscow, by the 1980s its reticence had gone and human rights became the dominant issue in the subsequent Helsinki review conferences in Belgrade, Madrid and Vienna.

It was accurate to describe East–West relations in Europe as tense during much of the Cold War, but as the process of détente between the superpowers began to take hold in the 1970s a growing number of writers began to remark on the stabilising features of the Cold War. Were they right? How stable was the Cold War? Gaddis (1987) and Waltz (1979) were right to point out that the Cold War had stabilising features, but their overall analysis suffered from its over-reliance on realist ideas. The

Box 10.3

## Arms control

Arms control agreements which still have relevance in the post-Cold War era include the following:

- The Non-Proliferation Treaty (NPT), signed in 1968, commits the five official nuclear states (USA, Russia, Britain, France and China) not to provide other states with nuclear weapons and commits all other states to abandon any claim to becoming independent nuclear powers. In 1995, the number of signatories had risen to 186, and they all agreed to extend the treaty indefinitely. However, the testing of nuclear weapons by India and Pakistan in May 1998 has raised doubts over the treaty's ability to contain nuclear proliferation in the future.

- The Intermediate Nuclear Forces Treaty (INF), signed in 1987, abolished all land-based intermediate nuclear weapons (300–3,000 mile range) in Europe.

- The Conventional Forces in Europe Treaty (CFE), signed in 1990, set ceilings on the numbers of tanks, combat vehicles, artillery, combat aircraft and attack helicopters, and also lowered force levels across Europe.

- The Strategic Arms Reduction Treaty I (START I), signed in 1991, reduced the number of Soviet and American long-range nuclear weapons by 30 per cent.

- The Strategic Arms Reduction Treaty II (START II), signed in 1993, calls for a reduction of the Russian and American long-range nuclear forces to 3,000–3,500 each by the year 2003.

- The Comprehensive Test Ban Treaty of 1996 bans all testing of nuclear weapons.

- The Chemical Weapons Convention, signed by 164 countries in 1998, called for the destruction of all chemical weapons by the year 2003.

- The Anti-Personnel Mine Treaty of 1998 bans the production and export of landmines and pledges plans to remove mines already in place.

assumption of bipolarity was that Moscow and Washington had roughly equal power. Yet this could only be assumed if only military factors, and most especially nuclear capability, were taken into account. In other aspects of power, including economic power, the USSR was far behind America and the West. Furthermore, Gaddis and Waltz offered a curiously static vision of the post-war world which paid little attention to the shift in power relations over time, and most particularly to the growing economic and political crisis inside the Soviet bloc. This omission became increasingly evident in the late 1970s as the Soviet economy slowed and the ideology of Marxism–Leninism lost its legitimacy and appeal both at home and abroad.

The importance of Mikhail Gorbachev, who came to power in the USSR in March 1985, was that he recognised the relative weakness of the Soviet Union. Gorbachev can be criticised for many things, but in foreign policy he was resolute and remarkably consistent. On coming to power, he sought to end the Cold War with the West, which he believed was no longer in the interest of the Soviet Union. For one thing, the Cold War was too costly. Soviet defence spending had risen in the 1970s to somewhere between 15 and 20 per cent of Soviet GNP, and this was depriving the civilian economy of much-needed investment. Yet the USSR had been unable to use its military power to good effect.

When Gorbachev came to power, he introduced a number of important defence and foreign-policy initiatives which ultimately led to the end of the Cold War. On defence, he offered unilateral and asymmetrical cuts in arms, opening the way towards a series of important arms control agreements with the West which, for the first time, significantly reduced the number of conventional and nuclear weapons on either side (see Box 10.3).

### Francis Fukuyama (born 1952)

Francis Fukuyama rose to fame in 1989 after publishing an article called 'The End of History?'. Using Hegelian philosophy, Fukuyama argued that the end of the Cold War represented not only the victory of liberal democracy over Soviet-style communism, but the final triumph of liberal democracy over all other ideologies and political systems for all time. This was a highly controversial view, but one Fukuyama has defended and

expanded on in a number of other articles and books; see, for example, *The End of History and the Last Man* (Harmondsworth: Penguin, 1992).

Gorbachev sought to end conflicts in the Third World through negotiation and diplomacy, and, to show it was not all talk, withdrew Soviet troops from the war in Afghanistan in February 1989. But most significant of all, the *Politburo* in November 1986 formally abandoned the Brezhnev Doctrine, which had proclaimed the right of Moscow to use force to suppress anti-communist rebellion throughout Eastern Europe (Bowker, 1997, p. 89). This did not mean that Gorbachev willed the end of communism in the region. Far from it, but he was effectively saying that Moscow would no longer use force to uphold unpopular East European governments. Although many doubted that Gorbachev would be willing, or able, to keep to these commitments in the event of a major crisis in the region, Moscow did indeed refuse to give military aid when communism began to collapse in Eastern Europe in the second half of 1989. For many, the turning-point came on 9 November 1989 when the Berlin Wall was breached, opening the way for the reunification of Germany in 1990 and the end to the political divisions which had been the central feature of post-war history in Europe. The debate henceforth centred over the question of what the new post-Cold War world would look like and whether it would increase the chance of peace and stability in Europe and around the globe.

## The post-Cold War system

In the debate over the post-Cold War world, there were two main schools of thought – universalists, who perceived an emerging 'one-worldism', and their critics, who emphasised further fragmentation and division. Universalists argued that the world was coming together after the divisions of the Cold War around a common agenda of shared values based on democracy and the market. Optimists, like the American academic Francis Fukuyama (1989) (see Portrait 10.1) believed that this major shift opened up historic opportunities for peace and prosperity throughout Europe and the world.

George Bush and Mikhail Gorbachev caught the mood with talk of a New World Order (see Box 10.4). Stability and security would no longer be based on power blocs and nuclear deterrence, they declared, but on more idealist concepts of international law and **collective security**. Although some saw the intervention in Kosovo as a new type of war where states intervene for altruistic reasons even when their national

**Collective security:** The core idea of collective security is that states should act together for the common good rather than acting alone or in military blocs in their own selfish national interests.

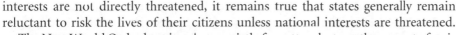

**Portrait 10.2**

### Immanuel Kant (1724–1804)

Kant was a German philosopher who continues to have a major influence on liberal thinking. In 1795, he published his book *Perpetual Peace*, in which he argued that democracies are less warlike than dictatorships because leaders are accountable to the people. Because the people would have to provide the money and the soldiers for waging war, Kant contended that the people would tend to favour peace.

interests are not directly threatened, it remains true that states generally remain reluctant to risk the lives of their citizens unless national interests are threatened.

The New World Order has since been quietly forgotten, but another aspect of universalist thinking has proved more lasting. This relates to the theory of the so-called democratic peace. According to this theory, democracies are less militarily aggressive, less expansionist and less willing to violate international law than dictatorships. Democracies do fight wars, but the proposition advanced by Michael Doyle, based on earlier observations by the philosopher Immanuel Kant (see Portrait 10.2), is that 'democracies do not fight each other' (Doyle, 1986). Therefore, as democracy spreads across Europe, the so-called 'peaceful union' is enlarged and the risk of war on the continent is greatly reduced. Although politicians tend to be rather suspicious of abstract theories, this is one that many Western leaders have embraced. Indeed, the expansion of the democratic peace has become official US policy towards Central and Eastern Europe. One criticism of the policy, however, is the fear that democratisation

**Box 10.4**

### The New World Order

The concept of the New World Order had at its heart the notion that security would be maintained not by the balance of mutual antagonism between power blocs but by collective security. Collective security rests on the idea that the behaviour of states will be governed by international law. If a rogue state should violate international law (as interpreted by the United Nations), all states are duty-bound to act in concert to punish the miscreant or make good the violation. *In extremis*, this could involve the use of military force, as Saddam Hussein discovered after Iraq invaded and annexed Kuwait in August 1990. Many observers were highly dubious, even at the time, that a collective security system was credible in the post-Cold War world (for example see Hurd, 1997, p. 190). It required states, and especially the great powers, to forgo their national interest and act collectively for the common good (which is often very difficult to define and agree on). Collective security had been tried in the interwar years, and been found wanting. In the post-Cold War world, it was scarcely more successful. There have been examples of the international community acting in the name of collective security – for example, in the Gulf War, but they have been the exception rather than the rule. Other violations of international law have occurred, and other conflicts have broken out around the world, without the international community taking action, although under the aegis of NATO Serbian repression in Kosovo was ended.

Portrait 10.3

### Eric Hobsbawm (born in 1917)

Born in 1917, Hobsbawm became Professor at Birkbeck College, London, until his retirement. He is now resident in the USA. A Marxist historian, highly respected amongst his peers, he was also popular amongst a much broader readership owing to his accessible writing style and penetrating insights. Of his many works, perhaps his greatest is a series of books on world history, entitled: *The Age of Revolution*, *The Age of Capital*, *The Age of Empire* and *The Age of Extremes* (all published by Michael Joseph).

during the difficult transition period is likely to foster populist politics, including intolerant forms of nationalism, as happened in the former states of Yugoslavia and the USSR (Snyder, 1995).

Nevertheless, universalists tend to be optimistic about the future. Some, however, take a bleaker view of the future. Eric Hobsbawm (1994) (see Portrait 10.3), for example, accepts that the end of the Cold War represented the victory of capitalism over communism, but argues that this will lead to instability and social disruption around the world. In the absence of any challenge from a rival social system, Hobsbawm has argued, international capitalism will be able to act in an unrestrained and irresponsible manner in its constant search to maximise profits. The result, according to Hobsbawm, will be growing income differentials between individuals within states, and between states themselves, resulting in social disruption and increasing anarchy within the international system. Whilst such an analysis may underestimate the ability of capitalism to adapt and create wealth, it does, however, act as a useful corrective to some of the more optimistic scenarios advanced by people like Fukuyama. It also points to the problems of regulating capitalism in the globalised international society of today, and the problem capitalism has in distributing wealth equitably. The nation-state is often found particularly wanting in this regard, and hence the search for international and regional organisations, such as the IMF, the World Bank, GATT and the EU.

Critics of universalist theory stress the divisions within the post-Cold War international system, but they are not united over where the most fundamental divisions lie. The realist scholar John Mearsheimer (1990) (see Portrait 10.4), for example, argued that national interest would still remain the driving force behind the behaviour of states in the international system. He feared, however, that the collapse of bipolarity would lead to greater instability than in the Cold War period. Other critics of **universalism** acknowledged, unlike Mearsheimer, that the world had undergone change during the Cold War period which went far beyond shifts in the balance of power. Such critics perceived the emergence of new fault-lines in the international system. Some, for example, argued that the state and the military were less important in the post-Cold War world, and placed more emphasis on economic strength as a source of power and influence. Fragmentists, however, detected new divisions and increasing tensions between the emerging economic blocs of the Americas (based around the US), Europe (based around Germany), and the Far East (based around China and Japan). The competition between these economic blocs was likely to

**Universalism:** A very general term which suggests that the end of the Cold War offered potential for the formation of a real international community based on the general acceptance of key principles governing international behaviour.

Portrait 10.4

## John Mearsheimer (born in 1947)

A professor at Chicago University, Mearsheimer has written extensively on military and security issues. In 1990, he wrote a highly influential article in *International Security*, called 'Back to the Future'. The title was taken from a popular Hollywood film of the time. Mearsheimer, a realist thinker, believed that the end of the Cold War would lead to a period of great instability. He expected the USA to withdraw from, or at least greatly reduce its commitment to, Europe and expected Germany to become a nuclear power at the centre of Europe. Mearsheimer saw the nuclearisation of Germany as a wholly positive development. For, according to his theory, peace and stability were only likely to be secured through the formation of a new balance of power in which nuclear deterrence would continue to play a key role.

intensify, it was argued, now that the unifying threat of Soviet communism had disappeared. However, although there have been disputes over such issues as trade protectionism and the environment, the level of division is easy to exaggerate. On the whole, leaders are well aware of the interdependent nature of the international capitalist system. Protectionism is perceived to have failed as a policy and free trade is generally believed to be the best means of stimulating growth. This has led to a more open and more co-operative international economic system than in the past.

Another theory critical of universalism is advanced by the American academic Samuel Huntington (see Portrait 10.5). He argues that the Western policy of promoting a democratic peace will fail because it is culture-bound. Western values, he argues, are not universally applicable, and the promotion of liberal democracy will lead to the inevitable accusations of **neo-imperialism**. Huntington sees cultural difference as the key to understanding the post-Cold War world and argues that differences among cultures represent the most important fissures in the new international system. Since culture has far deeper roots in society than ideology, according to Huntington, there is less room for the normal give-and-take of politics. As a result, Huntington predicts that the major conflicts of the new era will not be caused by nationalism or economic competition, but by what he calls 'the clash of civilizations' (1993). In particular, Huntington cites the potential for conflict in parts of the world where these great civilisations meet; for example, in the Balkans and parts of the former USSR where Christendom and Islam have often battled for supremacy. Although there are examples of conflict between cultures, Huntington's critics suggest that the differences between these civilisations are often less great than sometimes implied, and that it is, in any case, often a matter of dispute whether culture was the main cause of conflict. Furthermore, it would be wrong to suggest that the civilisations identified by Huntington are unified, coherent blocs with a clear set of political principles. On the contrary, both Islam and Christendom (as just two examples) are beset by fundamental divisions, and both religions throw up almost endless interpretations and reinterpretations of their sacred texts. It is nothing more than a truism to say that it is possible as a Christian or Muslim to be either conservative or radical (or, indeed, both in different contexts). Conflict within cultures (for example, in Northern Ireland) is just as common as conflicts between cultures.

So, how different is security in the post-Cold War era? The end of the Cold War had a deep impact on many aspects of security policy in Europe. Most notably, the

**Neo-imperialism:** This refers to the effects of imperialism on a state which exist without the political reality of colonisation.

Portrait 10.5

### Samuel P. Huntington (born in 1927)

Currently a professor at Harvard University, Huntington is a highly influential writer in America on international affairs. He founded the respected academic journal *Foreign Policy*, and he has written on a wide range of topics, including the important issue of Transition Theory (how dictatorships become democracies). In 1993, he wrote the article 'Clash of Civilizations?' in *Foreign Affairs*, in which he argued that wars in future were likely to take place between different cultures rather than between different ideologies or different nationalities. The response to his ideas was said to be the greatest since George Kennan's 'X' article some 45 years earlier. Huntington's ideas remain very controversial in academic circles but seem more popular amongst some officials and politicians in Western states.

political divide on the continent disappeared and, as a result, the threat of major war in Europe has also faded, at least for the moment. This does not mean that the end of the Cold War resolved all the security problems in Europe. Far from it. Some security issues which were only peripherally (if at all) to do with the Cold War, such as Cyprus and Northern Ireland, rumbled on. New problems have also emerged as a direct result of the Cold War ending, for example in Yugoslavia, leading to specific questions over the consequences of the collapse of communism and the end of the bipolar system. These include the following: how will Russia deal with its sudden and dramatic decline in status? Will the USA continue to play a key role in European security? How will Germany respond to reunification and its concomitant rise in power? What will be the role for the main regional organisations in terms of the future security architecture of Europe? And finally, what will happen to the small postcommunist countries of Central and Eastern Europe? These questions will be discussed in the remainder of this chapter.

# European security issues in the post-Cold War world

## 1  Post-Soviet Russia

Post-Soviet Russia is in a unique position. It is seen as both the primary risk to security in Europe and an integral part of any stable future security architecture. Russia, clearly, has the potential power to act either as a stabilising or destabilising force in Europe and beyond. It is strategically important, for Russia is a vast country, with a population of 146 million, which spans the two continents of Europe and Asia. Potentially, it has the natural and labour resources to emerge as a considerable economic power some time in the future. It remains a great military power, possessing a formidable nuclear capability and, even as it cuts its conventional military forces, the largest land army in Europe. In security terms, Russia is simply too important to ignore.

Yet its current situation domestically is highly unstable making future predictions over Russian foreign policy almost impossible to make. Its economy lies shattered, crime and corruption are rampant, and the people, unsurprisingly, have become disillusioned with reform and the whole democratisation process. The government has had to take account of this growing resentment and in an attempt to unify the country it began to adopt a more nationalist stance after 1993. After Yeltsin's resignation on New Year's Eve 1999, it was noticeable that Vladimir Putin, as acting President, gained public support for his commitment to increase defence spending and defeat the Chechens, whom he blamed for terrorist attacks in Russia, in the latest war with Moscow.

The military is desperate to restore its battered reputation and regain its influential position in Russia after the devastating effects of reform. The catastrophic state of government finances has meant there is little money to pay military personnel, to house them or train them. Military equipment, including nuclear weaponry, is inadequately stored, and it frequently fails to receive the maintenance and service required. This has led to an illegal trade in weaponry and frequent stories of dangerous practices at nuclear military bases and on board nuclear submarines (see Box 10.5). No one seriously believes that Russia wishes to launch a nuclear strike against the West today, but fears remain over an unofficial launch by terrorists, or some kind of nuclear accident which could well affect not only Russia but much of the European continent as well. There are also concerns that disillusioned nuclear experts or military officers could aid nuclear proliferation to rogue states (such as Iraq or Iran) through smuggling fissile material abroad, or by simply going abroad for employment.

Russia, according to most estimates, is not in a position militarily to threaten Europe in the foreseeable future. However, Russia still dominates the territory of the former Soviet Union. Twenty-five million Russians live outside the Russian Federation in neighbouring states of the former Soviet Union, which has created concern that this could provide the rationale for military action to undermine their newly won status as sovereign, independent states. The tiny Baltic States, for example, have applied for NATO membership to avert just such an occurrence. Russia has used military force on a number of occasions in ethnic conflicts on its periphery. It also used brutal force against Chechnya in 1994–6 and again from 1999, to prevent the Chechen Republic from seceding from the Russian Federation.

Nevertheless, the restoration of the Soviet Union, dominated by Russia, remains highly unlikely. First, it would only be possible through the use of military force. Quite apart from the cost and destabilising effects of war on its doorstep, it is unclear whether the Russian military has the power to enforce its will on recalcitrant nations. It proved enormously difficult in Chechnya, a small republic of only 1.2 million people. Why should it hope to have more success elsewhere? Secondly, Russia can maintain its influence in much of the region without undermining the formal independence of those states. The policy since 1993 has been to extend the CIS (Commonwealth of Independent States) to all Soviet successor states (with the exception of the three Baltic States, which were only brought into the USSR in 1940) and increase Russian influence within it. This would provide most of the benefits of political control whilst avoiding most of the costs. Although Moscow has manipulated conflicts in the Caucasus to entice reluctant members into the CIS, it has found its economic dominance to be the most useful means of furthering its policy in the region. Finally, Russia has no desire to take on the economic costs of a formal empire. Moscow clearly sees the Caucasus and the Slavic areas of the former Soviet Union as being of vital strategic interest to Russia, but it is unwilling to subsidise their collapsing economies. Moscow is keen, however, to benefit economically from oil in the Caucasus region, and this was another important reason why Moscow decided to use force to prevent Chechen independence.

## Box 10.5

### Safety concerns in the Russian nuclear arms industry

'Captain Alexei Tikhomirov of the Russian navy walked into the Sevmorput shipyard near Murmansk in the Arctic, entered a building in which unused submarine fuel was kept, took three pieces of the reactor core with about 10 pounds of highly enriched uranium and walked out. Eight months later, when Tikhomirov tried to sell the material (for $50,000), he was arrested.'

*Source*: John Lloyd, *Rebirth of a Nation: An Anatomy of Russia* (London: Michael Joseph, 1998), pp. 126–7.

In general terms, the West has turned a blind eye to Moscow's machinations over Chechnya and the CIS. It recognises Russia's interests in the area and has been unwilling to become militarily involved either as peacekeeper or as peace enforcer. The UN did, however, refuse to fund Russia's military operations in the CIS for fear it would be interpreted as supporting Russian neo-imperialism. On the other hand, the OSCE, a multinational pan-European body (see Box 10.2), has acted as a mediator in a number of conflicts on the soil of the former Soviet Union, for example in Chechnya and Moldova. Russia, however, has remained the key player in the CIS owing to its military dominance of the region.

On foreign policy outside the CIS, after a brief romance with the West, Moscow has adopted a more hard-headed, nationalist approach since 1993. Nevertheless, Russia's rather bellicose rhetoric has not always matched its actions. The relationship with the West is delicate and requires skilful handling. Western aid, to date, has had little impact on the fate of the Russian economy. Its support of democracy has been tempered by fears of what might follow Yeltsin. Thus, the West supported the forcible dissolution of the Russian parliament in 1993 and only registered mild rebukes in relation to Russian attacks on Chechnya. Nevertheless, the honeymoon with Russia is long over. But on most issues, from Iraq to Bosnia, Moscow has acted within the general parameters of the international consensus (see Bowker, 1997). It would be wrong to portray Moscow as unthinkingly obstructionist. There remains room and a necessity for co-operative relations with Russia.

## 2  Wars in Yugoslavia

The wars in the former Yugoslavia provided Europe with its first major security problem in the post-Cold War era. After the Yugoslav state (see Map 2.5) began to break up in 1991, wars erupted in the republics of Slovenia and Croatia. Diplomacy in Slovenia was successful in rapidly ending the war, but the war in Croatia (where a large number of Serbs lived) dragged on until a cease-fire was agreed in January 1992. However, the cease-fire did not create a stable peace. It was agreed only after the Serbs had partitioned Croatia by force, thereby creating the Serb-dominated state of Krajina on Croatian territory. The partition was never acceptable to the Croats and they remained committed to retrieving their land.

**Ethnic cleansing:** The practice of forcibly removing members of any different ethnic group from an area controlled by a particular group. The term, often no more than a euphemism for genocide, came into prominence during the war in Bosnia in the 1990s to describe the removal or destruction of Croats or Muslims from territories claimed by Serbs as part of 'Greater Serbia'. The term was then used to describe the forced removal of Serbs from territories that had become or were becoming independent states.

The temporary cease-fire in Croatia also had the effect of allowing the Serbs to turn their attention to Bosnia where approximately a third of the population was Serb. The Bosnian Serbs refused to accept the Bosnian declaration of independence in April 1992, and to live under the rule of its Muslim leader, Alija Izetbegovic. So they launched a military offensive to create their own, ethnically pure, Bosnian Serb republic (Republika Srpska). By Christmas, it appeared they had achieved their aim. They had taken about 70 per cent of Bosnian territory and, in the process, driven thousands of Muslim civilians from their homes in a deliberate policy of **ethnic cleansing**. It only remained for the Bosnian Serbs to integrate their new republic with Krajina and Serbia proper, for them to accomplish their ultimate aim of creating a Greater Serbia.

When the Croats (who made up about 17 per cent of the Bosnian population) launched their own land-grab in Bosnia in the winter of 1992–93, the war became a highly complex three-way affair with the Bosnian Muslims squeezed into an ever-diminishing parcel of land. The military action by the Bosnian Croats made it even more difficult for the international community to agree an acceptable end-goal in

Bosnia. The Bosnian Serbs and Bosnian Croats were the aggressors, but they had lived in Bosnia all their lives and had the basic right of self-determination. In the circumstances, what kind of political arrangement could be put in place which would be acceptable to all sides? How could the rights of the different ethnic groups in Bosnia be respected? Was a putative partition of Bosnia morally acceptable? Was an independent, sovereign Bosnia a viable option? These were major questions which were terribly difficult to answer, but without some agreement it was impossible for the West to do anything effective.

The course of the war only began to change in 1994 when the USA became more actively involved in diplomacy. The USA favoured putting pressure on the Serbs to compromise, but Washington was not prepared to back up its position with the deployment of US troops as peace enforcers. Instead, the Americans mediated an end to the Croat–Muslim war in Bosnia in March 1994, and the formation of a Muslim–Croat Federation on Bosnian territory. At the same time, the USA turned a blind eye to violations of the UN arms embargo on all states of the former Yugoslavia and allowed the anti-Serb forces in Croatia and Bosnia to re-arm. As a result, the relative power of the Serbs on the battlefield began to weaken. In May 1995, the Croats marched into Krajina forcing the majority of Croat Serbs to flee. This was the first major defeat for the Serbs on the battlefield and represented a turning-point in the wars of the former Yugoslavia.

When NATO finally acted in August 1995 and used a barrage of air strikes to destroy the Serbs' communications systems in Bosnia, the Muslim and Croat forces, now in alliance, had the strength to drive back the Serbs to approximately half the Bosnian land-mass. At this point, a cease-fire was called in Bosnia and a peace agreed at Dayton in November 1995, based on the new military positions on the ground. Zagreb had already won back Krajina from the Serbs to create an ethnically pure independent Croatian state. Bosnia, on the other hand, despite retaining its formal status as an integral sovereign state, was effectively cut in half by the Dayton Agreement with the formal recognition of the Muslim–Croat Federation and the Republika Srpska. The chances of such a peace holding have to be doubted, but a number of lessons were drawn by the international community from the conflict in Bosnia. First, it revealed the impotence of the West when it was divided. Secondly, it showed the continued importance of the USA to European security – only when the US became committed to a realistic peace proposal was a solution to the Bosnian tragedy possible. Thirdly, it showed the continued need for a military capability in Europe, at a minimum, for peace enforcement and peacekeeping purposes.

The resolve of the West was tested again shortly afterwards in the Serb province of Kosovo. At least 80 per cent of the Kosovan population is Albanian muslim, but the region is also perceived by Serbs, for historical reasons, as the cradle of the Serb nation. Nevertheless, Tito decided to reduce Serb power in his new 1974 constitution by granting Kosovo a considerable degree of autonomy within the republic of Serbia. This change was resented by the Serbs, and reversed by force by the Serb leader Slobodan Milosevic in 1989. Thereafter, the Albanian majority suffered widespread repression and increasingly gave its support to the radical KLA (Kosovo Liberation Army). In the spring of 1998, the KLA finally rose up against Belgrade, demanding complete independence for Kosovo. When Belgrade responded with force, war returned once more to the Balkans.

The international community attempted to negotiate a compromise peace based on the restoration of Kosovan autonomy and the deployment of international ground troops to protect the Albanian majority. When Belgrade rejected a final compromise deal at Rambouillet (near Paris) on 18 March 1999, NATO carried out its threat and started bombing Serb positions on 24 March. The bombing had two main objectives: first, to stop the Serb atrocities against the Albanians; and secondly, to force Milosevic to accept the Western-mediated deal on Kosovo. In the short term, at any rate, NATO was unable to achieve either objective. Yet, with the important exception of Greece (another Orthodox Christian country, like Serbia), public opinion in the West generally supported NATO's military action. The suffering of the Albanian Muslims, who were forced to flee from their homes in their hundreds of thousands, was shown daily on TV and elicited genuine outrage from people in the West.

Yet, even in a situation like Kosovo, where the humanitarian case against the Serbs was so relatively clear-cut, the crisis still revealed many of the problems of taking military action in defence of liberal principles. First, some critics doubted the legal basis for military action. NATO was bombing a sovereign state, which might be acting in the most appalling way towards an ethnic minority, but had still not violated any accepted international law. It had not attacked, or threatened, another state; it was not an exporter of state terrorism; nor had it committed genocide by any accepted definition of the term before the bombing began. Moreover, the West chose not to seek support for its military action from the international community via the UN Security Council (for fear of a Russian and Chinese veto), which further undermined the legitimacy of NATO's actions in the eyes of many. Secondly, there was the fundamental problem of using force to pursue humanitarian objectives. Many saw this as a contradiction in terms, whilst even those who accepted that force was an unfortunate necessity became increasingly concerned about the matter of proportionality as the Serb and Kosovan casualties mounted. The punishment had to be seen to fit the crime. How many casualties, how much destruction could be legitimised by the original Serb atrocities?

This leads on to a third problem. Since the international community will generally be unwilling to risk heavy casualties where vital interests are not threatened, any military action in such cases is likely to be limited. President Clinton announced even before the war started that ground troops would only enter Kosovo as peace-keepers after a cease-fire had been signed. As a result, NATO's main effort was limited to air strikes, which failed to bring the humanitarian outrage in Kosovo to a speedy conclusion, and it was only after 78 days of bombing that Milosevic was forced to the negotiating table. Why was Milosevic so slow to bend under Western pressure? Why did the Serb population rally to his side? The West tended to argue that it was mainly due to Serb propaganda. The Serb population, it was said, was simply unaware of the atrocities being committed in its name. But this could only ever be a partial answer at best. Kosovo, as explained earlier, was a highly sensitive, nationalist question for the majority of Serbs, and the West severely underestimated Serb attachment to the province. Even amongst those who were less committed to Kosovo and more aware of the Serb atrocities against the Kosovan Albanians, there was still deep resentment towards the West for their actions against the Serb nation. For Serbs felt picked on and singled out by the most powerful members of the international community. After all, Serbia was not the only state to repress an ethnic minority which sought secession. The Serbs themselves had suffered from ethnic cleansing after defeats in Krajina at the hands of the Croats in 1995, but on that occasion the international community had chosen to turn a blind eye. In another case with at least some parallels to Kosovo, Russian troops launched a massive assault on Chechnya in December 1994 after the republic sought independence from the Russian Federation, but there was never any suggestion of military retribution against Moscow. As a result of these apparent inconsistencies, the Serbs felt like victims, like martyrs. Why us? Why now? Why is NATO targeting the Serb nation? The Serbs charged the West with hypocrisy and double standards. How far were the Serb accusations fair?

It is clearly true that military action is not always undertaken whenever international law or human rights are violated, but supporters of NATO air strikes argued that this does not mean military action should never be taken. Not all crimes within a state are solved by the police, yet no one suggests that this means no criminals should be pursued and no punishment wrought. This is, of course, true, but the analogy is wrong. In the cases cited above, it is not a question of being unable to solve the crime. We know what was done, and we know which state perpetrated the crime. Yet in some cases the international community chose to do nothing, in others it decided to use military force. We know the Croats expelled thousands of Serbs from Krajina in 1995, but the West chose to ignore it because the Croats were its allies and effectively carrying out Western policy in the region. In the case of Chechnya, we know Moscow committed the most awful crimes against humanity, yet the international community argued it was an internal matter for Russia. In reality, Russia was simply too big and too powerful to be punished. Serbia, on the other hand, is a small and vulnerable state. NATO can attack Serbia without Belgrade being able to strike back. Thus, critics can view NATO not as acting in the name of common morality and in defence of the liberal democratic order, but as a bully out to prove its virility to the world.

It may be that military action in Kosovo was, none the less, a lesser evil, but military action is always going to be controversial. It polarises opinion and makes a compromise settlement more difficult to achieve. Thus, even after the withdrawal of Serb military forces from Kosovo (still formally a part of Serbia) in June 1999, it was clear that Western troops will have to remain in Kosovo for some considerable time to oversee the peace and help rebuild the province. NATO could claim a victory of sorts, but normalisation in the Balkans looks to be as far off as ever.

# 3 Central and Eastern Europe

No other region has been so affected by the end of the Cold War as the former communist states of Central and Eastern Europe. The end of communism and the withdrawal of Russian troops from their territory were important events which were welcomed by the vast majority of people in these countries. However, the states of Central and Eastern Europe found themselves in a security vacuum as they began the difficult process of reform. This was an uneasy position to be in, given their small size (Poland is the biggest state, with a population of 38 million, whilst most others have 10 million or under) and a history of conquest and occupation. As communism was abandoned, many feared the rise of nationalism in an ethnically mixed region with few natural borders. The Soviet Union, Yugoslavia and Czechoslovakia broke up as states, but only in the latter case was it accomplished without violence. Nationalist war seemed to many to be a portent for the future.

Thankfully, such fears have, as yet, not been realised. With the important exceptions of the former Soviet Union and the Balkans (noted above), the states of Central and Eastern Europe have largely contained the threat of nationalism. In part, this was due to Western influence since most Central and East European leaders have sought to buttress democracy through seeking closer relations with the West. After a prolonged period of reflection, the West decided the best way of integrating the former communist states into the Western community was through the enlargement of the EU and NATO. This should give a boost to democracy and economic development in the region, thereby increasing security for the whole of Europe. There are problems with enlargement, which will be discussed later in the chapter, but overall it is a positive step. More than anything, it symbolises the end of a divided Europe and the reintegration of the former communist states into the Western community.

## 4 The Islamic world

The importance of Islam first came to the attention of the West in 1979 after the Iranian Revolution of that year. The fundamentalist movement has spread rapidly in the Middle East and parts of Northern Africa and Asia, although the level of militancy has varied greatly. The reasons for this upsurge in Islam varies too, but in essence it was a rejection of the disruptive nature of Western-style modernisation and its continued failure to resolve the existing economic and social problems of the region.

Antagonism towards the West was a central part of Islamic fundamentalist thinking. It was a part which had resonance, especially amongst the young urban poor, who resented the Western dominance of the international system. It seemed to many that Western policy was motivated by an anti-Islamic bias (although NATO's actions in Kosovo may, at least in part, have been aimed at changing this common perception). For example, the West stood back whilst Muslims in Bosnia, Chechnya, Tajikistan and Azerbaijan were being slaughtered, but launched a massive military attack against Iraq after the invasion of Kuwait in 1990. It declared its support for the UN and international law, and yet did nothing when Israel defied UN resolutions on the occupied territories or when the Algerian authorities cancelled elections for fear of an Islamic fundamentalist victory at the polls. Turkey, a secular European state whose population is predominantly Muslim, has also felt the force of what it sees as double standards. It was thought good enough to join NATO in 1952 but it has been consistently refused membership of the EU. The EU cites human-rights violations (most notably its ill-treatment of the Kurds) and the Turkish occupation of Northern Cyprus as reasons for rejecting Ankara's application, but its strategic importance has meant that its continued membership of NATO has never been in doubt.

The states of southern Europe have become more concerned recently about relations with the Islamic world. Concerns persist over the possibility of terrorism and mass-migration if the conflict in some areas, such as Algeria, escalates. Greece and Turkey have also maintained their protracted stand-off over Cyprus with no sign of a compromise on either side. It remains more than an embarrassment to NATO that two of its members are involved in such a struggle; it also undermines its credibility as an effective security organisation for the post-Cold War era. Nevertheless, NATO and the Western European Union (WEU) have both started dialogue with a number of states in the Islamic world. There is little incentive, however, to extend security guarantees to such a volatile and unstable part of the world, although the EU has offered more economic aid and agreed to consider association agreements with Egypt,

Morocco, Jordan and Lebanon, whilst a full association agreement has already been formalised with Tunisia.

# The new security architecture in Europe

## 1  The USA

The role of the USA has long been crucial to European security and it is likely to remain so for a good few years yet. After some initial self-doubt, the USA emerged from the Cold War with its confidence renewed. America is recognised as being the single remaining superpower in the post-Cold War world. America's dominance of the current international system is due not only to its economic power, but to its military power as well. Now the Soviet military challenge has gone, Washington has been able to cut its defence spending by about 20 per cent since its peak in 1991, whilst still spending something like five times more on defence than its closest competitor and almost as much as the rest of the world combined (Kegley and Wittkopf, 1997, p. 383). America has a particular advantage, even over its more advanced allies in Europe, in high-technology weaponry, intelligence and logistics. As the USA has become recognised as the one true global power in the post-Cold War world, it seems that few conflicts, from Bosnia to Northern Ireland, can be resolved without a significant input from Washington. Add to this, America's pre-eminence in soft power too – that is, popular culture and political ideology – and it is not too much of an exaggeration to suggest that the USA has more power now than at any time since the early 1950s.

Few doubt America's current hegemonic position, but a question does still remain over whether the USA is willing and able to play a global role in the post-Cold War world. The US military commitment to Europe has been greatly reduced since the fall of the Berlin Wall and concerns have been expressed that the political commitment has weakened as well. The formal US link with Europe is through NATO. This can be problematic, because the immediate security threat from the USSR has gone. However, the USA perceives NATO in a positive light and it has revealed its commitment to the alliance through its initiatives on the enlargement programme (see below). Washington is keen to maintain its dominance within the alliance and see it expand its commitments beyond Europe. This reveals some of the tensions within NATO, since Europe wishes to play a greater role in the alliance whilst perceiving it as an organisation primarily concerned with European security alone.

## 2  Germany

When Germany was reunified in 1990, it looked like becoming one of the world's great powers. Its population of over 80 million was the biggest in Europe outside Russia, and its geopolitical position made it a pivotal state in the new Europe. Its economy was one of the strongest in the world, accounting for almost one-third of the total EU GNP. Yet, reunification put considerable pressures on the German economy. The East German economy was in a far worse state than early estimates had supposed. Bonn ploughed DM150 billion per year in financial transfers into the former East German republic, roughly equivalent to twice the total Irish GNP, over a prolonged period of time (Marsh, 1994, p. 65). Economic recovery in the former East German territory began in 1993–4, but it was accompanied by high unemployment and attendant social problems. The launch of the Euro, initially seen as a

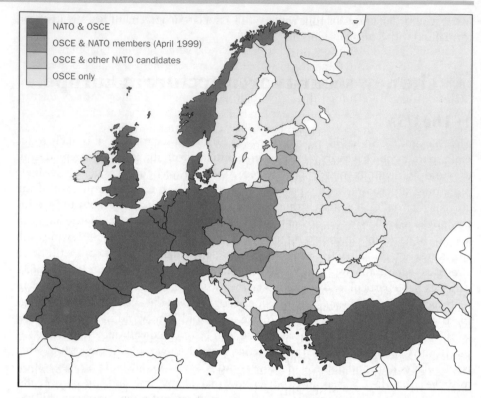

NATO & OSCE
OSCE & NATO members (April 1999)
OSCE & other NATO candidates
OSCE only

**Map 10.1** NATO and the OSCE

means of containing German economic power, is now viewed as the principal means of future economic recovery for the slumbering European giant.

Germany's power is also likely to be limited due to its general unwillingness to assert itself nationally in Europe. Germany has one of the biggest standing armies in Europe, but it is so deeply integrated in NATO, the WEU and Eurocorps that it is unable to act independently on the world stage. There appears little desire to do so either. Germany remains committed to the Non-Proliferation Treaty as a non-nuclear state and continues to support the US security commitment to Europe. The pressure on Germany to become more militarily active comes more from external rather than internal forces. Under such pressure, a parliamentary amendment to the constitution permitted German troops to participate in humanitarian or peacekeeping operations if approved by the UN. This allowed Germany to take part in the NATO-led operations in Bosnia and Kosovo. However, the constraints on German military activity beyond the borders of NATO allies remain tight. The Germans wanted, in the words of the former foreign minister Hans-Dietrich Genscher, to create a European Germany rather than a German Europe. This largely accords with the desires of its European allies.

## 3 NATO

The main regional organisation dealing with security matters in Europe is NATO (see Box 1.1). However, when the Cold War came to an end, inevitably NATO's future was hotly debated. Now that the Soviet Union had collapsed, what was the purpose of NATO? Was the time right for the people of Western Europe and America to ask NATO to fold up its tents and go home?

Although this did appear a possibility for a short while, it did not happen. NATO was not abolished; if anything, its position has been strengthened. Spain has joined its integrated military command, France has re-joined the Military Committee, and the Atlantic Alliance welcomed three new members from the former Warsaw Pact in April 1999. Why has NATO survived? First, as indicated earlier in the chapter, it soon became apparent that all security issues had not disappeared along with the Cold War. There was still room for a multinational military alliance like NATO which offered its members the security of collective defence. Secondly, Europe still needed the USA to contribute to its security, a fact brought home to European politicians by the events in Bosnia and Kosovo. The best way to ensure a continued American commitment was through NATO and its integrated military command. Thirdly, NATO retained a stabilising function. Through its integrated military command, it could prevent the re-nationalisation of the military in the different states of Europe and the possibility, as outlined by John Mearsheimer, of new power blocs forming.

Even though NATO quickly won the argument for its continued existence, it recognised the need to change radically to meet the new challenges of the post-Cold War world. Instead of deterring the threat of the USSR, it soon became clear that NATO's main function in future would be peacekeeping, crisis management and the provision of humanitarian aid. These new tasks required smaller, more flexible armies to deal with these less dangerous but less predictable security concerns. The absence of a common and agreed security threat also meant that it would be more difficult to reach a consensus amongst NATO members. To offset this problem, NATO set up the Combined Joint Task Force (CJTF) in 1994. The CJTF meant that not all NATO members would be required to take part in any NATO military action, but it could use NATO assets as long as the action received unanimous support from all alliance members. In essence, this was an attempt to resolve the problem of European members wishing to take military action when the USA was unwilling to act itself.

The other major change in NATO strategy involved enlargement. Initially, NATO was reluctant to offer security guarantees to Central and Eastern Europe (Holmes, 1997, p. 312), but this attitude began to change, under American influence, from early 1994. Enlargement, it was said, would not only offer security to former communist states but also help to reintegrate those countries into the community of Western states. Enlargement was permitted according to Article Ten of the Washington Treaty. If former communist states wanted to join the alliance, it was difficult to see how that could be ruled out, at least in principle. However, NATO did lay down some conditions – the new members should be democratic; they should allow transparency and civilian control over their military; they should have no outstanding border or ethnic disputes with their neighbours; and they should be in a position to contribute militarily to the Atlantic Alliance. At the Madrid summit in 1997, it was decided that Hungary, the Czech Republic and Poland had conformed to these conditions and they became members of NATO on its fiftieth anniversary in 1999.

However, enlargement remained a controversial decision within the security community. First, many believed that enlargement was not necessary. It was generally agreed that the threats to Central and Eastern Europe had disappeared or been greatly reduced when the Soviet Union collapsed. Why then the need to enlarge? Secondly, what would happen to those states excluded from membership? Was there a danger of creating new divisions in Europe as those left outside NATO sought new alliances to ensure their own security? And could Moscow argue that those excluded from NATO membership were within the Russian sphere of influence? Thirdly, there was a fear that enlargement could weaken NATO. NATO operates on the basis of consensus, but consensus in an enlarged NATO would be more difficult to achieve and, as a result, NATO might be less able to act decisively in times of crisis.

More than anything, however, critics feared the reaction from Moscow, which was strongly opposed to NATO enlargement. Moscow felt betrayed. It believed that commitments had been given by the West not to enlarge NATO, when Gorbachev approved NATO membership for a reunified Germany. Instead, a US-dominated, nuclear-armed military alliance seemed to be moving inexorably closer to Russian borders. The main danger of enlargement, according to its critics, was that it could help to create the scenario it was meant to deter – namely, an aggressive, nationalist, anti-Western Russia.

Moscow recognises that it cannot prevent enlargement, but although the door to new members remains open, Moscow clearly hopes that further enlargement will remain limited. It is particularly sensitive to the prospect of former Soviet republics, such as the Baltic States, joining NATO. However, supporters of enlargement have pointed out that relations between NATO and Russia have remained largely positive. In May 1997, Russia and NATO signed the Founding Act, which established the Russia–NATO Permanent Joint Council. This body gives Moscow an effective voice in NATO, but not the right of veto. Moscow also gained a pledge in the agreement that nuclear weapons would not be deployed on the territory of new members. Russian troops have played a useful role, under the command of the Americans, as part of the NATO-led peacekeeping forces in Bosnia, and Russia has also sent peace-keeping troops to Kosovo.

NATO has tried to finesse the problem of Russia. The implication is that Moscow has a crucial role to play in European security; NATO is not trying to isolate Russia or keep it out of important decisions on European security. However, Russia remains a central problem in the enlargement process. If NATO maintains collective defence rather than collective security as its guiding principle, it is hard to see how NATO can truly become a unifying force in Europe. The promise of membership has led to Hungary and Romania settling their border disputes, but when it becomes obvious to others that membership of Western institutions remains only a distant prospect, disillusionment might set in and new divisions may well emerge.

What are the prospects for the other regional institutions?

## 4  Western European Union (WEU) and EU

In the Cold War period, traditional security concerns were dealt with by NATO. Attempts to set up a West European alternative, which was not dependent on the USA, had largely failed. The European Defence Community initiative had come to nothing and was finally abandoned in 1954, and its successor, the West European Union, appeared virtually moribund by the 1970s despite a growing desire inside the EU at that time to improve the co-ordination of foreign policy. Due to some concern over American foreign policy under President Reagan, the WEU was revived in the 1980s and its institutions reactivated after the Rome summit in 1984. At the Maastricht summit of December 1991 the WEU members set out their views on creating a European security and defence identity (ESDI) and on greater European responsibility for defence matters. The WEU was designated as the organisation which would be developed as the defence component of the EU whilst also becoming the European pillar of the Atlantic Alliance. The following year, at Petersberg near Bonn in Germany, the WEU ministers agreed to extend its tasks beyond collective security to include humanitarian and rescue tasks, and tasks of combat forces in crisis management, including peacekeeping. The WEU was free to mount missions on its own initiative but it remained formally independent of the EU. According to the Petersberg agreement, the EU could request the WEU to take military action but it could not require it to do so (Flockhart and Rees, 1998, p. 64).

At present, the WEU has ten full members, all of whom are members of both the EU and NATO. At Maastricht, membership of the WEU was thrown open to states in either the EU or NATO at the level of observers or associate members respectively. In 1992, a Forum of Consultation was also set up to offer dialogue on security matters with former Warsaw Pact states, all of whom became associate partners of the WEU in 1994 with limited rights to participate in meetings and WEU peacekeeping operations. Full membership, however, is dependent on states satisfying the criteria for EU membership (similar to those for NATO). The former communist states are mostly eager to join the EU. The WEU, on the other hand, seems a second-best option to NATO. The WEU lacks the kudos of the EU and offers less in terms of military security than NATO since there is no equivalent to NATO's Article Five commitment on collective defence.

The EU has been heavily criticised for its inability to deal effectively with major security issues in Europe. It has been slow to enlarge its membership, allowing NATO to take the initiative on this issue, and it was unable to prevent the terrible wars in Croatia, Bosnia and Kosovo. Yet supporters argue that Europe has been trying to reform itself in the face of unprecedented change. Inevitably, this has taken longer than many would have wished. The Maastricht Treaty was only ratified by the EU in 1993, and the WEU was only formally permitted to provide humanitarian and peacekeeping services after the Petersberg summit of 1992. Therefore, in a sense, the break-up of Yugoslavia came too soon. Nevertheless, David Owen (1995), the EU representative in Yugoslavia, has forcibly argued that the EU was not as divided as is often suggested. Indeed, he says, the EU, despite all the difficulties, was able to strongly back the Vance–Owen Peace Plan in 1993 as well as all the other peace proposals put forward by the international community. The WEU also played a role in monitoring the arms embargo on Yugoslavia from 1993 and a joint EU/WEU administration, set up in July 1994, helped keep the peace between the Muslims and Croats in Mostar after the formation of the joint Federation on Bosnian territory.

Supporters also argue that the EU has done a lot more for Central and Eastern Europe than many suggest in terms of economic security (see Chapter 8). The enlargement of the EU will be difficult and costly, but it is a price Europe appears willing to pay for the benefit of greater stability and security across the continent. It may well be that the EU, rather than either the WEU or NATO, will prove to be the most important European security institution in the post-Cold War era.

# 5 OSCE

Moscow has always favoured the expansion of the role of the OSCE (see Box 10.2 and Map 10.1) at the expense of NATO, but its obvious weaknesses have undermined its case. Its size and the general commitment to consensus decision-making has weakened its ability to act effectively. Its willingness to accept the membership of the former Soviet republics of Central Asia was noble, but has led to problems. Central Asia is not a part of Europe and its values and cultures are very different. Central Asia is comprised of states at Third World levels of development, which have few if any democratic pretensions. The organisation has taken on more than it can cope with and has never been supplied with the money to undertake the task properly. The OSCE lacks both the economic clout of the EU and the military clout of NATO. It was asked to monitor the Serb troop withdrawal from Kosovo after the cease-fire agreement of October 1998. However, the withdrawal never took place and hostilities were soon resumed.

This does not mean that it has no role to play in European security matters. The OSCE remains unique as the only body which can be truly called pan-European. Untainted by the divisions of the Cold War, it has been viewed generally as an independent and largely well-intentioned body. The CFE (Conventional Forces in Europe) treaty was negotiated under the auspices of the OSCE and the treaty is still monitored by the organisation in its offices in Vienna. It has also played a role in the former Yugoslavia by monitoring the national elections in Bosnia in September 1996, and monitoring the human-rights situation in Kosovo. Russia has been prepared to allow OSCE missions to be sent to Chechnya and other conflicts on the territory of the former Soviet Union. The OSCE will not become a replacement for the EU or NATO, but if managed correctly it could become a useful adjunct to existing regional and international institutions. It is already viewed by the authorities as a potential European equivalent of the UN, in which its independence can be used as a means of legitimising peacekeeping or crisis management by NATO or the WEU (see, e.g., Hyde-Price, 1998a).

# ◼ The future of European security

The threat of a major nuclear war on European soil has faded since the Cold War ended, but security risks remain. These security risks, however, are less clear and less predictable than they used to be. The unifying aspect of the Soviet threat has gone. Europe is no longer divided politically, but it remains divided over security priorities in the post-Cold War world. What is the greatest security risk? Is it post-Soviet Russia? Is it the Balkans? Is it North Africa, Turkey or the Middle East? Europeanists hope these differences can be overcome through deeper integration. Realists believe that regional organisations will always be undermined in the long run by the re-emergence of national divisions. Integrationists hope that Western levels of security and development can be exported to the East through the enlargement of the EU and NATO. Realists (and some other pessimists) fear that this is unattainable and the attempts to enlarge will lead to the isolation of Russia and a new division in Europe. Universalists believe that security is best obtained through the promotion of economic development and democracy. Realists believe that security will continue to be maintained largely through military means. Yet, perhaps there is a middle way through all of this. Evidence suggests that Europe still requires an effective military capability in the post-Cold War era, but it must also reach out and welcome the former communist states into the community of liberal democratic states. This may include enlargement, but need not always do so. This balancing act may not always be easy. It may take some time with many bumps along the way, but it still remains the best hope for securing peace and security into the next millennium.

## Summary

◆ In the Cold War period, European security was mainly concerned with the containment of the Soviet Union. After the collapse of the USSR in 1991, however, this all changed. The threat of nuclear war all but disapppeared, but lesser security risks continued to exist.

◆ Europe bore witness to conflicts in the Balkans and on the territory of the former Soviet Union. These, and other security risks, are a result of: (a) the collapse of communism as an ideology, (b) the emergence of a power vacuum in Central Europe, and (c) political and economic instability in some parts of the continent.

◆ The military still has a large role to play in maintaining stability in Europe, but its tasks in the post-Cold War world will be less predictable and more varied. For example, in the Balkans, NATO or UN military forces have variously acted as peace-enforcers, peacekeepers, and the distributors of humanitarian aid to the people of the region. These are vital tasks which the military are best suited to carry out.

◆ Commentators increasingly acknowledge the importance of other non-military aspects of security, which include economic aid, the promotion of democracy and the closer integration of Europe. These latter measures can all promote security through stabilising states and encouraging co-operation across national boundaries.

◆ It is in these areas, in particular, that Western Europe and the EU have a vital role to play, although NATO and the USA will continue to dominate military aspects of European security for the foreseeable future.

## Questions for discussion

▶ To what extent should security concerns be extended to include issues such as poverty, AIDS and the environment?

▶ Was John Lewis Gaddis right in referring to the Cold War as the 'long peace'?

▶ What security risks and dangers exist in Europe today?

▶ Was NATO right to respond with force in Kosovo?

▶ What role should the USA, the EU and NATO play in maintaining peace and stability in Europe?

## Further reading

For a useful summary of the concept of security, see John Baylis, 'International Security in the Post-Cold War Era', in John Baylis and Steve Smith (eds), *The Globalization of World Politics* (Oxford: Oxford University Press, 1997).

For a good introduction to the more specific issues of security in Europe, see W. Park and G. Wyn Rees, *Rethinking Security in Post-Cold War Europe* (London and New York: Addison Wesley

Longman, 1998); and James H. Wyllie, *European Security in the New Political Environment* (London and New York: Addison Wesley Longman, 1997).

For a range of thought-provoking views on the nature of the post-Cold War world, see Francis Fukuyama, 'End of History?', *National Interest*, no. 16, Summer (1989); John Mearsheimer, 'Back to the Future: Instability in Europe after the Cold War', *International Security*, 12, 1 (1990); and Samuel P. Huntington, 'The Clash of Civilizations?', *Foreign Affairs*, 72: 3 (Summer 1993).

# The Cultural Dimension

John Coombes

# CHAPTER 11

'Je ne peins pas l'être; je peins le passage.'
(I do not show being. I show movement.)
MONTAIGNE, *Pensées*

## Contents

The problems of giving a comprehensive account of twentieth-century European **culture** are considerable. First, when we remember that twice as many books (in which, until recently, culture was principally lodged) were published in the 25 years after 1960, as in the whole previous recorded history of humanity; and secondly, when we reflect that culture is less satisfactorily defined as a series of isolated and conspicuous activities (concerts, exhibitions – though these definitely have their place) than, more widely, as the means by which humanity seeks to define itself and its relation to the world.

The scope of such an enquiry becomes even more daunting when we recognise that cultural history (if it is to be more than a mere series of facts and dates) always demands antecedents to its own starting point; and that its materials, in order to be explained, have to be placed in a context with which they may be contrasted. Much recent postmodernist thinking has attacked 'dualism' (the opposition of 'past' and 'present', 'fact' and 'fiction', 'subject' and 'object'). It has sought to replace it, and indeed notions of determination and contrast, with a kind of universal, random present without a history. Yet these contrasts, and their interaction, would seem to explain more about culture than a repeated statement of their absence. Such contrasts cannot, of course, be seen as consisting of *abstract* elements eternally ranged against each other, in some strange Tom and Jerry conflict of the world of ideas. They are better seen as forming a kind of web or network, each of whose components acts upon, and moves away from, its neighbours by turns.

Clearly no account of the cultural production of a whole century – let alone one as brief as this – can hope, so to speak, to unweave the web entirely and to lay bare all its constituents and their articulations. Rather, certain contrasting tendencies may be singled out, and their affinities, at various historical moments, with others, more or less overtly suggested. Three such contrasts – perhaps the most widely recognised of all – have already been instanced. Among others of specific relevance to the twentieth-century experience we might add:

    realism/modernism
    selfhood/collectivity
    convention/subversion

**Culture:** The relationship between ideas, relationships and institutions, reflection on the nature of which enables us to understand our relationship to the world.

**Denotation:** The act of marking or distinguishing something as separate or distinct.

**Connotation:** The process of noting something together with something else, the implication of something besides itself.

**Unconscious:** Simply, those operations of the mind of which we are not immediately aware. By extension, a reservoir of drives and motives which may run counter to, or threaten, the operations of the rational consciousness.

**Revolutionary:** In its strictly political sense, whatever furthers the transfer of power and wealth in society from one class to another; in artistic and cultural affairs, by analogy, whatever transforms the established patterns of aesthetic production and their recognition or consumption.

aesthetics/politics
**denotation/connotation**
structure/chance
rationality/**unconscious**
capital/labour
politics/mysticism

The tendencies of any cultural product of the twentieth century can probably be charted along more than one of these lines – and with more profit to the understanding of it than if it were to be represented as an ideal form and located exclusively along, or at the extremity of, any one of them. We shall not attempt to cover all areas of cultural endeavour but try to indicate the main themes through analysis of the media, education, architecture and cinema.

# Romanticism and positivism

Such tendencies – whether perceived *within* the cultural item or activity itself, or in its relation to the world which it inhabits – must be understood (unless we subscribe to an excessively simple notion of time and history as an eternal present) as, at any time, part of a complex process. What they are is to be understood as deriving from, and referring to (whether consciously or implicitly) the cultural moments which preceded them; and as in some sense meeting the cultural world which we, their interpreters, inhabit.

Here again, ways of connecting historical epochs are myriad. But when, in particular, we look back over the twentieth century as a whole, it is apparent that – turbulent and sanguinary though it has been – the period has not been, in the final analysis, a **revolutionary** one. In terms of the transformation of social relations and of ways of seeing, rather, we observe the global domination – in 2000 as in 1900 – of liberal capitalism. In oblique and dependent relationship to this multi-faceted phenomenon – as 100 years ago – remain a variety of archaic and/or authoritarian regimes; more directly subordinate to it, now as then, are the countries of the developing world of the South.

The dominance of liberalism – and its engagement with a series of powerful threats to it throughout the century – is, then, the context within which the culture of our times must be viewed. By comparison, the transitions effected from 1789 to 1911 – from France to Mexico and China, and from *ancien régime* and still more archaic forms to, at least, proto-democratic liberalism – mark out the nineteenth century as, indeed, a revolutionary epoch. It is not, then, surprising that the cultural movements of world-historical significance to which, more than to any other, subsequent developments in European intellectual life can be related, are the intellectual trends which attained dominance between 1800 and 1850: *romanticism* and *positivism*.

For most people *romanticism* evokes, quite appropriately, sexual passion – but there is more to it than that. In contrast to the world of classical values which it opposed, and which was centred on fixed forms and 'rules', whether political, social or aesthetic, romanticism lays stress on the authenticity and variability of personal experience – and indeed of the self both as a focus for human experience and in its changing relation to nature and to society. Rather than the human being seen as the measure of all things, as in the world of the classics, romanticism lays continual

## Pablo Ruiz Picasso (1881–1973)

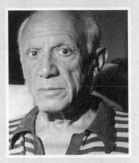

By perhaps the most prolific and versatile artist in history and certainly in the twentieth century, Picasso's work suggests from the outset a critical fusion of various painterly elements. If the works of the early Blue Period seem mawkish, this is perhaps because their debt to Gauguin and Toulouse-Lautrec is still offset by that of El Greco and a Christian ideology with which their author had nothing directly to do. The slightly later Rose Period bears the imprint of Picasso's writer friends in Paris, Max Jacob and Guillaume Apollinaire – both concerned with manipulating words and typography to new, disruptive effect, and Gertrude Stein, whose modernist prose is considerably more impenetrable than even Picasso's most innovatory forms. His great early cubist work *Les Demoiselles d'Avignon* (1907) continued fragmentations of planes and surfaces with a representation of the whores portrayed as sordid, appealing and vulnerable in their necessarily fragmented lives. Picasso's cubist painting – whether mono- or polychromatic – tends subsequently to increasingly radical fragmentation. Its effects are often heightened by the use of collage; related effects are achieved in experiments with sculpture, and with other 3-dimensional constructions which look forward to 1960s pop art. In the early 1930s Picasso's cubism goes through a particularly erotic phase (his women, however weird to some, are always lively and sexy in appearance). The Spanish Civil War ensured that joy in painting gave way to the grim panorama, combining dislocated elements of cubism and allegorical realism, of Picasso's most famous painting *Guernica* (1937). The same intensity is caught in the smaller anti-American painting of the Korean War *Massacre en Corée* (1951). Much of the production of Picasso's last years consists of reworkings of paintings by the great artists of the past, from Velázquez to Monet – not as imitations or embellishment but as a continuing dialogue.

stress upon otherness, upon the questionability of apparently fixed forms of existence (it is in this sense that Marx and Engels may be seen as Romantic thinkers as much as political economists). This is especially apparent in the mode, much used by Romantic writers and their successors, known as 'Romantic irony', whereby the text avows its own artificiality and questionability. The Romantic interrogation of the relationship of consciousness and the world (articulated in German idealist philosophy, notably by Hegel) provides the basis for *phenomenological* thinking, whether in Wordsworth's poetry or in Marx's interrogation of the social order.

This latter suggests an alternative to both idealistic and positivistic modes of thought, which propose, respectively, that it is the mind which constructs the world or that it is the world which determines the mind. Phenomenology opposes to these the proposition that mind and world, as interdependent elements, determine each other; it is thus closely related to *dialectics* (the investigation of forces in their conflict and possible resolution). It will be apparent that the effects of these conceptual derivatives of romanticism were potentially (and have been effectively) tremendously far-reaching, putting into question as they do fixed and traditional notions of personality and collectivity; text and reader; self and world.

Resonances of Romantic questioning are, as we shall see, to be perceived throughout the twentieth century. They are most generally apparent in revolutionary crises from St Petersburg to Barcelona, and from Mexico City to Shanghai. In every area of artistic practice, **modernism** – seeking as it does, whether in architecture or in drama, to display self-consciously both its contemporary nature and its situation within continuing history – has expanded the practices of Romantic irony. Movements such as *cubism*, *Dada*, **futurism** and **surrealism**, have worked on the notion of the work of art (and by implication that of our consciousness itself) as fragmented and diverse rather than as fixed and unitary (see Portrait 11.1). The philosophy of *existentialism*

**Modernism:** An aesthetic tendency which contrasts with realism (q.v.) in that, rather than an art work purporting to show an aspect of the world external to it, it draws attention to the devices by which it attains to that world.

**Futurism:** Italian aesthetic movement which rejected values of reason and progress in favour of the veneration of speed, violence and war; one of the early constituents of fascism.

**Surrealism:** An aesthetic movement which originated in France after the First World War; it was/is principally concerned with the dual (surreal) possibilities of perceptions in life and art, and with the exploration of the **unconscious** (q.v.) in the form of automatic writing.

### Jean-Paul Sartre (1905–80)

Philosopher, novelist and playwright, Jean-Paul Sartre is arguably the most central figure in twentieth-century French intellectual life. He first achieved recognition with *La Nausée* (1938), a novel whose central focus was the question of contingency (the apparent formlessness and lack of necessity of the world), which had been a preoccupation for him since the mid-1920s. The 1940s were a particularly productive period for Sartre, his brand of existentialism being elaborated both in his seminal philosophical work *L'Être et le néant* (1943), his novel cycle *Les Chemins de la liberté* (1945–9), his plays, notably *Les Mouches* (1943), *Huis clos* (1945), and *Les Mains sales* (1948), and through the controversial journal *'Les Temps Modernes'* (1945– ), which he inaugurated and edited. Sartre's existentialism of the 1940s, which came to characterise French existentialism in general, stressed individual choice and responsibility based on an affirmation of human freedom ontologically (at the level of the analysis and evaluation of being). Although a declared socialist by the 1940s, Sartre's emphasis on subjectivity brought him into conflict with his Marxist contemporaries and, following an abortive attempt to initiate a left-wing group in 1948, Sartre spent much of the next decade in an awkward position politically, at times close to communism whilst strongly critical of others. *La Critique de la raison dialectique* (1960), in which he sought to reconcile the concerns of subjectivity with a Marxist analysis of history and society, did much to dispel the tension between his philosophy and his politics. His last major work, *L'Idiot de la famille* (1971–2), was never completed; a study of the novelist Flaubert, it brings together many of his major concerns. His last years were mainly concerned with radically anti-authoritarian political activism.

continues romanticism's rejection of pre-cast forms in its insistence on man's responsibility to make sense of the world through the exercise of conscious choice, rather than through dependence on any more reassuring notion of intellectual tradition or inheritance (see Portrait 11.2). Even such widely divergent intellectual phenomena as *socialist realism* and *absurdism* show signs of a common Romantic ancestry; the former in its optimism as to the capacities of mankind to overcome its past; the latter in its notation of human experience as a performance generating – from moment to moment – its own meaning.

The contours of *positivism*, by contrast, are possibly easier to delineate. Its authority – even, its notoriety – derives in the main from two nineteenth-century thinkers, Auguste Comte in France, and Herbert Spencer in England. Whilst romanticism cannot be imagined apart from a context of revolutionary change in Europe, positivism represents the consecration of the newly established bourgeois order: it is, accordingly, as much a plan for the implications of philosophy as a network of philosophical concepts in themselves. The implications of positivism are – in distinction to the linguistic, formal and often political libertarianism of the Romantics – in many respects authoritarian; Comte's political and social thinking was hierarchical, and notably placed thinkers at the apex of the hierarchy. Further conceptual elements confirm this underlying tendency: the positivistic preoccupation with the cult of the fact (*le culte du fait*) with its tendency to limit the possibilities of human action to conformity to what is, rather than to a search for change; an epistemology, similarly, which asserts the determination of the mind, unilaterally, by the world and likewise limits the possibility of the transformation of either; an unimaginative and arbitrary division of knowledge into the 'known' and the 'unknowable' (*l'inconnaissable*) which similarly forecloses the limits of mental progress within the bounds of established utility; and an inordinate preoccupation with taxonomy – the ordering and classifica-

## George Bernard Shaw (1856–1950)

In 1930 Shaw was probably the best-known figure in the world after Gandhi and Charlie Chaplin. Born in Dublin in an economically insecure, bohemian milieu, he came to London as a young man and was entirely self-educated in the British Museum; circumstances which may well have enhanced his lack of respect for established intellectual categories and conventional political and social values. He had at least four overlapping careers of varying length and success. As a novelist (from the late 1870s to the mid-1880s) his critical esteem did not extend beyond a relatively small circle; he went on towards highly regarded music criticism throughout the rest of his life, and is principally remembered in this field for having made Wagner known in Britain. But the third career – for which he is best known – that of dramatic writer, displaced musical writing to some extent from the early 1890s on. His first plays (*Widowers' House*, 1892, etc.) are in the manner of the naturalism of Ibsen, whom Shaw had also introduced to Britain; later works prefigure much of later twentieth-century absurdism (*You Never Can Tell*, 1896; *Heartbreak House*, 1918); those for which he is best known are extended discursive debates in which various dramatic forms clash against each other (*Man and Superman*, 1903; *Saint Joan*, 1924; *The Apple Cart*, 1929). Finally, as an active socialist politician, he was continuously involved with the Fabian Society from 1886, with the founding of the London School of Economics and the *New Statesman* (1913), and in continuous political controversy, from attacks on stage censorship to accounts of a visit to Stalin (1931).

Shaw's significance lies not only in his breadth of interests but in the continued paradoxes which inform his life and writing, noticeably between anarchistic and subversive drives and a yearning for rational order.

tion of knowledge, by which those who have accumulated most may, in effect, transform its quantity into quality and secure their intellectual and social power.

Positivism's concern with regularity, order and classification of course predisposed it to absorption into the 'official' art of the twentieth century in many of its contexts and into forms of cultural production whose function was the legitimation and perpetuation of the status quo. At its most extreme this could lead back beyond Romanticism to a reversion to classicism as a supposedly 'objective' aesthetic yardstick; the trend was most consistently imposed in architecture by the fascist regimes, and subsequently, half-heartedly sustained by Anglo-Saxon conservative practitioners working for regimes sympathetic to aesthetic and political repression. But positivism's stress on linearity and clarity meant that artistic discourses could emerge from positivism which were not constrained by a tedious conformity to authority. After all, nineteenth-century **naturalism** – as variously exemplified by the novelist Émile Zola, the dramatists Henrik Ibsen and (the earlier) August Strindberg, and the polymath George Bernard Shaw (see Portrait 11.3) – often demonstrates the contradictory workings of positivism in practice; and the philosophy's connections with the extensive and varied world of pre-First World War social democracy (which comprised such diverse figures as Jean Jaurès (see Portrait 11.4), Karl Kautsky, Rosa Luxemburg and Lenin) generated a massively influential body of political, but also of politically committed painting and fiction – notably in the *roman fleuve* (saga fiction) tradition, and somewhat later in the various manifestations of socialist realism throughout Europe.

Our two major cultural tendencies in the modern world should not, then, be seen as confrontational opposites, nor as complementary forces; but rather as tendencies which, by turn, implicitly comment on, negate and confirm each other. The demands

**Naturalism:** A late nineteenth-century aesthetic movement which combines minute depiction of the external world with a wide preoccupation with the operation of heredity and environment as understood by nineteenth-century science.

### Jean Jaurès (1859–1914)

Without doubt the most influential socialist politician in Western Europe during the twentieth century. To some extent his contribution to French and European culture has been overshadowed by his political activities; but for Jaurès the two were always intimately connected. He studied at the École Normale Supérieure and was a professor of philosophy at the University of Toulouse before being elected as a centre-right deputy in 1885. Electoral defeat four years later led to completion of his doctoral theses – on realist epistemology and on German socialism – to involvement with strikes, the founding of a co-operative glass factory in his constituency at Carmaux and active participation in the renewal in the 1890s of French socialist politics (at this time largely the work of intellectuals). He rapidly became a leading figure in the movement together with Jules Guesde, with whom he frequently debated. Though both men were Marxists, Guesde believed in a socialism virtually restricted to working-class activity, whilst Jaurès saw it as the successor to the Enlightenment and the French Revolution (and

indeed, subsequently wrote and edited a socialist history of the French Revolution which broke new ground in its preoccupation with 'history from below'). Jaurès's participation in the campaign to free the unjustly condemned army officer Alfred Dreyfus earned him criticism from some on the Left, and the hatred of some of the Right, who called for his assassination. However, he went on to found and edit the socialist daily *L'Humanité* (1904) and to unite France's many socialist fractions in a united Socialist Party (1906), of which he became undisputed leader. He also continued to write extensively, notably developing materialist theories of the relation of education, socialism and culture. He may be considered as comparable in stature to those other great Europeans Voltaire, Victor Hugo and Goethe. As a socialist and anti-imperialist, he opposed nationalism and called for workers' unity against war in 1914. He was murdered at the end of July 1914 by Raoul Villain, a youth influenced by nationalist thinking and with links to the Russian embassy.

of both are so enormous that twentieth-century experience cannot possibly ignore them.

## The media

Relatively speaking, the greatest rate of growth of all cultural forces in the twentieth century has been that of the electronic media, transmission and recording. Here it is easy to forget – in a world of satellites and internet – that the quantum leap in mass communication was the invention of 'broadcasting' radio itself, of which subsequent inventions are mainly, after all, only sophisticated developments: the social and political organisation of radio thus merits particular attention.

First, however, some reference needs to be made to some of the social attitudes attendant upon the rapid technical advances of the twentieth century in general and their effects on culture. Opposition to them, it may be said, has tended to come in Europe from more or less marginalised groups – factions of the aristocracy, gentry and intelligentsia – for whom culture was their only capital and who, thus, felt disproportionately threatened by its wider dissemination. More rational fears concerning the dilution of artistic quality through its mass dissemination have largely proved unfounded; recorded music has neither, as was feared, killed off live music nor has it blighted the careers of practising musicians. Rather, throughout Europe and beyond, it has stimulated a widespread musical enthusiasm previously restricted to the geographically and financially privileged.

If there are indeed negative aspects to such cultural shifts, they are hardly new.

The world-wide success in the 1990s of the three tenors – Carreras, Domingo, Pavarotti – was deplored by nostalgics for cultural privilege on account of its transmission to the masses of opera arias out of context; and (more perceptively) by those who suggested that the inflatory effect of the vast investment and huge fees involved would eventually put opera still further out of the reach of the masses. But it should be remembered that attentive reverence for singing within the opera house only dates from the age of Wagner (the 1860s); and that commercialisation of single arias dates back to the invention of the gramophone record and its exploitation by Caruso (c. 1900) – the first recording star to become a millionaire.

The dissemination of all these cultural activities involves, of course, a range of electronic media activities whose development has, throughout the twentieth century, increased, stimulated and been stimulated by their interpretation in ways unthinkable in the epoch of European classicism, but which have considerable affinities with the world of Romanticism, especially with the Wagnerian mixed-media total work of art (*Gesamtkunstwerk*); and paradoxically (in form though obviously not in scale) with the carnivals of late medieval and early modern times. (Then the major ideology which dominated them was the church; now it is the logic and function of the media themselves.)

The process of such cultural production has in the twentieth century become increasingly self-referential and self-parodic. A contemporary manifestation of a mixed-media show may well arouse admiration for including a computer-generated image of Donald Duck – a simulation, in effect, of a 1930s simulation drawn with little concern for verisimilitude – not for its precise resemblance to its model, but for the technical achievement involved in – after all – an aesthetic banality.

Radio was of course the first means of simultaneous communication to a mass audience. In 1922, when the BBC, the first regular radio service, began, the cinema – its only mechanised rival – could, owing to the high cost of film, only reach a small audience simultaneously. There was until relatively late in the century a lack of homogeneous cinema audiences even in small, densely populated countries such as Britain and Belgium; populations which radio (and later TV) were later to homogenise. Again, film distribution (even with films, later, existing in multiple copies) remained decentralised; in Britain until the 1960s and in much of the rest of Europe throughout the century, small, independently owned cinemas and chains of cinemas were the norm, and ensured a multiplicity of viewing choice.

In the last quarter of the twentieth century, however, power over cinematic distribution – and thus consumption – became especially concentrated in agglomerative chains of cinemas; uniformity of programmes ensued. Britain was especially vulnerable to this development, having, as many others, its origins in the USA – on account moreover of similarity of language, and thus, supposedly, of cultural identity.

The same tendencies – to homogenisation resulting from capital agglomeration in the interests of large US or multinational concerns – are to be observed (especially but not solely in Great Britain) both in publishing and in the sale of books. In publishing, the 'gentleman' individual publisher has been replaced as decision-maker by the accountant; in distribution, guaranteed prices, profit-margins and choice have been cut, and turnover has increased, to the advantage of major capital and the disadvantage of independent ownership. The trend has continued in all areas of media sales, whether prices (with their effect on public access) have relatively increased (books, cinema entrance) or decreased (recorded music) in the latter part of the century.

**Fabian:** Fabianism was a tendency in British socialism dating from the 1880s, advocating the total but gradual transformation of society by administrative action under, largely, the control of the enlightened middle classes.

The development of radio (and later TV) throughout the twentieth century has been more complex. Whilst the production and circulation of books, recorded music and other materials (CD-Roms etc.) has in general become increasingly dominated by unambiguous market considerations (the origins of all these products were, after all, commercial if in varying ways), radio has seen the intersection of three basic models of organisation. These – the public-service, the commercial and the totalitarian – are not always as self-explanatory as this nomenclature may seem.

The major and innovatory example of public-service broadcasting, the BBC, initially gained its reputation from being the world's first public radio service. Afterwards to be partially imitated outside Europe in some of the countries of the British Empire/Commonwealth, and in the liberal democracies of Europe (notably being transplanted to the British zone of Germany after the Second World War), its ethos – imposed on the British Broadcasting *Company* (1922–6) by its first Director-General, John Reith – was initially one of, largely, benevolent authoritarianism. This was manifest as an élitism through which the cultural monopoly of a **Fabian**, liberal and conservative upper middle-class oligarchy, preserved by the absence of competition, was imposed on the nation as a whole.

Many of the BBC's earlier practices now seem ludicrously archaic – with their instigator Reith a bizarre as much as a benevolent despot – and its overall political practices (for at least half a century) seem to have been over-submissive to established power. The value of the model, however – easy clichés about its generating a sense of 'national community' apart – has resided in its durability and, eventually, its ability to develop and provide a natural forum for political and cultural discussion more effectively than other systems (in so far as these have not themselves imitated its forms). Further, the BBC TV – especially since the 1960s – has managed to produce 'quality' programmes which are also highly saleable overseas. And its radio World Service – directly funded by the government, antique in presentational format, radically independent (more so than its internal services) in its coverage of world affairs and universally respected – reflects the paradoxes of the BBC's origins and subsequent development.

The commercial model of radio developed rapidly throughout Europe in the later 1920s, and again in the years since 1945. More recently its practices have been, of course, taken up increasingly by cable, satellite and other commercial television. In essence the antithesis of BBC broadcasting, it was from the outset populistic, imposing on its mass public a diet of what was then called 'light music' as remorseless as the BBC's uplifting material; designed, with its rapid alternation of recorded music and adverts, for brief and casual attention; and of course cheaply produced, being financed from fluctuating advertising revenues as against the public service's relatively massive income from licence fees. In the television era, commercial broadcasting seemed, in the third quarter of the twentieth century, and in those countries (Britain, Holland, Italy, West Germany) with a relatively strong public broadcasting tradition, to attempt to imitate it. Later technical developments – satellite and cable broadcasting and the consequent multiplication of channels – led to a proliferation of viewing modes. Many channels do little but recycle programmes from the major producers; others – just as cheaply – run perpetual talk shows. Most of these are no doubt harmless enough, and undoubtedly viewed by their audience at home with a humorous distance which may be associated with the late twentieth-century post-modern condition in general.

More sinister implications of what can easily become a disquieting manifestation of manipulative populism – indeed brainwashing, as was apparent in Italy in the 1990s when the massive broadcasting apparatus of Silvio Berlusconi undoubtedly led to the (albeit temporary) political success of his Forza Italia movement – are shown in an apparently unstructured anti-intellectualism, the harbinger of a return to a politics of the extreme Right. In the English-language popular press, preoccupation with right-wing politics and with profits has been more evenly balanced.

Public broadcasting systems in continental Europe have in general withstood these pressures less adequately than the BBC (which it is not unduly Anglocentric to characterise, with all its faults, as the flagship of twentieth-century broadcasting). The contrasting history of the RTF – subsequently ORTF – in Europe's other major traditionally liberal democracy, France, with that of the BBC is instructive here. Before the Second World War, French broadcasting, unlike British, was largely commercial – stations like Tour Eiffel, broadcasting notably in English on Sunday to circumvent the sabbatarian gloom imposed on Britain by Reith's BBC. The war and the subsequent occupation of France (1940–4) convinced the politicians, both those of the Resistance in London and those of Vichy and the collaboration, of the importance of radio as a source of information and of propaganda. Accordingly the establishment of the RTF at the liberation was accompanied by that of a Minister of Information to control it; acceptance was general (amongst the political class at least) that the business of the RTF – apart from a genuine diversification of cultural activity modelled largely on the BBC – was to present the viewpoint of the government of the day.

This caused little concern so long as, under the Fourth Republic, the government changed fairly regularly every two or three months. With the 1960s however, two related phenomena became apparent: the advent of television with its greater possibilities of ideological impact; and the durability of the de Gaulle government whose power of control of the media – although the product of a previous dispensation – now gave it quasi-totalitarian potential. Freedom of the media from government control was a major demand of the workers' and students' movement of 1968; the subsequent relaxation of controls evolved until it coincided with the Socialist victory of 1981. For some years after this – until, in the late 1980s, its effectiveness was undermined by the dual process of partial denationalisation and the development (as elsewhere) of satellite and cable networks – the televisual production of the (by now) ORTF was equal in quality to any other.

Political pressures such as these were, of course, minor, compared with those operated in the totalitarian countries, and especially in the most efficiently organised of them, Nazi Germany. Here, totalitarian intensity was compounded by the absence of TV (the subjects being absorbed into the visually spectacular by obligatory attendance at rallies instead of receiving their impact passively at home – the technical lack doubtless proving ideologically effective); and especially by the relentless unity of the electronic message – the 'people's receiver' (*Volksempfänger*), commonly known as the 'Goebbels gob' (*Goebbelsschnauze*) – its price subsidised, and only capable of receiving one programme.

The 'Goebbels gob' – produced by the million – stands as a powerful symbol of what fascism threatened: the destruction altogether of politics, culture and technology. It may be seen as a grotesque parody of the early ideology of broadcasting with its hope to impose a national community. The other extreme alternative to that mode – random consumption, postmodern fragmentation – hardly empowers its recipients. Rather than mindless aggression, it stimulates inertia. Other developments in the media highlight perennial arguments, less about culture itself than about its valuation (in so far as the two can be separated). Rapid advances in the recording and reproduction of music have vastly increased its availability and simultaneously reduced its significance. The increasing tendency of radio stations to play single movements of classical works again puts the listener, effectively, back into the position of his predecessor at the eighteenth-century court, socially absorbing a few bars of Telemann or Vivaldi.

Finally, many of the developments which we have noted as achieved in the latter years of the century could hardly have come about without tremendous achievements in the field of cybernetics – after the revolution of steam around 1800 and that of electricity around 1880, the third great stage in the industrial revolution. Since the 1980s there has been talk of the 'revolutionary' impact of these developments for personal life, of 'empowerment' through their articulation with the individual subject through the internet. Yet whilst there is so far the sense that possibilities of communication have increased exponentially, it is not as yet clear how these processes have come to constitute a genuine popular force for cognisable change. As in other areas of the media – and indeed in most areas of cultural production – the technical is rarely harmonised with its use and administration.

# ■ Education

Educational theorists of the nineteenth century found themselves, in seeking to maintain the regular functioning of the societies in which they were operating, confronted by a paradox. First, these societies in the main were – since the industrial revolution – mass-societies in the sense of their modes of operation, production and (increasingly in the latter part of the century) dissemination of knowledge and information; yet secondly, in a period prior to the establishment of political (let alone social and economic) democracy, control of all these practices was restricted to a small minority of the population.

From this followed the contradictory motivation of all proposals for educational innovation which did not rest on more or less total opposition to the established nature of society. Education for the masses had to be developed broadly, to ensure their greater capacity, in literacy and numeracy, to operate the productive systems in which they were involved. Yet it had, as far as possible, to offset, notably through systems of moral education, the propensity of the increasingly stimulated mental capacities of the masses to question their ascribed place in the social order.

Outside the activities of such ruling-class educationists – whose theories, aptly summarised by Dickens's Mr Gradgrind in *Hard Times* as the exclusive domain of 'facts', impress us today principally by their monotony – there grew up in the nineteenth century a varied body of radical and working-class educational thinking. Whether inspired by Chartism, Trade Unionism or aesthetic socialism in Britain, by Marxism in Russia, Germany and Denmark, or by varieties of socialism and anarcho-syndicalism in France and Spain, questioning of the narrow norms of bourgeois utility in education had, by 1900, become extremely forceful. It could ensure that, in the European liberal (and subsequently social) democracies of the twentieth century, there continued an implicit negotiation between the elements of inherited utilitarianism and its radical critics.

Such utilitarianism has frequently manifested itself across Europe as an educational vulgarisation of what we have termed the positivist tradition. International in scope and linear in its objects and progress, it has throughout the twentieth century been a force for standardisation and measurement of achievement, for – at best – rationality and conscious purpose; and – at worst – for the monotonous subjugation of education to the supposed needs of industry and business. Nor are the modern reverberations of the Romantic tradition necessarily more inclined to see education as, fundamentally, the production of knowledge. More diverse (and notably more subject to national variation) than the modes of positivism, romanticism rejects its tendency to systemisation – often in the name of childhood spontaneity, but also in the name of tradition, heritage, and exclusive notions of **Literature** and Culture. In educational (as in other) politics, positivism tends in general to support of the status quo; whilst romanticism can move, sometimes bafflingly, between Left and Right.

Democratic advances in education – both to ensure its availability to the masses, and to maintain it as a critical function not pre-ordained to serve any particular group or social order – had quite a strong basis in previous practice in France. Revolutionary projects for the interrelation of educational and social transformation had been considerably cut back by Napoleon I, but the legislation establishing the *Université* in 1808 had at least established the principle of a total exam-based state **meritocracy**, and the abolition of all vestiges of *ancien régime* educational privilege. Throughout the nineteenth century the principle had been reinforced by the universalisation of primary education, and (in the 1880s) its patriotic extension through a system of scholarships to the secondary and higher sphere. The unequal nature of society, however, continued to ensure that the system, though rigorously uniform, only benefited a minority; and a growth of political awareness ensured, in the early years of the century, the development of a workers' educational movement, the *Universités Populaires*, of considerable breadth and vitality – though unlike its British equivalents, the Workers' Educational Association and the National Council of Labour Colleges, riven with internal dissension.

Initiatives in French education have in general been particularly dependent on general political developments; thus we observe, as consequences of moderate Left governments of the 1920s, an extension of possibilities for secondary education, the first steps towards comprehensive secondary education and the massive investment in sport, leisure and cultural facilities under the *Front Populaire* government of 1936. The politicisation of education and culture had its reverse side under the Vichy régime (1940–4). This attempted a total reversal of French educational history. First, it reinstated the dominance of the Church. Finally excluded from state schools by the law of separation of Church and State of 1904, the Catholic Church had maintained its own schools throughout the Republic; 'private', basically, in their religious teaching and finances – though state subsidy for Catholic schools will always be the most contentious issue in French politics – they necessarily follow the State curriculum for the *baccalauréat*. Moreover, every opportunity was used for the indoctrination of Pétainist, anti-Semitic and a bizarrely ruralist propaganda which may well appear more laughable to those reading it today than to those who fell foul of it at the time.

Since the liberation, France has continued to develop, in common with much of Western Europe, an increasingly egalitarian education system. As we have noted, the independent Church sector has continued to flourish; though, given its basis in belief rather than in class and money, it has very little of the aura of snobbery and privilege which still surrounds its counterpart in Britain. Though educational selection

**Literature:** Its definition will probably be forever a vexed question, but *literature* may perhaps be defined as what is written and read, and *Literature* as those texts which, for whatever reason, have remained continuously (or nearly) in print since their first publication.

**Meritocracy:** Rule by those deemed to be the most deserving, the brightest and/or the most successful.

has increasingly been delayed to 16+, the subsequent distinction between *Collèges d'Enseignement Général* and *Lycées* has to some extent affinities with the division in higher education between universities and *Grandes Écoles*. These latter, highly competitive, Napoleonic institutions represent the pinnacle of the State élitist system: they are, together with its evident centralisation, the aspect of French education which makes it closest to that of the USSR.

By comparison with such schematisation (positivist both in its negative rigidity and in its positive ability to organise knowledge effectively) the British educational system seems difficult to delineate. It has shared with the French system some notable similarities, such as the strange belief (held possibly later in Britain's public schools than in France) that a thorough knowledge of the Classics was the best possible preparation for a life in public affairs, and, more generally, a spasmodic commitment to the delay, at least, of selection to a later age. As in France, access to secondary education became more widely available between the world wars – though in keeping with a British propensity for hierarchical decentralisation, it was (until 1945) controlled in country towns largely by grocers rather than by ministry officials.

Since Britain's major reorganisation of education at the end of the Second World War – positivist, quite possibly without knowing it, in its division of 11-year-olds into the academic, the technically gifted (at 11!), and the rest – the tendency has, as in France, been towards the progressive elimination of these distinctions and a realisation that they involve social as well as academic factors; albeit, as with much in the British educational system, on a local and arbitrary basis. Against this tendency has been the imposition since 1986 of a national curriculum; though whereas in France a uniform syllabus is universally accepted, its introduction in Britain has proved politically contentious, both to those who resent the disappearance of their ancient local privileges, and to those who object to its reversion to utilitarianism.

The principal curiosity of British education is, however, the continued dominance of the private sector. The so-called 'public' schools constitute a hegemonic bloc not to be found elsewhere in Europe, and one which manages still to extract deference from other sectors (selective and even non-selective state schools) in terms of imitation of its organisation, nomenclature, and attitudes. Whilst certain areas of the French system embody élitism, the 'public' schools represent a privilege subject to virtually no external intellectual control, a dominance which quite probably goes back to 1688, of gentry, upper professional classes, business and – residually – aristocracy.

German education before 1914 reflected, as in France and Britain, the norms of a rigid social hierarchy, as well as the undemocratic hierarchies of the Wilhelmine state, with military academies as a more savage version of the British private sector. The transformations effected by the Weimar Republic, accordingly, going as they did further than contemporary Britain or France in terms of comprehensivisation and sexual equality at all levels, aroused ferocious opposition from nostalgics for 1900 and anti-Republicans in general. The clock was comprehensively put back by the Nazis with: selection reintroduced on traditional as well as political and racial grounds; abolition of 'modern' subjects like 'civics'; confusion of teaching the national literature with Nazi sloganising; garbled teaching of the Classics; an increase of rote-learning, and so on.

After 1945, and until reunification, the Federal Republic took as its model the less archaic aspects of the Second Empire; and the Democratic Republic, the advanced social-democratic ideology and practices of the Weimar Republic. Thus the nature of West German education could vary (though rather less than in Britain) from *Land*

## Anatoli v. Lunacharsky (1875–1933)

Lunacharsky is principally remembered for his activities as People's Commissar for Education from the moment of the Bolshevik Revolution in 1917, to 1929. His project during this period was unique in the twentieth century: extensively, to increase literacy in the new Soviet Union to the level of Western Europe (in which he sowed the seeds of considerable success), and intensively, to further new developments in Soviet literature, music and the visual arts. Here too, Soviet production in the 1920s was remarkable – modernist drama and the novel, acmeism and constructivism in painting, the engagement of Shostakovich and others with jazz, etc. But with the rise of Stalin and the officially sanctioned doctrines of socialist realism, Lunacharsky's positive attitude to modernism was given a hostile definition as collusion with formalism and he was sent into semi-exile as ambassador to Spain.

His earlier periods of exile (under Czarism) had been more productive; after 1905 he had edited the Bolshevik journal *Vpered* (Forward) and had developed a reputation as a publicist, orator and historian of literature and art. Later, in exile with Gorki on Capri, he wrote *Outlines of a Collectivist Philosophy* (1909) and, interestingly, planned an advanced school for a select élite of workers, which Lenin opposed. After the 1917 Revolution he also wrote dramas for the atheist theatre, *Oliver Cromwell* (1920) and *Campanella* (1922), and again with Gorki was involved in preserving art works during the Civil War. Lunacharsky's career and its eclipse may be seen to furnish an instance of the critical confrontation of Enlightenment values with radically new twentieth-century political and social forms.

to *Land*: in the social-democratic (urban) *Länder* there might be experiments in comprehensivisation; in the Christian-democratic areas, selection – and the concomitant social distinctions – were rigorously preserved (especially by the Catholic middle classes).

In East Germany, revival of the educational practices of Weimar were of course combined with political and cultural affinities with the USSR. The virtual absence of a Soviet-style *Nomenklatura*, however, had the result that universal (and centrally determined) comprehensive secondary education did not tail off at higher-education level, into a 'partially exclusive' 'private domain' for those with influence, as in the Soviet Union. The social constitution of the universities in the GDR was more socially comprehensive – certainly than that of their West German counterparts, but also than, for instance, those in Poland, where (even under the People's Republic) they remained largely colonised by nostalgics for the pre-war regime. In short, the norms of education in the GDR would seem closer to those of France than to those of other comparable countries.

Since reunification the GDR has been totally incorporated into the FRG, and most aspects of GDR culture, from their origins in the Berlin Enlightenment to the present, have been subordinated to those of the West. Division of the former unitary Republic into *Länder* has led to the reintroduction of selection in many areas; the teaching of literature has changed from relating text and context, to the immediate interpretation of texts ('practical criticism' on the Anglo-Saxon model); history is no longer social history but narrative history, paradoxically a new manifestation of positivism.

For all the tendencies manifested, essentially in its latter years, towards appropriation by corrupt officials of educational and cultural (as well as other) power, the educational achievements of the USSR cannot but appear impressive. It was long fashionable amongst – especially British – superior people to mock the Soviet passion for 'culture'. But the preoccupation becomes more accessible when we reflect that the Bolshevik founders of the Soviet Union were taking over a country of relative backwardness and one of enormous diversity (Soviet newsreel films show literacy classes for the women of central Asia – one of the regime's proudest achievements). From this, Soviet education achieved – in less than 50 years – parity with the nations of the West (see Portrait 11.5), before declining to some extent under the dual pressures of changes in the terms of world trade, and the cost of the Cold War. It can hardly be maintained that conditions have improved since the fall of the Soviet Union. In educational terms this has meant the diminution of higher educational opportunities for all but a wealthy few, and a disastrously under-funded system.

In the first half of the century we can see (with the exception of the fascist states) a general tendency for governments to incorporate workers' demands – familiar since the nineteenth century – into their practice. Since then a combination of factors – political reaction against social democracy, the collapse of regimes and currencies under external (and internal) pressure – has reversed the tendency. The consequences for the world may be incalculable.

# Architecture

European architecture between 1880 and 1920, in common with other domains of artistic production, seems a tangle of conflicting impulses from which, none the less, two major tendencies dominate: construction in the image of the past (a tendency not entirely without affinities with various kinds of representational **realism**); and modernist construction, which in many ways asserts its own independence of the past and the self-sufficiency of its own forms.

To the first type may be ascribed the massive German neo-Gothic bourgeois villas constructed in the expansionist years of the Wilhelmine Empire. Similar edifices – of the same period, though rather more slender and less overpowering – are to be found in what were, at the time, the more prosperous regions of Britain. Throughout Western Europe at the time, however, the dominant architectural style – for official construction and for the housing of the prosperous – occasioned a kind of classicism so diluted that it has rapidly come to be considered as a form hardly to be noted in any particular way: the habitat of a middle class whose increasing social diversity was, for most of the period, only matched by its growing political dominance. Significantly, its principal exponent in Britain, Edwin Lutyens, is remembered chiefly for a complex where such 'normality' asserts itself as extraordinary: the official British government buildings in New Delhi, whose arrogant disregard of their 'native' surroundings symbolises the motives of imperial power.

Different, though analogous, reflections are provoked by the town of Metz in Eastern France. Annexed into the German Second Empire from 1871 to 1918, the town was largely reconstructed in accordance with contemporary nationalist ideology and resembles a fascinating architectural icon, with a neo-Gothic Wilhelmine centre, surrounded by untouched French neo-classical building of the late eighteenth and early nineteenth centuries and, on the outskirts, all the eclectic paraphernalia of post-1918 construction.

The architecture which sought, against all this, to articulate new forms (and which accordingly figured in architectural textbooks) constituted a minority of building construction. Of most significance in the years before the First World War was the

**Realism:** An aesthetic which seeks to engage with the external world both in the depiction of its appearances and in an investigation of their history.

**Fig. 11.1** The Sagrada Familia in Barcelona, by Antonio Gaudí (1852–1926)

international movement known as *Art nouveau* (in French and English) and as *Jugendstil* (in German). It flourished, mainly, far from the major cities of Europe – in Brussels and in Helsinki, in Prague and in Barcelona, where the unfinished *Sagrada Familia* temple by Antonio Gaudí has a claim to be seen as its principal monument (see Figure 11.1). As in the similarly florid Parisian domestic architecture and Metro entrances of Hector Guimard, the reaction against rectilinear classicism could not be more pronounced; the decorated, intertwining, curving lines immediately evoke the Gothic Middle Ages and Grimms' fairy tales, yet are evidently supported by the most modern iron and steel construction. To some extent consequent upon the earlier painting and graphics of the English Pre-Raphaelites, and with roots in the contemporary writing of the Catholic revival in France – most notably in the dramas of Paul Claudel – *Art nouveau* presents us not with an ideology of medievalism but with a 'false middle ages' (*faux moyen âge*), evoking distance from the present rather than identification with the past.

Its affinities are, in Britain, with the work of Charles Rennie Mackintosh – principally in Glasgow rather than in London, reinforcing the impression of a movement largely confined to the peripheries of Europe by the force of metropolitan eclecticism – and the Arts and Crafts Movement. This was more concerned with design than with architecture, but derived significantly from the concerns of William Morris, probably the greatest British socialist thinker of the nineteenth century, with the identity of social and aesthetic transformation.

Yet for all of Morris's massive influence, both on thinking about aesthetics and on socialism, such innovatory architecture was only for a privileged few. Until the years following the First World War, innovations in housing for the masses were largely restricted to arranging a rapidly increasing urban population in such a manner as most efficiently to maximise profits. Increasingly, across Europe as a whole, working-class housing came to be indistinguishable, from the outside at least, from the barracks – or indeed the prison. The oppressiveness of such conditions at their worst is represented in a scene in the Soviet film *Strike* (1925) by Sergei Eisenstein (1898–1948) where the Czarist mounted police ride up the staircases of the apartment block in pursuit of the workers. Of course there were exceptions, of which the Karl Marx Hof in Vienna – constructed for the workers by their own organisations – is the most famous. But in general the benefits of new design, with its additional demands both on time and space for construction, remained marginal.

During the decades after 1918, however, the relationship between economics, class and design altered considerably. The middle classes and the possessors of capital across Europe maintained, in general, their economic advantages to a greater degree than has commonly been supposed – but the social and political adjustments of the post-war period included, to the advantage of the working classes, certain areas of social democracy of which publicly subsidised housing was one of the most significant.

It is in this context that new developments in modernist architecture emerged, with the work of the *Bauhaus* (*c*.1922–33) and Walter Gropius in Germany; and that of Le Corbusier in France. The collective political and aesthetic philosophy of the *Bauhaus* was close to that of the German Communist Party (its preoccupations having much in common with those of Morris 50 years earlier), whilst Le Corbusier's authoritarian individualism in many ways brought him close to fascism; the two centres of architectural activity had together an impact across Europe – in Italy, Britain and elsewhere.

The functionalism of *Bauhaus* architecture – with its steel-framed windows, flat roofs and rectilinear white-covered outer wall surfaces whose bevelled corners alone offset the effect of a cubic 'living machine' (to use Le Corbusier's phrase) – combined frequently, in Western Europe between 1920 and 1940, with the superficially similar 'Spanish colonial style'. The effect was a large volume of production of small box-like suburban dwellings whose inspiration was modernist, but whose living arrangements essentially differed little from the cottages of previous centuries. The mass of housing for the Western European upper-working and lower-middle class would seem, however, to have struck a lifeless compromise between such (modest) modernism, and other styles of architecture favoured by the dominant upper-middle classes of the period. In the 1930s, Nazism (having banned the *Bauhaus* in 1933) favoured the revival of traces of the Gothic; in Britain mock- (or as it became vulgarly known, 'stockbroker') Tudor building, complete with fake beams and mullioned windows, perhaps testified to a longing for past stability, as did the widespread imitation of the Norman manor-house in France.

Outside the liberal democracies at the time, non-domestic architecture was the centre of attention. Unlike Hitler (and in line with a general policy less dominating of business enterprise than the Third Reich), Mussolini, once sponsored by the futurists, permitted a limited amount of modernist activity, mainly in the private sector. Nazi architecture, however, seems to have been entirely preoccupied with its own giganticism, above all, the designs by Hitler and Speer for a new Berlin, with its physically impossible Assembly Hall (*große Halle*), and plans for new railway stations with doors (presumably to be opened by hand) 8 metres high. These were characterised by an uneasy mix of cultural indicators: primeval Germanic myth, the historic authority of classicism, the contemporary miracles of technology.

Soviet architecture of the Stalinist period (c.1932–53) has often been compared to this – and undoubtedly, in their shared neo-classicism and in the often injudicious decoration of buildings with monumental sculptures, there are notable similarities. But the differences are also to be noted; architectural production in the Soviet Union was less monolithic than in Nazi Germany and in spite of its increasing control in the 1930s by the Central Committee of the party, modernist impulses (dominant in the previous decade) survived to co-exist with 'official' classicism. From their co-existence emerged, on occasion, buildings far from the more bizarre excesses of Nazism and largely comparable with certain major Western European enterprises of the interwar period (such as the principal buildings of London University) – austerely functional and not without a certain drab grandeur.

In the 30 years after 1945 – in what may be termed the period of European reconstruction and social democracy – it now appears that, in both East and West Europe, the principal influence on housing styles for most people – whether acknowledged or not – was, especially for the public sector (and posthumously), the *Bauhaus*. Its stress on uncluttered functionalism was particularly appropriate to an era where speed of construction was essential; stress on utility of form rather than decoration was also suitable to a democratic age. Other contemporary developments in mass housing were noticeable – new versions of the perennial cottage, particularly in Great Britain, but also in the North of Europe generally, from northern France to Scandinavia – but remained overall a minority phenomenon.

Meanwhile housing for the more prosperous tended, through virtually all the rest of the century, to national – or at least regional – stereotypes. In France an attenuated classicism mostly prevailed, with smaller houses – especially those built identically on small estates, a tendency only to emerge in the last third of the century – affecting a self-conscious prettiness, presumably redolent of the eighteenth-century cottage. In Austria and Germany, and to some extent in Poland and even Scandinavia, architectural style often recalls the aristocratic past of hunting lodges and the cosy rusticity of the *White Horse Inn*. Most intriguingly of all, perhaps, there emerged around 1980 in Britain a kind of diluted resurrection of the interwar mock-Tudor style – now an imitation not so much of the sixteenth century as of the 1930s, a truly postmodern parody of a parody.

The last decades of the century produced little in the way of noteworthy monumental and public architecture. The reconstruction of Berlin after German reunification from 1989 onwards was notable, in a climate more in accordance with profit than with aesthetics, mainly for a style of office building which, whilst incorporating some modernist elements, might be termed international–bureaucratic, and for little else.

A contrast might be drawn, finally, between the two grandiose Paris edifices evolved in, respectively, the 1970s and 1980s – the *Centre Pompidou* of Richard Rogers (see Figure 11.2) and the *Pyramide du Louvre* of I. M. Pei – and the recent extension to London's *National Gallery*, an ill-proportioned work of neo-classicism, parasitic

**Fig. 11.2** Centre Pompidou in Paris, by Rogers and Piano (1972–6)

upon the elegant 1820s neo-classicism of the main building, which it seems to mimic ineptly. The difference is here extremely evident between an aesthetic activity which aims to see beyond the limitations of the present, and one which, necessarily engaged in that present as all art must be, immerses itself in a reversion to a falsely imagined past. A contrast which appears most visibly in architecture – but is by no means restricted to it.

# ■ Cinema

Together with jazz (principally a North American phenomenon and thus not, in general, a subject for this volume) cinema is the quintessentially twentieth-century art form. Its history, from its beginnings in Paris with the Lumière brothers in the late 1890s to the present day, is dramatic, as is its rise from side-show curiosity and simple item in a music-hall programme to gigantic mechanism for mass entertainment, dramatic enlightenment and propaganda. Then follows its relative decline (first the diminution of its audiences – from the 1950s – through the competition of television; secondly, the dispersal of cinema audiences themselves – from the 1980s – by the use of video). Yet in spite of these vicissitudes it remains the most powerful force for the dissemination of culture in the world.

Technical advances in the industry have been prodigious. Yet, as opposed to many which have proved relatively short-lived (cinerama, Todd-Ao, 3D etc.), only two innovations can be confidently stated to have had a significant and long-lasting effect on cinematic form as a whole – the introduction of sound (1928–9) and, soon after, that of colour (c.1935). Use of sound had the effect – principally in Hollywood but also in the European cinema – of effecting a reversion to the representational naturalism from which, paradoxically, the European theatre was at almost the same time emerging. Colour took much longer to catch on, and it was almost 30 years after its first use that it became, as now, practically universal. Partly this was due to the crudity of North American colour systems (licensed throughout Western Europe); in the early post-war decades its indiscriminate use was partly responsible for the division of cinema production (and presumably its hitherto relatively heterogeneous audiences) into two categories: light comedy and 'spectacular' (in colour) and 'serious' or 'intellectual' films (in black and white). It is difficult to judge the original impact of films of the silent/black and white era; as ever, we can only attempt a relation of our contemporary reactions with our general aesthetic and historical preoccupations. However, it can be safely assumed that the element of the extraordinary in early cinema must have militated against any simple, realist response to screen images as a 'slice of life'; both the gestures of the actors and the insertion of captions (from which Brecht borrowed for the theatre) must have given, as to some extent they do now, the effect of opera rather than anything more everyday, whatever the ostensible setting.

The effectiveness of these conditions for the 'de-realising' drama of the early 1920s – for German expressionism and French surrealism – is apparent in films such as Robert Wiene's *Dr Caligari's Cabinet* (*Das Kabinett des Doktor Caligari*, 1919). Here the strangeness of the youthful medium is correlated with bizarre distortions of plot and of visual perspective – and Caligari emerges as the manipulator of these distortions, but in a lunatic asylum – a prescient foretaste, perhaps, of the Third Reich. René Clair's *Entr'acte* (1929) and Germaine Dulac's *The Seashell and the Clergyman*

(*La Coquille et le Clergyman*, 1928) both involve a ludicrous dreamlike chase – the mourners after a runaway coffin, the unfortunate portly clergyman along a beach. Each film thus celebrates modernism (the speed of the camera a source of the futurism from which surrealism derived) whilst simultaneously rendering it ludicrous.

The vicissitudes of German cinematic expressionism are, of course, tortuous. Fritz Lang, whose *Metropolis* (1926) is supremely cinematic in that the class and social conflicts it shows occur within a gigantic closed, 'layered' townscape, emigrated to Hollywood in 1933 and subsequently produced films closer to the US social realist norm of the period. Leni Riefenstahl, the best-known Nazi film-maker, incorporated expressionist elements (choric unison, rapidly clashing images) in her film of the Nazi Party rally, *Triumph of the Will* (*Triumph des Willens*, 1934). The progress of French surrealism through the century has been more serene: elements of it subsist in Jean Cocteau's *Orphée* (1950) and *Le Testament d'Orphée* (1960) and in the comic-satirical mode of Jean-Pierre Mocky's *Snobs* (1961).

Affinities can be observed between the work of German expressionists and that of their Soviet near-contemporary, Sergei Eisenstein. The revolutionary impact of his films – e.g. *Battleship Potemkin* (1925) and *October* (1928) – is of course much more direct, but not, for that matter, simple. Notably Eisenstein's innovatory use of *montage* (cutting rapidly from scene to scene, image to image) builds a complex network of representations of political conflict, of which the film may be seen, retrospectively, as the resolution.

The 1930s look now like the period when the centre of world film production moved to Hollywood (though this was not to be a permanent development), when the 'dream factory' seemed capable of producing a virtually inexhaustible supply of comedies, fantasies and social dramas – still a source of considerable interest. One factor in this was, of course, the emigration not just of German directors, but of actors, administrators and technicians of all sorts. What was now produced in Germany was not, in the main, direct fascist propaganda on film (and this was true of fascist Italy too): apart from the notorious Riefenstahl and one or two others, production centred on banal 'feel-good' comedies and mediocre musicals – the 'dream factory' of Hollywood without the imagination or the tools.

The British film industry of the time – without suffering the repressions of its German counterpart – hardly survived the world economic crisis much better. Emigration to Hollywood was, unlike that from Germany, more economic than political – but virtually as disastrous. Severity of censorship, extraordinary for a supposedly liberal democracy, was also doubtless to blame. When Alfred Hitchcock left in 1939, he was only continuing an established trend (see Portrait 11.6). Meanwhile, the production of comedies, versions of that British speciality the comedy murder mystery (satirised indeed by Hitchcock in *The 39 Steps*, 1935), Gracie Fields and George Formby musicals, and the historical biographies of Alexander Korda, produced material now principally of antiquarian interest. One field of film-making was, however, genuinely innovatory – the documentaries of Herbert Grierson, which incorporated into their dramatic investigations of British working life music by Benjamin Britten and texts by W. H. Auden.

The only European country to come near to rivalling Hollywood in technical and discursive cinematic power, at this period, was France. The legacy of surrealism was extended with the Prévert brothers' *It's Buttoned Up* (*L'Affaire est dans le sac*, 1932) and with Jean Vigo's hilarious and bizarre *Nought for Behaviour* (*Zéro de Conduite*, 1933) and off-beat, lyrical *l'Atalante* (1934). In addition there evolved a series of

### Charlie Chaplin (1889–1977)

The best-known figure in the world for half a century, from his film *The Kid* (1921), was that of Chaplin's little tramp, with the precarious dignity of his bowler hat and umbrella constantly under threat from his baggy trousers, always seemingly on the point of coming down. Perhaps it is this contrast – as in the case of the circus clown with whom Chaplin has so often been compared – that in some way appealed to a vast audience, especially the lower-middle classes in the first half of the century, increasingly (or so they felt) at the mercy of forces over which they had no control. The negative product of their fear is marvellously rendered in *The Great Dictator* (1940), where Chaplin the harmless Jewish barber *becomes* Hitler and is then magically transformed back to normality; the film greatly influenced Bertolt Brecht's *Arturo Ui* (1941), a satirical attack on Hitler in the guise of a small-time Chicago gangster. The positive image of the bowler-hatted tramp is reworked in Samuel Beckett's *Waiting for Godot* (1953) where the amiability of the tramps is equalled by their steadfast resistance to an alien world. Chaplin's comic-satiric view of US society is perhaps most evident in *Modern Times* (1935), with not only its image of dehumanising modernity but its motif of the police van, ever returning to scoop up dissidents. Though he worked in the USA for nearly 40 years, Chaplin was born in London and sought political exile in Switzerland when threatened for his leftist views, and his achievement moreover, is always very much that of a European.

subtly argued and brilliantly shot films of critical social realism – of which the most striking were those of Jean Renoir: *The Great Illusion* (*La Grande illusion*, 1937) and pre-eminently *The Rules of the Game* (*La Règle du Jeu*, 1939), the free adaptation of an early Romantic comedy by Alfred de Musset. The genre, with its epic range and persistent interrogation of social relationships, has, though not continually dominant in French cinema, continued to produce isolated masterpieces ever since – the panoramic history of nineteenth-century art and politics in Marcel Carné's *Children of the Gods* (*Les Enfants du Paradis*, 1944) and Claude Berri's Zola adaptation, *Germinal* (1992).

After the Second World War, epic realism emerged as the dominant mode in much of Europe. In the Soviet Union, Eisenstein's *Ivan the Terrible* (1945–58) showed a narrative more monumental than his earlier work, as in a different register did Sergei Bondarchuk's *War and Peace* (1966–7), which outgunned in every way the 1956 US version by King Vidor. In Eastern and Southern Europe, in countries where hitherto political circumstances had largely excluded the possibility, film dramas of epic proportions concerned with the interplay of historical and personal forces were dominant for at least a quarter-century. In Poland, Andrzej Wajda's trilogy (*A Generation*, 1954; *Kanal*, 1957; *Ashes and Diamonds*, 1958) chronicled the Occupation and Resistance with both respect and scepticism; later, his *Man of Marble* (1977) gave an account – dynamic and panoramic – of a whole society with few equivalents in the West. In Hungary something of a similar epic breadth and intensity was manifest in Miklós Jancsó's accounts of successive moments in Hungarian history: pathetic in *The Round-up* (1965); heroic in *Reds and Whites* (1967); ironic in *The Confrontation* (1969). And from Greece, where the national culture was twice virtually destroyed by the pre-war and post-war dictatorships, came one of the most remarkable films of this type: Theodor Angelopoulos's *The Travelling Players* (1975) not only chronicled more than two critical decades of Greek history, but the changing relation to them of Greek classical and artistic performance in general, through the varying stories of the actors in the title.

But it is in Italy that the most varied developments from French critical realism are to be found. Italian neo-realism dates from the fall of Mussolini, and is largely defined through the work of two directors: the former fascist Roberto Rossellini, whose major contribution to the movement, *Rome, Open City* (*Roma, Città aperta,* 1945) is none the less remarkable for its combination of fluid actuality with denunciation of repression and torture; and Luchino Visconti, a Communist whose more consistent work in the idiom began with *Ossessione* (1942). This version of the James M. Cain story *The Postman Always Rings Twice* is distinguished from the three Hollywood versions (1944 as *Double Indemnity*, 1946 and 1981) by its treatment of its characters as social agents rather than as individual demons. Visconti's later films – *The Earthquake* (*La Terra Trema*, 1948) and *Rocco and his Brothers* (*Rocco e i suoi fratelli*, 1960) – developed these tendencies on a wider canvas; *The Damned* (*Götterdämmerung*, 1969), on an industrial dynasty in early fascist Germany, contrives to combine them with an appropriately Wagnerian intensity.

In contrast to the uncompromising depiction of conflict in Visconti stand the films of Federico Fellini. Though *La Strada* (1954), with its peasant girl dominated by a circus strong-man, may be seen as an allegory of Italy under fascism, later films – *Satyricon* (1969), *Fellini's Rome* (*Roma*, 1972), *Amarcord* (1973) – deploy a somewhat unctuous political ambiguity, together with cynical manipulation of images of the cruel and the bizarre. The latter characteristics are also prominent in the work of Pier Paolo Pasolini, but with a very different accent. *The Gospel According to St Matthew* (*Il Vangelo secondo Matteo*, 1964) gives – partly through the distanced sound of the Bach *Passion* which accompanies it – a sympathetic atheist version of the Gospel story, of poor peasants in social and existential isolation; and *The 120 Days of Sodom* (*Salò*, 1975) conflates the imagined horrors of de Sade with those of the last days of Italian fascism, to an extent that has ensured its prohibition in Britain.

Most affinities with the work of Visconti, however, are to be found in that of Bernardo Bertolucci. *The Conformist* (*Il Conformista*, 1970) examines, in the mode of a thriller, the relation between mythology, sexuality and fascist repression; and the gigantic *1900* (*Novecento*, 1976) explores twentieth-century Italy – in a way which also recalls Wajda and Angelopoulos – through the changing terms of class and personal relations represented by the two protagonists, landowner and labourer.

To turn from the violent drama of Italian history and cinema to the work of Ingmar Bergman in the relative isolation and apparent calm of Sweden seems to involve a vast transition. True, Bergman's early films, especially, seem claustrophobic by comparison with the Italian panoramas of Visconti or Bertolucci; but their preoccupation with Protestant guilt (as early as *Frenzy* [*Hets*], 1944, the issue is of ethical collusion with Nazism), personal violation and the failure of transcendental mythologies achieves – in films such as *The Seventh Seal* (*Det Sjunde Inseglet*, 1957) *Winter Light* (*Nattsvardsgästerna*, 1962) and *The Silence* (*Tystnaden*, 1963) – a discursive intensity comparable with their more expansive Italian contemporaries; subsequently Bergman has moved to wider political scenes, as in the denunciation of the Vietnam War, *The Shame* (*Skammen*, 1968).

The relationship between fantasy and politics, and between 'personal vision' and social realism, is, as we have seen it in Italy and elsewhere, a complex one in which no rigid dividing lines can, ultimately, be drawn. In Germany (East and West) the tremendous influence of Brecht on all subsequent artistic production has ensured that the treatment of 'social' topics in the cinema was achieved through a cinematic rhetoric which induced the spectator to see the circumstances of those topics as strange and questionable. This is the case in the work of Rainer Werner Faßbinder, about racism and political persecution – *Fear Eats the Soul* (*Angst essen Seele auf*, 1974) and *The Marriage of Maria Braun* (*Die Ehe der Maria Braun*, 1979). It also characterises Margarethe von Trotta's feminist *The German Sisters* (*Die Deutsche Frauen*, 1980). On the other hand, the more 'personal' dramas of Werner Herzog's films – often concerned with demented and marginal characters – have a social reference of violence and oppression which evidently reaches back, implicitly, into a recent political past.

The most prominent cinematic phenomenon of the latter half of the twentieth century, the French *nouvelle vague* of the late 1950s and 1960s, seems, in retrospect, to have initiated the formulation of ambiguities. It was never clear what constituted the *ancienne vague* which the young directors and critics of *Cahiers du Cinéma* were (if only in terms of journalistic speculation) to reject. A 'staged' romantic panorama like Carné's *Children of the Gods* maybe (though obviously they would not dismiss it as negligible)? But other 'monuments' of older French cinema – parts of Renoir's *The Rules of the Game* and particularly his *A Day in the Country* (*Une Partie de Campagne*, 1936) – had the inconclusive thematics and close depiction of character and situation through intimate camera-work which the *nouvelle vague* generation were to take up.

Claude Chabrol's thrillers and dramas of the everyday – *The Girls* (*Les Bonnes Femmes*, 1960), *The Butcher* (*Le Boucher*, 1969) – have much in common with these antecedents, as they do with the *film noir* productions of Henri-Georges Clouzot during and after the war period – *The Wages of Fear* (*Le Salaire de la Peur*, 1953), *Diabolique* (*Les Diaboliques*, 1951). François Truffaut, similarly, made his name with *The 400 Blows* (*Les 400 Coups*, 1959), a semi-autobiographical narrative of the problems of an isolated and increasingly delinquent boy, which now seems more innovative for its understanding of its subject than for its cinematography, which is not radically distinguishable from that of 'old wave' directors such as Claude Autant-Lara – *Thou Shall Not Kill* (*Tu ne tueras pas*, 1962). Later, Truffaut was to direct a series of films continuing the life-story of his first protagonist, Antoine Doinel – sympathetic without being condescending, but essentially repetitive.

The most contentious and varied of the *nouvelle vague* directors are Louis Malle and Jean-Luc Godard. Malle's achievements have included a combination – in *The Lovers* (*Les Amants*, 1959) – of sexual intensity and direct evocation of place which seemed to fuse the archetypal with the local; *Lacombe Lucien* (1973) maintained a dispassionate lucidity in its account of a young French farm boy drifting into collaboration with the Gestapo. The work of Godard, the most avowedly 'Brechtian' of the group, has ranged from the confrontational, anti-élitist satire of *Les Carabiniers* (1963) to the consideration of the interplay of cinema illusion and natural reality as expressive of a world without values in *Contempt* (*Le Mépris*, 1963). *Two or Three Things That I Know About Her* (*Deux ou trois choses que je sais d'elle*, 1967) gave brief presentations of part-time prostitutes as characteristic of contemporary relations; *Weekend* (1968) went further in presenting universal carnage on the roads as the essential reality of social life.

Meanwhile, the social realism which had been, ever since the war, the strength of the British cinema was renewed in the 1960s. Its greatest achievements in the epoch of post-war social democracy had been transformations of nineteenth-century texts from Dickens to Stevenson (notably David Lean's unsurpassed *Great Expectations*, 1946). Now Karel Reisz (*Saturday Night and Sunday Morning*, 1960) set a trend which had many undistinguished imitators (for instance, John Schlesinger's *A Kind of Loving*, 1962) and some less literal-minded successors capable of uniting the bizarre and the fantastic in a project of social denunciation, as in Reisz's *Morgan – A Suitable Case for Treatment* (1966) and Lindsay Anderson's *If* (1968).

But the innovatory impact of this British 'new wave', as it soon became known, was to a large extent, like that of its French counterpart, the effect of its contrast with the anodyne nature of the cinema immediately preceding it. Just as there are major affinities between French cinema of the 1940s and 1960s, so in Britain identical themes emerge. The disaffection of youth from the inauthentic routine of society, the oppressiveness of the urban scene and yet the impossibility of escape – all of this is to be found in films such as Robert Hamer's *It Always Rains on Sunday* (1947) or Charles Crichton's *Dance Hall* (1950).

These films are nowadays forgotten: I cite them in conclusion, not as a display of erudition, but to make the point that the cinema is not just a series of 'masterpieces' (which will, by reason of their continued availability, none the less continue largely to determine our view of its evolution) but, like other cultural forms, a network of relationships across theme and technique, geography and time.

# ■ Postmodernism and deconstruction: towards the end of the century

We have examined some cultural tendencies – whether we designate them by turns as realism or modernism, representation or self-questioning, harmony or dissonance – whose meanings are, by and large, within the conceptual limits set by the European Enlightenment of the eighteenth century. That is to say, both the cultural products of the first two-thirds of the twentieth century and the efforts of interpretation directed at them have, in the main, inhabited a mental universe in which reason and the viability of the search for truth went together with notions of the mutual determination of phenomena in the context of historical progression.

These principles (or conventions according to preference) have, in the last third of the twentieth century, been increasingly challenged by tendencies in thinking variously known as post-structuralism, postmodernism or deconstruction. These share characteristics which, though largely novel in themselves, have seemed, in a new configuration, to dominate European intellectual life at the expense of more established models of thinking, whether positivist, Marxist or aesthetic. Their effect would appear to derive from a combination of the following: an irrationalism which comprises a denial not just of the supremacy of human reason, but also of the validity of the notions of historical determination or of progress; a radical scepticism which denies both the significance of the thinking subject and the attainability of truth; an extreme eclecticism which sees all phenomena as of equal importance and the relations between them as infinite – thus seeing our world as a location of indifference, where choice and value are ultimately of no significance.

The proponents of this thinking have been mainly French, although taken up enthusiastically by some others elsewhere. At the risk of conglomerating figures from varying intellectual spheres (but who none the less seem to have a great deal in common, in both their actuality and their effect) we might single out four thinkers. Michel Foucault's preoccupation with the relationship between intellect and power

(*The Birth of the Clinic, Naissance de la clinique*, 1963; *Discipline and Punish, Surveiller et punir*, 1977) led him to apparent revulsion from the notion of power in itself, from the general reforming tendencies of the Enlightenment and after, and towards the supposition that viable political activity could only consist in little local struggles for power, in minor agitation against universal, large-scale domination. His anti-intellectualism was effectively underwritten by Jean-François Lyotard (*The Post-modern Condition; La Condition postmoderne*, 1982) whose project of combating what he termed the 'grand narrative' of history (*le grand récit*) was to reduce the understanding of society and the past to moments of insight rather than any wider speculation. Jean Baudrillard (*The Mirror of Production, Le Miroir de la production*, 1973) has more recently reflected this scepticism in his affirmation that the Gulf War never happened (that is to say, because we cannot distinguish between a plethora of media images of a phenomenon, its particular significance is to be discounted); the perception coincided to some extent with Baudrillard's fascination with the 'emptiness' of the USA. The radical scepticism of Jacques Derrida (*De la grammatologie, Grammatology*, 1967; *Spectres of Marx, Les Spectres de Marx*, 1993) seeks to dismiss logocentrism (the functional centrality of language and reason) as well as the phenomenon, supposedly associated with it throughout modern history, of binary thinking (thinking in terms of contrasts). These he characterises (fallaciously) as specifically European modes of thinking, and proposes a preoccupation with language, centrally, as a system of displacements, its relation to its objects infinitely questionable and obstructive of any notion of truth.

It is hard not to see the political consequences of such thinking. The relationship of the self to the world is in many respects radically altered and – so the proponents of the new thinking would assert – opened up. Yet in the absence of any preoccupation with the determination – or the mediation/transformation – of one phenomenon by another, the possibilities of any substantive change in a world which seems effectively to be there as it is, nowhere and everywhere at once, are small.

What results is a kind of universal conservative inertia. In speaking briefly of postmodern artistic production it is not appropriate to generalise in the same way as in discussing the legislative statements of postmodern philosophers. We may, however, note, finally, that a significant tendency in postmodern art is towards minimalism. Yves Klein painted one-colour canvases around 1960; in 1978 Carl André achieved notoriety by arranging a row of bricks in London's Tate Gallery; in 1998 Per Kirkeby's *Brick Work* repeated the exercise. It rather looks as if the tendency of postmodern art may take us back to the naturalism with which we started at the beginning of the century – always different, yet always the same.

## ■ Summary

◆ Culture may perhaps be stated to be the way in which humanity defines itself in its relation to the world; the statement may then be broken down into further contrasts manifest as between aesthetics and politics, personality and collectivity, etc.

◆ Twentieth-century cultural developments may be charted in many ways; one is to examine the effects of the intellectual relations of *romanticism* (which stresses personal feeling over general structure, a sense of distance from established reality, the possibility of otherness and revolt and the interrelation of mind and world);

and *positivism* (the practical philosophy of the nineteenth-century classes, stressing intellectual and social order, the significance of facts, categorisation and classification, the determination of mind by world).

◆ In the media, the new organisation of technical advances (notably in the field of electronic reproduction) have brought the most ambitious romantic forms (the total work of art) closer to a mass audience; their administration has, however, shown conflict between fixed attitudes inherited from the nineteenth century and the rise of new forms of organisation appropriate to such wider audiences.

◆ Education is evidently the crucial site for the transmission of knowledge and for the generation of conditions for the furtherance of cultural activities. The relation between the authority of knowledge and the possibility of its free development is always a complex one, never separable from political conditions.

◆ In architecture a contrast is evident between work which evidently recapitulates past forms, and that which aims to be of its own time and to display its own processes of construction – a contrast which indicates similarly a complicated series of relationships to history and power.

◆ The conditions of cinema were set in the first third of the twentieth century through the eventual relation of early silent film (often fantastic, quasi-abstract) and sound film (for some time exclusively preoccupied with the chronicle of external reality). Out of these tendencies various forms of modern cinema have emerged.

◆ So far we have counterposed general cultural tendencies in terms of the rational analysis of opposing and inter-determining forces, as practised in European thought since the Enlightenment. In the last third of the twentieth century influential thinking has emerged (postmodernism, deconstruction) which is radically eclectic and sceptical and which negates the possibility of determination, truth itself and, presumably, judgement.

◆ It is too early to say whether such thinking will outlive the immediate historical circumstances which engendered it. At any event, the details which such thinking examines are infinite; what it derives from them is always the same.

## Questions for discussion

▶ Explain the difference between romantic and positivist approaches to culture.

▶ What have been the main tendencies in the development of the media?

▶ Can the educational system of a country be politically 'neutral'?

▶ Is architecture a good case study demonstrating the tension between romanticism and positivism?

▶ How has film been used for propaganda purposes?

▶ What are the distinctive features of the postmodern approach to culture?

## Further reading

Barthes, Roland, *Mythologies*, trans. Annette Lavers (London: Jonathan Cape, 1972). Barthes generates a vivid field of experience for us between theories of society and images of everyday life.

Benjamin, Walter, *Illuminations*, ed. Hannah Arendt (London: Fontana, 1982). Quirky and stimulating; reflections on what and how we think by the most visionary Marxist of them all.

Bloch, Ernst, *Heritage of our Times* (Cambridge: Polity Press, 1991). Meditations on culture and history, progress and barbarism by one of the most strenuous of central European thinkers.

Camus, Albert, *The Rebel* (Harmondsworth: Penguin, 1969). Liberal thought at its defining moment of crisis in mid century.

Gasset, José Ortega y, *The Dehumanization of Art* (Princeton, NJ: Princeton University Press, 1972). An elegant summation of conservative thinking.

Harby, Howard (ed.), *European Music in the Twentieth Century* (Harmondsworth: Penguin, 1961). Music, the least referential of the arts, seems difficult to connect with other art forms. A careful and comprehensive work such as this helps.

Hughes, Stuart, *Consciousness and Society – The Reorientation of European Social Thought, 1890–1930* (New York: Alfred A. Knopf, 1961). Undogmatic, perceptive and inclusive – an attractive introduction to the history of twentieth-century thought.

Hughes, Robert, *The Shock of the New – Art and the Century of Change* (London: BBC/Thames and Hudson, 1991). Determined in its opinions, wide-ranging and with an eye for significant detail.

Krakauer, Siegfried, *Theory of Film*: *The Redemption of Physical Reality* (New York: Oxford University Press, 1979). The daddy of all film theorists – sophisticated, embattled and lucid.

Sartre, Jean Paul, *Critique of Dialectical Reason*: *I* (London: Verso, 1976). The paradoxes of personality, society and history and our need to articulate them.

Tompkins, Calvin, *Ahead of the Game – Four Versions of Avant-Garde* (Harmondsworth: Penguin, 1968). An enthusiasm which provides a way in to sometimes the most obscure of twentieth-century artistic production.

Williams, Raymond, *Keywords* (London: Fontana, 1996). Not just a lexicon of intellectual terms but a means to their critical evaluation.

# Conclusion

Richard Sakwa and Anne Stevens

## Contents

Contemporary Europe presents a picture of complexity and challenges. Europe is no longer the measure of modernity and a synonym for progress. The passage into the next century is fraught with dangers, whether in the shape of 'simplistic populism and ethnic obscurantism' (Jenkins, in Chapter 3, above), of imbalances in the mechanisms for political participation and accountability (Chapters 5 and 6), of failures in the processes of integration (Chapters 7 and 8) or of unpredictable but probably violent risks to security (Chapter 10). We cannot fully subscribe to Francis Fukuyama's (Portrait 10.1) optimistic proclamation of 'the end of history'. Some form of representative democracy and an economy 'run on the basis of a competitive capitalism which looks to the market for its instructions' may indeed be 'the only viable options for modern society' (Beedham, 1999). However, not only is democracy far from axiomatic or inevitable in Europe (Mazower, 1998), but it is in itself not always a bar to more or less authoritarian rule (Zakaria, 1997). As Dieter Rucht and Thomas Saalfeld both remind us (Chapters 5 and 6), a wider process of political participation than the mere casting of a vote may be required, even where political competition is relatively unfettered, if individuals and minorities are to be confident that their contribution to debates will not go unheeded and their rights will be respected.

Many of the cleavages identified in Chapter 1, which have shaped the identity of Europe, continue to run very deep. Some of them have for much of the twentieth century been overshadowed by the monolithic ideologies which underpinned so many of the bloody conflicts of the period. Two of the most influential of these, fascism and communism, have greatly diminished and no longer enjoy political dominance anywhere. Ideologies which proclaim a total and all-embracing worldview – religious fundamentalism is another – have not altogether disappeared as political forces within as well as outside Europe. Secularisation, democracy and liberal values, on the other hand, are more pluralist. But that in itself opens up the possibility of widespread, if less total and bloody, conflict.

Identity has to some extent replaced ideology. Reactions to globalisation (Chapter 9) involve assertions of distinctiveness. This runs from the local level (Scottish nationalism and devolution, Corsican violence) to claims to 'Europeanism'. Whilst 'Eurosceptics' combat what they see as a centralisation and unacceptable uniformity, others attempt to insist upon the preservation and development of distinctively European models of protectionism, taxation, economic organisation and welfare-state provision. However, as the multi-faceted transformation of Central and Eastern Europe demonstrates, there are no panaceas nor any invariably successful recipes. At the heart of the discussion lies the question of what Europe is becoming and what it should be.

# ■ The three Europes

If the slogan of the anti-communist insurgency in 1989 was 'return to Europe', we need to examine which Europe the demonstrators in those stirring events had in mind. The EU is only one vision of Europe, and itself is divisive in that it is unlikely in the near future to encompass countries like Russia and Turkey. The EU is only one form of European integration, although by far the most important. The principles on which the EU itself will be built are still not entirely clear, with no formal constitution enshrining principles of federalism and political accountability. And what about the outsider countries? Are they to remain eternal supplicants grateful for whatever crumbs might fall from the European table? This is not a recipe for European solidarity and a broader European identity to develop.

There remain fundamental tensions between the dynamics of official European integration, processes of pan-European unity that bring together the whole of the continent, and forms of cultural coherence that reflect the distinctive features of a separate continent-wide European civilisation. Three concepts of European solidarity, if not unity, can be identified.

## Official Europe

West European integration is central to the concept of Europe that we can call 'official Europe'. Chapters 2 and 7 have described its beginnings and current form. The fifteen-member EU of the late 1990s had become one of the most successful supra-national institutions in European history. The extent of its eastward enlargement remained problematic (see Chapter 8) with Ukraine, for example, left out of official definitions of what constituted 'Europe'. While Russia sought to make the CIS an official counter-Europe, most of its members sought to distance themselves from the idea, which they viewed as a way of projecting Russian hegemony over the former Soviet space. The enlargement of NATO and the EU threatened to isolate Russia, a concern that was voiced in the summer of 1999 by the then Russian prime minister Sergei Stepashin, warning the EU not to marginalise Russia as it brought Eastern Europe into its fold (*Financial Times*, 2 July 1999).

The programmes for EU and NATO enlargement were powerful catalysts of change in Eastern Europe, and in turn fed back and forced an agenda of reform and adaptation on the enlarging institutions themselves. EU enlargement challenged the whole continent to rethink what it meant to be 'European'. Deepening (that is, intensification of the pace of institutional integration within the existing membership) took precedence over widening (the incorporation of new members), a priority that many have argued to have been wrong (e.g. Garton Ash, 1999), leaving the East Europeans in the lurch. According to Garton Ash (1996), 'EU-rope' caught the wrong bus in the 1990s; as he put it elsewhere, 'Instead of seizing the opportunities, and preparing to confront the dangers, that would arise from the end of communism in half of Europe, they set about perfecting the internal arrangements of an already well-functioning, peaceful and prosperous community of states in western Europe' (*Prospect*, July 1999, p. 24).

## Pan-Europe

The idea of the establishment of a European federation had long been part of the European intellectual agenda, and was most eloquently advocated by Count

Box 12.1

## The Council of Europe

The Council of Europe (which should not be confused with the European Council, the meeting of Heads of State and Government of the member states of the European Union, see Chapter 7) was established on 5 May 1949, by 10 Western European states (Belgium, Denmark, France, Ireland, Italy, Luxembourg, the Netherlands, Norway, Sweden and the United Kingdom); 13 more West European states joined before 1990 (Austria, Cyprus, Finland, West Germany, Greece, Iceland, Liechtenstein, Malta, Portugal, San Marino, Spain, Switzerland and Turkey). After 1990 former East Germany was incorporated as a result of German unification, and since then 16 Central and East European states have joined (Albania, Bulgaria, Croatia, the Czech Republic, Estonia, Hungary, Latvia, Lithuania, Macedonia, Moldova, Poland, Romania, Russia, Slovakia, Slovenia and Ukraine), along with Andorra. The Council is based in Strasbourg, France. It consists of four principal bodies: the Committee of Ministers, which meets twice annually; the Parliamentary Assembly, which meets four times a year; the Congress of Local and Regional Authorities of Europe; and the Secretariat.

The Council of Europe issues reports and consultative documents, and draws up conventions, which are binding only on those member states that ratify them, and become operative when a minimum number of member states have done so. The most important of these is the European Convention on Human Rights, which established the European Court of Human Rights (not to be confused with the European Court of Justice, a body of the European Union).

Coudenhove-Kalergi in 1923 in his book *Pan-Europa*. Mikhail Gorbachev's espousal of the 'Common European Home' from the Atlantic to the Pacific (the trans-Urals region is European in all but name) appeared to signal a new reconciliation of all parts of the continent, not opposed to North America but separate from it, in a deepening process of pan-European integration. Mitterrand in early 1990 floated the idea of a European confederation, and the idea was later taken up by other French leaders and President Václav Havel of the Czech Republic, but the Gorbachevian ideal of pan-European unity and of a 'common European home' has been eclipsed in the post-Cold War era. Instead, while some pan-European institutions continue to develop, the ideal itself has been marginalised.

The institutions of pan-Europe are inter-governmental rather than supra-national. They include the Council of Europe, established in May 1949, together with its European Commission on Human Rights and the European Court of Human Rights, both responsible for the enforcement of the European Convention on Human Rights of 1950. Supported by the Council of Europe's European Social Charter, the pan-European space is now a uniquely intense arena of human-rights development. The Parliamentary Assembly of the Council of Europe (PACE) brings together deputies from all 40 member states. With the fall of communism the Council has gradually extended its reach to the East as countries are deemed to have fulfilled certain conditions of democracy and human and civil rights, including the abolition of the death penalty. The vigorous human-rights agenda raised sharp questions about the balance to be drawn between national and supra-national rights.

The Organisation for Security and Co-operation in Europe (OSCE) (see Box 10.2) is another of the founding blocs of pan-Europe. The OSCE played a crucial part in the final days of communism, above all at its Vienna follow-up meeting from November 1986. By 1989, Gorbachev had accepted the whole agenda of human-rights and civil society formulated by the concluding document of the Vienna conference. He assumed that this ethical individualism could be grafted onto the communist system to create a more humane form of socialism. Perhaps in different circumstances this might have been possible, but by this time the repressive legacy of communism and its systematic denigration of representative democracy meant that few were willing to give this new experiment the benefit of the doubt.

The wars in the Balkans starkly revealed the inadequacies of the OSCE even in its new form (see Box 10.2). Above all, the tension between the core OSCE principles of national self-determination and the inviolability of borders has still to be reconciled. Russia's aspirations to make the OSCE the main security body in Europe to replace NATO were not fulfilled (Chapter 10). Instead, NATO became the dominant security body, and in the sphere of integration the EU began the long process of enlargement (Chapter 8).

## Civilisational Europe

While Europe has been divided politically, and new sources of division remain, there can be no doubt that Russia, for example, is part of a broader European civilisation. Its literature and art have embellished European culture, its music and philosophy are part of the currency of European thinking, and its people are firmly part of the European tradition. As Viktor Loshak, the editor of *Moscow News*, put it, 'The role of Russian culture in the world is large, even larger than we can imagine' (Itar-Tass, 22 June 1999), and he went on to note that no theatre in the world is without works by Chekhov, Gogol and Ostrovsky in its repertoire. This cultural unity transcends political divisions and geographical barriers.

Of the three Europes, the civilisational one is perhaps the weakest. Economic globalisation and the Western-centred process of European integration cannot conceal an underlying unease about the loss of national and regional identities. In spite of the end of overt organised ideological conflict, above all between capitalism and socialism, and despite rhetorical support for the view that there were no winners or losers at the end of the Cold War, Europe has remained divided, but in new ways. Ideological conflict gave way to amorphous 'culture wars' where issues of identity and separateness came to the fore. In a landmark article, Samuel Huntington (1993, and see also 1996; see Portrait 10.5) suggested indeed that the new era would be characterised by 'the clash of civilisations'. In Europe he identified an Orthodox civilisation and a Western European one. While this division might be questionable, the fact of tensions between the various parts of Europe, in particular in the Balkans and in the former Soviet Union, confirmed the view that just as one set of conflicts came to an end, a new set emerged. Although Huntington failed to address those elements that unite Europe culturally, he raised important issues. Above all, the end of the Cold War division of the continent allowed its peoples to argue that 'we are all Europeans now'; but the history of the post-Cold War years brought home that there was no unanimity over who *we* were, quite apart from the question of what was distinctively *European* about Europe.

Thus, three conceptions of Europe are in tension. One, the official Europe represented by European integration in the form of the EU and its predecessors, has traditionally served to fulfil French strategic aims, the German search for rehabilitation after the war, and Italian hopes for good governance and participation in Europe, while for the Benelux countries it has provided them with markets and a political stature quite incommensurate with their size. Only Britain has not perceived any vital national interest in membership, other than fear of exclusion from the most dynamic market in Europe, and thus has traditionally been Europe's 'awkward partner' (George, 1998). Western Europe, and above all the EU, has become the 'ideal' to which the rest of the continent aspires. Enlargement after the fall of communism, however, has been a concession granted, as it were, by sufferance rather than conceded as a right, and thus represents a very different political dynamic. This is 'official' Europe at its starkest, contrasted with the more amorphous universalistic concept embedded in the pan-European ideal. The second conception, associated with pan-Europe, is based on inclusivity and the principle of the universal applicability of human-rights and democratic aspirations. Although the Council of Europe had been established in Western Europe, it became a genuinely pan-European body after the fall of communism and was not dominated by any single state or alliance of states. The origins of the OSCE were even more genuinely pan-European, it having originally been sought by the Soviet Union and its allies to enshrine by treaty what it had achieved at the end of the Second World War by force, but then it went on to become one of the main instruments to overcome the Cold War. By contrast with official Europe, pan-Europe was inclusive and consensual. The third Europe is that of peoples and cultures, where gradually the outline of a single cultural space, not only at the elite but also at the mass level, is beginning to emerge. Mass tourism, electronic communications, student exchanges, cheaper air flights and much else are gradually creating a single European people.

## The reinvention of Europe

The 'post-war' period in European history, an era marked by the division of the continent into two hostile military and ideological blocs, ended in 1989–91. The features of the new epoch are not yet clear. What is already evident, however, is that the high hopes of the early postcommunist years have not been fulfilled. Aspirations for a new European order to be established through the joint endeavours of both parts of the continent, the pan-European reconstitution of the continent, gave way to a process whereby the existing instruments of Western European integration and security were extended to the East. The belief that the end of the Cold War saw neither 'victors' nor 'vanquished' but a common victory over suspicion and ideological blindness gradually gave way to an understanding that there remained profound divisions on the continent; of economic development, wealth, civilisational aspirations and geopolitical concerns. In economic terms, the gap between most states in the former Soviet Union, together with countries like Albania and Romania, and Western Europe had increased rather than diminished in the first decade after the fall of communism. Europe's demons, above all those of nationalism, had not been laid to rest, and in former Yugoslavia took the form of wars of ethnic cleansing. If the American President George Bush, in the period immediately following the fall of the Berlin Wall, talked of the establishment of a New World Order (see Box 10.4), his failure to give the idea any substance was symptomatic of a larger failure of leadership in the post-Cold War era.

Europe is in a constant process of reinvention. Its very diversity of peoples, cultures, geography and history allows new combinations to emerge that stamp each age with a different view of 'what is Europe'. We are witnesses perhaps to one of the greatest acts of reinvention, one no longer born out of the destruction and chaos of the Second World War but out of the fall of communism and the rise of globalisation. While there are many acts involved in this play, one of them being the development of what we have called 'official Europe' in bodies like the European Union, and another, the reconfiguration of pan-European political space through the Council of Europe and the OSCE, these are only part of a larger picture associated with the reforging of European identity itself.

There are many elements to this new identity. One of them involves changes to the identities of the countries themselves. In drawing attention to these changes we are arguing for the continued crucial importance of individual states as the framework both for internal policy-making and for international relations. Interdependence and diffused authority (Chapters 3 and 9) are inescapable features of the environment to which states are adapting. But there is no sign of the emergence of any real alternative to the nation-state as the main unit which provides for the organisation of society and the provision of those collective services which most affect individual citizens – education, health and social services in particular. Nation-states are the main units between which international relations are conducted. This is because despite the movements towards a common foreign and defence policy it is the nation-states that control the two key resources, force and money. It is by and within the nation-states that armies and police forces are raised and commanded, and it is nation-states who raise and spend large, and not diminishing, proportions of GDP (see Table 12.1). In comparison, the amount of money raised and spent by, for example, the European Union, is almost insignificant. In 1999 it amounted to 1.11 per cent of the member states' GNP and about 2.5 per cent of their total public expenditure (Nugent, 1999, p. 390).

Nation-states remain the basic units. But their identities are changing. This is apparent above all in France, Germany and Russia. The enormous sacrifices of the First World War in France gave way to an era of disappointment, and then rapid

**Table 12.1** Government spending: percentage of GDP spent by national governments

|  | Spending | | | Tax revenue | | |
|---|---|---|---|---|---|---|
|  | 1960 | 1980 | 1988 | 1960* | 1980 | 1997 |
| Australia | 21.2 | 31.4 | 32.9 | 22.4 | 28.4 | 30.3 |
| Britain | 32.2 | 43.0 | 40.2 | 28.5 | 35.1 | 35.3 |
| Canada | 28.6 | 38.8 | 42.1 | 23.8 | 32.0 | 36.8† |
| France | 34.6 | 46.1 | 54.3 | na | 41.7 | 46.1 |
| Germany | 32.4‡ | 47.9† | 46.9 | 31.3† | 38.2† | 37.5 |
| Italy | 30.1 | 42.1 | 49.1 | 34.4 | 30.4 | 44.9 |
| Japan | 17.5 | 32.0 | 36.9 | 18.2 | 25.4 | 28.4‡ |
| Spain | na | 32.2 | 41.8 | 14.0 | 23.9 | 35.3 |
| Sweden | 31.0 | 60.1 | 60.8 | 27.2 | 48.8 | 53.3 |
| United States | 26.8 | 31.4 | 32.8 | 26.5 | 26.9 | 28.5‡ |
| **Average§** | **28.3** | **40.5** | **43.8** | **25.1** | **33.1** | **37.6** |

*Estimated  †West Germany  ‡1996  §Unweighted
Source: OECD, reproduced from The Economist, 31 July 1999.

defeat in 1940 as the continent once again plunged into war. Liberated in 1944 by Anglo-American forces, the country began to see that the only way out of defeat and dependency was through Europe itself, and to do this there had to be co-operation with Germany. And thus the plans for 'official Europe' were drawn up, although the EEC was only part of the larger attempt to reforge an autonomous European politics. Nevertheless, the view of an unidentified German statesman remains potent: 'Europe is the continuation of France by other means.'

For West Germany, Europe was a way of escaping from its own past. It did so not only by maintaining a strong relationship with France but by remaking the entirety of its domestic political arrangements and social organisation. After 1945 Germany purged itself of the militarism that had brought to it and the continent so much horror, and became a thoroughly civilian state, perhaps the most pacific on the continent. Ironically, its very peacefulness allowed the goal of unification to be achieved in 1990 without the 'blood and iron' that Bismarck had imposed on German foreign policy the previous century.

For Russia there was to be no such happy ending to the century. Defeat at the hands of an emerging Asian power, Japan, in 1905, had precipitated the first of the revolutions that would sweep away the Romanov dynasty in 1917 after yet more defeats in the First World War. Coming to power in October 1917, the Bolsheviks promised a way out of backwardness and dependency by the adoption of Western technological civilisation accompanied by the rejection of Western political values. The great experiment with revolutionary socialism in Russia, however, proved incapable of delivering on its promises. An industrial power was created, one capable of taking the brunt of the war effort against Nazi Germany, but communist power was unable to create a complex, self-sustaining system of economic and political development. Stagnatory tendencies were well in evidence long before Gorbachev came to power in 1985, and his attempts to reform the system precipitated its collapse in 1991. The fall of communism, however, was not to inaugurate an era of full-scale democracy and economic prosperity but a decade of unprecedented economic and social crisis. The unfinished agenda of democratisation and coming to terms with the Russian and Soviet past made Russia an uncomfortable partner of the West and a potentially unstable member of the pan-European community.

All other countries are having to 'reinvent' themselves to adjust to the post-Cold War world. Italy finally overcame the paralysis that appeared to have settled on its political evolution for half a century after the end of the war, and by the end of the 1990s was governed by a coalition including former communists. Turkey remained torn between Europe and Asia, but its fundamental choice to the West (secular, modernising and Europe-oriented) taken by Kemal Ataturk in the early 1920s remained under strain. In Scandinavia the Nordic 'third way', based on developed welfarism and neutrality between the blocs, was challenged by processes of economic and security integration, with Finland and Sweden joining the EU, while Norway voted to remain outside the EU but remained a member of NATO.

The second element in the reinvention of Europe is the development of a dense network of non-governmental institutions. We have examined the development of multilateral organisations like the EU and NATO (Chapters 2, 7 and 10), but it must be stressed that 'official Europe' is only part of the development of a more coherent European community. There is a dense infrastructure of agencies, businesses, and human movements across borders that suggests the emergence of Europe as a single community. In this the borders that had appeared so impermeable for most of the twentieth century began to return to what they had been before the onset of the modern era, no more than frontiers between different zones of state activity. The danger here was that while Europe's internal borders might become more open, in particular between the Schengen countries (those that had signed up to the Schengen Agreement of 1985 to dispense with border controls between themselves: by 1999 these were Austria, Belgium, France, Germany, Holland, Italy, Luxembourg, Portugal and Spain), the external borders would become more tightly controlled in compensation, above all to the East and South. It appeared that Europe was turning inwards, to the general disadvantage of countries beyond the narrow confines of 'official' Europe.

A third element of the reinvention of Europe in the eyes of some European leaders is the development of a specifically European model of capitalist society. The Soviet model of a centrally planned economy has been decisively rejected, and socialist parties across Europe are turning away from those definitions and symbols of socialism that carry such connotations. The British Labour Party's rejection of Clause Four of its constitution, which pledged it to work for the common ownership of the means of production and exchange, was an important moment in Tony Blair's drive to create 'New Labour'. But many European leaders equally reject what can be seen as an American-inspired neo-liberal version of intensely competitive and unrestrained capitalism.

Different countries have different traditions. French capitalism was long based on a tradition of *dirigisme* – state direction – where the state played a crucial role as the depository for the savings of its citizens, and played an active role in managing credit and providing investment. Privatisation during the 1980s and 1990s, the legalisation of unit trusts during the 1980s, the deregulation and expansion of the stock market and the impact of the free movement of capital and services introduced by the Single European Market since 1992 have all changed the nature of French capital structures. Hostility to inward investment has declined, and French firms have been active in expanding outside France. For example, French-owned utility companies are active in the United Kingdom. But government regulation still provides for protective holdings of core or 'golden' shares and the close relationships between the elite groups at the top of both state and private financial institutions still provide for a good deal of formal and informal influence.

In Germany, capital has been to a very marked extent provided and managed through the Banks, with a great deal of cross-shareholding. Consequently, for example, hostile take-overs until recently were virtually unknown. The model of capitalism which this implies is sometimes called 'Rhineland' capitalism. Its proponents, and those who, like former European Commission President Jacques Delors, insist that Europe must be an organised social, as well as economic space, regard it as a more humane and socially responsible form of capitalism than the 'Anglo-Saxon' version, which they disparage.

In Eastern Europe, as Chapter 8 suggests, the proponents of these contending versions of capitalism have offered their nostrums to societies in transition. The movement from central planning to capitalism has undoubtedly been brutal and a source of great disillusionment to many, but no clear 'third way' has emerged. The forces of globalisation (see Chapter 9), the need to move away from pay-as-you-go, state-funded pensions and to rely more on individual savings to finance the old age of an ageing population, and the impact of the common currency, all seem likely to drive towards greater uniformity of economic systems, though it is perhaps symptomatic that the EU has not yet managed to agree on a common framework for company structures. There will certainly continue to be powerful voices insisting that the social dimensions, the fight against exclusion, social solidarity and the collective good must not be forgotten or neglected as economic policies and frameworks continue to evolve.

Fourthly, more broadly, the reinvention of Europe involves changes to the very idea of Europe. If the continent was forged in war between the peoples of which it was composed, and then in imperial adventures abroad, together with an extraordinary economic and political dynamism, today the continent's vision of itself is as a post-military zone of peace, welfare and prosperity. Old conceptions of international relations such as the arena of alliances, balances of power and the pursuit of national interests have by no means disappeared, but a new layer encompassing values and identity has emerged to become at least as important. Values may well be drawn from tradition but they, too, like national identity, are in a constant process of change. The problem for much of Europe, however, is that the absence of over-riding goals, challenges or even a sense of purpose may undermine the very values with which it now seeks to identify itself. The very notion of 'the West', a concept Europe now shares with North America and some other parts of the world, is challenged by the rise of powerful economies in the East with distinctive value systems of their own (see Coker, 1998), and by the disarray within its own borderlands in the East. If the notion of 'European solidarity' was so weak that it could not rise to the postcommunist challenges in Russia and other former Soviet republics and in the Balkans, then what hope was there for the new Europe to transcend a divisiveness and materialism that could not but sooner or later dissolve into a new age of disappointment?

## The distinctiveness of Europe

This process of reinvention constitutes the main element of European distinctiveness. As William Outhwaite points out (Chapter 4) and Ian Manners also suggests in a different context (Chapter 9), the values which took shape in particular during and after the sixteenth century and as a consequence of the French Revolution were widely exported through the processes of empire-building and colonisation, and are, in some forms, now being re-imported. So Europe can claim no exclusive ownership. It is not attachment to the so-called 'Western' approach to liberal democracy, the role of the market, economic forces and human-rights which distinguishes the nation-states of Europe from much of the rest of the world. They are distinguished by the scope and scale of the transformations that they have undergone in the last 50 years, and their ability to adapt to these. Some of these transformations are social: the advent of secularism, the relation between town and country, the nature of the family, the role, status and rights of women. All these features have changed and are changing in directions that cannot always be foreseen. These, and, even more, the end of colonialism and empire, the passage from fascism or autocracy for Italy, Germany, Greece, Spain and Portugal, and the 'triple transformation' after communism in Central and Eastern Europe, have required greater or lesser adjustments in all European states. In comparison, other 'Western' countries, and especially the United States, fixed as it is within the firm corset of its constitutional discourse and values, seem more static and less flexible.

Pluralism and flexibility, however, are as likely to generate friction as harmony. Diverging interests and conflicting claims may degenerate into violent clashes, since the lust for territory, the desire for cultural domination and the temptation to ethnic cleansing have by no means disappeared from Europe, as wars in Bosnia, Kosovo and Chechnya and the appalling rise in displacement of persons and refugees remind us.

Several factors may in the long term mitigate these pressures. One, as Brian Jenkins points out (Chapter 3), is the 'hollowing out of the nation-state' and the 'fluid and dynamic politics of multi-level governance'. Another may be a growing aversion to traditional face-to-face warfare on the part of the general public. Young men, as well as their girl-friends, partners and mothers, who can benefit from the changing status of women to voice their views more assertively, now see in vivid and visual representation via the electronic media just what fighting will mean. The consequence seems to be, as in Kosovo, some deterrence at least to the use of land-fighting forces, and possibly to war at all.

Globalisation is a further factor. While differing patterns of development (Chapter 9) increase economic tensions, the network of global institutions also provides a framework, through bodies such as the G8, for the management of some of the tensions.

A final factor which may limit and control the forces for fragmentation, violence, domination and oppression is the political choice of the nation-states of Europe. The development of the European Union is one example of the impact of fundamentally political choices often in quite humdrum and technical areas. 'Low' politics of this sort will continue to enmesh countries both inside and outside the European Union. If the international system agreed at the Congress of Vienna in 1815 failed to secure lasting peace, the accompanying convention on river traffic on the Rhine has had a much more enduring existence. Air traffic and high-speed trains may be the modern equivalent; since the early 1990s the territory covered by the member states of the European Civil Aviation Conference has run from Reykjavik to Vladivostok. If the transformations of contemporary Europe succeed in lengthening the list of states who 'seriously want not to fight each other. . . [and] are willing to take a wide range of economic decisions by collective action' (Beedham, 1999), then the future of Europe may yet be both distinctive and hopeful.

It is in recognition of this ability to regenerate, reinvent and choose, that we do not wish to paint a picture of unmitigated gloom. While still at an unacceptably high level, deaths in Europe from war and violence have amounted to only one million in the second half of the century compared with 60 million in the first half (Mazower, 1998). The 'muddling through' that a pluralistic society has preferred is producing in contemporary Europe notable progress in cross-border trade and movement, in economic stability, in the development of welfare states and of human-rights, and in the creation of a single European people referred to above. There is still a chance that the reinvention of the nation-state and of Europe will result in the gradual evolution of a set of political relationships of a new sort: functional, complex, multilingual, geared to supporting economic development and controlling it, attentive to the social dimension, and concentrating at inter-state level on the management of tasks which transcend the local, whether – to take examples amongst many others – the movement of people or trade, or facing environmental issues and threats. The achievement of this new set of relationships, which will be both unprecedented and unparalleled elsewhere, will depend upon the ability of the states of Europe, within the European Union and outside it, to manage conflict without resorting to violence. Peace, even if sometimes a partial and punctured peace, and, despite all the disappointments and setbacks, may still be a realistic vision and hope for Europe.

## Summary

◆ Three Europes can be identified: an official Europe made up above all of the EU and NATO; pan-Europe, comprised of bodies like the Council of Europe, the OSCE and other institutions expressing universal norms of human-rights and freedoms; and a civilisational Europe, the weakest of the three but no less important for that, based on shared history, cultural values and understanding.

◆ Europe is now once again reinventing itself, coming to terms with its past, its identity and aspirations, together with a sense of responsibility not only for its own fate but for the world as a whole, but any survey of Europe's past cannot view the future with any great optimism.

◆ Nevertheless, the distinctiveness of Europe's future lies precisely in the ability of its states to adapt and adjust, both internally and to new pattterns of external relations. There are forces which militate against the use of violence as a means for solving conflict. An increasing enmeshing of states through pragmatic functional responses to common problems may be one pointer to a more hopeful future.

## Questions for discussion

▶ Are the three Europes compatible with each other?

▶ What are the main features of the reinvention of Europe today?

▶ Can we identify a distinctively European identity?

▶ Do the grounds for pessimism about fragmentation and conflict outweigh the arguments for optimism about the future of Europe?

# Glossary

**Accountability** The requirement for agents (or representatives) to answer to the principals (or represented) on the exercise of their powers and duties. Political systems typically employ certain institutional arrangements ('mechanisms' such as parliamentary investigations, public inquiries, ministerial responsibility, collective responsibility, etc.) to ensure at least a degree of accountability.

**Additional and compensatory member systems (AMS)** Electoral systems with at least two tiers of electoral districts used, for example, in Germany as well as in the elections for the Scottish Parliament and the Welsh Assembly. They involve a lower-level local constituency, with which a representative can maintain personal contact, and a higher-level regional or even national district in which minority interests can be proportionately represented. Voters have two votes, one for each district. The party vote at the upper level (e.g., the national level) is used to calculate the percentage of parliamentary seats a party will receive. The mandates won in the lower-level constituency contests are then deducted from this total. Thus, parties winning a less than proportional share of seats at the lower level are compensated with a higher number of seats from the party lists at the higher level.

**Alternative vote (AV)** Electoral system where voters rank the candidates in single-member districts according to their preferences. In a first step, all first preferences are counted, and any candidate with more than half of the votes is elected. If no candidate achieves half of the vote, the candidate with fewest first preferences is eliminated and their second preferences are redistributed. This is repeated with third, fourth, etc. preferences as often as required until a candidate wins more than half of the valid votes. AV is used in elections to the Australian parliament.

**Anarchy** A term frequently used in International Relations theory. It refers to the fact that no legitimate world government exists, a fact which is perceived by realists and idealists alike as inherently dangerous and destabilising.

**Austro-Hungarian Empire** A multinational empire which comprised, among other political units, Austria proper, the Kingdom of Hungary, Bohemia, northern Italian provinces such as Lombardy, etc. The people who inhabited the Empire differed in language, customs, and historical background, and included Germans, Czechs, Slovaks, Poles, Magyars, Croats, Serbs and Slovenes, among others. The Empire fell at the end of the First World War.

**Autarchy** Strictly, autarchy means rule or government by a single person. The word is also sometimes used as an alternative spelling of autarky, which means a policy of being economically self-sufficient as a nation or community. Such self-sufficiency is often protected by various measures to hamper or discourage cross-border trade.

**Autocracy** Government by a single person having unlimited power.

**Bipolarity** An arrangement of international relations in which two actors or 'poles' are each vying for dominance over the other. Often refers to the division of the world into roughly equal military blocs. In the Cold War period, the two superpowers leading these two blocs were the USA and the USSR

**Bolshevik Party** A revolutionary Marxist party which originated from the part of the Russian Social Democratic Labour Party which supported Lenin after 1903. Under Lenin the Bolsheviks seized control of Russia during the October Revolution in 1917. Renamed the Communist Party of the Soviet Union in 1951.

**Brezhnev Doctrine** Named after the violent suppression of socialist reforms in communist Czechoslovakia in 1968. According to the doctrine, Moscow arrogated the right to intervene in the internal affairs of Warsaw Pact members to protect the supposed gains of communism.

**Cleavages** Cleavages separate social or political groups that, having a relatively stable and coherent view on fundamental aspects of society, take opposite stances on issues such as religion, individual liberties and state intervention, social justice, and market economy.

**Clientelism** A structure of relations between powerful patrons such as landlords or political leaders and those dependent on them for services, who reward them by political or other forms of support.

**Cold War** A state of hostility, animosity and tension between the Communist bloc and the Western World, embodied particularly in the relationship between the USSR and the USA. It lasted from the period soon after the end of the Second World War until the end of the Communist regimes in 1989.

**Collective security** The core idea of collective security is that states should act together for the common good rather than acting alone or in military blocs in their own selfish national interests.

**Colonialism** The practice of holding land as a form of

colony in order to increase the wealth of a colonial state. The colonies had little political independence and primarily served an economic purpose.

**Connotation**   The process of noting something together with something else, the implication of something besides itself.

**Containment**   The US-inspired doctrine of the Cold War aimed at stopping the spread of Communist influence, through the use of military alliances, subversion, and diplomatic and economic isolation.

**Co-ordination, positive and negative**   'Positive coordination is an attempt to maximize the overall effectiveness and efficiency of government policy by exploring and utilizing the joint strategy options of several ministerial portfolios. . . . Negative coordination, by contrast, is associated with more limited aspirations. Its goal is to assure that any new policy initiative designed by a specialized subunit within the ministerial organization will not interfere with the established policies and the interests of other ministerial units. ... Procedurally, positive coordination is associated with multilateral negotiations in intra- or interministerial task forces. . . . By contrast, negative coordination is more likely to take the form of bilateral "clearance" negotiations between the initiating department and other units whose portfolios might be affected – but whose own policy options are not actively considered.' Scharpf (1993, pp. 143–4)

**Culture**   The relationship between ideas, relationships and institutions, reflection on the nature of which enables us to understand our relationship to the world.

**Decolonisation**   The retreat of European powers from their colonies during the twentieth century.

**Democracy**   Rule by the people. According to Abraham Lincoln in his address at Gettysburg in 1864, 'government of the people, by the people and for the people'. Democracy is a much contested concept, subject to many varying interpretations.

**Denotation**   The act of marking or distinguishing something as separate or distinct.

**Depression**   An economic contraction resulting in high unemployment. The Great Depression was triggered by the stock market crash on Wall Street in New York in October 1929 and lasted throughout the 1930s.

**Détente**   Literally this means loosening, but it is used to describe the relaxation of tension between antagonistic states, for example between the USA and USSR following the Cold War.

**Developed world**   Those parts of the world which can be considered to have undergone industrialisation and have developed primary, secondary and tertiary sectors of their economy. Also termed the 'first world' or the 'north', it includes most of Europe.

**Developing world**   Those parts of the world which have not undergone industrialisation and usually rely on their primary economic sector. Also termed the 'Third World' or the 'south', this includes most of the former European colonies.

**Direct democracy**   A form of government where those entitled to decide do so directly in sovereign assemblies or referendums.

**Enlightenment**   The name given to a period of intellectual history during the eighteenth century when philosophers and other thinkers stressed the importance of reason, of freedom of thought and of proceeding by observation and deduction.

**Ethnic cleansing**   The practice of forcibly removing members of any different ethnic group from an area controlled by a particular group. The term, often no more than a euphemism for genocide, came into prominence during the war in Bosnia in the 1990s to describe the removal or destruction of Croats or Muslims from territories claimed by Serbs as part of 'greater Serbia'. The term was then used to describe the forced removal of Serbs from territories that had become or were becoming independent states.

**Ex-ante/ex-post controls**   When political authority is delegated from a principal (for example, a government minister) to an agent (for example, a civil servant), the principal has two fundamental ways of controlling the agent. *Ex-ante* controls apply before the delegation takes place. Principals may screen agents for their suitability or set out the agents' duties in contracts. *Ex-post* controls apply after the delegation has taken place. Principals may monitor their agents' performance by requiring them to report on their activities or by using independent bodies to audit agent performance.

**Fabian**   Fabianism was a tendency in British socialism dating from the 1880s, advocating the total but gradual transformation of society by administrative action under, largely, the control of the enlightened middle classes.

**Fascism**   An ideology characterised by a belief in anti-rationalism, struggle, charismatic leadership, elitism and extreme nationalism; associated historically with the Mussolini regime in Italy.

**Federal states**   States in which regional governments have substantial, constitutionally guaranteed powers. The term is often used to describe political systems which are less centralised than unitary states, but without the extreme decentralisation of a confederation. Federal states are often characterised by a complex web of checks and balances between the national government and regional governments. Examples of federal states in Europe are Belgium and Germany.

**First-past-the-post electoral system**  A way of describing simple-plurality electoral systems. They are commonly used to allocate seats in single-member districts. In order to win a seat, a candidate is required to get more votes than each of the others (plurality). The candidate is not required to have the vote of a majority of those voting in the constituency. In Europe, the simple-plurality system is used only in the United Kingdom. Its main advantage is its simplicity. Its main disadvantage is that it is likely to produce disproportionate outcomes.

**Fordism**  Named after the early twentieth-century US carmaker Henry Ford, refers to standardised and mechanised mass production: the term 'post-Fordism' has been used since the 1980s to denote more specialised and flexible forms of production, often involving the co-ordination of small-scale producers and catering to small niche markets.

**Free trade**  The notion that the pursuit of barrier-free trade will benefit all those involved, regardless of relative economic strength.

**Fundamentalism**  Religious believers who see literal meanings in their sacred texts are usually referred to as fundamentalists. Often perceived by outsiders as extremists, fundamentalists usually wish to see their religion playing a bigger role in politics and society.

**Futurism**  Italian aesthetic movement which rejected values of reason and progress in favour of the veneration of speed, violence and war; one of the early constituents of fascism.

**Glasnost**  Literally this means 'openness', but was used to describe the relaxation of censorship and cultural repression during Gorbachev's time in power in the USSR, 1985–91.

**Gross domestic product (GDP)**  Common indicator of the level of a country's economic activity. It represents the total value of the goods and services produced by a country's economy during a specified period of time excluding the income of the country's residents from investment abroad.

**Hegemonic power**  A state possesses hegemonic power when it is able to create and enforce rules to maintain the international status quo and its own dominance within the existing system.

**Hegemony**  In global terms this refers to the pre-eminence or domination of one power over others.

**Highly Indebted Poor Countries**  The world's most indebted countries and the plan to reduce their outstanding debt to 'sustainable' levels, assuming they adopt 'good' economic policies.

**Human Development Index**  A means used by the United Nations Development Program for rating the quality of life, based on life expectancy, education and real GDP per capita.

**Human Rights Index**  An index developed by the *Observer* newspaper as a means of drawing attention to the worst human rights abusers in the world.

**Humanism**  A system of thought and belief which rejects dependence upon the notion of the existence of God as the source of values and ethics and sees human beings as containing within themselves the highest values.

**Idealism**  A normative International Relations theory which accepts the problems and dangers of anarchy in the international system but, unlike realist theories, seeks to overcome them through the creation of an international community based on international organisations and a greater emphasis on international law.

**Imperialism**  The seizing of territory by military means involving the subjugation of its peoples. The empires created were based on hostility and conflict for political and economic gain.

**Individualism**  The cluster of doctrines that assert the importance of individual persons and their opinions, rights, welfare, etc. rather than collective structures such as families, churches, states, etc.

**Interdependence**  A condition of great mutual dependence involving exchanges of an economic, social and political nature.

**Interest groups**  Interest groups are more or less formal associations that represent a particular group/clientele or promote collective demands – be they very specific or very general – in the political process, predominantly by public statements, bargaining and lobbying.

**Internal market**  A concept from the field of New Public Management (NPM), which has come to dominate debates about the reform of the public sector in the United States of America, the United Kingdom, New Zealand and Sweden in the 1980s. Traditional state functions are increasingly 'contracted out' to external providers competing for a contract from government as a service 'purchaser'. Even within the public sector, funders are systematically separated from providers of services. For example, public health authorities contract with providers – such as hospitals – to supply health care on agreed terms. Public providers compete with other outside providers for the award of a contract.

**Liberal democracy**  A form of democracy which incorporates limited government, accountability of government to the legislature and the people, and a system of regular and competitive elections.

**Literature**   Its definition will probably be forever a vexed question, but *literature* may perhaps be defined as what is written and read, and *Literature* as those texts which, for whatever reason, have remained continuously (or nearly) in print since their first publication.

**Marshall Plan**   Officially named the European Recovery Program, this US initiative involved massive financial aid and loans to European countries totalling some $14 billion in contemporary prices in order to hasten their economic recovery following the Second World War, and thereby, hopefully, strengthen their political stability. Although offered to East European countries as well, most recipients were Western European.

**Mercantilism**   The pursuit of trade surpluses in order to increase the wealth of a state. It emphasised the importance of exports and decreasing imports as well as attempting to accumulate wealth in the form of precious metals.

**Meritocracy**   Rule by those deemed to be the most deserving, the brightest and/or the most successful.

**Modernism**   An aesthetic tendency which contrasts with realism (q.v.) in that, rather than an art work purporting to show an aspect of the world external to it, it draws attention to the devices by which it attains to that world.

**Multilateralism**   International relations involving more than two participants in an attempt to achieve common goals.

**Multipolar**   An arrangement of international relations in which there are many actors or 'poles', none of which is predominant.

**Multipolarity**   Refers to the division of the world into three or more power blocs.

**National self-determination**   The possibility for any nation to determine for itself by whom and how it should be governed. The implications are that the nation is sovereign and that government should be both independent and democratic.

**Nationalism**   A set of beliefs, which may take varied forms, which asserts the primacy of the nation as the source of sovereignty and the main basis for politics and government.

**Naturalism**   A late nineteenth-century aesthetic movement which combines minute depiction of the external world with a wide preoccupation with the operation of heredity and environment as understood by nineteenth-century science.

**Neo-imperialism**   This refers to the effects of imperialism on a state which exists without the political reality of colonisation.

**Neo-colonialism**   The continued exploitation of former colonies through other means, usually involving aid, technical assistance and foreign direct investment.

**Neocorporatism**   Neocorporatism is an arrangement in which the leaders of interest groups, together with representatives of the state, jointly make policies and justify these *vis-à-vis* their respective members or clientele.

**New World Order**   A term used by President Bush at the end of the Cold War which called for a world governed by international law, the respect of human rights and the renewed authority of the United Nations.

**Newly industrialising countries**   Those countries which have recently undergone industrialization and do not have to rely on their primary economic sector. These countries are currently found only in South-East Asia.

**Oligarchy**   Rule or government by a small group or a few people.

**Parliamentary system of government**   In a general sense any system of government which operates through a popularly elected parliament. In a more specific sense, 'parliamentary systems of government' are systems in which the heads of government are selected by the assembly and govern through a majority in the assembly.

**Participatory democracy**   This connotes decentralisation of power for the direct involvement of amateurs in authoritative decision-making.

**Party list systems**   A proportional electoral system which distributes the seats on a national (such as in the Netherlands) or regional basis (for example, in Germany or Italy). This order is often determined by party bodies. Once the parties' share of the vote is established, the parliamentary seats are filled using the party lists. Seats are allocated to candidates, starting from the top of the lists. Such lists can be 'open' (that is, the voters may change the ranking on the lists by indicating preferences for certain candidates) or 'closed' (the voters can only accept or reject the list as drawn up by the parties, as in the 1999 European Parliament elections in Britain). Party list systems are used in most countries of continental Western Europe, with varying degrees of party control over the ranking of candidates and openness to changes through the voters.

**Patronymics**   Names derived from a father or other ancestor, for example by suffixes such as -son, -ovich.

**Perestroika**   This literally means 'restructuring' but was used by Gorbachev to describe his attempts to reform the Soviet Union between 1985 and 1991, suggesting plans to liberalise and democratise the Soviet system within a communist framework.

**Plurality (or majority) systems**   Electoral systems which emphasise the powers of political candidates or parties backed by an absolute or relative majority (plurality) of the voters. The winner in elections 'takes all' in such systems. Normatively such systems are based on the belief that a government formed this way offers the most effective and accountable form of government.

**Policy communities**   Networks of government ministries, executive agencies, interest groups and other non-government actors in a particular policy area. These networks cut across the formal divide between governmental and non-governmental actors and are 'communities' in so far as they share expertise and a common definition of the problems in a particular area. A great deal of public policy, especially uncontroversial and routine legislation, is typically made in such 'communities'.

**Polis**   The Greek word for a city state. Used to denote a complete set of political arrangements, usually with the implication that the existence of such arrangements is desirable.

**Postmaterialism**   Postmaterialism is a set of values such as freedom of speech and protection of the environment that are supposed to gain relevance after basic material needs (e.g., food and shelter) are satisfied.

**Presidential system of government**   A system of government in which the head of government is a president whose office is politically and constitutionally separate from the legislature.

**Proportional representation (PR)**   Electoral systems with multi-member districts, in which parties are represented in an assembly in proportion to their overall electoral strength. Most continental West European electoral systems (except France and Italy) are more or less pure systems of proportional representation.

**Protectionism**   The use of trade barriers such as tariffs, taxes, technical rules and invisible barriers in order to protect a state's economy from imports.

**Realism**   An aesthetic which seeks to engage with the external world both in the depiction of its appearances and in an investigation of their history.

**Realist**   Realist thinkers argue that states always pursue their own national interests in the world, both to maximise their own power and to defend their own territory.

**Realpolitik**   A policy emanating from realist ideas in international relations. It argues for a state to pursue its own national interests rather than act in an ethical way or for the common good.

**Referendum**   An election which allows voters to make a choice between alternative policies on a particular issue. Referendums (**referenda**) are important instruments of direct democracy.

**Reformation**   The historical period during the sixteenth century which saw the emergence in Western Europe of Christian denominations, most of them described as 'Protestant', which broke away from the leadership of the papacy and rejected what they saw as the excesses, abuses and errors of the Roman Church.

**Renaissance**   The historical period during the fifteenth and sixteenth centuries which saw the rediscovery of Classical literature and thought, and the development of new forms of art, music, architecture and literature.

**Representative government**   A form of government where a legislature with significant decision-making power is freely elected. Political decisions are made by elected representatives on behalf of the represented.

**Revolutionary**   In its strictly political sense, whatever furthers the transfer of power and wealth in society from one class to another; in artistic and cultural affairs, by analogy, whatever transforms the established patterns of aesthetic production and their recognition or consumption.

**Second ballot systems**   A form of plurality or majority electoral system requiring a winning candidate to get a majority of the votes cast (50 per cent of the vote in a constituency plus 1) in a first round. If no candidate gains a majority of the votes in the first round, a second ballot is held for the strongest of the first-round candidates. This system is used in France. The candidate with the plurality of votes wins this second ballot.

**Single transferable vote (STV)**   A system of proportional representation for multi-member districts. It is used in the Irish Republic and Malta. Each voter lists a number of candidates in order of preference. In a first step, first preferences are counted. Those candidates who have achieved at least a certain quota of votes (usually the 'Droop quota' [named after a Belgian mathematician] of the number of total votes divided by the number of available seats plus 1) are elected. Their 'surplus votes', i.e., the number of votes by which they exceed the quota, are transferred to the next candidate on those voters' lists. When no further candidates can be elected by this route, the candidate with the fewest first preferences is eliminated and their second preferences are transferred. The process continues until all seats in a district are filled.

**Social capital**   Two different meanings prevail. In the understanding of the French sociologist Pierre Bourdieu, social capital consists of an individual's intangible resources based on personal ties with other people – resources that can be used to enhance the individual's social status and career. The US political scientist David Putnam means by 'social capital' the associational life of a society that creates bonds of solidarity and a sense of responsibility for the common good and the functioning of democracy.

**Social mobility** The 'upward' or 'downward' movement from one position in a social scale to another, e.g. from 'working class' to 'middle class' – either within an individual's lifetime or from one generation to another.

**Social movements** Social movements are loosely coupled networks of groups and organisations that, over a considerable period of time, mobilise to achieve or resist social change and/or change society predominantly by means of collective and public protest.

**Stagflation** A combination of stagnating output and inflationary pressures which typified the depression of the late 1970s and early 1980s.

**Subsidiarity** The principle, developed from Roman Catholic social thought, that public policy decisions should be made, and action taken, at as low a level and as close to the citizen as possible. It is enshrined in the Treaty of European Union, which requires that the Community act only if, and in so far as, the desired objectives cannot be sufficiently achieved by the member states. Some argue that the principle also requires devolution from central to local government.

**Surrealism** An aesthetic movement which originated in France after the First World War; it was/is principally concerned with the dual (sur-real) possibilities of perceptions in life and art, and with the exploration of the **unconscious** (q.v.) in the form of automatic writing.

**Technocratic rule** A tendency in complex, modern states to delegate more and more powers to bureaucratic experts rather than elected politicians, who cannot match the former's expertise.

**The Triad** Kenichi Ohmae's 1985 description of the world's three economic giants – the United States of America, the European Union and Japan.

***Trente glorieuses*** Literally the 'thirty glorious years' of economic expansion in France, this phase of post-Second World War economic growth ended in the mid-1970s, and was characterised by rising personal incomes, affluence and low unemployment.

**Truman Doctrine** Ideologically expressed commitment made by US president Truman in 1947 to maintain freedom throughout the world by 'containing' the spread of communism. The Doctrine laid the basis for subsequent US involvement in the Greek civil war, the creation of NATO, and long-term US global military presence.

**Unconscious** Simply, those operations of the mind of which we are not immediately aware. By extension, a reservoir of drives and motives which may run counter to, or threaten, the operations of the rational consciousness.

**Unipolar** An arrangement of international relations in which one actor or 'pole' is dominant over all others.

**Universalism** A very general term which suggests that the end of the Cold War offered potential for the formation of a real international community based on the general acceptance of key principles governing international behaviour.

***Wirtschaftswunder*** Literally the 'economic miracle' of West German post-war economic expansion, characterised by rising incomes and affluence. This unprecedented economic performance helped to legitimise the new West German state in the first few decades after the end of the Second World War. The 'miracle' ended in the mid-1970s.

**World System** Immanuel Wallerstein's description of a single world arrangement of economic and political relations which expanded from Europe in the sixteenth century to encompass the globe.

# Bibliography

Agh, A. (1998) *The Politics of Central and Eastern Europe* (London: Sage).

Albert, M. (1991) *Capitalisme contre capitalisme* (Paris: Seuil). Translated as *Capitalism Against Capitalism* (London: Whurr, 1993).

Allum, Percy (1995) *State and Society in Western Europe* (Cambridge: Polity Press).

Amin, Ash and Nigel Thrift (eds) (1994) *Globalization, Institutions, and Regional Development in Europe* (Oxford: Oxford University Press).

Amin, A. and J. Tomaney (1995) *Behind the Myth of European Union* (London: Routledge).

Amsden, A., H. J. Kochanowicz and L. Taylor (1994) *The Market Meets its Match: Restructuring the Economies of Eastern Europe* (London: Harvard University Press).

Andersen, S. S. and K. A. Eliassen (1996) *The European Union: How Democratic is it?* (London: Sage).

Anderson, B. (1983) *Imagined Communities: Reflections on the Origins and Spread of Nationalism* (London: Verso).

Andeweg, R. B. (1997) 'Collegiality and Collectivity: Cabinets, Cabinet Committees and Cabinet Ministers', in P. Weller, H. Bakvis and R. A. W. Rhodes (eds) *The Hollow Crown: Countervailing Trends in Core Executives* (Basingstoke: Macmillan) pp. 58–83.

Andeweg, R. B. (2000) 'The Delegation Process between Government and Ministers in Western Democracies', *European Journal of Political Research*, 34 (forthcoming).

Andeweg, R. B. and L. Nijzink (1995) 'Beyond the Two-Body Image: Relations between Ministers and MPs', in H. Döring (ed.) *Parliaments and Majority Rule in Western Europe* (Frankfurt am Main: Campus, and New York: St Martin's Press) pp. 152–78.

Appadawai, Arjan (1996) *Modernity at Large: Cultural Dimensions of Globalisation* (Minneapolis: University of Minnesota Press).

Arnason, J. P. (1993) *The Future That Failed: Origins and Destinies of the Soviet Model* (London: Routledge).

Aron, R. (1962) *Dix-huit leçons sur la société industrielle* (Paris: Gallimard).

Artobolevskiy, S. S. (1997) *Regional Policy in Europe* (Regional Studies Association, London: Jessica Kingsley).

Avery, G. and F. Cameron (1998) *The Enlargement of the European Union* (Sheffield: Sheffield Academic Press).

Axelrod, R. (1984) *The Evolution of Cooperation* (New York: Basic Books).

Axtmann, Roland (ed.) (1998) *Globalization and Europe: Theoretical and Empirical Investigations* (London: Pinter).

Ayoob, M. (1995) *The Third World Security Predicament: State Making, Regional Conflict and the International System* (Boulder, CO: Lynne Rienner).

Bachrach, Peter (1969) *The Theory of Democratic Elitism* (London: University of London Press).

Bagehot, W. (1963 [1867]) *The English Constitution* (Glasgow: Fontana/Collins).

Bailey, J. (ed.) (1992; 2nd edn 1998) *Social Europe* (London: Longman).

Baldwin, R. (1994) *Towards an Integrated Europe* (London: Cambridge University Press).

Balibar, E. and I. Wallerstein (1991) *Race, Nation, Class: Ambiguous Identities* (London: Verso).

Barber, Benjamin (1985) *Strong Democracy: Participatory Politics for a New Age* (Berkeley: University of California Press).

Barnes, Samuel (1998) 'The Mobilization of Political Identity in New Democracies', in Samuel Barnes and János Simon (eds) *The Postcommunist Citizen* (Budapest: Erasmus Foundation and IPS of HAS) pp. 117–37.

Barnes, Samuel, Max Kaase et al. (1979) *Political Action: Mass Participation in Five Western Democracies* (Beverly Hills and London: Sage).

Barthes, Roland (1972) *Mythologies*, tr. Annette Lavers (London: Cape).

Baun, Michael (1999) 'Enlargement', in Laura Cram, Desmond Dinan and Neill Nugent (eds), *Developments in European Union Politics* (London: Macmillan) pp. 269–89.

Beck, U. (1986) *Risikogesellschaft* (Frankfurt: Suhrkamp). Translated as *Risk Society: Towards a New Modernity* (London: Sage, 1992).

Beck, U., A. Giddens and S. Lash (1994) *Reflexive Modernization* (Cambridge: Polity Press).

Bell, D. (1987) 'The World and the United States in 2013', *Daedalus*, vol. 116, no. 3, pp. 1–32.

Benjamin, Walter (1982) *Illuminations*, ed. Hannah Arendt (London: Fontana).

Berger, J. (1981) 'Changing Crises-Types in Western Societies', *Praxis International*, vol. 1, no. 3, pp. 230–9.

Bergman, T. (1993) 'Formation Rules and Minority Governments', *European Journal of Political Research*, 23, pp. 55–66.

Bernhard, W. (1998) 'A Political Explanation of Variations in Central Bank Independence', *American Political Science Review*, 92, 2, pp. 311–28.

Black, Cyril E., Jonathan A. Helmreich, Pal C. Helmreich, Charles P. Issawi and A. James McAdams (1992) *Rebirth: A History of Europe since World War II* (Boulder, CO: Westview Press).

Bloch, Ernst (1991) *Heritage of our Times* (Cambridge: Polity Press).

Bluth, C. (1994), 'Strategic Nuclear Weapons and US–Russian Relations: From Confrontation to Co-operative Denuclearization', *Contemporary Security Policy*, vol. 15, no. 1, April.

Bollerup, Søren Rinder and Christian Dons Christensen (1997) *Nationalism in Eastern Europe: Causes and Consequences of the National Revivals and Conflicts in Late-Twentieth-Century Eastern Europe* (Basingstoke: Macmillan).

Booth, K. and N. Wheeler (1992) 'Contending Philosophies about Security in Europe', in C. McInnes (ed.) *Security and Strategy in the New Europe* (London: Routledge).

Borg, Sami (1995) 'Electoral Participation', in Jan W. van Deth and Elinor Scargrough (eds) *The Impact of Values: Beliefs in Government*, vol. 4 (Oxford: Oxford University Press) pp. 441–60.

Bourdieu, P. (1970) *La reproduction.* Translated as *Reproduction in Education, Society and Culture* (London: Sage).

Bowker, M. (1997) *Russian Foreign Policy and the End of the Cold War* (Aldershot: Dartmouth).

Bowles, Samuel and Herbert Gintis (1986) *Democracy and Capitalism: Property, Community and the Contradictions of Modern Thought* (London: Routledge and Kegan Paul).

Brittan, Leon (1998) *Globalisation vs. Sovereignty? The European Response* (Cambridge: Cambridge University Press).

Brubaker, R. (1992) *Citizenship and Nationhood in France and Germany* (Cambridge, MA: Harvard University Press).

Bryce, Lord (1921) *Modern Democracies*, 2 vols (London: Macmillan).

Buckley, Richard (ed.) (1999) *The Global Village: Challenges for a Shrinking Planet* (Cheltenham: Understanding Global Issues).

Budge, Ian et al. (1997) *The Politics of the New Europe: Atlantic to Urals* (London and New York: Longman).

Bugajski, Janusz (1993) *Nations in Turmoil: Conflict and Co-operation in Eastern Europe* (Boulder, CO: Westview Press).

Bullman, U. (1997) 'The Politics of the Third Level', in C. Jeffery (ed.) *The Regional Dimension of the European Union: Towards a Third Level in Europe?* (London: Frank Cass).

Buzan, B. (1991) *People, State and Fear*, 2nd edn (Hemel Hempstead: Harvester Wheatsheaf).

Cadot, O. (1994) *Adusting to Another Enlargement* (Paris: INSED).

Calvocoressi, P. (1992) *Resilient Europe: A Study of the Years 1870–2000* (London: Longman).

Carr, E. H. (1939) *The Twenty Years' Crisis, 1919–1939: An Introduction to the Study of International Relations* (London: Macmillan).

Castles, S. et al. (1984) *Here for Good: Western Europe's New Ethnic Minorities* (London: Pluto).

Cerby, P. (1980) *The Politics of Grandeur: Ideological Aspects of de Gaulle's Foreign Policy* (Cambridge: Cambridge University Press).

Cheles, L., R. Ferguson and M. Vaughan (eds) (1991) *Neo-Fascism in Europe* (Harlow: Longman).

Clark, A. (1993) *Diaries* (London: Phoenix).

Coker, Christopher (1998) *Twilight of the West* (Boulder: Westview Press).

Coleman, D. (1996) *Europe's Population in the 1990s* (Oxford: Oxford University Press).

Coleman, William and Geoffrey Underhill (eds) (1998) *Regionalism and Global Economic Integration: Europe, Asia and the Americas* (London: Routledge).

Collier, D. and S. Levitsky, quoted in A. Agh (1998) *The Politics of Central and Eastern Europe* (London: Sage) p. 20 and p. 21n.

Cornick, M. (1996) 'French Intellectuals, Neutralism and the Search for Peace in the Cold War', in T. Chafer and B. Jenkins (eds) *France from the Cold War to the New World Order* (London: Macmillan) pp. 39–52.

Cotta, M. (1991) 'Conclusions', in J. Blondel and J.-L. Thiébault (eds) *The Profession of Government Minister in Western Europe* (Basingstoke: Macmillan) pp. 174–98.

Cram, Laura (1997) *Policy-Making in the EU* (London: Routledge).

Cram, Laura (1999) 'The Commission', in Laura Cram, Desmond Dinan and Neill Nugent (eds) *Developments in the European Union* (London: Macmillan) pp. 44–61.

Crewe, Ivor and David Denver (eds) (1985) *Electoral Change in Western Democracies: Patterns and Sources of Electoral Volatility* (London: Croom Helm).

Crick, Bernard (1970) 'Parliament in the British Political System', in Allan Kornberg and Lloyd D. Musolf (eds) *Legislatures in Developmental Perspective* (Durham, NC: Duke University Press) pp. 33–54.

Crouch, C. (1993) *Industrial Relations and European State Traditions* (Oxford: Clarendon Press).

Crouch, C. and W. Streeck (eds) (1997) *Political Economy of Modern Capitalism* (London: Sage).

Crozier, M. (1964) *The Bureaucratic Phenomenon* (Chicago: University of Chicago Press).

Csaba, L. (1995) 'The Political Economy of Trade Regimes in Central Europe', in L. A. Winters, *Foundation of an Open Economy, Trade Laws and Institutions for Eastern Europe* (London: Centre for European Policy Research).

Dahl, R. (1971) *Polyarchy, Participation and Oppression* (London: Yale University Press).

Dahl, Robert A. (1994) 'A Democratic Dilemma: System Effectiveness versus Citizen Participation', *Political Science Quarterly*, 109, pp. 23–34.

Dalton, Russell J. (1996) *Citizen Politics: Public Opinion and Political Parties in Advanced Industrial Democracies*, 2nd edn (Chatham, NJ: Chatham House).

Davies, Norman (1996) *Europe: A History* (Oxford: Oxford University Press).

De Porte, A. W. (1979) *Europe Between the Superpowers* (New Haven, CT: Yale University Press).

De Winter, L. (1995) 'The Role of Parliament in Government Formation and Resignation', in H. Döring (ed.), *Parliaments and Majority Rule in Western Europe* (Frankfurt am Main: Campus, and New York: St Martin's Press) pp. 115–51.

Delanty, G. (1995) *Inventing Europe: Idea, Identity, Reality* (Basingstoke: Macmillan).

Delanty, G. (1999) 'Die Transformation nationaler Identität und die kulturelle Ambivalenz Europäischer Identität', in R. Viehoff and R. T. Segers, *Kultur, Identität, Europa* (Frankfurt: Suhrkamp).

della Porta, Donatella, Hanspeter Kriesi and Dieter Rucht (1999) *Social Movements in a Globalizing World* (London: Macmillan).

della Porta, Donatella and Herbert Reiter (eds) (1998) *Policing Protest: The Control of Mass Demonstrations in Western Democracies* (Minneapolis and London: University of Minnesota Press).

Dent, Christopher (1997) *The European Economy: The Global Context* (London: Routledge).

Dewatripont, M. et al. (1995) *Flexible Integration: Towards a More Effective and Democratic Europe* (London: Cambridge University Press).

Diamond, L. (1996) 'Is the Third Wave Over', *Journal of Democracy*, vol. 7, no. 3.

Diamond, Jareed (1997) *Guns, Germs and Steel* (London: Jonathan Cape).

Dinan, Desmond (1994) *Ever Closer Union? An Introduction to the European Community* (London: Macmillan).

Döring, H. (1995) 'Time as a Scarce Resource: Government Control of the Agenda', in H. Döring (ed.) *Parliaments and Majority Rule in Western Europe* (Frankfurt am Main: Campus, and New York: St Martin's Press) pp. 223–46.

Downs, Anthony (1957) *An Economic Theory of Democracy* (New York: Harper & Row).

Doyle, M. (1986) 'Liberalism and World Politics', *American Political Science Review*, vol. 80, no. 4, December.

Dryzek, Jon S. (1996) 'Political Inclusion and the Dynamics of Democratisation', *American Political Science Review*, 90 (1), pp. 475–87.

Dunford, M. (1998) 'Differential Developments, Institutions, Modes of Regulation and Comparative Transitions to Capitalism', in A. Pickles and A. Smith (eds) *Theorising Transition: The Political Economy of Post-Communist Transformations* (London: Routledge).

Dunford, Mick and Grigoris Kafalas (1992) *Cities and Regions in the New Europe: The Global–Local Interplay and Spatial Development Strategies* (London: Belhaven Press).

Duprat, Gerard, Noel Parker and Alain-Marc Rieu (eds) (1995) *European Democratic Culture* (London: Routledge).

Dussen, Jan van der and Kevin Wilson (eds) (1995) *The History of the Idea of Europe* (London: Routledge).

Duverger, M. (1954) *Political Parties* (London: Methuen).

Economic Europe and the Commonwealth of Independent States (Geneva: ECE).

Economist Intelligence Unit (1999) *Yugoslavia*, Country Report 3rd Quarter.

Ehlermann, Claus-Dieter (1995) 'Increased Differentiation or Stronger Uniformity', *Robert Schuman Centre European University Institute, Working Paper*, no. 95/21 (Florence: European University Institute).

Einhorn, B. (1993) *Cinderella Goes to Market* (London: Verso).

Eley, G. and R. G. Suny (eds) (1996) *Becoming National* (New York: Oxford University Press).

Elias, N. (1988) *Die Gesellschaft der Individuen*. Translated as *The Society of Individuals* (Oxford: Blackwell, 1992).

Elster, J., C. Offe and U. K. Preuss (1998) *Institutional Design in Post-Communist Societies* (Cambridge: Cambridge University Press).

Eriksson, R. and J. Goldthorpe (1992) *The Constant Flux. A Study of Class Mobility in Industrial Societies* (Oxford: Clarendon Press).

Etzioni, Amitai (1970) *Demonstration Democracy* (New York: Gordon and Breach).

European Commission (1995), Directorate General VI (Agriculture), *Agricultural Situation and Perspectives in the Central and Eastern European Countries, Summary Report* (Brussels: European Commission at http://europa.eu.int/comm/dg06/publi/peco/summary/index_en.htm).

European Commission (COM) (1997) *Agenda 2000: For a Stronger and Wider Union* (Brussels: Bulletin of the European Union), Supplement 5/97.

— *Commission Opinion on Hungary's Application for Membership of the European Union*, Supplement 6/97.

— *Commission Opinion on Poland's Application for Membership of the European Union*, Supplement 7/97.

— *Commission Opinion on Romania's Application for Membership of the European Union*, Supplement 8/97.

— *Commission Opinion on Slovakia's Application for Membership of the European Union*, Supplement 9/97.

— *Commission Opinion on Latvia's Application for Membership of the European Union*, Supplement 10/97.

— *Commission Opinion on Estonia's Application for Membership of the European Union*, Supplement 11/97.

— *Commission Opinion on Lithuania's Application for Membership of the European Union*, Supplement 12/97.

— *Commission Opinion on Bulgaria's Application for Membership of the European Union*, Supplement 13/97.

— *Commission Opinion on Czech Republic's Application for Membership of the European Union*, Supplement 14/97.

— *Commission Opinion on Slovenia's Application for Membership of the European Union*, Supplement 15/97.

European Council (1997) Luxembourg European Council Press Release: Luxembourg (12 December 1997), Nr: SN400/97 at http://ue.eu.int/Newsroom paragraphs 4–9.

European Union Council of Ministers (1995) 1883rd Council Meeting – General Affairs, Brussels, 20 and 21 November 1995 Press Release: no PRES/95/328 Date: 21 November 1995 at http://www.europa.eu.int/rapid.

Eyal, G., I. Szelenyi and E. Townsley (eds) (1998) *Making Capitalism without Capitalists: Class Formation and Elite Struggles in Post-Communist Central Europe* (London: Verso).

Fieldhouse, David (1999) *The West and the Third World* (Oxford: Blackwell).

Fingleton, J., E. Fox, D. Neven and P. Seabright (1996) *Competition Policy and the Transformation of Central Europe* (London: Cambridge University Press).

Fischer, M. E. (ed.) (1996) *Establishing Democracies* (Boulder, CO: Westview Press).

Flenley, P. (1996) 'From Soviet to Russian Identity: The Origins of Contemporary Russian Nationalism and National Identity', in B. Jenkins and S. Sofos, *Nation and Identity in Contemporary Europe* (London: Routledge) pp. 223–50.

Flockhart, T. and G. W. Rees (1998) 'A Core Europe? The EU and the WEU', in W. Park and G. W. Rees (eds) *Rethinking Security in Post-Cold War Europe* (London and New York: Addison Wesley Longman).

Fuchs, Dieter (1991) 'The Normalization of the Unconventional: Forms of Political Action and New Social Movements', in Gerd Meyer and Franciszek Ryszka (eds) *Political Participation and Democracy in Poland and West Germany* (Warsaw: Wydawca) pp. 148–65.

Fuchs, Dieter and Dieter Rucht (1994) 'Support for New Social Movements in Five Western European Countries', in Chris Rootes and Howard Davis (eds) *A New Europe? Social Change and Political Transformation* (London: UCL Press) pp. 86–111.

Fukuyama, F. (1989) 'End of History?', *National Interest*, no. 16, Summer.

Gaddis, J. L. (1987) *The Long Peace: Inquiries into the History of the Cold War* (Oxford: Oxford University Press).

Gaddis, J. L. (1992) *The United States and the End of the Cold War: Implications, Reconsiderations, Provocations* (New York and Oxford: Oxford University Press).

Gallagher, M., M. Laver and P. Mair (1995) *Representative Government in Modern Europe*, 2nd edn (New York: McGraw-Hill).

Garcia, S. (1993) *European Identity and the Search for Legitimacy* (London: Pinter).

Garton Ash, T. (1994) *In Europe's Name: Germany and the Divided Continent* (London: Vintage).

Garton Ash, T. (1996) 'Catching the Wrong Bus?', in Peter Gowan and Perry Anderson (eds) *The Question of Europe* (London: Verso) pp. 117–25.

Garton Ash, T. (1999) *History of the Present: Essays, Sketches and Despatches from Europe in the 1990s* (Harmondsworth: Penguin Books).

George, Stephen (1998) *An Awkward Partner: Britain in the European Community*, 3rd edn (Oxford: Oxford University Press).

Gerth, H. H. and C. Wright Mills (eds) (1948) *From Max Weber: Essays in Sociology* (London: Routledge & Kegan Paul).

Giddens, A. (1991) *Modernity and Self-Identity* (Cambridge: Polity).

Giddens, A. (1998) *The Third Way: The Renewal of Social Democracy* (Cambridge and Oxford: Polity Press).

Gilroy, P. (1993) *The Black Atlantic: Modernity and Double Consciousness* (London: Verso).

Glenny, M. (1990) *The Rebirth of History: Eastern Europe in the Age of Democracy* (London: Penguin Books).

Goetz, K. H. (1996) 'The Federal Constitutional Court', in G. Smith, W. E. Paterson and S. Padgett (eds) *Developments in German Politics*, 2 (Basingstoke and London: Macmillan) pp. 96–116.

Gowan, P. (1995a) 'The Visegrad States and the EU', *Social Democracy in the East: Labour Focus on Eastern Europe*, no. 50.

Gowan, P. (1995b) 'Neo-Liberal Theory and Practice for Eastern Europe', *New Left Review*, 213.

Gowan, P. (1995c) 'Analysing Shock Therapy', *New Left Review*, no. 213.

Gowan, Peter and Perry Anderson (eds) (1996) *The Question of Europe* (London: Verso).

Grabbe, H. and K. Hughes (1997) *Eastwards Enlargement of the European Union* (Royal Institute of International Affairs).

Grabher, G. and D. Start (1998) 'Organising Diversity: Evolutionary Theory, Network Analysis and Post Socialism', in A. Pickles and A. Smith (eds) *Theorising Transition: The Political Economy of Post-Communist Transformations* (London: Routledge).

Gray, V. (1996) 'Identity and Democracy in the Baltics', *Democratization*, vol. 3, no. 2.

Greenwood, Justin and Mark Aspinall (1998) *Collective Action in the European Union* (London: Routledge).

Griffiths, Paul (1988) *A Concise History of Modern Music from Debussy to Boulez* (London: Thames and Hudson).

Gundelach, Peter (1995) 'Grass-Roots Activity', in Jan W. van Deth and Elinor Scargrough (eds) *The Impact of Values: Beliefs in Government*, vol. 4 (Oxford: Oxford University Press) pp. 412–40.

Guyomarch, Alain, Howard Machin and Ella Ritchie (1998) *France and the European Union* (London: Macmillan).

Habermas, J. (1973) *Legitimationsprobleme im Spätkapitalismus* (Frankfurt: Suhrkamp). Translated by Thomas McCarthy as *Legitimation Crisis* (London: Heinemann, 1976).

Habermas, J. (1990) *Die nachholende Revolution* (Frankfurt: Suhrkamp).

Habermas, Jürgen (1992) *Daktizität und Geltung* (Frankfurt/M.: Suhrkamp).

Habermas, Jürgen et al. (1961) *Student und Politik. Eine soziologische Untersuchung zum politischen Bewußtsein frankfurter Studenten* (Neuwied: Luchterhand).

Hague, R., M. Harrop and S. Breslin (1998) *Comparative Government and Politics: An Introduction* (Basingstoke: Macmillan).

Hailsham, Lord (1976) *Elective Dictatorship* (London: BBC).

Hainsworth, P. (ed.) (1992) *The Extreme Right in Europe and the USA* (London: Frances Pinter).

Hall, Stuart (1997) 'The Local and the Global', in Anthony King (ed.) *Culture Globalization and the World-System* (Minneapolis: University of Minnesota Press).

Haller, Max and Rudolf Richter (1995) *Towards a European Nation? Political Trends in Europe – East and West, Center and Periphery* (New York: M. E. Sharpe).

Harby, Howard (ed.) (1961) *European Music in the Twentieth Century* (Harmondsworth: Penguin).

Hayward, Jack and Edward C. Page (eds) (1995) *Governing the New Europe* (Cambridge: Polity Press).

Held, D. (1995) *Democracy and the Global Order* (Cambridge: Polity Press).

Henderson, Karen (ed.) (1999) *Back to Europe: Central and Eastern Europe and the European Union* (London: UCL Press).

Heywood, A. (1997) *Politics* (Basingstoke: Macmillan).

Hildebrandt, Kai and Russell J. Dalton (1977) 'Die neue Politik – Politischer Wandel oder Schönwetterpolitik?' *Politische Vierteljahresschrift*, 13 (2), pp. 165–77.

Hirschmann, A. O. (1995) 'Social Conflicts as Pillars of Democratic Societies', in A. D. Hirschmann (ed.) *A Propensity to Self Subversion* (London: Harvard University Press).

Hirst, Paul (1994) *Associative Democracy: New Forms of Economic and Social Government* (Cambridge: Polity Press).

Hirst, Paul and Grahame Thompson (1996) *Globalization in Question* (Cambridge: Polity Press).

Hix, Simon (1999) *The Political System of the European Union* (London: Macmillan).

Hobsbawm, E. (1990) *Nations and Nationalism since 1780* (Cambridge: Cambridge University Press).

Hobsbawm, E. (1994) *Age of Extremes: The Short Twentieth Century, 1914–1991* (London: Michael Joseph).

Hobsbawm, E. and T. Ranger (eds) (1993) *The Invention of Tradition* (Cambridge: Cambridge University Press).

Holland, Martin (1999) 'The Common Foreign and Security Policy', in Laura Cram, Desmond Dinan and Neill Nugent (eds) *Developments in European Union Politics* (London: Macmillan) pp. 230–46.

Holmes, L. (1997) *Post-Communism: An Introduction* (Cambridge: Polity Press).

Hopkins, T. K. and I. Wallerstein (1996) *The Age of Transition* (London: Zed Books).

Houbert, Jean (1998) 'Decolonization in Globalization', in Roland Axtmann (ed.) *Globalization and Europe: Theoretical and Empirical Investigations* (London: Pinter) pp. 43–58.

Huber, E., C. Ragin and J. D. Stephens (1993) 'Social Democracy, Christian Democracy, Constitutional Structure, and the Welfare State', *American Journal of Sociology*, 99, pp. 711–49.

Hudson, R. and A. M. Williams (1999) *Divided Europe: Society and Territory* (London: Sage).

Hughes, Robert (1991) *The Shock of the New – Art and the Century of Change* (London: BBC/Thames and Hudson).

Huntington, S. (1993) 'The Clash of Civilizations?' *Foreign Affairs*, 72 (3), pp. 22–49.

Huntington, Samuel P. (1996) *The Clash of Civilizations and the Remaking of World Order* (New York: Simon & Schuster).

Hurd, D. (1997) *The Search for Peace: A Century of Peace Diplomacy* (London: Little, Brown).

Hyde-Price, A. (1996) *The International Politics of East Central Europe* (Manchester: Manchester University Press).

Hyde-Price, A. (1998a) 'The OSCE and European Security', in W. Park and G. Wyn Rees (eds) *Rethinking Security in Post-Cold War Europe* (London and New York: Addison Wesley Longman).

Hyde-Price, Adrian (1998b) 'Patterns of International Politics', in Stephen White, Judy Batt and Paul G. Lewis (eds) *Developments in Central and East European Politics*, 2 (London: Macmillan) pp. 255–75.

Inglehart, R. (1977) *The Silent Revolution: Changing Values and Political Styles among Western Publics* (Princeton, NJ: Princeton University Press).

Inglehart, Ronald (1981) 'Post-Materialism in an Environment of Insecurity', *American Political Science Review*, 75 (4), pp. 880–9.

Inglehart, R. (1990) *Culture Shift in Advanced Industrial Society* (Princeton, NJ: Princeton University Press).

Jeffery, C. (1997) 'Conclusions: Sub-national Authorities and "European Domestic Policy"', in C. Jeffery (ed.) *The Regional Dimension of the European Union: Towards a Third Level in Europe?* (London: Frank Cass) pp. 204–19.

Jenkins, B. and S. Sofos (1996) 'Introduction', in B. Jenkins and S. Sofos, *Nation and Identity in Contemporary Europe* (London: Routledge).

Jennings, Kent M., Jan W. van Deth et al. (eds) (1990) *Continuities in Political Action: A Longitudinal Study of Political Orientations in Three Western Democracies* (Berlin and New York: de Gruyter).

Jjöorgo, Tore and Rob Witte (eds) (1993) *Racist Violence in Europe* (Basingstoke: Macmillan).

Jones, Morris (1954) 'In Defense of Political Apathy', *Political Studies*.

Kaase, Max (1984) 'The Challenge of the "Participatory Revolution" in Pluralist Democracies', *International Political Science Review*, 5, pp. 299–318.

Kaase, Max (1990) 'Mass Participation', in Kent M. Jennings, Jan W. van Deth et al. (eds) *Continuities in Political Action: A Longitudinal Study of Political Orientations in Three Western Democracies* (Berlin and New York: de Gruyter) pp. 23–64.

Kaelble, H. (1991) *Nachbarn am Rhein. Entfremdung und Annäherung der französischen und deutschen Gesellschaft seit 1880* (Munich: C. H. Beck).

Katz, Richard S., Peter Mair et al. (1992) 'The Membership of

Political Parties in European Democracies, 1960–1990', *European Journal of Political Research*, 22, pp. 329–45.

Keane, John (ed.) (1988) *Civil Society and the State: New European Perspectives* (London: Verso).

Kegley, C. W. and E. R. Wittkopf (1997) *World Politics: Trend and Transformation*, 6th edn (New York: St Martin's).

Kegley, C. W. and E. R. Wittkopf (1999) *World Politics: Trend and Transformation*, 7th edn (New York: St Martin's).

Keim, Donald W. (1975) 'Participation in Contemporary Democratic Theories', in J. Roland Penncock and John W. Chapman (eds), *Participation in Politics* (New York: Lieber, Atherton) pp. 1–38.

Kennedy, Paul (1987) *The Rise and Fall of the Great Powers: Economic Change and Military Conflict from 1500 to 2000* (New York: Random House).

Keohane, R. O. and J. S. Nye (1977) *Power and Interdependence: World Politics in Transition* (Boston: Little Brown).

Key, V. O., Jr (1958) *Politics, Parties, and Pressure Groups*, 4th edn (New York: Crowell).

Khan, Usman (1999) *Participation Beyond the Ballot Box* (London: UCL Press).

Kiewiet, D. R. and M. D. McCubbins (1991) *The Logic of Delegation: Congressional Parties and the Appropriations Process* (Chicago: University of Chicago Press).

King, A. (1975) 'Executives', in F. I. Greenstein and N. W. Polsby (eds), *Handbook of Political Science*, vol. 5 (Reading, MA: Addison-Wesley).

King, A. (1976) 'Modes of Executive–Legislative Relations: Great Britain, France and West Germany', *Legislative Studies Quarterly*, 1, pp. 11–36.

Kirchheimer, Otto (1966) 'The Transformation of the Western European Party Systems', in 'Political Parties and Political Development' in La Palombara, Joseph and Myron Weiner (eds) *Political Parties and Political Development* (Princeton, NJ: Princeton University Press).

Kitschelt, Herbert (1990) 'New Social Movements and the Decline of Party Organization', in Russell Dalton and Manfred Küchler (eds) *Challenging the Political Order: New Social and Political Movements in Western Democracies* (Cambridge: Polity Press) pp. 179–208.

Kitschelt, Herbert (1993) 'Social Movements, Political Parties, and Democratic Theory', *Annals of the AAPSS*, no. 528, pp. 13–29.

Kornhauser, William (1959) *The Politics of Mass Society* (New York: Free Press).

Krakauer, Siegfried (1979) *Theory of Film: The Redemption of Physical Reality* (New York: Oxford University Press).

Krause, K. (1998) 'Theorizing Security: State Security and the "Third World" in the Post-Cold War World', *Review of International Studies*, vol. 24, no. 1, January.

Kriesi, Hanspeter, Ruud Koopmans, Jan Willem Duyvendak and Marco Giugni (1995) *New Social Movements in Western Europe: A Comparative Analysis* (Minneapolis: University of Minnesota Press).

Laczko, F. (1994) *Older People in Eastern and Central Europe: The Price of Transition to a Market Economy* (London: HelpAge International), quoted in A. Mayhew (1998) *Recreating Europe: The European Union's Policy towards Central and Eastern Europe* (Cambridge: Cambridge University Press).

Laffan, Brigid (1992) *Integration and Cooperation in Europe* (London: Routledge).

Lane, C. (1989) *Management and Labour in Europe: The Industrial Enterprise in Germany, Britain and France* (Aldershot: Elgar).

Lane, Jan-Erik and Svante O. Ersson (1996) *European Politics: An Introduction* (London: Sage).

Lash, S. and J. Urry (1987) *The End of Organized Capitalism* (Cambridge: Polity Press).

Laslett, Peter (1965) *The World We Have Lost* (London: Methuen; 2nd edn, 1971; 3rd edn, 1983).

Lawson, Kay (1988) 'When Linkage Fails', in Kay Lawson and Peter H. Merkl (eds) *When Parties Fail: Emerging Alternative Organizations* (Princeton: Princeton University Press) pp. 13–38.

Lehman, Peter (ed.) (1997) *Defining Cinema* (London: Athena Press).

Lehmbruch, Gerhard and C. Philippe Schmitter (eds) (1982) *Patterns of Corporatist Policy-making* (London: Sage).

Lenoir, D. (1994) *L'Europe sociale* (Paris: La Découverte).

Lewis, Bernard (1982) *The Muslim Discovery of Europe* (New York: Norton).

Leibert, U. and M. Cotta (eds) (1990) *Parliament and Democratic Consolidation in Southern Europe* (London: Pinter).

Lichtenberg, Judith (ed.) (1990) *Democracy and the Mass Media* (Cambridge: Cambridge University Press).

Light, M. (1991) 'Soviet Policy in the Third World', *International Affairs*, vol. 67, no. 1, April.

Lijphart, A. (1984) *Democracies: Patterns of Majoritarian and Consensus Government in Twenty-One Countries* (New Haven and London: Yale University Press).

Lijphart, A. (ed.) (1992) *Parliamentary versus Presidential Government* (Oxford: Oxford University Press).

Lijphart, A. (1994) *Electoral Systems and Party Systems: A Study of Twenty-Seven Democracies, 1945–1990* (Oxford: Oxford University Press).

Lijphart, Arend (1997) 'Unequal Participation: Democracy's Unresolved Dilemma', *American Political Science Review*, 91 (1) pp. 1–14.

Lintner, Valerio, and Clive Church (forthcoming) *The European Union: Economic and Political Aspects* (London: McGraw Hill).

Linz, J. J. (1992) 'The Perils of Presidentialism', in A. Lijphart (ed.), *Parliamentary versus Presidential Government* (Oxford: Oxford University Press) pp. 118–27.

Lipset, Seymour M. and Stein Rokkan (1967) 'Cleavage Structures, Party Systems, and Voter Alignments: An Introduction', in S. M. Lipset and S. Rokkan (eds) *Party Systems and Voter Alignments: Cross-National Perspectives* (New York: Free Press) pp. 1–64.

Loughlin, John (1997) 'Representing Regions in Europe: The Committee of the Regions', in C. Jeffery (ed.) *The Regional Dimension of the European Union: Towards a Third Level in Europe?* (London: Frank Cass).

Luhmann, Niklas (1969) 'Komplexität und Demokratie', *Politische Vierteljahresschrift*, 11, pp. 314–25.

Lupia, A. and M. D. McCubbins (1998) *The Democratic Dilemma: Can Citizens Learn What They Need to Know?* (Cambridge: Cambridge University Press).

Majone, Giandomenico (1996) *Regulating Europe* (London: Routledge).

Mann, M. (1986, 1993) *The Sources of Social Power*, 2 vols (Cambridge: Cambridge University Press).

Marceau, J. (1977) *Class and Status in France* (Oxford: Oxford University Press).

Marks, G. (1997) 'An Actor-centred Approach to Multi-level Governance', in C. Jeffery (ed.) *The Regional Dimension of the European Union: Towards a Third Level in Europe?* (London: Frank Cass) pp. 20–38.

Marsh, David (1983) *Pressure Politics: Interest Groups in Britain* (London: Junction Books).

Marsh, D. (1994) *Germany and Europe: The Crisis of Unity* (London: Heinemann).

Massey, A. (1999) 'Public Policy in the New Europe', in F. Carr and A. Massey (eds), *Public Policy in the New Europe: Euro-governance in Theory and Practice* (Cheltenham: Edgar).

Mastny, Vojtech (1993) 'The Helsinki Process and a New Framework of European Security', in Jonathan Story (ed.) *The New Europe* (Oxford: Blackwell) pp. 421–42.

Mayhew, Alan (1998) *Recreating Europe: The European Union's Policy towards Central and Eastern Europe* (Cambridge: Cambridge University Press).

Mazey, Sonia and Jeremy Richardson (1993) *Lobbying in the European Community* (London: Routledge).

Mazower, M. (1998) *The Dark Continent: Europe's Twentieth Century* (London: Allen Lane/Penguin).

McCubbins, M. D. and T. Schwartz (1984) 'Congressional Oversight Overlooked: Police Patrols versus Fire Alarms', *American Journal of Political Science*, 28, pp. 165–79.

McLean, Iain (ed.) (1996) *Oxford Concise Dictionary of Politics* (Oxford: Oxford University Press).

Meadows, Donella (1996) 'If the World were a Village', *Independent on Sunday*, 20 October, pp. 4–5.

Mearsheimer, J. (1990) 'Back to the Future: Instability in Europe after the Cold War', *International Security*, vol. 12, no. 1.

Mendras, H. (1997) *L'Europe des Européens* (Paris: Gallimard).

Mendras, H. (1988) *La seconde révolution française* (Paris: Gallimard). Translated by H. Mendras and A. Cole as *Social Change in Modern France* (Cambridge: Cambridge University Press).

Mény, Y. (1996) 'France: The Institutionalization of Leadership', in J. M. Colomer (ed.) *Political Institutions in Europe* (London: Routledge) pp. 99–137.

Mestrovic, Stjepan G. (1994) *The Balkanization of the West: The Confluence of Postmodernism and Postcommunism* (London: Routledge).

Meyer, David and Sidney Tarrow (eds) (1997) *The Social Movement Society: Contentious Politics for a New Century* (Boulder, CO: Rowman & Littlefield).

Mezey, M. L. (1998) 'Executive–Legislative Relations', in G. T. Kurian (ed.) *World Encyclopedia of Parliaments and Legislatures*, vol. II (Washington, DC: Congressional Quarterly) pp. 780–6.

Miall, Hugh (ed.) (1994) *Redefining Europe: New Patterns of Conflict and Cooperation* (London: Pinter).

Michels, Robert (1962 [orig. 1911]) *Political Parties* (New York: Free Press).

Middlemas, Keith (1995) *Orchestrating Europe* (London: HarperCollins/Fontana).

Milbrath, Lester (1965) *Political Participation: How and Why do People Get Involved in Politics?* (Chicago: Rand McNally).

Millan, B. (1997) 'The Committee of Regions: In at the Birth', *Regional and Federal Studies*, vol. 7, no. 1, Spring, pp. 5–10.

Milward, Alan S. (1984) *The Reconstruction of Western Europe, 1945–51* (London: Routledge).

Milward, Alan S. et al. (1993) *The Frontier of National Sovereignty* (London: Routledge).

Milward, Alan S. (1994) *The European Rescue of the Nation-State* (London: Routledge).

Mitchell, P. (2000) 'Voters and their Representatives: Electoral Institutions and Delegation in Parliamentary Democracies', *European Journal of Political Research*, 34 (forthcoming).

Möckli, S. (1998) 'Direktdemokratische Einrichtungen und Verfahren in den Mitgliedsstaaten des Europarates', *Zeitschrift für Parlamentsfragen*, 29, 1, pp. 90–107.

Molle, W. (1994) *The Economics of European Integration* (Aldershot: Dartmouth).

Moore, B. (1966) *Social Origins of Dictatorship and Democracy: Landlord and Peasant in the Making of the Modern World* (Boston: Beacon Press).

Moore, B. (1978) *Injustice: The Social Bases of Obedience and Revolt* (London: Macmillan).

Morgenthau, H. (1978) *Politics Among Nations*, 5th edn (New York: Knopf).

Müller, W. C. and K. Strøm (1997) 'Schluß: Koalitionsregierungen und die Praxis des Regierens in Westeuropa', in W. C. Müller and K. Strøm (eds) *Koalitionsregierungen in Westeuropa: Bildung, Arbeitsweise und Beendigung* (Vienna: Signum) pp. 705–49.

Münch, R. (1993) *Das Projekt Europa. Zwischen Nationalstaat, regionaler Autonomie und Weltgesellschaft* (Frankfurt: Suhrkamp).

Nagle, J. D. and A. Mahr (1999) *Democracy and Democratization* (London: Sage).

Nairn, T. (1977) *The Break-up of Britain* (London: New Left Books).

Neidhardt, Friedhelm and Dieter Rucht (1993) 'Auf dem Weg

in die "Bewegungsgesellschaft"? Über die Stabilisierbarkeit sozialer Bewegungen', *Soziale Welt*, 44 (3), pp. 305–26.

Nugent, Neill (1999) *The Government and Politics of the European Union*, 4th edn (London: Macmillan).

O'Donnell, G., P. Schmitter and L. Whitehead (eds) (1996) *Transitions from Authoritarian Rule* (London: Johns Hopkins University Press).

OECD (1993) *Integrating Emerging Market Economies into the International Trading System* (Paris: OECD).

OECD (1994) 'Report to the Working Party no. 1 on Competition and International Trade: Anti-Dumping Policy', chapter 5 in *Competition and the EC Anti-Dumping Regulations* (Paris: OECD).

OECD (1997) *Agricultural Policies in Transition Economies, Monitoring and Evaluation* (Paris: OECD).

Offe, C. (1985) *Disorganized Capitalism* (Cambridge: MIT).

Ohmae, Kenichi (1996) *The End of the Nation State: The Rise of Regional Economies* (London: HarperCollins).

Olsen, D. and P. Norton (eds) (1996) *The New Parliaments of Eastern and Central Europe* (London: F. Cass).

Orloff, Ann Shola (1996) *Gender and the Welfare State* (Madrid: Instituto Juan March de Estudios e Investigaciones).

Owen, D. (1995) *The Balkan Odyssey* (London: Gollancz).

Parry, Geraint, George Moyer and Neil Day (1992) *Political Participation and Democracy in Britain* (Cambridge: Cambridge University Press).

Pateman, Carole (1970) *Participaton and Democratic Theory* (London: Cambridge University Press).

Pateman, Carole (1996) 'Democracy and Democratization', *International Political Science Review*, 17 (1), pp. 5–12.

Peterson, John and Elizabeth Bomberg (1999) *Decision-Making in the European Union* (London: Macmillan).

Peterson, John and Margaret Sharp (1998) *Technology Policy in the European Union* (London: Macmillan).

Pickles, A. and A. Smith (eds) (1998) *Theorising Transition: The Political Economy of Post-Communist Transformations* (London: Routledge).

Picq, Jean (1995) *Il faut aimer l'état* (Paris: Flammarion).

Piening, Christopher (1997) *Global Europe: The European Union in World War Affairs* (Boulder, CO: Lynne Rienner).

Pinder, J. (1991) *The European Community and Eastern Europe* (London: Royal Institute of International Affairs/Pinter).

Pohoryles, R. et al. (eds) (1994) *European Transformations: Five Decisive Years at the Turn of the Century* (Aldershot: Avebury).

Pridham, G. (ed.) (1995) *Transitions to Democracy* (Aldershot: Dartmouth).

Prodat: data set on protest events in West Germany from 1950 to 1994, produced under the guidance of Dieter Rucht at the Wissenschaftszentrum Berlin für Sozialforschung.

Putnam, Robert D. (1993) *Making Democracy Work: Civic Traditions in Modern Italy* (Princeton, NJ: Princeton University Press).

Putnam, Robert D. (1995) 'Bowling Alone: America's Declining Social Capital', *Journal of Democracy*, 6 (1), pp. 65–78.

Radaelli, Claudio (1999a) *Technocracy in the European Union* (London: Longman).

Radaelli, C. (1999b) 'The Public Policy of the European Union: Whither Politics of Expertise?', *The State of the Art: Theoretical Approaches to the EU in the Post-Amsterdam Era*, Aston University, Birmingham, 6–7 May.

Ray, Douglas and Michael Taylor (1970) *The Analysis of Political Cleavages* (New Haven, CT: Yale University Press).

Renan, E. (1882) *Qu'est-ce qu'une nation?*, reproduced and translated in S. Woolf (ed.) *Nationalism in Europe, 1815 to the Present* (London: Routledge, 1996) pp. 48–60.

Richardson, Dick and Chris Rootes (eds) (1994) *The Green Challenge: The Development of Green Parties in Europe* (London: Routledge).

Richardson, Jeremy (1995) 'The Market for Political Activism: Interest Groups as a Challenge to Political Parties', *West European Politics*, 18 (1), pp. 116–39.

Rieu, A.-M. and G. Duprat (eds) (1993) *European Democratic Cultures* (Milton Keynes: Open University, and London: Routledge, 1995).

Rogers, G. et al., (1995) *Social Exclusion* (Geneva: International Institute for Labour Studies).

Rokkan, Stein (1997) *State Formation, Nation-Building, and Mass Politics in Europe* (Oxford: Oxford University Press).

Rokkan, S. and D. Urwin (1983) *Economy, Territory, Identity* London: Sage).

Roller, Edeltraud and Berhard Weßels (1996) 'Contexts of Political Protest in Western Democracies: Political Organization and Modernity', in Frederick Weil et al. (eds) *Extremism, Protest, Social Movements, and Democracy. Research on Democracy and Society*, vol. 3 (Greenwich/London: JAI Press) pp. 91–134.

Rollo, J. M. C. et al. (1990) *The New Eastern Europe: Western Responses* (London: RIIA/Pinter).

Rootes, Christopher (1999) 'Acting Globally, Thinking Locally? Prospects for a Global Environmental Movement', in C. Rootes (ed.) (1999) *Environmental Movements: Local, National and Global* (London: Frank Cass) pp. 290–310.

Rootes, C. and H. Davis (eds) (1994) *Social Change and Political Transformation: A New Europe?* (London: UCL Press).

Rose, Richard (1996) *What is Europe? A Dynamic Perspective* (New York: HarperCollins).

Rosanvallon, P. (1981) *La crise de l'état-providence* (Paris: Seuil).

Ross, K. (1995) *Fast Cars, Clean Bodies: Decolonization and the Reordering of French Culture* (Cambridge: MIT Press).

Rucht, Dieter (1995) 'Parties, Associations and Movements as Systems of Political Interest Mediation', in Josef Thesing and Wilhelm Hofmeister (eds) *Political Parties in Democracy* (Sankt Augustin: Konrad Adenauer Stiftung) pp. 103–25.

Rucht, Dieter, Barbara Blattert and Dieter Rink (1997) *Von der Bewegung zur Institution? Alternative Gruppen in beiden Teilen Deutschlands* (Frankfurt am Main: Campus).

Rustow, D. (1970) 'Transitions to Democracy: Towards a Dynamic Model', *Comparative Politics*, vol. 3.

Sachs, J. (1995) 'Consolidating Capitalism', *Foreign Policy*, no. 98 (Spring 1995; September/October 1995).

Sagan, C. and R. Turco (1993) 'Nuclear Winter in the Post-Cold War Era', *Journal of Peace Research*, no. 30, November.

Sartori, Giovanni (1987) *The Theory of Democracy Revisited* (Chatham, NJ: Chatham House Publishers).

Sassoon, Donald (1996) *One Hundred Years of Socialism: The West European Left in the Twentieth Century* (London: I. B. Tauris).

Saunders, P. (1995) *Capitalism: A Social Audit* (Buckingham: Open University Press).

Scharpf, F. W. (1993) 'Coordination in Hierarchies and Networks', in F. W. Scharpf (ed.) *Games in Hierarchies and Networks: Analytical and Empirical Approaches to the Study of Governance Institutions* (Frankfurt am Main: Campus, and Boulder, CO: Westview).

Schmidt, M. G. (1996) 'Germany: The Grand Coalition State', in J. M. Colomer (ed.) *Political Institutions in Europe* (London: Routledge) pp. 62–98.

Schmidt, M. G. (1997) *Demokratietheorien: Eine Einführung*, 2nd edn (Opladen: Leske and Budrich).

Schmitter, Philippe C. and Gerhard Lehmbruch (eds) (1979) *Trends towards Corporatist Intermediation* (London: Sage).

Schmitter, Philippe C. and Wolfgang Streeck (1991) 'Organized Interests and the Europe of 1992', in Norman J. Ornstein and Mark Perlman (eds), *Political Power and Social Change: The United States Faces a United Europe* (Washington, DC: The American Enterprise Institute Press) pp. 46–67.

Schumpeter, Joseph (1966 [orig. 1942]) *Capitalism, Socialism, and Democracy* (London: Allen and Unwin University Books).

Schwengel, H. (1999) 'Europäische Sozialstruktur und Globaler Wandel' (University of Freiburg: http://www.zmk.uni-freiburg.de).

Seccombe, W. A. (1992) *A Millennium of Family Change: Feudalism to Capitalism in Northwestern Europe* (London: Verso).

Senghaas, D. (1982) *Von Europa Lernen. Entwicklungsgeschichtliche Betrachtungen* (Frankfurt: Suhrkamp).

Shelley, Monica and Margaret Winck (eds) (1995) *Aspects of European Cultural Diversity* (London: Routledge).

Shugart, M. S. and J. M. Carey (1992) *Presidents and Assemblies: Constitutional Design and Electoral Dynamics* (Cambridge: Cambridge University Press).

Smith, Adam (1784) *An Inquiry into the Nature and Causes of the Wealth of Nations*, general editors R. H. Campbell and A. S. Skinner; textual editor W. B. Todd, 3rd edn (Oxford: Clarendon Press, 1976).

Smith, A. and A. Swain (1998) 'Regulating and Institutionalising Capitalism', in A. Pickles and A. Smith (eds) *Theorising Transition: The Political Economy of Post-Communist Transformations* (London: Routledge).

Smith, A. D. (1979) *Nationalism in the Twentieth Century* (Oxford: Martin Robertson).

Smith, Bernard (ed.) (1975) *Concerning Contemporary Art: The Powe Lectures, 1968–1973* (Oxford: Clarendon Press).

Snyder, J. (1995) 'Myths, Modernization, and the Post-Gorbachev World', in R. N. Lebow and T. Risse-Kappen (eds) *International Relations Theory and the End of the Cold War* (New York: Columbia University Press).

Sofos, S. (1996) 'Culture, Politics and Identity in Former Yugoslavia', in B. Jenkins and S. Sofos, *Nation and Identity in Contemporary Europe* (London: Routledge) pp. 251–82.

Sperling, J. and E. Kirchner (1997) *Recasting the European Order* (Manchester: Manchester University Press).

Steiner, Jurg (1997) *European Democracies*, 4th edn (Harlow: Addison Wesley Longman).

Sternhell, Z. (1978) *La Droite révolutionnaire 1885–1914: Les Origines françaises du fascisme* (Paris: Éditions du Seuil).

Story, Jonathan (ed.) (1993) *The New Europe: Politics, Government and Economy since 1945* (Oxford: Blackwell).

Strøm, K. (1990) *Minority Government and Majority Rule* (Cambridge: Cambridge University Press).

Strøm, K. (1995) 'Parliamentary Government and Legislative Organisation', in H. Döring (ed.) *Parliaments and Majority Rule in Western Europe* (Frankfurt am Main: Campus, and New York: St Martin's Press) pp. 51–82.

Strøm, K. (1997) 'Democracy, Accountability, and Coalition Bargaining. The 1996 Stein Rokkan Lecture', *European Journal of Political Research*, 31, pp. 47–62.

Strøm, K. (2000) 'Delegation and Accountability in Parliamentary Democracies', *European Journal of Political Research*, 37(3) (forthcoming).

Stuart-Hughes, H. (1961) *Consciousness and Society – The Reorientation of European Social Thought, 1890–1930* (New York: Knopf).

Szelenyi, I. (1988) *Socialist Entrepreneurs: Embourgeoisement in Rural Hungary* (Cambridge: Polity Press).

Taagepera, R. and M. S. Shugart (1989) *Seats and Votes: The Effects and Determinants of Electoral Systems* (New Haven and London: Yale University Press).

Tangermann, S. and T. Josling (1994) *Pre-accession Agricultural Policies for Central Europe and for the European Union* (Brussels: European Commission).

Tarrow, Sidney (1994) *Power in Movement: Social Movements, Collective Action and Politics* (Cambridge: Cambridge University Press).

Tarrow, Sidney (1995) 'The Europeanization of Conflict: Reflections from a Social Movement Perspective', *West European Politics*, 18 (2) pp. 223–51.

Therborn, G. (1995) *European Modernity and Beyond: The Trajectory of European Societies, 1945–2000* (London: Sage).

Thomas, W. I. and D. S. (1928) *The Child in America: Behavior Problems and Programs* (New York: Knopf).

Tompkins, Calvin (1968) *Ahead of the Game – Four Versions of Avant-Garde* (Harmondsworth: Penguin).

Tönnies, F. (1955 [1887]) *Gemeinschaft und Gesellschaft.* Translated as *Community and Association* (London: Routledge, 1955).

Topf, Richard (1995) 'Beyond Electoral Participation', in Hans-Dieter Klingemann and Dieter Fuchs (eds) *Citizens and the State* (Oxford: Oxford University Press) pp. 52–91.

Touraine, A. and Ragazzi, O. (1961) *Ouvriers d'origine agricole* (Paris: Seuil).

Uçarer, Emek (1999) 'Cooperation on Justice and Home Affairs Matters', in Laura Cram, Desmond Dinan and Neill Nugent (eds) *Developments in European Union Politics* (London: Macmillan) pp. 247–67.

United Nations Development Program (1998) *Human Development Index 1998* (New York: United Nations Development Program).

Urwin, Derek (1991) *The Community of Europe: A History of European Integration since 1945* (London: Longman).

van Deth, Jan (ed.) (1997) *Private Groups and Public Life: Social Participation and Political Involvement in Representative Democracies* (London: Routledge).

Verba, Sidney, Norman Nie and Jae-on Kim (1978) *Participation and Political Equality: A Seven-Nation Comparison* (Cambridge: Cambridge University Press).

Visser, Jelle (1986) 'Die Mitgliederentwicklung der westeuropäischen Gewerkschaften. Trends und Konjunkturen 1920–1983', *Journal für Sozialforschung* 26 (1) pp. 3–33.

Waites, Bernard (ed.) (1995) *Europe and the Wider World* (Milton Keynes: Open University Press).

The United Nations Development Program (1998) *Human Development Index 1998* at www.undp.org/hdro/98hdi.htm.

Wallerstein, Immanuel (1972) *The Modern World System: Capitalist Agriculture and the Origins of the European World Economy in the Sixteenth Century* (London: Academic Press).

Waltz, K. J. (1979) *Theory of International Politics* (New York: Random House).

Weber, Max (1920) *Gesammelte Aufsaetze zur Religionssoziologie* (Tubingen: Mohr); reprinted as 'Author's Introduction' to Weber, *The Protestant Ethic and the Spirit of Capitalism*, translated by Talcott Parsons (London: Allen & Unwin, 1976).

White, Stephen (1991) *Gorbachev and After* (Cambridge: Cambridge University Press).

Wallace, Helen and William Wallace (eds) (1996) *Policy Making in the European Union*, 2nd edn (Oxford: Oxford University Press).

Whyte, W. H. (1960) *The Organisation Man* (London: Penguin).

Williams, G. A. (1979) 'When was Wales?' (BBC Wales Annual Radio Lecture, 12 November 1979), reproduced in S. Woolf (ed.) *Nationalism in Europe, 1815 to the Present* (London: Routledge, 1996) pp. 203–4.

Williams, Raymond (1993) *Drama from Ibsen to Brecht* (London: Hogarth).

Williams, Raymond (1996) *Keywords* (London: Fontana).

Williamson, P. J. (1989) *Corporatism in Perspective* (London: Sage).

World Bank (1997) *World Development Report 1997* (Washington, DC: IBRD/The World Bank).

World Bank (1998) *World Development Report 1998/99* (Washington, DC: IBRD/The World Bank).

World Bank (1999) *World Development Indicators 1999* (Washington, DC: IBRD/The World Bank).

Young, H. and A. Sloman (1982) *No, Minister: An Inquiry into the Civil Service* (London: British Broadcasting Corporation).

Zakaria, Fareed (1997) 'The Rise of Illiberal Democracy', *Foreign Affairs* 76: 6 (November/December) pp. 22–43.

Zloch-Christy, I. (1987) *Debt Problems of Eastern Europe* (Cambridge: Cambridge University Press).

Zweig, Stefan (1943) *The World of Yesterday* (London: Cassell).

# Index